*To Sarabeth,*
*who lived it all*

# AGE OF AMBITION

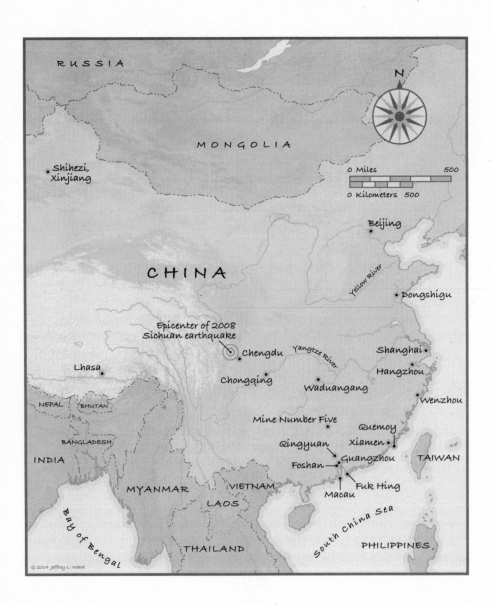

RUSSIA

MONGOLIA

Shihezi,
Xinjiang

0 Miles        500
0 Kilometers  500

Beijing

CHINA

Yellow River

Dongshigu

Epicenter of 2008
Sichuan earthquake

Chengdu

Yangtze River

Shanghai

Lhasa

Hangzhou

Chongqing

Waduangang

Wenzhou

NEPAL   BHUTAN

Mine Number Five

Quemoy

BANGLADESH

Qingyuan

Xiamen

INDIA

Foshan

Guangzhou

TAIWAN

MYANMAR

VIETNAM

Fuk Hing

LAOS

Macau

Bay of Bengal

South China Sea

THAILAND

PHILIPPINES

© 2014 Jeffrey L. Ward

# AGE OF AMBITION

## CHASING FORTUNE, TRUTH, AND FAITH IN THE NEW CHINA

## EVAN OSNOS

THE BODLEY HEAD
LONDON

Published by The Bodley Head 2014

2 4 6 8 10 9 7 5 3 1

First published in Great Britain in 2014 by
The Bodley Head
Random House, 20 Vauxhall Bridge Road,
London SW1V 2SA

www.bodleyhead.co.uk
www.vintage-books.co.uk

Addresses for companies within The Random House Group Limited can be found at:
www.randomhouse.co.uk/offices.htm

The Random House Group Limited Reg. No. 954009

A CIP catalogue record for this book
is available from the British Library

ISBN 9781847922786 (Hardback)
ISBN 9781847922793 (Trade Paperback)

The Random House Group Limited supports the Forest Stewardship
Council® (FSC®), the leading international forest-certification organisation.
Our books carrying the FSC label are printed on FSC®-certified paper. FSC is the only
forest-certification scheme supported by the leading environmental organisations,
including Greenpeace. Our paper procurement policy can be found at:
www.randomhouse.co.uk/environment

Printed and bound in Great Britain by Clays Ltd, St Ives plc

Why should I be like everyone else, just because I was
born to a poor family?            —Michael Zhang, teacher


The commander of a mighty army can be captured, but
the aspiration of an ordinary man can never be seized.
                                                    —Confucius

# CONTENTS

Prologue    3

## PART I: FORTUNE

1. Unfettered    11
2. The Call    21
3. Baptized in Civilization    34
4. Appetites of the Mind    50
5. No Longer a Slave    60
6. Cutthroat    76
7. Acquired Taste    95

## PART II: TRUTH

8. Dancing in Shackles    117
9. Liberty Leading the People    131
10. Miracles and Magic Engines    149
11. A Chorus of Soloists    163
12. The Art of Resistance    181
13. Seven Sentences    194
14. The Germ in the Henhouse    207
15. Sandstorm    218
16. Lightning Storm    232
17. All That Glitters    248
18. The Hard Truth    264

**PART III: FAITH**

19. The Spiritual Void    277
20. Passing By    294
21. Soulcraft    307
22. Culture Wars    319
23. True Believers    333
24. Breaking Out    343


Epilogue    357


*Notes on Sources*    373
*Acknowledgments*    385
*Index*    389

# AGE OF AMBITION

# PROLOGUE

Whenever a new idea sweeps across China—a new fashion, a philosophy, a way of life—the Chinese describe it as a "fever." In the first years after the country opened to the world, people contracted "Western Business Suit Fever" and "Jean-Paul Sartre Fever" and "Private Telephone Fever." It was difficult to predict when or where a fever would ignite, or what it would leave behind.

In the village of Xiajia (population 1,564) there was a fever for the American cop show *Hunter*, better known in China as *Expert Detective Heng Te*. When the show appeared on Chinese television in 1990, the villagers of Xiajia started to gather to watch Det. Sgt. Rick Hunter of the Los Angeles Police Department go undercover with his partner, Det. Sgt. Dee Dee McCall. And the villagers of Xiajia came to expect that Det. Sgt. Rick Hunter would always find at least two occasions to utter his trademark phrase, "Works for me"—though, in Chinese, he came across as a religious man, because "Works for me" was mistranslated as "Whatever God wants." The fever passed from one person to the next, and it affected each in a different way. Some months later, when the police in Xiajia tried to search the home of a local farmer, the man told them to come back when they had a warrant—a word he had learned from *Expert Detective Heng Te*.

When I moved to China in 2005, I was accustomed to hearing the story of China's metamorphosis told in vast, sweeping strokes involving one-sixth of humanity and great pivots of politics and economics. But, up close, the deepest changes were intimate and perceptual, buried in daily rhythms in ways that were easy to overlook. The greatest fever of all was aspiration, a belief in the sheer possibility to remake a life. Some who tried succeeded; many others did not. More remarkable was that they defied a history that told them never to try. Lu Xun, China's most celebrated modern author, once wrote, "Hope is like a path in the country-side: originally there was no path, but once people begin to pass, a way appears."

I lived in China for eight years, and I watched this age of ambition take shape. Above all, it is a time of plenty—the crest of a transformation one hundred times the scale, and ten times the speed, of the first Indus-trial Revolution, which created modern Britain. The Chinese people no longer want for food—the average citizen eats six times as much meat as in 1976—but this is a ravenous era of a different kind, a period when people have awoken with a hunger for new sensations, ideas, and re-spect. China is the world's largest consumer of energy, movies, beer, and platinum; it is building more high-speed railroads and airports than the rest of the world combined.

For some of its citizens, China's boom has created stupendous for-tune: China is the world's fastest-growing source of new billionaires. Several of the new plutocrats have been among the world's most dedi-cated thieves; others have been holders of high public office. Some have been both. For most of the Chinese people, however, the boom has not produced vast wealth; it has permitted the first halting steps out of pov-erty. The rewards created by China's rise have been wildly inconsistent but fundamentally profound: it is one of the broadest gains in human well-being in the modern age. In 1978, the average Chinese income was $200; by 2014, it was $6,000. By almost every measure, the Chinese people have achieved longer, healthier, more educated lives.

Living in Beijing in these moments, I found that confidence in one's ideas, especially about China's future, seems to vary inversely with the time one spends on the ground. The complexities blunt the impulse to impose a simple logic on them. To find order in the changes, we seek refuge, of a kind, in statistics: in my years in China, the number of airline passengers doubled; cell phone sales tripled; the length of the Beijing subway quadrupled. But I was less impressed by those numbers than by a drama that I could not quantify: two generations ago, visitors to China marveled most at the sameness of it all. To outsiders, Chairman Mao was the "Emperor of the Blue Ants," as one memorable book title had it—a secular god in a land of matching cotton suits and "production teams." Stereotypes about the Chinese as collectivist, inscrutable drones endured in part because China's politics helped sustain them; official China reminded its guests that it was a nation of work units and communes and uncountable sacrifice.

But in the China that I encountered, the national narrative, once an ensemble performance, is splintering into a billion stories—stories of flesh and blood, of idiosyncrasies and solitary struggles. It is a time when the ties between the world's two most powerful countries, China and the United States, can be tested by the aspirations of a lone peasant lawyer who chose the day and the hour in which to alter his fate. It is the age of the changeling, when the daughter of a farmer can propel herself from the assembly line to the boardroom so fast that she never has time to shed the manners and anxieties of the village. It is a moment when the individual became a gale force in political, economic, and private life, so central to the self-image of a rising generation that a coal miner's son can grow up to believe that nothing matters more to him than seeing his name on the cover of a book.

Viewed one way, the greatest beneficiary of the age of ambition is the Chinese Communist Party. In 2011 the Party celebrated its ninetieth birthday—a milestone unimaginable at the end of the Cold War. In the years after the Soviet Union collapsed, Chinese leaders studied that history and vowed never to suffer the same fate. When Arab dictatorships fell in 2011, China's endured. To survive, the Chinese Communist Party shed its scripture but held fast to its saints; it abandoned Marx's theories but retained Mao's portrait on the Gate of Heavenly Peace, peering down on Tiananmen Square.

The Party no longer promises equality or an end to toil. It promises only prosperity, pride, and strength. And for a while, that was enough. But over time the people have come to want more, and perhaps nothing more ardently than information. New technology has stirred a fugitive political culture; things once secret are now known; people once alone are now connected. And the more the Party has tried to prevent its people from receiving unfiltered ideas, the more they have stepped forward to demand them.

China today is riven by contradictions. It is the world's largest buyer of Louis Vuitton, second only to the United States in its purchases of

Rolls-Royces and Lamborghinis, yet ruled by a Marxist-Leninist party that seeks to ban the word *luxury* from billboards. The difference in life expectancy and income between China's wealthiest cities and its poorest provinces is the difference between New York and Ghana. China has two of the world's most valuable Internet companies, and more people online than the United States, even as it redoubles its investment in history's largest effort to censor human expression. China has never been more pluralistic, urban, and prosperous, yet it is the only country in the world with a winner of the Nobel Peace Prize in prison.

Sometimes China is compared to the Japan of the 1980s, when a hundred square feet in downtown Tokyo sold for a million dollars, and tycoons were sipping cocktails over ice cubes shipped from Antarctica. By 1991, Japan was in the largest deflation of assets in the modern history of capitalism. But the similarities run thin; when Japan's bubble burst, it was a mature, developed economy; but China, even overheated, remains a poor country in which the average person earns as much as a Japanese citizen in 1970. At other moments, China's goose-stepping soldiers, its defectors and its dissidents, recall the Soviet Union or even Nazi Germany. But those comparisons are unsatisfying. Chinese leaders do not threaten to "bury" America, the way Khrushchev did, and even China's fiercest nationalists do not seek imperial conquest or ethnic cleansing.

China reminds me most of America at its own moment of transformation—the period that Mark Twain and Charles Warner named the Gilded Age, when "every man has his dream, his pet scheme." The United States emerged from the Civil War on its way to making more steel than Britain, Germany, and France combined. In 1850, America had fewer than twenty millionaires; by 1900 it had forty thousand, some as bumptious and proud as James Gordon Bennett, who bought a restaurant in Monte Carlo after he was refused a seat by the window. As in China, the dawn of American fortune was accompanied by spectacular treachery. "Our method of doing business," said the railway man Charles Francis Adams, Jr., a grandson and great-grandson of presidents, "is founded upon lying, cheating and stealing." Eventually, F. Scott Fitzgerald gave us the slippery tale of James Gatz of North Dakota, who catapulted himself into a new world, in doomed pursuit of love and fortune. When I stood in the light of a new Chinese skyline, I sometimes thought of Gatsby's New York—"always the city seen for the first time, in its first wild promise of all the mystery and the beauty in the world."

In the early years of the twenty-first century, China encompasses two universes: the world's newest superpower and the world's largest authoritarian state. Some days, I spent the morning with a new tycoon and the evening with a dissident under house arrest. It was easy to see them as representing the new China and the old, distinct realms of economics and politics. But eventually I concluded that they were one and the same, and the contrast was an unstable state of nature.

This book is an account of the collision of two forces: aspiration and authoritarianism. Forty years ago the Chinese people had virtually no access to fortune, truth, or faith—three things denied them by politics and poverty. They had no chance to build a business or indulge their desires, no power to challenge propaganda and censorship, no way to find moral inspiration outside the Party. Within a generation, they had gained access to all three—and they want more. The Chinese people have taken control of freedoms that used to be governed almost entirely by others—decisions about where they work and travel and whom they marry. But as those liberties have expanded, the Communist Party has taken only halting steps to accommodate them. The Communist Party's commitment to control—to ordain not only who leads the country but also how many teeth a train attendant shows when she smiles—contradicts the riot of life outside. The longer I lived in China, the more I sensed that the Chinese people have outpaced the political system that nurtured their rise. The Party has unleashed the greatest expansion of human potential in world history—and spawned, perhaps, the greatest threat to its own survival.

This is a work of nonfiction, based on eight years of conversations. In my research, I gravitated most of all to the strivers—the men and women who were trying to elbow their way from one realm to another, not just in economic terms, but in matters of politics, ideas, and the spirit. I came to know many of them when I was writing stories in the *Chicago Tribune* and, later, *The New Yorker*. I followed them as their lives evolved and veered in and out of my own. For an American writing abroad, it is tempting to envy China's strengths where America feels weak, and to judge the country harshly where it grates against my values. But I have tried, above all, to describe Chinese lives on their own terms.

I have used real names, except in several cases that I have noted, in which I obscured an identity because of political sensitivities. All the dialogue is based on the accounts of one or more people present. Part I begins at the earliest moments of the boom; I introduce several men and women who were swept up in China's rise from poverty, and describe the risks they took and the ideas that animated them. The more that people succeeded in their economic lives, the more they demanded to know about the world around them, and in part II, I describe the rebellion against propaganda and censorship. In the final part, those pursuits converge in the search for a new moral foundation, as men and women on the bottom rung of the middle class set out in search of what to believe.

The story of China in the twenty-first century is often told as a contest between East and West, between state capitalism and the free market. But in the foreground there is a more immediate competition: the struggle to define the idea of China. Understanding China requires not only measuring the light and heat thrown off by its incandescent new power, but also examining the source of its energy—the men and women at the center of China's becoming.

# PART I

# FORTUNE

# ONE

# UNFETTERED

*May 16, 1979*

Under a sliver of moon, on an island off the coast of China, a twenty-six-year-old army captain slipped away from his post and headed for the water's edge. He moved as calmly as possible, over the pine scrub to a ledge overlooking the shore. If his plan were discovered, he would be disgraced and executed.

Capt. Lin Zhengyi was a model soldier, one of the most celebrated young officers in the army of Taiwan, the island province ruled by opponents of the Chinese Communist Party. For three decades Taiwan had defied Communist control, and Captain Lin was a symbol of that resistance: in college, he had been a star student who'd given up a placid civilian life to join the military, a decision so rare that Taiwan's future president made a point to shake his hand, and the picture was splashed all over the newspapers, turning Lin into a poster boy for the "Holy Counterattack," the dream of retaking mainland China.

Lin Zhengyi (pronounced "Jung-yee") stood nearly six feet tall, with ramrod posture, a broad, flat nose, and jug ears that protruded from the rim of his hat. His devotion had earned him the assignment to the most sensitive place on the front line: the tiny island of Quemoy, known in Mandarin as Jinmen, barely one mile, across the water, from the rocky coast of mainland China.

But Captain Lin had a secret so dangerous to him and his family that he did not dare reveal it even to his wife, who was home with their son and pregnant with their second child. Captain Lin had awoken to a sense of history gathering around him. After thirty years of turmoil, China was appealing to the people of Taiwan to reunify the "great Motherland."

Any soldier who tried to defect to the mainland would be shot on sight. The few who tried were exceedingly rare, though the consequences were vivid; the most recent case had occurred less than a month ago. But Lin had heard his calling. China would prosper again, he believed. And he would prosper with it.

In the darkness he found the sandy path that could lead him safely down a hill laden with land mines. The wind off the sea had bent the gnarled island pines. The water, a brilliant crystal green by day, was now an endless black mass, surging and withdrawing with the waves. To ward off an invasion, the beaches had been fitted with long metal spears that protruded from the sand to face the sea.

Just before the captain left the tree line for the dash to shore, he loosened the laces of his shoes and stepped barefoot onto the soil and stone. He was ready to abandon his fellow soldiers, his family, and his name.

Virtually everyone else who had tried to swim those waters had headed in the opposite direction. In 1979, mainland China was a place to flee.

In the eighteenth century, imperial China controlled one-third of the world's wealth; its most advanced cities were as prosperous and commercialized as Great Britain and the Netherlands. But in the nineteenth and twentieth centuries, China was crippled by invasion, civil war, and political upheaval. After taking power in 1949, the Communist Party conducted a "land reform" campaign that grouped China's small family farms into collectives, and led to the killing of millions of landlords and perceived enemies. In 1958, Chairman Mao launched the Great Leap Forward, attempting to vault his country past Britain in just fifteen years. Some advisers told him it was impossible, but he ignored and humiliated them; the head of the national technology commission jumped out a window. The propagandists hailed one fantastical harvest after another, calling them "Sputnik harvests," on par with the success of the Soviet satellite. But the numbers were fiction, and as starvation spread, many who complained were tortured or killed. The Party barred people from traveling to find food. Mao's Great Leap Forward resulted in the world's worst famine, which killed between thirty and forty-five million people, more than World War I. By the time Captain Lin defected from Taiwan, the People's Republic was poorer than North Korea; its per capita income was one-third that of sub-Saharan Africa.

Deng Xiaoping had been China's paramount leader for less than six months. At seventy-five, he was a persuasive but plainspoken statesman, and a survivor—repeatedly purged from the leadership by Chairman Mao, twice rehabilitated. In the years since, he has often been described as the sole architect of the boom that followed, but that view is the handiwork of Party historians. Deng understood the limitations of his knowledge. On matters of the economy, his shrewdest move was to unite with Chen Yun, a fellow Party patriarch who was so skeptical of the West that he greeted the idea of reform by rereading Lenin's *Imperialism*; and with Zhao Ziyang, a younger, progressive Party boss whose efforts to reduce poverty had spawned a saying among peasants: "If you want to eat, look for Ziyang."

When change came, it came from below. The previous winter, in the inland village of Xiaogang, the local farmers had been so impoverished by Mao's economic vision that they had stopped tilling their communal land and had resorted to begging. In desperation, eighteen farmers divided up the land and began to farm it separately; they set their own schedules, and whatever they sold beyond the quota required by the state, they sold at the market and reaped the profits. They signed a secret pact to protect one another's families in the event of arrest.

By the following year, they were earning nearly twenty times as much income as before. When the experiment was discovered, some apparatchiks accused them of "digging up the cornerstone of socialism," but wiser leaders allowed their scheme to continue, and eventually expanded it to eight hundred million farmers around the country. The return of "household" farming, as it was known, spread so fast that a farmer compared it to a germ in a henhouse. "When one family's chicken catches the disease, the whole village catches it. When one village has it, the whole county will be infected."

Deng and the other leaders squabbled constantly, but the combination of Deng's charisma, Chen's hesitation to move too fast, and Zhao's competence was startlingly successful. The model they created endured for decades: a "birdcage economy," as Chen Yun called it, airy enough to let the market thrive but not so free as to let it escape. As young revolutionaries, the elders had overseen the execution of landlords, the seizure of factories, and the creation of people's communes. But now they preserved their power by turning the revolution upside down: permitting private enterprise and opening a window to the outside world even if it allowed, as Deng put it, "a few flies" to get in. China's reforms had no blueprint. The strategy, as Chen Yun put it, was to move without losing control—to "cross the river by feeling for the stones." (Deng, inevitably, received credit for the expression.)

In 1979 the Party announced that it would no longer tag people as "landlords" and "rich peasants," and later Deng Xiaoping removed the final stigma: "Let some people get rich first," he said, "and gradually all the people should get rich together." The Party extended the economic experiment. Officially, private businesses were permitted to hire no more than eight employees—Marx had believed that firms with more than eight workers were exploitative—but eventually small enterprises began popping up so fast that Deng Xiaoping told a Yugoslav delegation that it was "as if a strange army had appeared suddenly from nowhere." He did not take credit. "This is not the achievement of our central government," he said.

All over the country, people were exiting the collective farms that had dominated their lives. When they talked about it, they said they had been *songbang*—"unfettered"—a term more often used for a liberated prisoner or an animal. They began to talk of politics and democracy. But Deng Xiaoping had his limits. In March 1979, not long before Lin Zhengyi embarked on his adventure to the mainland, Deng spoke to a group of senior officials and demanded, "Can we tolerate this kind of freedom of speech which flagrantly contravenes the principles of our constitution?" The Party would never embrace "individualist democracy." It would have economic freedom but political control. For China to thrive, there must be limits on "emancipating the mind."

When change began to take hold on the mainland, Lin Zhengyi watched it from afar. He was born in 1952, three years after Taiwan and the mainland had embarked on the ideological and political standoff that would endure for decades. After losing China's civil war to the Communists in 1949, the Nationalist Party fled to the island of Taiwan, where it declared martial law over the islands and prepared, in theory, for the day that it might return to power over China. Life in Taiwan was harsh and circumscribed. Lin grew up in the lush river delta town of Yilan, in a remote corner of Taiwan's main island. His family was descended from earlier migrants from the mainland. The arriving Nationalist forces viewed the earlier migrants as low-class and politically unreliable, and they were subject to widespread discrimination in jobs and education.

His father, Lin Huoshu, ran a barbershop, and his mother took in laundry from the neighbors. The family lived in a shanty on the edge of town. But the father taught his children about ancient Chinese science and statecraft, about a civilization once so advanced that it started printing books four hundred years before Gutenberg. He read aloud from the old books—*The Three Kingdoms, Journey to the West*—and he drilled into his children the dream of China's revival. He named his fourth child Zhengyi because it meant "justice."

As a boy, Lin wondered why, despite China's glorious history, his family could barely feed itself. His older brother did not ask their mother if they would have lunch, because it was an uncomfortable question, Lin recalled. "He would lean on the stove. If it was warm, that means we had lunch." Otherwise, they went hungry. For Lin, the experience fostered a highly pragmatic streak. He came to view issues of human dignity primarily through the lenses of history and economics.

In his teens, he gravitated to tales about engineering—the exploits of ancient Chinese leaders such as Li Bing, a governor in the third century B.C.E., in today's Sichuan Province, who set out to control deadly floods by devoting eight years to digging a water channel through a mountain. He relied on thousands of workers, who heated the rocks with hay fires and cooled them with water to make them crack. The result was an irrigation system so vast and durable that it is often compared to the wonders of the world; it transformed one of the country's poorest stretches into a region so fertile that it is known today as the "Land of Heaven."

Lin was the most promising of the sons, and in 1971 he won a coveted seat at National Taiwan University, to study irrigation. To pay his tuition, his three brothers left school and worked in their father's barbershop. Lin entered college just as the campus was roiling with debate over the future of Taiwan and mainland China. For years, young people in Taiwan had been taught that the mainland was run by "Communist bandits" and "demons." The Nationalist Party used this threat to justify martial law, and it committed widespread human rights abuses against political opponents and Communist sympathizers.

But as Lin arrived on campus, Taiwan's status was eroding. In July 1971, U.S. president Richard Nixon announced his visit to Beijing. The mainland was gaining influence. In October the United Nations voted to take away Taiwan's seat at the UN General Assembly and give it to the People's Republic, acknowledging that government as the lawful representative of the Chinese people. In this climate, Lin Zhengyi found his voice. He became president of the freshman class and emerged as one of Taiwan's most ardent young activists. At a student rally called "Fight the Communist Bandits Sneaking into the United Nations," he took the microphone and appealed for an island-wide protest, an idea so radical in the era of martial law that even his fellow activists couldn't bring themselves to support it. At another event, he vowed to go on a hunger strike, until the dean talked him out of it.

When he announced that he was transferring to a military academy, he told reporters, "If my decision to join the military can arouse nationalism in every youth . . . then its impact will be immeasurable." He had practical reasons as well: at the military academy he could study for free and receive a stipend.

At a friend's house one day during college, Lin met a young woman named Chen Yunying, an activist who was studying literature at National Chengchi University. After they graduated, they married and had a son. Lin spent two years studying for an MBA and then he was assigned to lead a company on the island of Quemoy, known during the Cold War as the "lighthouse of the free world," because it was the final spit of land before the Communist shoreline. The two sides had once shelled each other so ferociously that Taiwan's military honeycombed the island with bunkers, underground restaurants, and a hospital carved so deep into the mountain that it was designed to survive a nuclear strike.

By the time Lin arrived in 1978, the war was more psychological than physical. The armies still shelled each other, but only on schedule: the mainland fired on odd-numbered days; Taiwan returned fire the rest of the week. Mostly they dueled with propaganda. They blasted each other with enormous, high-powered speakers, and they dropped leaflets from hot-air balloons. They floated softball-sized glass containers to the opposing shores packed with bundles of goods intended to lure defectors with glimpses of prosperity. Taiwan sent pinups and miniature newspapers describing the outside world, clean underwear, pop music cassettes, instructions on how to build a simple radio, and promises of gold coins and glory for anyone willing to defect. The mainland replied with liquor, tea, sweet melons, and pamphlets with photos of smiling Taiwanese diplomats and scientists who had defected to the mainland—or, as the Party put it, "traded darkness for light."

In December 1978, Jimmy Carter announced that the United States was officially recognizing the Communist government in Beijing, and severing formal diplomatic ties with Taiwan. The news buried any remaining hope that the island might regain control of the mainland. In Taiwan, as a correspondent put it, people were "as nervous as a cat trying to cross a busy road with the traffic getting worse by the moment." On New Year's Day 1979, the Beijing government announced that it was ending its military bombardment of Quemoy, and broadcast an appeal to the people of Taiwan that "the bright future . . . belongs to us and to you. The reunification of the motherland is the sacred mission that history has handed to our generation." It boasted that "construction is going ahead vigorously on the motherland."

On February 16, Lin was reassigned even closer to the mainland; he was put in charge of a tiny command post on a lonesome, windswept outcropping called Mount Ma, known among the soldiers as "the front line of the universe." It was a prestigious post, but, according to military investigators, Lin resented the assignment because he was marooned on the outer islands when he could be teaching at the military academy, or taking the exam for senior military office. His post was a favorite stop for political grandees who wanted to be photographed on the front line with the young patriots in uniform. In April he took a leave to see family and friends; one night, he told an old college classmate, Zhang Jiasheng, that he believed Taiwan could prosper only if the mainland thrived.

When he returned to Mount Ma, Lin was so close to the mainland that he could see the faces of People's Liberation Army soldiers through his binoculars. His thinking had already begun to take a sharp turn.

Although Taiwan and the Communists were enemies, ordinary people considered them two halves of the same clan, with a shared history and destiny. As in the American Civil War, some families were physically divided. In one case, a man sent by his mother to go shopping on the mainland just before the Communists cut off boat traffic did not get home for forty years.

In the first years after the separation, some soldiers had tried to swim to the mainland, but fierce currents swirled around the islands, and the defectors washed back up, exhausted, and were arrested as traitors. To deter others, the army destroyed most of the island's fishing boats, and the few that remained were required to lock up their oars at night. Over the years, anything that might be turned into a flotation device—a basketball, a bicycle tire—had to be registered, like a weapon, and the army conducted spot checks around the island, knocking on doors and demanding to see that all balls and inner tubes were accounted for.

Earlier in the spring of 1979, a soldier had made the rare attempt to defect, but he, too, was caught. Lin was undeterred. He believed his plan was better, but he wanted to minimize the effects on his commanding officers. He was scheduled to move from one command to another in May; he believed that if he defected at the time of the transition, senior officers could plausibly blame each other for missing the clues and avoid much blame. What's more, spring on the island was the season of fog, when the humid air met the cold water of the sea and draped the shoreline in a curtain of gray, a shroud that just might be heavy enough to conceal a figure slipping into the waves.

With each spring day, the currents were growing, and by summer they would be strong enough to push a man back to shore, no matter how hard he fought against the waves. If Lin was going to swim to mainland China, he had to go immediately.

On the morning of May 16 he was at his command post. He asked the company secretary Liao Zhenzhu for the latest tide chart. High tide would come at four o'clock in the afternoon and then begin to withdraw.

That night, after sunset, Lin attended a meeting at battalion headquarters and returned to Mount Ma for dinner. At 8:30 a company secretary named Tung Chin-yao visited his table to say he was going over to the battalion headquarters to pick up a new soldier. Tung returned an hour later, but Lin was no longer in the dining hall.

He wasn't in the barracks, either. At 10:50 p.m., two captains from the division recorded his absence in the log and organized a search party. By midnight, commanders had launched a full-scale search of the island—a Thunderbolt Operation, as they called it—involving a hundred thousand people, including soldiers and civilians, men, women, and children. They tore open farmers' storehouses and probed the ponds with bamboo poles. Then searchers found the first clue: at the end of the mine-laden trail, from Mount Ma to the shore, were his sneakers, stenciled with the characters for "Company Commander." They searched his room and discovered that items were missing: a canteen, a compass, a first-aid kit, the company flag, and a life jacket.

By then, Lin was far ahead of them. From the command post, he had to cross just three hundred yards to reach the gray-brown boulders on the shore. From there, he slid into the waves. He had calculated that he needed to enter the water before low tide at 10:00 p.m., so that the force of the sea would draw him away from the land. He had taken one other crucial step: According to military investigators, two days before he swam, Lin inspected the sentry posts along the coast, and he addressed the young recruits assigned to watch the horizon. He told them an odd joke: if, at night, you see swimmers who show no signs of attacking, don't bother to shoot; they're probably just "water spirits," and if you shoot, you'll tempt them into retribution. Superstitions about omens and spirits thrived in Taiwan, and an offhand comment from a commander might have been just enough to make a nervous teenager think twice before raising the alarm over a mysterious flutter on the night sea.

In the water, Lin swam hard and fast. The current tugged at him, but soon he was clear of the shallows and alone on the black depths, enveloped in water and sky. He needed only to make it to the middle of the channel, and then the rising tide would carry him the rest of the way.

He swam freestyle until he was exhausted, and then floated on his back to regain energy. After three hours, with his legs throbbing and numb with cold, he was nearing land. It was the easternmost edge of Chinese soil—Horn Islet. It was just sixty acres of sand and palmetto scrub, home to nothing but Chinese guard posts and artillery guns. The shore, he knew, was laced with land mines. He reached into his clothing, where, sealed in a plastic bag, he had stowed a flashlight. His frozen fingers fumbled with the button. He flicked it on and signaled to Chinese troops, who began to mass on the shore.

Lin reached the shallows. He had much to look forward to: the Communist pamphlets had promised a hero's welcome and rewards of gold and cash. But in the darkness, a lone Chinese soldier waded into the water, edged toward Lin Zhengyi, and placed him under arrest.

# TWO

# THE CALL

Every journey into China begins with a story of gravitational pull. The American writer John Hersey, who was born to missionaries in Tianjin, named it "the Call."

In my first year of college, I wandered into an introductory class on modern Chinese politics: revolution and civil war; the tragic, protean force of Chairman Mao; the fall and rise of Deng Xiaoping, who led China out of seclusion and into the world. Only five years had passed since the 1989 democracy demonstrations at Tiananmen Square, when students, barely older than I was, built a tent city in the very citadel of Party power, a mini-state-within-a-state, alive with impulsive idealism. On television, they looked torn between East and West; they had shag haircuts and boom boxes and quotes from Patrick Henry, but they sang the Internationale and knelt to deliver their demands to men who were still buttoned up in Mao suits. A student protester told a reporter, "I don't know exactly what we want, but we want more of it." Their movement ended in bloodshed on the night of June 3–4, when official loudspeakers blared, "This is not the West; it is China," and the Politburo turned the People's Liberation Army on their people for the first time since the revolution. The Party was proud of suppressing the challenge but aware of the damage to its image, and in the years that followed, the Party scrubbed those events so systematically from its history that only the ghostliest outline has remained.

Once I became interested in China, I flew to Beijing in 1996 to spend half a year studying Mandarin. The city stunned me. Cameras had failed to convey how much closer it was, in spirit and geography, to the windswept plains of Mongolia than to the neon lights of Hong Kong. Beijing smelled of coal and garlic and work-stained wool and cheap tobacco. In a claptrap taxi, with the windows sealed and the heat cranked up, the smell stuck to the roof of your mouth. Beijing was cradled by mountains, high on the North China plain, and in the winter the wind that rose in the land of Genghis Khan whistled down and lashed your face.

Beijing was a clanging, unglamorous place. One of the nicest buildings in town was the Jianguo Hotel, which the architect proudly described as a perfect replica of a Holiday Inn in Palo Alto, California. China's national economy was smaller than that of Italy. The countryside felt near: most nights, I ate in a Muslim neighborhood known as Xinjiang Village, which belonged to the Uighurs, an ethnic group from far western China. Their tiny gray-brick restaurants had jittery sheep tied out front, and the animals vanished in the kitchens, one by one, at dinnertime. After the crowds thinned out each day, the waiters and cooks climbed on the tables and went to sleep.


The Internet had reached China two years earlier, but there were just five telephone lines for every hundred people. I had brought a modem from the United States, and plugged it into my dorm room wall; the machine let out a sharp *pop!* and never stirred again.

When I visited Tiananmen Square for the first time, I stood in the center and saw, on three sides, Mao's mausoleum, the Great Hall of the People, and the Gate of Heavenly Peace. There was no trace of the demonstrations, of course, and nothing in the square had changed since Mao's remains were embalmed in a glass case in 1977. As a foreigner, I found it tempting to look at the Stalinist monuments built by the Party and conclude that the Party was doomed. That summer, *The New York Times* ran a piece headlined THE LONG MARCH TO IRRELEVANCE, in which it observed that "the once-omnipresent party has almost no presence at all."

One side of the square was dedicated to the future: a giant digital clock, fifty feet tall and thirty feet long, counted down the seconds until, as it read across the top, "The Chinese Government Regains Sovereignty over Hong Kong." In less than a year, Great Britain was scheduled to return the islands of Hong Kong, which it had controlled ever since China's defeat in the First Opium War in 1842. The Chinese bitterly resented the history of invasion, of being, as they put it, "cut up like a melon" by foreign powers, so the return of Hong Kong was to be a symbolic restoration of Chinese dignity. Underneath the clock, Chinese tourists were taking photos, and the local paper carried stories about couples who stood at the base of it to take their wedding photos.

The return of Hong Kong fed a burst of patriotism. After nearly two decades of reform and Westernization, Chinese writers were pushing back against Hollywood, McDonald's, and American values. A best seller that summer was entitled *China Can Say No*. Written by a group of young intellectuals, it decried China's "infatuation with America," which, they argued, had suppressed the national imagination with a diet of visas, foreign aid, and advertising. If China didn't resist this "cultural strangulation," it would become "a slave," extending the history of humiliating foreign incursions. The Chinese government, wary of volatile, fast-spreading ideas even when they were supportive, eventually pulled the book off the shelves, but not before a raft of knockoffs sought to exploit the same mood: *Why China Can Say No, China Still Can Say No,* and *China Should Always Say No*. I was there that fall when China celebrated its National Day on October 1. An editorial in the *People's Daily,* the flagship of the state-run media, reminded people, "Patriotism requires us to love the socialist system."

Two years later, I returned to China to study at Beijing Normal University. Most of what I knew about the school was from the history of 1989, when it was one of China's most active campuses during the Tiananmen Square demonstrations; there were days when 90 percent of the student body marched to the square to protest. But by the time I arrived, the most urgent priority for practically everyone I met that summer was a pent-up desire to consume. It's hard to overstate how large a change this was. In the heyday of socialism, there had been a movie called *Must Never Forget,* which told the story of a man whose lust for a new wool suit drives him insane. Now there was a Chinese magazine called the *Guide to Purchasing Upscale Goods,* with features such as "After the Divorce, Who Gets the House?" An article on beverages had an entry called

"Men Who Choose Club Soda," which explained that they were known to have "strong self-respect, ideals, and ambitions, and a low tolerance for mediocrity."

The government was offering its people a bargain: prosperity in exchange for loyalty. Chairman Mao had railed against bourgeois indulgences, but now Chinese leaders were actively promoting the pursuit of the good life. The first winter after the democracy demonstrations, work units in Beijing gave employees overcoats, blankets, Coke, instant coffee, and extra meat. There was a new government slogan around town: "Borrow Money to Realize Your Dreams."

People were still adjusting to the idea of a life outside of labor. Only two years had passed since China reduced the workweek from six days to five. Then it had redrawn the old socialist calendar to create something previously unimaginable: three weeks of vacation. Chinese academics greeted it with a new genre called "leisure studies," dedicated to this "important stage in the social evolution of mankind." One weekend, I joined Chinese classmates on a trip to Inner Mongolia. The train was overcrowded, and the ventilation system inhaled diesel exhaust and exhaled it into the cabins. But nobody complained, because it was a small pleasure simply to be on the move.

After college, I went to work as a newspaper reporter in Chicago, New York, and the Middle East, and in 2005 the *Chicago Tribune* asked if I wanted to return to China. I packed up an apartment in Cairo, and landed in Beijing on an airless night in June. China still had a quarter of a billion people living on less than $1.25 a day. The fact that this population, nearly the size of the United States, was often left out of descriptions of the new China was a mistake, but it was an understandable one, given the scale and pace of change going on around it. The city was unrecognizable to me. I went looking for the night stalls and the sheep of Xinjiang Village, but they had been swept away in a bout of beautification. Income had begun to soar at a rate never experienced in a big country. The last time I had been in China, per capita income was three thousand dollars a year—equivalent to the United States in 1872. The United States took fifty-five years to get to seven thousand dollars. China did it in ten.

Every six hours, the People's Republic was exporting as much as it did in the calendar year 1978, just before Captain Lin Zhengyi swam to the mainland. Economics led me to Lin's front door. I was tracking down academics, trying to unravel what was driving China's changes. By that point, Lin was a prominent economist in his late fifties with a gray brush cut, thick eyebrows, and wire-rim glasses that slipped down his nose. I knew nothing of his background. When I mentioned his name to another economist, he suggested that Lin's own path might tell me more about the engine of China's boom than my stack of books could.

When I first asked Lin about it, he said politely, "This is an old story." He rarely spoke about his defection. I understood, though my curiosity lingered. After our first meeting, I visited Lin many times; we'd catch up on his latest writings, and eventually he resigned himself to my questions about his past. I collected documents about his case, and I visited the shoreline where he started his swim. When he left Taiwan, he said, he had simply wanted to "evaporate."


In the hope of finding the China that I recognized, I clung at first to the countryside. It was the China of literature and ink paintings. One month, I did nothing but walk and hitch rides beside the rivers of Sichuan Province. I slept in small towns that felt half-abandoned, because the call of the city had swept away everyone who was not too old or too young to feel its pull. The village ancients liked to joke that, when they died, there would be nobody strong enough to carry their casket.

But if there was a time when Chinese cities felt like exceptions, like islands in a sea of impoverished countryside, this was less true all the time. China was building the square-foot equivalent of Rome every two weeks. (In 2012 the country became, for the first time, more urban than rural.) I began to sense something charged about entering an instant city, with its miles of unlined, untrammeled black asphalt, flanked by buildings with nobody yet inside. The endless churn was the only constant. When a Chinese friend asked which American cities to visit on his next trip to the United States, I suggested New York, and he responded as tactfully as he could, "Every time I go, it looks the same." In Beijing, I never passed up an invitation, because places, and people, vanished before you had a chance to see them again.

When I went looking for somewhere to live, there were advertisements for Merlin Champagne Town and Venice Water Townhouses and

Moonriver Resort Condo. I chose the Global Trade Mansion. It was an outcropping in a sea of construction, and whoever had built it had installed soundproof windows, since it would be surrounded, for the foreseeable future, by constant noise. I was on the twenty-second floor, and in the mornings before work, I studied Chinese beside the window, peering down on a small army of workers in orange hard hats moving beneath a restless crane. At night, another shift took their place, and the light from the welders' torches flared in the windows. The Global Trade Mansion seemed as good a place as any to figure out what the Communist Party meant by "socialism with Chinese characteristics."

Nine years after the *Times* had heralded the Communist Party's long march to irrelevance, the Party was richer and larger than ever, with eighty million members—one in every twelve adults—and no organized opposition. It was opening Party cells inside even the most Westernized technology companies and hedge funds. China was a high-functioning dictatorship—a dictatorship without a dictator. The government answered to the Party; the Party appointed CEOs and Catholic bishops and newspaper editors. It advised judges how to decide sensitive court cases, and it directed the nation's military generals. At the lowest levels, the Party felt like a professional network. A talented young journalist I knew in Beijing told me that she became a Party member in college because it doubled the number of jobs available, and because one of her favorite professors had pleaded with her to help fill a quota for female recruits.

When I arrived, the Party was freshening itself up with what it called the "Educational Campaign to Maintain the Advanced Nature of the Chinese Communist Party." This was upbeat by Party standards. Unlike the public denunciations and confrontations of the 1960s and '70s, the Party was encouraging people to celebrate their "Red birthday" (the anniversary of the day they joined), and every member was expected to write a two-thousand-word self-evaluation. The market sensed an opportunity, and soon there were websites offering to sell "model" self-evaluations. They came drafted with the requisite apologies, such as "I didn't pay enough attention to establishing a scientific worldview." My journalist friend who joined the Party while in college tried to write her own self-evaluation, but when she read it aloud at the monthly meeting, she was criticized for failing to include the approved phrases, so she went back to the standard list.

In the seven years I had been gone, the language had changed. The word for "comrade," *tongzhi*, had been wryly adopted by gays and lesbians to describe one other. I was in line at the bank one afternoon when an old man, peering ahead impatiently, said, "*Tongzhi*, let's hurry up!" and two teenagers cracked up. The word for waitresses and shopgirls, *xiaojie*, had been repurposed to refer mostly to prostitutes. And the new kind of *xiaojie* were suddenly everywhere in a country overrun with cash-rich new entrepreneurs on business trips.

But the change that startled me most surrounded the word for "ambition," *ye xin*—literally, "wild heart." In Chinese, a wild heart had always carried the suggestion of savage abandon and absurd expectations—a toad who dreams of devouring a swan, as an old saying had it. More than two thousand years ago, a collection of political advice called the *Huainanzi* had warned rulers to "keep powerful positions out of the hands of the ambitious, just as one keeps sharp tools out of the hands of the foolish." But suddenly I was seeing references to "wild hearts" everywhere—on television talk shows and in the self-help aisles. Bookstores carried titles such as *Great Wild Hearts: The Ups and Downs of Pioneering Entrepreneurial Heroes* and *How to Have a Wild Heart in Your Twenties*.

When the summer heat began to break, I set off to see a man I had read about named Chen Guangcheng. Chen was the youngest of five brothers in a peasant family in the village of Dongshigu, which had a population of five hundred. A childhood illness had left him blind, and he received no schooling until he was seventeen years old. His family read literature and adventure novels to him. He listened to the radio, and he took inspiration from his father, who had been illiterate until adulthood, when he went to school and earned a job as a teacher.

Chen studied massage and acupuncture—virtually the only education available to the blind in China—but he was more interested in the law, and he applied to audit legal courses. His father gave him a copy of *The Law Protecting the Disabled*, and he asked his parents and siblings to read it to him repeatedly. Chen discovered that his family was not receiving the tax breaks that it deserved. Chen ventured to Beijing to file his grievance, and to everyone's astonishment, he won. Not long after that, he married a woman he heard speaking on a radio call-in show.

Her parents, like most in China, did not approve of her marrying a blind man, but she did it anyway.

In Dongshigu village, where people grew wheat, soybeans, and peanuts, the masseur knew about the law, so people turned to him for help. In one case, he prevented local leaders from gaining control of land and renting it back to peasants at higher prices. In another, he closed a paper mill that was polluting the local river. When a reporter visited him, he said, "The most important thing is for ordinary people to know that they have the right" to complain. Chen was an oddity in the world of Chinese politics, not only because of the circumstances of his life but because he was a new kind of activist, something more ambiguous than a conventional dissident.

When I heard about him in 2005, he was collecting accounts of women forced to undergo abortions and sterilizations after defying China's one-child policy. When they refused or fled, the local government locked up their parents and siblings in an attempt to force the women out of hiding. When Chen helped the women file a suit, local officials locked him in his house.

One day in late summer, I took a plane to Shandong, and then one taxi after another until I reached Dongshigu village. It was a drowsy afternoon by the time I reached the narrow dirt road into town. I left the cab and continued up the sloping path on foot. Chen lived in a single-story farmhouse, with a weeping willow over the front gate and flowering vines that reached up the home's stone walls. There were faded red paper holiday banners hung beside the gate. Just before I reached it, a pair of men blocked my path. One was lean and bony, with red chapped cheeks; the other was stout and smiling.

"He's not home," the stout man said. He smiled and stepped close enough that I could smell the remnants of his lunch.

"I think he might be," I said. "He's expecting me."

Even if Chen was home, he said, Chen did not want any visitors. Other men began to arrive, in groups of two and three. One took my wrist and walked me back toward the taxi. A police car pulled up, and the officers asked for my passport. I was not permitted to be there, they said. They gave me a choice: I could go to the station with them "to rest for a while," as they put it, or I could leave town.

The stout fellow was no longer smiling. He wanted to know where I had heard about the blind man in Dongshigu village. "From the Internet," I said. He blinked back at me, and from his expression, I sensed that the Internet meant as much to him as if I'd said I had been led there by fairies. He opened the door of the taxi and pressed me toward it.

I slumped back into the cab, and we inched out of town, trailed by the police. The taxi driver was curious about the fuss. I explained that Chen was collecting complaints about abuses of the one-child policy, and the driver said he knew of another place nearby where people had similar complaints. He took me to a town called Nigou, where we pulled up beside a line of shops on the main street. There was a fertilizer store on the first floor, and above it, a fenced-in window. When I got out of the taxi and stood beneath the window, a woman stepped to the inside of the fence and peered down at me.

I asked why she was there. "We cannot leave. We have no freedom," she said. She was calm. She said that local family-planning officials had locked her there, above the fertilizer store, because her daughter-in-law would not agree to a forced sterilization or pay the fees for having too many children, the equivalent of about a year's income.

I peered up at the woman and asked, "How long have you been there?"

"Three weeks," she said.

"How many of you are up there?"

"Fifteen," she said.

It was an odd arrangement for an interview. I was standing beneath the window, and she was looking down through the fence. I looked up and down the block, where people were going about their lives. There was a hair salon on one side and a fruit stand on the other.

The local family-planning office occupied a storefront across the street. I walked in and asked about the people detained above the fertilizer store. A man behind a desk named Wan Zhendong, the head of the office's statistics department, said he knew nothing about any detention center, adding that people who complain about being detained are usually trying to avoid paying fines for having too many children. "The policy," Wan said, "is accepted by ninety-nine-point-nine percent of the people here."

Once I returned to Beijing, I called Chen Guangcheng, the blind masseur. Every time I dialed, the line was dead. I didn't get through for months. A lawyer named Teng Biao wasn't surprised when I described the scene in Nigou. People were beginning to call these detention centers "black jails." It was difficult to figure out how many there were or where they were located. You had to look for them, town by town. "It is very hard for people there to get information to lawyers and the media," he told me. "The local authorities will try their best to make sure nobody knows about it."

The Internet was largely a mystery in Dongshigu village, but no longer in Beijing. Initially, the Chinese government had regarded the Internet as an opportunity: the country had arrived late to the Industrial Revolution, and Chinese leaders hoped that the information revolution could help the country close the gap with the West. But the enthusiasm cooled. In 2001, President Jiang Zemin identified the Internet as a "political, ideological, and cultural battlefield." The week I returned from Shandong, the Ministry of Public Security expanded a list of information officially "prohibited" from the Web. Whenever possible, the government liked to organize the world by category, and it had already banned a list of nine types of information, including "rumors" and anything that "damages the credibility" of the state. Now it expanded the list from nine to eleven, including "information inciting illegal assemblies" and "information concerning activities of illegal civic associations."

The scale of available information was soaring. At the beginning of 2005, China had about one million bloggers; by the end, this figure had quadrupled, and the government ordered Internet companies to set up a system of "self-discipline" to censor and monitor the way people used the Web. Bit by bit, the Party was erecting what came to be known as the Great Firewall—a vast digital barricade that prevented Chinese users from seeing newspaper stories critical of China's top leaders or reports from human rights groups; eventually, it blocked social networking sites such as Twitter and Facebook. Unlike the physical Great Wall, the digital version grew or shrank to meet new challenges or convey a sense of openness. Often, I didn't know something was off-limits until I typed it in and received an error code such as HTTP 404—the page cannot be found.

The Party grew more determined to punish those who tried to undermine its control of information. The previous year, 2004, a journalist named Shi Tao, who worked at Contemporary Business News in Hunan Province, attended a staff meeting in which an editor relayed the latest instructions about what subjects could not be published around the anniversary of the Tiananmen Square protests. That night, Shi logged on to his e-mail account (huoyan1989@yahoo.com.cn) and sent a summary of the Party document to an editor of Democracy Forum, a pro-democracy website based in New York. Two days later, the Beijing State Security Bureau contacted Yahoo! China and asked for the name behind the account, the contents of the e-mail, and the locations from which the e-mail was accessed. Yahoo! complied, and on November 23, 2004, Shi Tao was arrested and later charged with "leaking state secrets." His trial lasted two hours; he was found guilty and sentenced to ten years.

The case was the clearest demonstration of the force with which the government would seek to maintain control over an uncertain new challenge. When human rights groups criticized Yahoo! for handing over the information, the company's cofounder Jerry Yang replied, "If you want to do business there you have to comply." Members of the U.S. Congress took note. At a subcommittee hearing on the Internet in China, Rep. Chris Smith, a Republican from New Jersey, wondered, "If the secret police a half century ago asked where Anne Frank was hiding, would the correct answer be to hand over the information in order to comply with local laws?" Yahoo! held firm, and when Shi Tao's mother sued the company for exposing her son to harm, Yahoo! filed a motion to dismiss.

Over time, the pressure on the company became unbearable. In the fall of 2007, Rep. Tom Lantos, the only Holocaust survivor to have served in Congress, called Yang and other Internet executives before the House Foreign Relations Committee and said, "Morally you are pygmies." Shi Tao's mother gave tearful testimony, and when it was over, Yang bowed to her three times and said, "I want to personally apologize." Yahoo! settled with her family, but the son remained in jail. Inside China, the message was indelible: the Internet would never be a domain of free expression.

———

The Global Trade Mansion was too quiet and too expensive, and I needed more chances to practice Chinese: When I called my landlord to suggest that he keep the security deposit as my final month's rent, I mistakenly told him to keep the security deposit as my final month's "menstruation."

Large parts of the city had been demolished and rebuilt in preparation for the 2008 Olympics. The Beijing-born author Zha Jianying, who returned to the capital after studying in the United States, quoted a friend describing the city as a place where it was becoming impossible to find a place "to hang up one's birdcage." The few surviving sections of old Beijing consisted mostly of tiny alleyways lined by single-story homes of gray brick, wood, and tile. The arrangement had remained more or less the same for seven centuries, when sections of the city were laid out under the Yuan dynasty, which gave these streets the name *hutong*, a Mongolian term that came to mean "alley" in Chinese. The Mongols had designed the *hutong* to uniform widths of twelve or twenty-four paces. In 1980 the city had six thousand *hutong*; over the years, all but a few hundred were leveled to make way for office buildings and apartment complexes. Only one of the city's forty-four princely palaces had survived intact.

I asked around and found a one-story house for rent at No. 45 Caochang Bei Xiang. Most people in these old homes used a communal public toilet around the corner from my front door. But this house had been fitted with indoor plumbing, and renovated to comprise four modern rooms surrounding a small courtyard that contained a date tree and a persimmon tree. When I reported my new address to the *Chicago Tribune*'s driver, Old Zhang, he did not approve. "You're going the wrong direction," he said. "You should be moving from the ground into an apartment up in the air, not the other way around."

The walls of the house were porous; when it rained, the ceiling leaked, and when the winter overwhelmed the heating, I wore a ski hat around the house. Underfoot, there was a steady traffic of mice and beetles and geckos, and now and then I had to wallop a scorpion with a magazine. But it was a relief to live with the windows open, and I loved it. Across the alley, my neighbor kept a pigeon coop on his roof, as a hobby. He attached wooden pipettes to the birds' feet so they whistled as they flew in great circles above our heads.

The window above my desk was filled with a view of Beijing's ancient Drum Tower, a soaring wooden pavilion built in 1272. For hundreds of years the Drum Tower, and its neighbor the Bell Tower, kept time for the people of the city, telling them when to sleep and when to rise. They were the tallest buildings for miles around. The Drum Tower contained twenty-four giant leather-covered drums, large enough that their thundering could be heard in the farthest reaches of the capital.

Chinese emperors were obsessed with controlling the passing of the seasons and the hours of the day. In the spring, the emperor decreed the precise moment when members of the court could change out of their furs and into their silk; in the fall, the emperor decreed the right moment for the raking of leaves. Controlling time was so closely associated with imperial power that when foreign armies invaded Beijing in 1900, they made a point to climb the Drum Tower and slash the leather drums with bayonets. For a while, the Chinese renamed it the Realizing Humiliation Tower.

# THREE

# BAPTIZED IN CIVILIZATION

The soldiers hauled Lin Zhengyi from the water and onto the beach. It was the dead of night, May 16, 1979. They suspected he was a spy; they had never encountered a soldier who had swum from Taiwan.

Back in Taiwan, Lin's commanders didn't know what to think. They suspected he had tried to defect, but had he succeeded, the loudspeakers across the water, they thought, would be gloating about his arrival. Perhaps he had drowned. Or perhaps he had been a mainland spy all along. Regardless, the abrupt disappearance of one of Taiwan's most celebrated soldiers was humiliating. The army classified Lin as missing, then dead, and awarded his wife, Chen, the equivalent of thirty thousand dollars in benefits. She was pregnant and alone, raising their three-year-old son. To protect her from retaliation, Lin had told her nothing of his plans. At the family shrine, Lin's parents added a memorial tablet inscribed with his name.

On the mainland, Lin was held in custody and questioned for three months. Once he had persuaded them that he was not a spy, he was released and allowed to travel. In a country where most people were still reeling from the Cultural Revolution, he regarded Mao's legacy with the passion of the convert, and he made a pilgrimage to Yan'an, the wartime headquarters of the Communist Party, "to be educated," he told me.

He also went to Sichuan to see the ancient dam built by his hero Li Bing. From a ledge overlooking the roiling waters, he peered into the channel, which was often described as a symbol of how far China had fallen in the two thousand years since the dam was built. But Lin took it as a source of inspiration to do something bold. "I think that if we do something, we can change the fate of people, change the fate of the nation for a thousand years."

The exhilaration of defection was tempered by the shameful fact that he had left his family behind. "I love my wife. I love my children. I love my family. I feel responsibility for them," he told me. "As an intellectual, I also feel strongly my responsibility for the culture and the prosperity in China. If I have a strong belief in what is right, then I need to follow that."

In the months after he arrived, contacting his wife was out of the question. Taiwan's military government was undoubtedly monitoring her for clues about Lin's fate. He remembered a cousin who was studying in Tokyo and he wrote him a letter: "You are now the only relative I can contact. But you must be careful. Don't give the Nationalists any evidence they could use against you. I have a message to pass along, but you must deliver it verbally, and leave no traces." Lin asked him to buy birthday presents for Chen and the children, and to sign them "Fang-fang," his family nickname. In his letter, Lin confessed, "Even though a man must have great aspirations, and be aware of his duties beyond emotions and attachments to family, I am more and more homesick by the day." He worried about his parents, his son, and his newborn daughter. Of his son, he said, "Xiao Long is three years old now, the age when he most needs a father, but he only has his mother. Xiao Lin has never even laid eyes on her father . . . To all of them, words cannot express my apology." He remained bitter that Taiwan's government had assigned him tasks that were more about propaganda than advancement. "The Nationalists were only using me, never nurturing me," he wrote. He gushed about the changes under way in China in the early months of the economic boom unleashed by Deng: "Almost everyone has enough food and clothing these days . . . Things are flying ahead in leaps of progress. People are full of vitality and confidence. I truly believe that China's future is bright. Someday you'll be proud to be Chinese, to stand up in the world with your head held high and your chest puffed out."

But once the novelty wore off, life for defectors was hard. Huang Zhi-cheng, a Taiwanese pilot who landed his plane on the mainland in 1981, recalled, "At first, it's hello, hello, and then they leave you to fend for yourself."

Lin applied to study economics at People's University in Beijing and was rejected. His official file, the *dang'an*, contained every suspicion ever raised about his political history. For Lin, defection would always be a cause for suspicion; in the language of the day, people said he had "origins unclear." After the rejection, he applied to Peking University. Dong Wenjun, an administrator, worried that Lin might turn out to be a spy, but ultimately decided, as he put it later, that there was "no intelligence to be gathered in the economics department anyway." Lin was accepted.

Lin told his classmates that he was a student from Singapore. In return for his defection, he had asked the People's Liberation Army not to publicize his story for propaganda purposes. He had seen the brochures that washed up in Quemoy, heralding defectors, but he didn't want to be featured that way. He gave up the name Lin Zhengyi. From now on he would be Lin Yifu, which meant "a persistent man on a long journey."

In his office one afternoon, I mentioned to Lin that people in Taiwan speculated that he had given military secrets to the People's Liberation Army, to prove that he was trustworthy. He had heard this, too. He laughed wearily. "That's nonsense," he said. "I didn't come with anything other than what I wore." He noted that by the time he fled, China was calling for reunification, and a junior officer's secrets would have been of limited use. He disputed the military investigators' reports that he'd defected partly out of professional frustration, and that he had misled the sentries in order to conceal his departure. He framed his swim as an act of idealism. "I still believe that my friends in Taiwan had the same aspiration to make a contribution to China. I respect their aspiration. This is just the way I think I can contribute to China's history. It was my personal choice."

It was, by mainland Chinese standards, a radical act: historically, personal choice was a low priority for the Chinese, for reasons both modern and ancient, including, in the beginning, the land itself. Richard Nisbett, a psychologist at the University of Michigan who studies cultural differences in how people see the world, found that in ancient China, fertile plains and rivers lent themselves to rice farming that required irrigation and compelled people "to cultivate the land in concert with one another." By contrast, the ancient Greeks, who lived amid mountains and coastlines, relied on herding, trading, and fishing, and they were able to be more independent. In that history, Nisbett saw the makings of Greek ideas about personal freedom, individuality, and objective thought.

The sense that an individual was embedded in larger forces ran through Chinese art, politics, and society. The philosopher Xunzi, in the third century B.C.E., believed that only social rituals and models could control individual "wayward" appetites, just as steam and pressure could straighten a warped slab of wood. One of China's most famous classical paintings, an eleventh-century scroll by Fan Kuan entitled *Travelers Among Mountains and Streams*, is often called China's Mona Lisa. But compared to Leonardo's full-frame portrait, Fan Kuan's work depicts a tiny figure of a horseman enveloped by vast, misty mountains. In imperial Chinese law, the courts considered not only motive but also the damage to the social order, so a defendant received a harsher sentence if he murdered someone of a higher social rank than someone of a lower rank. Punishment was collective: judges sentenced not just the guilty individual but also family members, neighbors, and community leaders.

Liang Qichao, one of China's leading reformers of the early twentieth century, hailed the importance of the individual in national development, but renounced that view after he visited San Francisco's Chinatown in 1903 and concluded that the competition between separate Chinese clans and families was preventing Chinese people from prospering. "If we were to adopt a democratic system of government now," he wrote, "it would be nothing less than committing national suicide."

He dreamed of what he called a Chinese Cromwell, "to carry out harsh rule, and with iron and fire to forge and temper our countrymen for twenty, thirty, even fifty years. After that we can give them the books of Rousseau and tell them about the deeds of Washington." Sun Yat-sen, the revolutionary who became president after the fall of the empire in 1911, concluded that China was weak because its people were a "sheet of loose sand." His prescription? "The individual should not have too much liberty," he said, "but the nation should have complete liberty." He encouraged people to think of the government as a "great automobile" and its leaders as essential "chauffeurs and mechanics" who require a free hand to operate.

China had always had poets, writers, and revolutionaries—whom the authors Geremie Barmé and Linda Jaivin have called the "unbound feet" of Chinese history—but Chairman Mao was determined to enshrine the idea that "the individual is subordinate to the organization." The Party, he declared, must "eradicate all tendencies towards disunity." It organized people into work units and collective farms. Without a letter from your *danwei* ("work unit"), you couldn't get married or divorced, you couldn't buy a plane ticket or stay in a hotel, or, for that matter, visit another *danwei*. Most days, you lived, worked, shopped, and studied within its confines. To identify and correct individualistic thinking, Mao relied on propaganda and education—"Thought Reform," as he called it, which became known colloquially as *xinao*, or "mind-cleansing." (In 1950, a CIA officer who learned of it coined the term *brainwashing*.)

To enliven its message, the Party promoted models of sacrifice. In 1959, newspapers highlighted a soldier named Lei Feng who was five feet tall and called himself a "tiny screw" in the revolutionary machine. He appeared in a traveling photo exhibition, with images such as "Shoveling Manure to Help the Liaoning People's Commune" and "Lei Feng Darning Socks." After the army announced that the young soldier had died in an accident (struck by a falling telephone pole), Chairman Mao advised people to "learn from Comrade Lei Feng," and for decades to come, local museums displayed replicas of his sandals, his toothbrush, and other effects—like the bones of saints.

The pressure to conform was profound. A doctor who was terrorized during the Cultural Revolution—exiled to the western desert, where his wife committed suicide—later said, "To survive in China you must reveal nothing to others. Or it could be used against you . . . That's why I've come to think the deepest part of the self is best left unclear. Like mist and clouds in a Chinese landscape painting, hide the private part behind your social persona. Let your public self be like rice in a dinner: bland and inconspicuous, taking on the flavors of its surroundings while giving off no flavor of its own."

As change gathered speed in the 1980s, Chinese leaders warned that the nation must cross the river by "feeling for the stones." In reality, many people swept into the current of China's transformation found they had no choice but to plunge in and swim as fast as possible, with only the vaguest sense of what might lie on the other side.

On paper, China remained suspicious of the individual; even after reforms were under way, the 1980 edition of the country's authoritative dictionary, *The Sea of Words,* defined *individualism* as "the heart of the Bourgeois worldview, behavior that benefits oneself at the expense of others." And nothing was more abhorrent to the Communist Party than the language of Thatcherist free-market fundamentalism. But China was enacting some of its most basic ideas: the retreat of public services, hostility to trade unions, national and military pride.

All over China, people were embarking on journeys, joining the largest migration in human history. China's extraordinary growth relied on a combination of abundant cheap labor and a surge of investment in factories and infrastructure—a recipe that uncorked economic energy stored up during the years of turmoil under Mao. Party leader Zhao Ziyang surrounded himself with economists who sought to emulate the growth of South Korea and Japan. To thrive, they had to be flexible. Wu Jinglian, a researcher in a state think tank, had begun his career as an orthodox socialist who persuaded his high school to give up teaching English and Western economics. But during the Cultural Revolution, his wife, the director of a kindergarten, was labeled a "capitalist roader" because her father had been a general in the Nationalist Army; Red Guards shaved half of her head. Wu himself was tagged an "antirevolutionary" and sent off to "reform through labor." "I experienced a drastic change in ideology," he told me. By the eighties, Wu was a leading expert on the free market, even though that term was too controversial to utter. Wu had to call it "the commodity economy."

Beginning in 1980, China designated special economic zones, which used tax advantages to attract foreign investment, technology, and links to customers abroad. The zones needed workers. Since the fifties, the Party had controlled where people lived by dividing households into two types: rural and urban. The distinction ordained where you were born, schooled, employed, and, most likely, buried. With few exceptions, only the Public Security Bureau could change your household registration, or *hukou.* But new machines and fertilizers demanded fewer hands in the fields, and in 1985 the government officially permitted rural people to live and work temporarily in cities. In the next eight years, the number of rural migrants reached a hundred million. In 1992, Deng Xiaoping let it be known that prosperity was paramount: "Development," he said, after visiting a refrigerator factory that had expanded sixteenfold in seven years, "is the only hard truth." Between 1993 and 2005, state-owned enterprises cut more than seventy-three million jobs, sending another flood of workers off to find a new source of income. Chinese leaders kept their currency undervalued, which made exports cheap, and these soared. In 1999, China's exports had been less than a third of America's. A decade later, China was the world's largest exporter.

Autonomy was creeping into daily life. In Mao's day, it had been considered immoral to take a second job, because spare time belonged to the state. By the nineties, so many people were moonlighting that there was a boom in the business of printing business cards. The state media, which had once encouraged everyone to be "a rustless screw" in the machine, now acknowledged the new reality of competition: "You must rely on yourself," the *Hebei Economic Daily* wrote. "Blaze your own path, and fight." People made money in whatever ways they could. In poor areas, door-to-door blood buyers offered to help cover the cost of taxes and school fees. Jing Jun, a Harvard-trained anthropologist, found that people were donating so often that they ran up against physical limits. "So the blood contractors would hang people upside down by their feet against a wall to make the blood flow down into the arms," he wrote. (The business proved disastrous; by the mid-nineties, the blood collectors had caused China's worst outbreak of HIV. An estimated fifty-seven thousand people were infected.)

The language of the individual filtered out through movies and fashions and music. Jia Zhangke, a filmmaker, recalled to me that when he was growing up in Shanxi coal country in the eighties, he would ride the bus for four hours just to buy a cassette of mushy pop ballads by Deng Lijun, a Taiwanese star so popular that Lin Yifu's military unit on Quemoy had played her music over the radio to attract defectors. Since she had the same surname as Deng Xiaoping, the soldiers on the mainland joked that they listed to Old Deng all day and Young Deng all night. "Before that, the songs we sang were 'We Are the Heirs of Communism' and 'We Workers Have Power.' It was always 'we,'" Jia told me. "But in Deng Lijun's song 'The Moon Represents My Heart,' it was about 'me.' *My* heart. And of course we loved it!"

Companies reinforced that message. China Mobile sold cell phone service aimed at people under twenty-five, using the slogan "My Turf, My Decision." Even in rural areas, where things changed slowly, people spoke of themselves in different ways. Mette Halskov Hansen, a Norwegian sinologist who spent four years in a countryside school, found that teachers were trying to prepare their students for a world in which survival required "self-reliance, self-promotion, and the self-made individual." Hansen watched a pep rally in 2008 in which students recited a pledge: "Ever since God created all things on earth, there has not been one person like me. My eyes and my ears, my brain and my soul, all are exceptional. Nobody speaks or behaves like me, no one before me and no one will after me. I am the biggest miracle of nature!"

The desire to leave—to "go out," as it was known—swept through villages. It didn't necessarily engulf the men and women who were most successful or confident. On the contrary, it often settled on the misfits— the restless, the willful, the unblessed. On the day the teenager Gong Hainan was seized by the desire to leave, her mother and her father hesitated. She was their only daughter, and they were country people with no knowledge of the city. But once their daughter had an idea in her mind, she drove it like a mule. "They had no choice but to agree," Gong told me.

Gong Hainan was born at the foot of a mountain in the village of Waduangang, in Hunan, the home province of Chairman Mao. Her parents met under benighted circumstances. During the Cultural Revolution, they were paired with each other because they shared a political affliction: their families had been classified as "well-off peasants." A village matchmaker put them together. Gong's family raised peanuts and cotton and chickens and pigs. She was the elder of two children, and she was small and sickly. She had narrow shoulders and thin lips, and her face at rest carried a wary expression. In the hierarchy of village life, this did her no favors. The local boys wanted girls with plump cheeks, and lips in the shape of a rosebud. "If anyone ever liked me, I have yet to hear about it," Gong told me years later, when we got to know each other in Beijing.

But even as a child, Gong had a restless energy. When her neighbors began to open tiny businesses, Gong badgered her parents to let her join the trend. They laughed. "We have three neighbors, and a mountain behind us. Who is going to shop here?" they asked. Undeterred, Gong enlisted her little brother, Haibin, into a business proposition: They would buy ice pops and resell them door-to-door. After one day of lugging a thirty-pound Styrofoam cooler around the rutted village paths, her brother quit. "I could've beaten him half to death and he wouldn't go out again," she said. But Gong made a map of the village that identified which parents were known to cave in to their kids' demands, and she charted the optimal route. Soon she was selling two boxes a day. "Whatever you're doing," she concluded, "you have to be strategic."

There was something different about her generation, the young men and women born in the seventies. You could hear it in their speech, their comfort with saying "I" and "me," where their parents would have used the plural: "our work unit" and "our family." (Older Chinese took to calling her cohort the *wo yi dai*—the "Me Generation.")

When Gong was sixteen, her test scores earned her a place at the top local high school, a transformative moment for a farming family. Shortly before school was to start, she was riding into town on a tractor-taxi, on her way to restock her ice pop supply, when the tractor plunged into a ditch. The other passengers were thrown clear, but she had been sitting on the front bench. Her right leg was crushed, and her nose was nearly severed. She would recover, but when she got out of the hospital, wearing a hip cast, she discovered that a rural school could not accommodate a student unable to walk. The school suggested she withdraw.

Gong's mother, Jiang Xiaoyuan, would have none of it. She moved into the dorm and carried her daughter on her back—up and down the stairs to the classrooms, back and forth to the toilet. (Gong trained herself to use the bathroom no more than twice a day.) While Gong was in class, her mother hustled outside to the street to sell fruit from baskets to make extra money. I wondered if the story was a metaphor, until I met her mother. "There was one especially tall building, the laboratory, and her class was up on the fourth floor," Jiang said, scowling at the memory of it. Gong had never seriously considered an alternative. "School was the only way out," Jiang told me. "We never wanted for her to work in the fields like us."

———

Gong's medical bills plunged her parents into debt. "My accident made a mess of the family," she said. It was 1994, and China's epic labor migration was gathering. In 1978, nearly 80 percent of the Chinese population had been working on a farm; by 1994 this figure had fallen to less than 50 percent. Gong dropped out of the elite local high school and set off for the factories on the coast.

As migration grew, the government tried to manage the course of the flood. One slogan urged rural people to find work close to home: "Leave the Land, but Not the Countryside! Enter the Factories, but Not the Cities!" The state officially named the new migrants the "floating population"—a term that shared Chinese characters with the words for hooligans and stray dogs. Police blamed crime on what they called "Triple Withouts"—migrants without a home, a job, or a reliable source of income. Cities sought to limit the number of new arrivals. In Beijing, the local government barred various categories of people, including "beggars and buskers, fortune tellers and other people engaged in feudal superstitious activities." If they were found, they would be sent home. Beijing offered official "green cards" to parcel out access to public schools and housing, but it set the standards so high that only 1 percent of the new migrants qualified. Shanghai published a handbook called *The Guide to Entering Shanghai: For Brothers and Sisters Who Come to Shanghai to Work*, in which the opening chapter was entitled "Do Not Blindly Come to Shanghai for Work."

Still, they came. By 2007, 135 million rural migrants were living in the cities, and the "floating population" became known by the government as the "outside population." The State Council ordered governments to improve insurance and workplace-injury protections, and to ensure the migrants were "baptized in civilization," as the Party press liked to put it.

In the city of Zhuhai, Gong found work on an assembly line making Panasonic televisions. She soldered two wires together, two thousand times a day, and sent money back to her family. If she finished early, the foreman raised her quota for the next day. The factory had an in-house newspaper, and after a few months Gong wrote a piece of spectacular propaganda entitled "I Love Panasonic, I Love My Home." It had the desired effect; she was taken off the assembly line and promoted to editor. She'd found a kind of contentment in her job. Then one day a former classmate visited and spent the weekend regaling her with news of their old friends rising up through college and moving to exotic new places. In the confines of the factory, she'd come to see herself as a success; she worked with her mind, not her fingers. Yet hearing about what she was missing was shattering.

She cursed her decision to drop out of school. "It was weak and naïve," she said. China's economy was rising on all sides of her, and she was trapped in the basement. Factories making televisions and clothes needed uncomplaining workers with no promise of job security or training or progress. Migrants like her were earning just half of what regular residents of Guangdong were earning, and the gap was widening. If she stayed in Guangdong, she could look forward to a life of second-class health care and education. She would have to pay five or six times what local parents paid to educate a child with a local *hukou*. More than three-quarters of all women who died in childbirth in the province were migrants with no access to prenatal care.

In the electronics businesses, assembly-line bosses preferred female employees, because they were more conscientious about detail work. The only men in her factory were security guards and truck loaders and cooks. "If I ever wanted to settle down, those were going to be my choices," Gong said. She knew the dangers of going back to the village. It was 1995, and already the income gap between the countryside and the city in China was wider than anywhere else in the world except Zimbabwe and South Africa. She had to get to a city. She said, "I decided to go back to school."

"Everyone in the village was against the idea," she went on. "They said, 'You're a twenty-one-year-old woman. Go and get married!'" In the village hierarchy, the only person who ranked lower than a young woman was a young woman who had something better in mind for her future. But her parents supported her decision, and the school allowed her to reenroll in the eleventh grade. She scored the highest rank in the county on the national college entrance test, and earned a coveted spot at Peking University, where Chairman Mao, who arrived as a twenty-four-year-old in the capital, once said, "Beijing is like a crucible in which one cannot but be transformed."

Before she enrolled, she, like Lin Yifu, changed her given name. She became Haiyan, a reference to the small, hardy seabird in an old revolutionary poem by Maxim Gorky, "The Song of the Storm Petrel." It was one of Lenin's favorites. She cared nothing about the revolution, but she loved the image of a bird that turns to face the storm—"one free soul," as Gorky put it, that "floats unharmed above the chaos."

At Peking University, Gong studied Chinese literature and went on to Fudan University, in Shanghai, for a master's degree in journalism. By her second year, she had gained a sense of professional momentum. But something was lacking: a love life.

Of all the upheavals in Chinese life, there was none more intimate than the opportunity to choose one's mate. For centuries, village matchmakers and parents paired off young people of comparable social and economic status—of "family doors of equal size"—with minimal participation from the bride and groom.

Confucius has exhaustive advice about justice and duty, but he mentions emotion, *qing*, only once in the *Analects*, a record of his teachings. Love stories didn't become popular in China until the twentieth century. While European protagonists occasionally found happiness, Chinese lovers typically succumbed to forces beyond their control: meddling parents, disease, miscommunication. The stories were categorized so that readers knew which doom to expect: Tragic Love, Bitter Love, Miserable Love, Wronged Love, and Chaste Love. A sixth genre, Joyous Love, was not as successful. (The tendency to see love as a problem endured. In the 1990s, the researchers Fred Rothbaum and Billy Yuk-Piu Tsang analyzed the lyrics of eighty Chinese and American pop songs and discovered that the Chinese songs made many more references to suffering and "negative expectations"—a sense that if destiny did not ordain a relationship, it could not be salvaged.)

In China, romance had a political side: In 1919, when Chinese students demonstrated for what they called Mr. Democracy and Mr. Science, they also demanded an end to arranged marriage. They called it "the freedom of love," and from then on it was tied to a sense of individual autonomy. Mao outlawed arranged marriages and concubines, and established a woman's right to divorce, but the system left little room for desire. Dating that did not lead to the altar was "hooliganism," and sex was so stigmatized in the Maoist period that doctors met couples who struggled to conceive because they lacked a firm grasp of the mechanics. When the magazine *Popular Films* ran a photo of Cinderella kissing a prince, readers wrote in to denounce it. "I heard the masses of workers, peasants, and soldiers condemning you for being so shameless!" one wrote.

Though arranged marriages were banned in 1950, factory bosses and Communist cadres still did much of the matchmaking, and when a young intellectual named Yan Yunxiang was sent down from Beijing to the village of Xiajia, in China's northeast, in 1970, he found an abundance of miserable love. Local women had so little say in whom they married that there was a village tradition of sobbing when you left home on your wedding day. It wasn't until the eighties that the village elders began to relinquish control over local marriages. Yan Yunxiang eventually became an anthropologist and continued to visit the village over the years. He attended a wedding where the bride was marrying for love, and she confided to Yan that she was too happy to sob. She rubbed hot pepper on her handkerchief in order to summon the tears that her parents' generation expected.

In the heyday of socialism, every man in Yan's village wanted to be seen as *laoshi*, "frank and simple"; the worst thing a bachelor could be was *fengliu*, "rebellious and romantic." But all of a sudden, the *laoshi* men were known as dowdy and gullible, and everyone wanted to be as *fengliu* as Leonardo DiCaprio aboard the *Titanic*, in the most popular pirated movie of the day.

In much of the world, marriage is in decline; the proportion of married American adults has dropped to 51 percent, the lowest ever recorded. But in China, even as rates of divorce have climbed, so much of the culture revolves around family and offspring that 98 percent of the female population eventually marries—one of the highest levels in the world. (China has neither civil unions nor laws against discrimination, and it remains a very hard place to be gay.)

The sudden freedom had its problems. China had few bars or churches, and no coed softball, for example, so pockets of society were left to improvise. Factory towns organized "friend-making clubs" for assembly-line workers; Beijing traffic radio, 103.9, set aside a half hour on Sundays for taxi drivers to advertise themselves; and CCTV-7, the military channel, organized a dating show for grunts. But those practices merely reinforced existing barriers, and for vast numbers of people, the collision of love, choice, and money was a bewildering new problem.

China's one-child policy had exerted unexpected forces on marriage. By promoting the use of condoms on an unprecedented scale, it de-linked sex from reproduction and spurred a mini sexual revolution. But it also heightened competition: When sonogram technology spread in China in the 1980s, couples aborted female fetuses in order to wait for a boy. As a result, China has twenty-four million men who will be of marrying age by 2020 but unable to find a spouse—"bare branches" on the family tree, as they're known in Chinese. Women were barraged with warnings in the Chinese press that if they were still single at thirty, they would be considered "leftover women."

"In China's marriage market," Gong explained to me one day, "there are three species trying to survive: men, women, and women with graduate degrees." She discovered, while studying for her master's degree, that Chinese men were wary of women who'd surpassed them in education. And in Shanghai, she said, "I didn't know a soul in the city. My parents had an elementary school education. I could never be interested in the kinds of people they had access to."

Men and women with different *hukou* rarely married; this frustrated her. "Even though 'free love and marriage' was written into the law, we don't actually have the freedom to choose," she told me. In 2003 the Internet had just sixty-nine million users (5 percent of the population), but it was growing at 30 percent a year. That fall, a Web portal called Sohu reported that the most-searched-for name on its site, once "Mao Zedong," was now "Mu Zi Mei," a sex blogger. When Mu Zi Mei posted an audio recording of one of her assignations, demand crashed her server. (To those who gasped, she replied, "I express my freedom through sex.")

Gong Haiyan paid five hundred yuan (about sixty dollars at the time) to an early online dating service. She selected twelve men and sent them messages. When she got no response and complained to the company, she was told, "Look at yourself—you're ugly, and you go after these high-quality men? No wonder you got no replies." She tracked down one of the bachelors and learned that he hadn't even registered with the site. The

photograph, the vitals, the contact info—all had been cobbled together
from other online sites. China had mastered the fake Polo shirt, and
now it was turning to the counterfeit date. "I wasn't thinking about being
an entrepreneur—I was just so angry," Gong said. "I wanted a site for
people who were in the same position I was in."

She mapped out a simple design on Front Page, the website software.
She named her business Love21.cn. To sell ads, she hired her brother
Haibin, who'd taken some computer classes after dropping out of high
school. She signed up her friends, and other customers followed. A software developer agreed to invest the equivalent of fifteen thousand dollars. (Later, he met his wife on the site.) Gong used the money to expand,
and she discovered that there was more demand than she had imagined.
In remote areas, where computer scanners were still hard to come by,
customers began to send photographs by post. People were signing up at
a rate of nearly two thousand a day.

Gong was nothing like the other Web entrepreneurs I knew in China.
For one thing, the top ranks of Chinese technology were dominated by
men. And unlike others who glimpsed the potential of the Internet in
China, she didn't speak fluent English. She didn't even have a degree in
computer science. She still had a trace of the countryside about her. She
spoke at high volume, except before crowds, when her voice trembled.
She was five feet three, still with narrow shoulders, and when she talked
about her business, I got the feeling that she was talking about herself.
"We're not like you foreigners, who make friends easily in a bar or go
traveling and chat up a stranger," she told me. "This is not about messing
around for fun. Our membership has a very clear goal: to get married."

In her spare time, she wrote. The Internet was taking off as a forum
for all kinds of ideas, and she carved out a reputation for herself as the
"Little Dragon Lady," an advice columnist who was attuned to the problems of the People's Republic. She flipped through messages from an-
guished bachelors, concerned parents, and anxious brides—many of them
current or former members of her dating service.

Often, her advice read like an argument against China's ancient pi-
eties. If your mother-in-law sees you as "nothing but a baby-maker" and
your husband won't help, she told one new wife, forget the husband, "get
some courage, and get out of that family." In the case of a newly rich
couple, in which the husband had taken to sleeping around, she ap-

plauded the wife for not becoming a "blubbering, feeble, pitiful creature," and advised her to make him sign a contract that would cost him
all his assets if he cheated again. Above all, Gong framed the search for
love as a matter of self-reliance. Heaven, she wrote, "will never throw you
a meat pie."

# FOUR

# APPETITES OF THE MIND

Not long after Gong Haiyan launched her business, a posting caught her eye: "Seeking a wife, 1.62 meters tall, above-average looks, graduate degree."

The seeker was a postdoc, studying fruit flies. He liked to exercise, and he attached a jokey photograph of himself flexing his triceps in front of his lab bench. "He had the whole package," Gong told me. Then she looked at his requirements and discovered, "I didn't meet a single one." She decided to answer him anyway, in a pose of high confidence. "Your announcement is not well written," she wrote. "Even if someone meets all those requirements, she'll think you're picky."

The man's name was Guo Jianzeng, and he was embarrassed. "I've never written anything like this, and I don't quite know what I'm doing," he replied. Gong volunteered to polish his announcement. "After polishing," she told me, "I could think of exactly four girls in the world who met the criteria, including me."

Guo Jianzeng was thirty-three and shy. When they met, his phone had eight numbers stored in it. He was not a born romantic—his first gift to her was a replacement for a pair of broken spectacles—and he was not rich; he had less than four thousand dollars to his name. But Gong asked him to take an IQ test. She was surprised when he beat her score by five points. She was also moved by the way he cared for his widowed father. On their second date, he proposed marriage to her on the subway.

She rode sidesaddle on the back of his bicycle to the Ministry of Civil Affairs, where they paid nine yuan for a marriage certificate. The ceremony took ten minutes. Instead of a wedding ring, he bought her a laptop. They rented a speck of an apartment for a hundred dollars a month and shared a bathroom with an elderly neighbor.

By 2006, Gong's dating site had a million registered users; the following year, venture capitalists invested. She began to charge a fee (about thirty cents) for sending or receiving a message. By her seventh year in business, the site had fifty-six million registered users and was ranked first in China in time spent online and in the number of unique visitors. It was China's largest online dating service. She dropped the name Love21.cn and adopted something grander: Jiayuan ("Beautiful Destiny"). She gave it a tagline that suited her disposition: "The Serious Dating Website."

I was at her office one morning when Gong slipped into a conference room for an orientation meeting with new employees. It was just before the Chinese New Year holiday. Single men and women across the country would be returning home to visit relatives—and would be interrogated relentlessly about marriage prospects. For some, the pressure would be unbearable. Afterward, Jiayuan's enrollment experienced a surge similar to the New Year's boom at fitness clubs in America.

Speaking before groups, even small ones, still made her nervous, and she carried her notes on a typewritten page. Before she spoke, the employees heard from the chief operating officer, a soft-spoken man named Fang Qingyuan, who told them, "Don't bother looking for favoritism or nepotism here. Work hard, and your success will be clear in your results. Don't bother kissing ass."

When it was Gong's turn, she took a seat at the head of the conference table and informed the new hires that they were now in "the happiness business." She did not smile. She rarely did when she talked about the happiness business. She focused instead on "price/performance ratios" and "information asymmetry." She was in office attire: glasses, ponytail, no makeup, and a pink Adidas jacket with a ragged left cuff. The young men and women before her were joining a staff of nearly five hundred. Your customers, she told them, will be virtually indistinguishable from you: migrants, alone in the city, separated from love by "three towering mountains"—no money, no time, and no connections. The goal was simple: give people choices.

In China, people had yet to acclimate to the proliferation of choices. In the local press, Gong was often described as "China's No. 1 match-maker," even though her business was a rebuke to the very idea of match-making. Despite the name of her company, Beautiful Destiny, she projected nothing more plainly than her belief that destiny was obsolete. "Chinese people still put their faith in destiny," she told the new employees. "They say, 'Oh, I'll get used to whatever happens.' But they don't need to do that anymore! Desire can lead them now. We're giving people the freedom of love."

After so many years without much say in one of life's great decisions, people seemed to be making up for lost time. I read an online personal ad by a graduate student named Lin Yu in which she itemized her expectations for her future husband:

> Never married; master's degree or more; not from Wuhan; no rural registration; no only children; no smokers; no alcoholics; no gamblers; taller than one hundred and seventy-two centimeters; ready for at least a year of dating before marriage; sporty; parents who are still together; annual salary over fifty thousand yuan; age between twenty-six and thirty-two; willing to guarantee eating four dinners at home each week; track record of at least two ex-girlfriends, but no more than four; no Virgos. No Capricorns.

The greatest difference between Internet dating in America and in China was conceptual: in America, it had the power to expand your universe of potential mates; in China, a nation of 1.3 billion people, online dating promised to do the opposite. "I once watched a twenty-three-year-old woman search for dates in Beijing, where there are four hundred thousand male users," Lu Tao, Gong's chief engineer, told me. "She narrowed it down by blood type and height and zodiac sign and everything else until she had a pool of eighty-three men." (A Chinese banker told me that he used Jiayuan to filter for a single criterion, height, which provided him with a list of gangly fashion models.)

When I signed on to Jiayuan to get a sense of Gong's business, I answered thirty-five multiple-choice questions. The Communist Party had spent decades promoting conformity, but the questionnaire left little doubt that, now, a man was expected to be able to define himself as precisely as possible. After height, weight, income, and other vitals, I was asked to describe my hair, first by color (black, blond, brunet, hazel, gray, red, silver, highlights, bald, or other) and then by style (long-straight, long-curly, medium-long, short, very short, bald, or other). For the shape of my face, I had nine choices, including as oval as a "duck egg" or as narrow as a "sunflower seed." For a moment, I wondered whether a "national character face" was the choice for patriots, but then I realized that it was for those with a lantern jaw in the shape of the Chinese character for "nation": 国.

I was asked to indicate my "most attractive feature," for which I had seventeen options, including my laugh, my eyebrows, and my feet. For "religious faith," I had sixteen choices; for variety's sake, I checked "Shamanism." For a question about "Life Skills," I worked my way through twenty-four options, including home renovations and business negotiations. By the time I was done, I had been asked for my views on vacation destinations, reading material, prenuptial agreements, smoking, pets, personal space, household chores, and retirement plans. Then I reached a question that asked me to choose from a list of labels with which to describe myself:

1. A dutiful son
2. A cool guy
3. Responsible
4. A penny-pinching family man
5. Honest and straightforward
6. A perceptive man
7. A career-driven man
8. Wise and farsighted
9. An unsightly man
10. A humorous man
11. A travel lover
12. A solitary shut-in man
13. Considerate
14. Gutsy
15. Loyal
16. Managerial

  17.  A handsome devil
  18.  Steady, staid, sedate

A page later, I was asked to choose the best description of my personal aesthetic. I thought back to the era of the "blue ants" and then examined the options:

  1.  I am gentle and urbane.
  2.  I am a cowboy from the Wild West.
  3.  I am graceful and sunny.
  4.  I am handsome and suave.
  5.  I am mature and charming.
  6.  I am tall and muscular.
  7.  I am simple and unadorned.
  8.  I am reserved and cool.

Gong Haiyan had good timing in entering the business of choice. The Chinese were spending more and more of their lives choosing. When private income began to climb in the eighties, shoppers moved in herds, surging after the same products as their neighbors with a force that became known as "tidal wave consumption."

In the village of Xiajia, the unofficial center of town moved from the headquarters of the Communist Party to the village's one and only shop. Young people began to speak admiringly of the quality they called *gexing*, "individuality." The young men in town started buying gel for their hair and cowhide loafers. They drove to the village store rather than walking, a distance of only about three hundred yards. Families rearranged their houses so that couples no longer shared a communal bed with grandparents and children, and the generations started sleeping in separate rooms. The local Communist Party secretary gave up calling himself a "rustless screw in the revolutionary machine" and said plainly, "Why am I doing this job? Simple—money."

Now that the state had phased out the direct assignment of jobs, it had to shepherd college graduates through the unfamiliar experience of choosing a profession. The new job market (and marriage market) created demand for new clothes and health clubs and cosmetics and razors and shaving cream. In 2005, Chinese television broadcast the first *American Idol*–style program—the *Mongolian Cow Sour Yogurt Super Girl Contest*. Its success spawned a new genre known as "choice shows," in which contestants could choose or be chosen by one another and the audience.

Shopping, or at least browsing, became a principal hobby. The average Chinese citizen was dedicating almost ten hours a week to shopping, while the average American spent less than four. That was partly because the process was less efficient in China—public transportation, cost comparisons—and partly because it was a novel form of entertainment. A study of advertising found that the average person in Shanghai saw three times as many advertisements in a typical day as a consumer in London. The market was flooded with new brands seeking to distinguish themselves, and Chinese consumers were relatively comfortable with bold efforts to get their attention. Ads were so abundant that fashion magazines ran up against physical constraints: editors of the Chinese edition of *Cosmopolitan* once had to split an issue into two volumes because a single magazine was too thick to handle.

My cell phone was barraged by spam offering a vast range of consumption choices. "Attention aspiring horseback riders," read a message from Beijing's "largest indoor equestrian arena." In a single morning, I received word of a "giant hundred-year-old building made with English craftsmanship" and a "palace-level baroque villa with fifty-four thousand square meters of private gardens." Most of the messages sold counterfeit receipts to help people file false expense reports. I liked to imagine the archetypal Chinese man of the moment, waking each morning in a giant English building and mounting his horse to cross his private garden, on the way to buy some fake receipts.

Western companies raced to add choices they hoped would appeal to Chinese tastes. Wrigley created cucumber-mint-flavored gum; Häagen-Dazs sold mooncakes. Not every angle succeeded: Kraft tried, and failed, to make a Ritz cracker flavored with fish boiled in spicy Sichuan peppercorn oil. The toy company Mattel opened a six-story Barbie megastore in downtown Shanghai, with a spa and a cocktail bar—only to discover that Chinese parents did not approve of Barbie's study habits. Home Depot found that the last thing the sons and daughters of farmers and laborers wanted was DIY.

Some of the choices that Chinese consumers made did not translate easily to outsiders. A brand of stylish eyeglass frames appeared on the market, named "Helen Keller." Reporters asked the company why it had chosen to advertise its eyeglasses with the world's most famous blind person. The company replied that Chinese schools teach the story of Helen Keller primarily as an icon of fortitude, and sure enough, sales of the frames were brisk. Helen Keller glasses were selling under the slogan "You see the world, and the world sees you."

Money and love had always been linked more explicitly in China than in the West, but the finances were simpler when almost everyone was broke. By tradition, a Chinese bride's parents paid a dowry, and the groom's parents paid a larger sum, known as the "bride wealth." Under Mao, this exchange was usually made in grain, but in the 1980s, couples came to expect "three rounds and a sound": a bicycle, a wristwatch, a sewing machine, and a radio. Or, in some cases, "thirty legs": a bed, a table, and a set of chairs. In much of China, the custom persisted (in cash), but the financial stakes were growing.

The greatest shock to the marriage tradition came from an unlikely source: in 1997 the State Council restored the right for people to buy and sell their homes. Under socialism, employers had assigned city workers to indistinguishable concrete housing blocks. When the government restored the market, Chinese bureaucrats didn't even have an official translation for the word *mortgage*. Before long, the world's largest accumulation of real estate wealth was under way.

Traditionally, young Chinese couples moved in with the groom's parents, but by the twenty-first century less than half of them stayed very long, and the economists Shang-Jin Wei and Xiaobo Zhang discovered that parents with sons were building ever larger and more expensive houses for their offspring, to attract better matches—a real estate phenomenon that became known as the "mother-in-law syndrome." Newspapers encouraged it with headlines such as A HOUSE IS MAN'S DIGNITY. In some villages, a real estate arms race began, as families sought to outdo one another by building extra floors, which sat empty until they could afford to furnish them. Between 2003 and 2011, home prices in Beijing, Shanghai, and other big cities rose by up to 800 percent.

The age of ambition sorted people not by their pasts, but by their futures. In the socialist era, the Chinese had evaluated the "political reliability" of parents and ancestors, but now men and women evaluated each other based on their potential, especially their earning potential. But it was becoming clear that, in the new marriage market, general expectations and reality did not coincide: only 10 percent of the men in Gong's dating service owned a home, but in an outside survey, nearly 70 percent of the women polled said they would not marry a man without one. The precise details of housing were so central to the prospect of romance that I was asked to choose from the following options:

1. I do not own a home.
2. I will buy a home when necessary.
3. I already own a home.
4. I rent with others.
5. I rent alone.
6. I live with my parents.
7. I live with friends and relatives.
8. I live in the dorm of my work unit.

Of all the questions, this was the most important. "If you're a man who rents or shares a place with roommates, you're almost out of the game from the beginning," Gong told me. Men who had a good answer did not bother with subtlety: in their singles ads, they adopted a new phrase: *chefang jibei*, which meant "car-and-home-equipped."

The pressure to keep up created a kind of language inflation. A few years earlier, a "triple without" was a migrant worker without shelter, a job, or a source of income. By the time I started hanging around Gong Haiyan's office, a "triple without" referred to a man without his own house, car, or nest egg. If a triple without got married, it was called a "naked wedding." In 2011 this was the title of a Chinese miniseries about a privileged young bride who married her working-class husband over the objections of her parents, and moved in with his family. It became the most popular show in China. If it had been a novel in the 1930s, it would have been listed under Tragic Love: by the series' end, the couple had divorced. Another popular program was a "choice show" called *If You Are the One*, in which single young men and women evaluated each other. On screen, pop-up bubbles indicated if the man was car-and-home-equipped. In one episode, a Triple Without offered a woman a ride on his bicycle, but she brushed it off, saying, "I'd rather cry in a BMW than smile on a bicycle." That line was too much for the censors. They soon restructured the show by adding a matronly cohost who counseled virtue and restraint.

Once or twice a week, Gong's company held singles mixers, and one night I filed into a ballroom in Beijing with three hundred carefully groomed men and women. They had been issued battery-powered blinking lights, in the shape of puckered lips, to be pinned to their clothing. An emcee bounded onstage and summoned the crowd's attention. "Please put your hand over your heart and repeat after me . . . 'I swear that I do not come here with any deceptive or ill intent.'"

Twelve women assembled onstage in a game show setup, each holding a red wand with a heart-shaped light on top: on, interested; off, not interested. It was a lineup of accomplished people: engineers, graduate students, and bankers in their late twenties and early thirties.

One by one, men took the stage to be questioned, but in the exchanges, I sensed the gulf of expectation. A barrel-chested bank employee in a cotton sweater attracted considerable interest until he said that he would be stuck in the office six and a half days a week. Next up was a physics professor in a tweed jacket, who generated little excitement by describing his life's ambition as "no marvelous accomplishment, just nothing I'll regret." Last came a laconic criminal lawyer with a fondness for hiking, who was doing well until he informed the panelists that he would place a heavy emphasis on "obedience." Lights blinked off. He left the stage alone.

The New Year holiday, days away, loomed like a deadline. That evening, I met a man named Wang Jingbing, a thirty-year-old with a friendly national-character face, who was bracing for the encounter with his family. "They will give me pressure. That's the reason I came here tonight," he told me as we sat along one wall. After college, Wang had become a salesman, exporting napkins and other paper products. The work had left an imprint on his English vocabulary; when he described a bad date, he would say he'd been "returned." The singles events baffled his relatives in the countryside. "My sister doesn't agree with my coming here," he told me. "She said, 'You'll never find a girl here.'" What did he think? "I have to follow my heart. My sister had a different educational background and life experience, so we have different ideas."

His sister, who never studied beyond junior high school, still lived in their home village, where she sold soda and noodles out of a storefront. When she was twenty, she married a man she'd been introduced to by relatives; he was from a neighboring village. Wang, by contrast, had studied English at Shandong University and migrated to Beijing for work. By the time we met, he had been in the capital for five years. He was on the verge of climbing out of the working class. As we chatted, I filled out his questionnaire in my mind: *1. A dutiful son . . . 4. A penny-pinching family man . . . 14. Gutsy.*

Wang had told himself he would attend at least one mixer a week until he found someone. "To tell you the truth, yesterday I was returned by a girl because she said I'm not as tall as she hoped," he said. I asked him if he agreed with the idea that he should have a house and a car before he marries. "Yes, because a house and a car are the signs of civility," he said. "A woman marrying a man is partly marrying his house and his car. I'm a renter, so I feel a lot of pressure." He was quiet for a moment, and said, "But I have potential, you know? In my opinion, to buy a house and a car will take me about five more years. Five more years."

# FIVE

# NO LONGER A SLAVE

When Deng Xiaoping declared that it was time to "let some people get rich first," he didn't say *which* people. It was up to them to figure it out.

Before that, the Party's first and most enduring target had been the tyranny of class. Mao dismantled four million private businesses, nationalized assets, and flattened society so thoroughly that China's income inequality fell to the lowest level in the socialist world. Students were taught that the bourgeoisie and other "class enemies" were "blood suckers" and "vermin." The zeal reached its greatest intensity during the Cultural Revolution, when the military went so far as to eliminate rank, until this created chaos on the battlefield and soldiers had to identify one another by the number of pockets on their uniforms. (Officers had two more than enlisted men.) Any effort to improve one's lot was not only pointless but dangerous. The Party banned competitive sports, and athletes who had won medals in the past found themselves accused, retroactively, of "trophy mania"—the crime of pursuing victory instead of mass fitness. People took to saying, "You'll earn less building rockets than you'll earn selling eggs."

But nowadays one of the running themes in the local papers was the dream to *baishou qijia*, to build a "bare-handed" fortune. Over lunch, I liked to spread out the pages on the kitchen table and read about street food vendors who became fast-food barons and other first-generation tycoons. There was nothing uniquely Chinese about rags-to-riches tales, but they had become central to China's self-image. The Chinese now talked about them the way that Americans mythologized garage start-ups in Silicon Valley. The first to make good on Deng's declaration became known as the *xianfu qunti*—the "Got Rich First Crowd." Despite the new reverence for bare-handed fortunes, China had spent so many decades railing against landlords and "capitalist roaders" that most of the Got Rich First Crowd chose to remain ciphers. "A man getting famous is like a pig fattening up," they liked to say, and when *Forbes* published its list of China's richest people in 2002, it illustrated their secrecy with a photograph of men and women wearing paper bags on their heads. Lottery winners were so worried about attention that Chinese newspapers published photos of the winners picking up their oversize checks while disguised in hoods and sunglasses.

For the Communist Party, the return of class presented an opportunity: the Party came to believe that co-opting those with property would buttress it against agitation toward democracy. Officials took to quoting the ancient sage Mencius, who said, "Those with a constant livelihood have a constant heart, those lacking a constant livelihood lack a constant heart." But relying on prosperity to ensure a "constant heart" posed a problem that would grow into the Chinese Communist Party's essential paradox: How could the heirs of Marx and Lenin, the rulers of the People's Republic, who had risen to power denouncing bourgeois values and inequality, baldly embrace the new moneyed class? How could it retain its ideological claim to rule?

This, however, was a time of self-creation, and so it was for the Party as well. The task fell to the president and general secretary of the Party, Jiang Zemin. At the Party's most important meeting, in 2002, he executed a major rhetorical contortion: he couldn't bring himself to use the term *middle class*, but he declared that, from then on, the Party would dedicate itself to the success of the "New Middle-Income Stratum." The New Middle-Income Stratum was everywhere, hailed by apparatchiks and enshrined in new slogans. An author at China's Police Academy described the New Middle-Income Stratum as "the moral force behind civilized manners. It is the force necessary to eliminate privilege and curb poverty. It is everything."

At the same meeting, the Party also made an important change to its constitution: it stopped calling itself a "revolutionary party" and started calling itself the "Party in Power." China's rulers had altered their reason for being; by becoming the Party in Power, the former rebels who'd spent decades lambasting their enemies as "counterrevolutionaries" turned themselves into such ardent defenders of the status quo that even the word *revolution* was now problematic. The Museum of Revolutionary History, beside Tiananmen Square, lost its name and was absorbed into the National Museum of China. In 2004, the prime minister, Wen Jiabao, said, "Unity and stability are really more important than anything else."

If the change struck ordinary Chinese as hypocritical, they didn't have much choice but to accept it. What's more, people had been so deprived for so long that they had little love for the old dogma. The Party and the people were now facing in opposite directions: Chinese society was becoming more diverse, raucous, and freewheeling, and the Party was becoming more homogenous, buttoned-down, and conservative.

In October 2007, I filed into the Great Hall of the People to watch the opening of the Seventeenth National Congress of the Communist Party—the most hallowed event on the political calendar, a week of speeches and ceremonies convened once every five years. Officially, the Congress would decide the leadership of the People's Republic. (In fact, those decisions had been reached already in private.) Onstage, the president and general secretary of the Party, Hu Jintao, stepped to the lectern. Like many of his peers at the top of the Party, he was an engineer by training, a technocrat who had imbibed the belief that "development is the only hard truth." At sixty-five, he was such a muted, affectless presence that his citizens had nicknamed him Wooden Face. This was only partly his fault: After the horrors of the Cultural Revolution, the Party had dedicated itself to preventing its leaders from developing a cult of personality. It succeeded. When Hu was younger, his official biography had included the fact that he enjoyed ballroom dancing; but once he reached the top of the Party, that detail, the only color about his likes or dislikes, was removed.

Hu looked out over a sea of two thousand loyal delegates. It was a tableau of conformity, bathed in the color of communism: a wall-to-wall red carpet, red drapes, and an enormous red star shining down from the ceiling. Behind him, rows of VIP officials were seated in hierarchical order, many of them wearing red ties, just as he was. The choreography was flawless: every few minutes, a team of young women carrying thermoses of hot water passed through the rows of VIPs, pouring tea with the precision of synchronized swimmers. Hu spoke for two and a half hours in a vocabulary removed from the language of the public. He spoke of "socialist harmonious society" and the "scientific outlook on development" and, as always, "Marxist-Leninism." He vowed to permit only incremental political change. The Party, he said, must remain "the core" that "coordinates the efforts of all quarters."

Outside the Great Hall, China embraced the return of class. In 1998 a local publisher translated Paul Fussell's 1982 cultural satire, *Class: A Guide Through the American Status System*, which makes such observations as "the more violent the body contact of the sports you watch, the lower the class." In Chinese, the satire fell away, and the book sold briskly as a field guide for the new world. "Just having money will not win you universal acclaim, respect, or appreciation," the translator wrote in the introduction. "What your consumption reveals about you is the more critical issue."

David Brooks's book *Bobos in Paradise: The New Upper Class and How They Got There* was translated into Chinese in 2002, and it became a best seller. It describes a distant world—one of American bourgeois bohemians, who mix sixties counterculture with Reagan-era economics— but, in China, it captured the strivers' self-perception, and "Bobos," or "*bubozu*," became one of the year's most-searched-for terms on the Chinese Internet. Soon there were *bubozu* bars, *bubozu* book clubs, and a laptop with ads that promised to give the *bubozu* "a jazzy sense of romance." Then the Chinese press tired of the *bubozu* and moved on to DINK—*ding ke*, in Mandarin—"Double Income, No Kids," followed by a succession of other new labels and identities: netizens, property kings, mortgage slaves. A popular Chinese essay by an anonymous author carved out an archetype of the young white-collar class, the men and women who

> sip cappuccino, date online, have a DINK family, take subways and taxis, fly economy, stay in nice hotels, go to pubs, make long phone calls, listen to the blues, work overtime, go out at night, celebrate Christmas, have one-night-stands . . . keep *The Great Gatsby* and *Pride and Prejudice* on their nightstands. They live for love, manners, culture, art, and experience.

In the age of ambition, life sped up. Under socialism, there had rarely been any reason to rush. Except for Mao's fantasies of leaping forward, people worked at the pace of the bureaucracy and the seasons. Moving faster or more efficiently, taking greater risks, would add little to the dinner table. Like the imperial court in the days of the Drum Tower, the socialist central planners decided when to turn on the central heating in the fall and when to turn it off in the spring. But all of a sudden, China was gripped by a sense that the country was running late. He Zhaofa, a sociologist at Sun Yat-sen University, published a manifesto in favor of speed, reporting that, in Japan, pedestrians were walking at an average speed of 1.6 meters per second. He criticized his fellow Chinese. "Even American women in high heels walk faster than young Chinese men." He called on his countrymen to adopt an urgent appreciation of every second. "The nation that wastes time," he wrote, "will be abandoned by time itself."

Some of the strivers achieved extraordinary fortune before they knew exactly what to do with it. In 2010, China was experiencing "Foreign IPO Fever," and in May of the following year, the dating entrepreneur Gong Haiyan took her company public on the NASDAQ. By the end of the day, her shares were worth more than seventy-seven million dollars. Her husband left his job researching fruit flies.

She invited me over for dinner. They had bought a place in the suburbs north of Beijing. The sun was setting as we pulled off the highway. We passed a Pet Spa and a compound called Chateau de la Vie, and turned into a lush gated community that evoked New Jersey more than Hunan. Her house was beige stucco with Tuscan details. Her two-year-old daughter, in pajamas, bounded out the front door and hugged her mother's legs. Gong's husband ushered us to the dining room, where her parents and her grandmother, who lived with them, were sitting down.

I was struck by the presence of four generations of women in the house. Gong's grandmother, who was ninety-four, had been brutalized during the Cultural Revolution because she was classified as a well-off peasant. She was born just after China ended the practice of foot binding, and while we ate I made a mental inventory of all the drama that she had survived in China's twentieth century, on the way to her granddaughter's mansion in the suburbs. "Women used to say, 'If you want clothes on your back and food to eat, get married,'" Gong said, poking at her rice with her chopsticks. "As long as you had the most basic require- ments, I'd marry you. But not anymore. Now I can live a good life, an independent life. I can be picky. If there's anything I don't like about you, well, you're out of luck."

For years, the family had bounced between rented apartments, six people in two bedrooms. Now they were in a home sandwiched between European diplomats and Arab businessmen. Nine months after they moved in, the walls of the villa were still bare and white. They had yet to buy any art or decorations, but those would come. A moped was parked in the front hall, in the village tradition, to protect the bike from thieves, though I didn't expect Gong's neighbors posed much of a threat. It looked as if the family had packed up its belongings from a farmhouse in Hunan and unloaded them at a CEO's villa in Beijing.

The age of ambition demanded new skills and knowledge. To help rookie entrepreneurs navigate the heavy toasting that comes with build- ing a business in China, a night school called the Weiliang Institute of Interpersonal Relations, in the city of Harbin, offered a "drinking strat- egy" course. (One tip: after a toast, discreetly spit the liquor into your tea.) What could not be learned could be bought: Zhang Dazhong, a home electronics tycoon, employed a three-member "reading staff" to summarize the books he wished he had read.

Long before Westerners were reading about the habits of hard-driving "tiger moms," the most popular Chinese parenting guide was *Harvard Girl*, in which a mother named Zhang Xinwu documented how she got her daughter into the Ivy League. The regimen had begun before birth, when Zhang forced herself to eat a high-nutrition diet, though it made her sick. By eighteen months, Zhang was helping her daughter memo- rize Tang dynasty poems. In primary school, Zhang took her to study in noisy settings to hone her concentration, and kept her on a schedule: for every twenty minutes of studying, five minutes of running stairs. To build fortitude, Zhang had her daughter clench ice cubes in her hands for fifteen minutes at a time. It was easy to see it as absurd, but for a population still fighting its way out of poverty, virtually any sacrifice sounded reasonable.

Nobody coveted the cultural capital of an elite education more assiduously than members of the Got Rich First Crowd. Many of them had come from nothing, and they knew that urban intellectuals considered them rubes. The size of China's population made college admissions so brutally competitive that people compared it to "ten thousand horses crossing a river on a single log." To create more opportunities, the government doubled the number of colleges and universities, in just ten years, to 2,409. Even so, only one in every four aspiring college students was able to earn a place.

An American education carried extra cachet, and Got Rich First parents channeled their anxieties into their children. In the fall of 2008, I had lunch with a woman named Cheung Yan, better known to the public as the Queen of Trash. Every year, the *Hurun Report*, a Shanghai magazine, released a ranking of China's richest people. In the 2006 list, Cheung was the first woman to rank number one. She was the founder of Nine Dragons Paper, China's largest paper manufacturer, and had earned her nickname by conquering an obscure niche that tuned global trade to peak efficiency: she bought mountains of filthy American wastepaper, hauled it to China at cheap rates, recycled it into cardboard boxes bearing goods marked "Made in China," and sold those goods to America. The 2006 rich list estimated her fortune at $3.4 billion. The following year, Cheung's wealth ballooned further, to more than $10 billion, and the magazine calculated that she was the richest self-made woman in the world, ahead of Oprah and J. K. Rowling.

Cheung, and her husband, Liu Ming Chung, a former dentist who worked as her company's CEO, met me in the managers' cafeteria at the largest paper mill in the world, one of Cheung's factories in the southern city of Dongguan. At fifty-two, Cheung was an unreconstructed factory boss. She spoke no English, and her Chinese carried a heavy Manchurian accent. She was barely five feet tall; in conversation, she was propelled by bursts of exuberance and impatience, as if she were channeling China's industrial id. "The market waits for no one," she said. "If I don't develop today, if I wait for a year, or two or three years, to develop, I will have nothing for the market, and I will miss the opportunity. And we will just be ordinary, like any other factory!"

As we ate, she didn't want to talk about business; they wanted to talk about their two sons. The older one was in New York, getting a master's degree in engineering at Columbia. The younger boy was at a prep school in California, and at one point mid-meal, her assistant passed her a copy of a college recommendation a teacher had written on her son's behalf. Cheung examined it and handed it back.

"His GPA is four-point-zero to four-point-three," she told me. Then, with the pride of an autodidact, she added, "His head is full of American education. He needs to accept some Chinese education as well. Otherwise, he'll be out of balance."

When I'd arrived in China in 2005, there were only sixty-five Chinese students in American private high schools, according to the U.S. Department of Homeland Security. Five years later, there were nearly seven thousand. I stopped being surprised when Communist Party grandees told me their offspring were at Taft or Andover. (Eventually, a group of elite Chinese parents cut out the commute and sent their kids to a lavish new prep school in Beijing. They hired former headmasters of Choate and Hotchkiss to run it.)

Of all the pathways to self-creation, nothing galvanized people as broadly as the study of English. "English fever" settled on waiters, CEOs, and professors, and elevated the language into a defining measure of life's potential—a force strong enough to transform your résumé, help attract a spouse, or vault you out of a village. Men and women on Gong's dating site often included their English proficiency in descriptions of themselves, alongside mention of cars and houses. Every college freshman had to meet a minimal level of English comprehension, and it was the only foreign language tested. In a novel called *English,* the author, Wang Gang, a teacher in a rural school, says, "If I rearranged the words in the [English] dictionary, the entire world would open up before me."

This was a sharp reversal from the past. In nineteenth-century China, English was held in contempt as the language of the middlemen who dealt with foreign traders. "These men are generally frivolous rascals and loafers in the cities and are despised in their villages and communities," the reformist scholar Feng Guifen wrote in 1861. But Feng knew that China needed English for diplomatic purposes, and he called for the creation of special language schools. "There are many brilliant people in China; there must be some who can learn from the barbarians and surpass them," he wrote. Mao favored Russian for the country, and he expelled so many English teachers that, by the sixties, China had fewer than a thousand high school English teachers nationwide. After Deng opened China's doors to the world, English fever took hold. Eighty-two percent of those polled in 2008 thought it was vital to learn English. (In America, 11 percent thought it was vital to learn Chinese.) By 2008 an estimated 200 million to 350 million Chinese were studying English. China's largest English school system, New Oriental, was traded on the New York Stock Exchange.

I wanted to meet a man named Li Yang, China's most popular English teacher and perhaps the world's only language instructor known to bring students to tears of excitement. Li was the head teacher and editor in chief of his own company, Li Yang Crazy English. His students recited his biography with the consistency of an incantation: he grew up the son of Party propagandists whose harsh discipline left him too shy to answer the telephone; he nearly flunked out of college but then he prepared for an English exam by reading aloud and found that the louder he read, the bolder he felt and the better he spoke; he became a campus celebrity and turned it into an empire. In the two decades since he began teaching, he had appeared in person before millions of Chinese adults and children.

In the spring of 2008, I visited him when he was overseeing an intensive daylong seminar at a small college on the outskirts of Beijing. He arrived accompanied by his photographer and his personal assistant. He stepped into a classroom and shouted, "Hello, everyone!" The students applauded. Li wore a dove-gray turtleneck and a charcoal-colored car coat. He was thirty-eight years old, and his black hair was set off by a faint silver streak.

Li peered at the students and called them to their feet. They were doctors in their thirties and forties, selected by Beijing hospitals to work at the following summer's Olympic Games. But like millions of English learners in China, they had almost no confidence speaking the language that they had spent years studying by textbook. Li had made his name with an ESL technique that a Hong Kong newspaper called English as a Shouted Language. Shouting, Li argued, was the way to unleash what he called the "international muscles." Li stood before the students, his right arm raised in the manner of a tent revivalist, and launched them into English at the top of their lungs. "I!" he thundered. "*I!*" they thundered back.

"Would!"

"*Would!*"

"Like!"

"*Like!*"

"To!"

"*To!*"

"Take!"

"*Take!*"

"Your!"

"*Your!*"

"Tem! Per! Ture!"

"*Tem! Per! Ture!*"

One by one, the doctors tried it out. A woman in stylish black glasses said, "I would like to take your temperature." Li gave a theatrical shake of his head and made her do it again. Her cheeks flushed, and in a sudden burst, she bellowed, "*I would like to take your temperature!*" Then came a thickset man in a military uniform who needed no encouragement—"*I would like to take your temperature!*"—followed by a tiny woman, who let out a paint-peeling scream. Around the room we went, each voice a bit more confident than the one before. I wondered how a patient might react, but before I could ask, Li was out the door, and on to another group in the adjoining classroom.

Li routinely taught in arenas, to classes of ten thousand people or more. The most ardent fans paid for a "diamond degree" ticket, which included bonus small-group sessions with the great man. The list price was $250 a day—more than a full month's wages for the average Chinese worker. Students thronged him for autographs. On occasion, they sent love letters, wrapped around undergarments.

There was another widespread view of Li's work. "The jury is still out on whether he actually helps people learn English," Bob Adamson, an English-language specialist at the Hong Kong Institute of Education, told me. Li's patented brand of shouting occupied a specific register: to my ear, it was not quite the shriek reserved for alerting someone to an oncoming truck, but it was more urgent than a summons to the dinner table. He favored flamboyantly patriotic slogans such as "Conquer English to Make China Stronger!" On his website, he declared, "America, England, Japan—they don't want China to be big and powerful! What they want most is for China's youth to have long hair, wear bizarre clothes, drink soda, listen to Western music, have no fighting spirit, love pleasure and comfort! The more China's youth degenerated, the happier they are!" Wang Shuo, one of China's most influential novelists, was put off by Li's nationalist rhetoric. "I have seen this kind of agitation," he wrote. "It's a kind of old witchcraft: Summon a big crowd of people, get them excited with words, and create a sense of power strong enough to topple mountains and overturn the seas." Wang went on: "I believe that Li Yang loves the country. But act this way and your patriotism, I fear, will become the same shit as racism."

But I started spending time around his students and found that they regarded him less as a language teacher than as a testament to the promise of self-transformation. Li gave classes in the Forbidden City and atop the Great Wall. His name appeared on the cover of more than a hundred books, videos, audio boxed sets, and software packages. Most of Li's products bore one of his portraits: rimless glasses, a commanding grin, an archetypal Chinese citizen for the twenty-first century. In conversation, Li was grandiose, comparing his fame to Oprah's and claiming that he had sold "billions of copies" of his books. (The truth was hardly worth embroidering: one of his publishers estimated to me that his book sales were in the millions.) A columnist in the state-run *China Daily* pronounced Li a "demagogue." The *South China Morning Post* asked whether Crazy English was becoming "one of those cults where the leaders insist on being treated like deities." (*Cult* is a dangerous word in China, where the spiritual group Falun Gong was given that label in 1999, and the government has rounded up its followers ever since.)

When I asked Li about the *South China Morning Post* piece, he said, "I was pissed off." He had no interest in being worshipped, he said. His motivations were nothing more than mercenary. "The secret of success," he said, "is to have them continuously paying. That's the conclusion I've reached." For all his students' devotion, his goal was simple: "How can we make them pay again and again and again?"

Li's cosmology tied the ability to speak English to personal strength, and personal strength to national power. It was a combination that produced intense, sometimes desperate, adoration. A student named Feng

Tao told me about the time he realized he had enough cash for tuition to one of Li's lectures but not enough for the train fare to get there. "I went and sold blood," he said. Collect a crowd of those fans, and the atmosphere could be overwhelming. Li's wife, an American named Kim Lee, told me, "There have been times when I've had to run in, or ask someone bigger, a guy, to go pull my daughter out of a crowd that is just pushing so much that I'm scared." She said, "Those aren't like a 'Wow, he's famous' moment. Those are like an 'Oh God, this is out-of-control famous' moment."

Kim Lee struck me as an oasis of normalcy in the world of Crazy English. "I'm just a mom who came into a bizarre life by happenstance," she said, laughing. She was a teacher in Florida when she met Li Yang during a trip to China with the Miami teachers' union in 1999. They married four years later, had two children, and she started teaching beside Li onstage. Her dry wit and all-American looks were the perfect foil to her husband's style: an American Alice Kramden to his Chinese Ralph. At first, she had been baffled by Li's antics and nationalist fire-breathing, but when she noticed how students responded, she was taken with his ability to connect with them. She said, "This guy is really passionate about what he's doing, and as a teacher, how can you not be moved by that?"

A few weeks after the class in Beijing, I attended Li's most anticipated event of the year: the Crazy English Intensive Winter Training Camp. That weekend, China was hit with its worst winter weather in half a century. The blizzards coincided with the travel weekend for Lunar New Year, the most important family holiday in the Chinese calendar. The havoc was unprecedented; in Guangzhou, hundreds of thousands of travelers were left stranded in the streets around the train station. Somehow, seven hundred adults and children managed to make it to a college campus in the southern city of Conghua. A ten-year-old boy told me that he had traveled by car for four days, with his older brother at the wheel.

At the English camp, supervisors dressed in camouflage and used megaphones; they escorted students in formation around the campus. Li's face could be seen everywhere, on oversize posters accompanied by English phrases. Above the stairs to the cafeteria: HAVE YOU THOUGHT

ABOUT WHETHER YOU DESERVE THE MEAL? Along the plaza where students lined up before lectures: NEVER LET YOUR COUNTRY DOWN! Above the doorway leading into the arena: AT LEAST ONCE IN YOUR LIFE, YOU SHOULD EXPERIENCE TOTAL CRAZINESS.

Shortly before nine o'clock on opening day, the students filed into the arena. It was unheated and frigid, like their dormitories. (The previous night, I had slept in a full set of clothes and a hat.) Li associated the ability to speak English with physical toughness based on his fundamental principle: the gap between the English-speaking world and the non-English-speaking world was so profound that any act of hard work or humiliation was worth the effort. He ordered his students "to love losing face." In a video for middle and high school students, he said, "You have to make a lot of mistakes. You have to be laughed at by a lot of people. But that doesn't matter, because your future is totally different from other people's futures."

A long red-carpeted catwalk cut through the center of the crowd, and after a burst of firecrackers, Li bounded onstage. He carried a cordless microphone and paced back and forth on the catwalk, his feet shoulder height to the seated crowd staring up at him.

"One-sixth of the world's population speaks Chinese. Why are we studying English?" he asked. He turned and gestured to a row of foreign teachers seated glumly behind him. "Because we pity them for not being able to speak Chinese!" The crowd roared.

For the next four hours, in numbing cold, Li swooped from hectoring to inspiring; he preened for the camera; he mocked Chinese speakers with fancy college degrees. The crowd was rapt. In the days afterward, students would run together at dawn, shouting English. On the final night, they walked on a bed of hot coals. Between classes, the campus was scattered with learners muttering like rabbinical students, Li's books pressed to their faces, their lips racing.

One afternoon, I wandered outside for some fresh air. By the door, I met Zhang Zhiming, a slim, inquisitive twenty-three-year-old with a plume of hair in the front that made him look like Tintin. He preferred to use the name Michael, and he told me he had studied Crazy English for five years. He was the son of a retired coal miner and couldn't afford a ticket to the camp, so the previous year he had worked as a camp security guard and strained to hear as much as he could from the sidelines. This year, he was promoted to teaching assistant at the camp and was receiving a small stipend.

"Usually when I see Li Yang, I feel a little nervous," Michael told me as we sat outside in the sun. "He is a superman."

Michael's enthusiasm was infectious. "When I didn't know about Crazy English, I was a very shy Chinese person," he said. "I couldn't say anything. I was very timid. Now I am very confident. I can speak to anyone in public, and I can inspire people to speak together."

Michael's older brother had worked for Li as an assistant. The brother never learned much English, but Michael began spending as much as eight hours a day on the language, listening over and over to a tape of Li's voice, which sounded to him "like music."

His favorite book was *Li Yang Standard American Pronunciation Bible*, which helped him hone his vowels and punch up his consonants. Eventually, he got a job teaching at an English school, with the hope that someday he might open a school of his own. I met scores of Li Yang students that winter, and I always asked them what purpose English had served in their lives. A hog farmer wanted to be able to greet his American buyers; a finance worker, studying during his vacation, wanted to get an edge in the office. Michael had no doubts about what English might do for him. A few years earlier, his brother got involved in a direct-sales network, pushing health drinks and potions. Schemes such as these, known in Mandarin as "rats' societies," proliferated in China's era of surging growth, fueled by get-rich-quick dreams and a population adrift between ideological faiths.

"He always wanted me to be involved in that," Michael went on, and I tried to picture him extolling the benefits of a health tonic with the same passion that he now expressed about English. "I spent half a year doing this business, and I gained nothing." Michael's brother eventually made it to the United States to try to earn money to repay his creditors. He was working as a waiter in New York, Michael said, and until he returned, it would be up to Michael to support their parents.

As Michael talked, the vigor in his voice faded. His brother wanted him to go to America, too. "He has big dreams," he said. "But I don't really want to go there, because I want to have my own business. If you are a worker, you can't be a rich man. You can't buy a house, buy a car, support a family."

Michael stared at his feet and said, "I have no choice. This is life. I should always keep smiling. But actually I feel I'm under a lot of pressure. Sometimes I want to cry. But I'm a man."

He stopped. The air was silent except for a warm wind that carried a trace of Li's voice, booming in the stadium behind us.

A few weeks later, Michael invited me for lunch at the apartment he shared with his parents in Guangzhou. It was in a cluster of modern high-rises on Gold Panning Road. When Michael met me at the gate, he was in a good mood. "I got promoted to teaching supervisor," he said. "I got a raise." The family's apartment consisted of a living room, two small bedrooms, and a kitchen. His parents were cooking, and the air smelled of ginger. Michael and his father shared a bunk bed in one room, and his mother and his older sister occupied the other. Michael's room was cluttered with English study books and an overfilled desk. English felt tangible, like a third, and messy, roommate. He rooted around in a box to show me the homemade vocabulary cards he carried, just as Li Yang once did. He pulled out a card marked "Occupations: Astronomer, Baker, Barber, Barkeeper, Biologist, Blue-Collar Worker, Boss/Superior, Botanist . . ."

When Michael was a child, the family lived in a coal mining town called Mine Number Five. His parents, who had survived the harshest years of poverty and political turmoil, had only "one goal in life," Michael said: "to pass the days normally." But Michael was desperate to get out of Mine Number Five. In a passage he used for language practice, he wrote:

> I couldn't stand eating steamed bread, leftover greens, and sweet potatoes every day. I couldn't stand wearing the same patched clothes year after year, when I was laughed at by my classmates. I couldn't stand walking one hour on foot to get to that old shabby school.

With the help of loans from the coal mine boss and others, Michael went to college, where English became his obsession. In his journal, he wrote, "Some nights I can't even sleep, I want to wake up so badly and practice English." He watched American movies and emulated the booming voice of Mufasa, the father lion in the animated film *The Lion King*. Mufasa was voiced by James Earl Jones, and on campus, the young Chinese man who sounded a bit like Darth Vader did not go unnoticed. "He was like a little weed," his friend Hobson told me.

In college, Michael worked at a local radio station, at KFC, as a dishwasher, but even with the loan from the coal mine boss, tuition was expensive, and Michael dropped out after two years to study Crazy English full time. He had absorbed the promise of self-creation more thoroughly than anyone I had met. He took to calling himself a "born-again English speaker." In his journal, he stopped dwelling on his frustration. "The growth of a tree depends on the climate, but I make my own weather. I control my own fate," he wrote, adding, "You can't change the starting point of your life, but with study and hard work, you can change the endpoint!" His bookshelves were heavy with business how-to books and self-help guides. He had picked up a salesman's habit of peppering his comments with ingratiating questions such as "Can you believe it?"

As we sat in his bedroom, he decided to play some recordings he'd been making for his students, as models of pronunciation. He clicked on a recording called "What Is English?" He had layered the sounds of waves and seagulls into the background and recorded it with a girl named Isabell, the two trading sentences as they went: "English is a piece of cake. *I can totally conquer English.* I will use English. *I will learn English.* I will live in English. *I am no longer a slave to English.* I am its master. *I believe English will become my faithful servant and lifelong friend . . .*"

It went on for another minute, and while Michael listened intently, my eyes settled on a small handwritten Chinese sign taped to the wall at the foot of his bed: THE PAST DOES NOT EQUAL THE FUTURE. BELIEVE IN YOURSELF. CREATE MIRACLES.

SIX

# CUTTHROAT

The age of ambition swept inland from China's coast, reversing the route of migration; it moved from the cities to the factory towns, and from the factory towns to the villages. As it reached people who had long waited for a chance to escape their origins, the pursuit of fortune intensified into magical thinking. Farmers in remote villages embarked on audacious inventions, earning the nickname "Peasant da Vincis." Some ideas were grimly pragmatic—a man with kidney disease built his own dialysis machine out of kitchen goods and medical parts, including clothespins and a secondhand blood pump. But more often, the inventors were animated by a pervasive sense of possibility: They built race cars and robots, and a grandfather named Wu Shuzai built a wooden helicopter. His neighbors said his helicopter looked like a chicken coop, but Wu kept at it in the hope, as he put it, that he might "fly it out of this mountain and see the world."

Yet, for all the talk of Peasant da Vincis and bare-handed fortunes, it was becoming clear that the Got Rich First Crowd was pulling ahead far faster than others could catch up. By 2007 the top 10 percent of urban Chinese were earning 9.2 times as much as the bottom tenth, up from 8.9 times the previous year. Public protests, often staged by workers angry about unpaid wages or by farmers whose land had been seized for development, soared to 87,000 in 2005, up from 11,000 a decade earlier. The more that people became aware of the widening gap, the more desperate they became. Michael, the English teacher, concluded that he needed to work a greater portion of each day, so he decided to limit himself to four hours of sleep a night. "Money, I can make. But time, I can't make," he told me.

The race to catch up inspired creativity, but occasionally with disastrous results. Wang Guiping, a tailor in the Yangtze River Delta, joined his neighbors in the new business of chemical production, telling another villager that it would "put my son in a good school and make us city people." At night, while his family slept, the tailor, who had a ninth-grade education, experimented with the help of a chemistry book and found that he could disguise a solvent as a more expensive variety and save the difference in cost. "Before selling it, I drank some," he recalled later. "It burned my stomach a bit, but nothing too strong." He found other cheap substitutes for chemical components, and his profits rose. But his concoctions turned out to be poison, and when they ended up in cough syrup in 2006, they killed fourteen people at a hospital in Guangdong, and the tailor went to jail. China closed down more than four hundred small-time medicine makers that year; in all, their tainted products had killed hundreds of people, some as far away as Panama.

The race to catch up affected each person in a different way. A fifty-year-old former barber named Siu Yun Ping found that it stirred his appetite for risk. In the summer of 2007 he began making regular visits from his village in Hong Kong to the city of Macau, the only Chinese territory where it is legal to gamble in a casino. Macau sits on a horn of rocky coastline where the Pearl River washes into the South China Sea. It's about a third the size of Manhattan, covering a tropical peninsula and a pair of islands that look, on a map, like crumbs flaking off the mainland. Chairman Mao banned gambling in China long ago, but it endures in Macau because of a historical wrinkle: for nearly five hundred years, the city was a Portuguese colony, and when it returned to Chinese control, in 1999, it was entitled to retain some of the flamboyantly libertine traditions that led W. H. Auden to christen it "a weed from Catholic Europe." The infusion of China's new riches triggered an unprecedented surge in construction; by 2007, when Siu began to visit, Macau's casino revenues had surpassed those of Las Vegas, until then the world's largest gambling town. Within a few more years, the quantity of money passing through Macau would exceed that of Las Vegas six times over.

Siu Yun Ping had known little good fortune. He grew up in a tin-roofed hut in a squatters' settlement on the mudflats of rural Hong Kong. The year he was born, a fatal flood swept through his neighborhood; subsequent years brought drought, then typhoons. "It was as though the gods wished to destroy us by driving us mad," a local official wrote in his memoirs about the period. Siu had five siblings, and his education ended in primary school. Before he was a barber, he found employment as a tailor and construction worker. Gambling was technically illegal in Hong Kong, but as in many Chinese communities, it was a low-key fixture of life, and by the age of nine, Siu was pushing his way into the crowd to watch local card games. At thirteen, he was playing for small stakes, and an underground gambling den hired him to hang around and keep an eye on the players' hands. "I'm good at observing people's movements," he told me. "Whenever I saw someone cheating, I told the boss."

As an adult, he continued to play cards, though with little success. He was an unglamorous presence—trim and wiry, with plump cheeks, bushy hair, and the fast, watchful eyes of a man accustomed to looking out for himself. He married at nineteen, had three children, divorced, and married again. Around his home village, Fuk Hing, which means "Celebrating Fortune," he was known by a nickname that he did not much care for: Lang Tou Ping, or Inveterate Gambler Ping.

While working as a barber, he befriended a skinny local teenager named Wong Kam-ming. Wong had grown up in the same district as Siu, one of the poorest places in Hong Kong, and had also dropped out of school to find work. They occasionally met for supper at a café where Wong worked for his mother. Siu was trying to become a small-town developer, building and selling houses among the paddy fields near his village, and Wong opened his own restaurant. They became even closer after Wong began working on the side in Macau, as a "junket agent," recruiting gamblers, giving them lines of credit, and earning commissions on how much they bet. One of the people he recruited was Siu.

Once or twice a week, Siu boarded the public ferry for the trip across the rolling gray waters of the Pearl River estuary. Seventy thousand people went to Macau each day to try their luck, more than half of them from mainland China. Siu had no illusions about whether his habit was in his favor. "Out of every ten people who gamble, maybe three will win," he said. "And when those three keep on gambling, only one will win." He played baccarat, the Chinese gamblers' favorite. (It offered slightly better odds than the alternatives and was easy to master.) The *punto banco* style, favored in Macau, involved no skill; the result was determined as soon as the cards were dealt.

In August of 2007, within weeks of beginning his regular trips, Siu hit a hot streak. Some days, he won thousands of dollars. Others, he took home hundreds of thousands. With Wong's recommendation, he was invited into opulent VIP rooms, which were open only to the biggest bettors, and he became a regular on the high rollers' helicopter trips across the water. The more Siu played, the more Wong earned in commissions and tips. As winter approached, Siu's success set in motion a chain of events that showed why, in China's new landscape of money and power, Macau is a place where it is easy to get into trouble—whether you are a former barber in Hong Kong or one of the richest men in America.

Gambling towns are shrines to self-invention. Las Vegas was a desert outpost bedeviled by sandstorms and flash floods—a land that "the Lord had forgotten," in the view of nineteenth-century Mormon missionaries, who abandoned it—before it grew into the city that now attracts more people each year than Mecca. Hal Rothman, the late historian of the American West, wrote that Las Vegas posed the same question to every visitor: "What do you want to be, and what will you pay to be it?"

The ferry to Macau is greeted by a crowd of touts. When I arrived on a fall afternoon, a young woman handed me a Chinese advertisement for "USA Direct," which offered a toll-free number for Mandarin speakers to buy American real estate at cut-rate prices. My phone buzzed. It was an automated message from a casino:

> The City of Dreams congratulates the lucky winner of the "$1-to-Get-Rich, Rich, Rich" Giveaway on the grand prize of $11,562,812 Hong Kong Dollars! Climb abroad the Fortune Express. The next millionaire could be you.

With a population of just half a million, Macau feels like China amplified and miniaturized. It is animated by the same combination of ambition, risk, and self-creation, but the sheer volume of money and people passing through distilled the mixture into an extract so potent that it can seem to be either the city's greatest strength or its greatest liability. Macau used to manufacture fireworks, toys, and plastic flowers, but once the casinos arrived, the factories vanished. The average citizen now earns more than the average European. Construction is ceaseless. When I checked into a hotel, the scene outside reminded me of my first months in China, with welders' torches flashing against the windows twenty-four hours a day.

Even by China's standards, the speed of Macau's growth was breathtaking. In 2010, high rollers in Macau wagered about six hundred billion dollars, roughly the amount of cash withdrawn from all the ATMs in America in a year. But even all that cash changing hands on the tables was only part of the picture. "The growth of gambling in Macau, fueled by money from mainland Chinese gamblers and the growth of U.S.-owned casinos, has been accompanied by widespread corruption, organized crime, and money laundering," according to the 2011 annual report by the U.S. Congressional-Executive Commission on China. The place had become the "Macau Laundry Service," as U.S. diplomats put it in an internal cable in 2009. David Asher, who was a State Department senior adviser for East Asian and Pacific affairs in the Bush administration, told me it had "gone from being out of a James Bond movie to being out of *The Bourne Identity*."

In 2005 the FBI infiltrated a smuggling ring involving a Macau citizen named Jyimin Horng, by posing as representatives of Colombian FARC (Fuerzas Armadas Revolucionarias de Colombia) guerrillas. When an FBI agent named Jack Garcia asked for weapons, Horng sent him a catalogue; Garcia ordered antitank missiles, grenade launchers, submachine guns, and AK-47s. To lure Horng and others to the United States for arrest, the agency staged a mock wedding for a male and a female agent involved in the sting. Horng and other guests received elegant invitations to a celebration aboard a yacht moored off Cape May, New Jersey. "I was the best man," Garcia told me. "We picked them up for the bachelor party and drove them straight to the FBI office." Fifty-nine people were arrested. Based on that case and on other information, the Treasury Department blacklisted Banco Delta Asia, in Macau, for participating in money laundering with links to the North Korean regime, charges the bank denied.

Games of chance had been a part of Chinese history since the Xia dynasty (2000–1500 B.C.E.). "The government often imposed rules against them, and yet officials themselves were the ones who gambled the most," Desmond Lam, a marketing professor at the University of Macau, told me. "They would get stripped of their titles, caned, jailed, exiled, but we still see the trend across the dynasties." Lam studied Chinese attitudes toward risk. He and I were taking a walking tour of the City of Dreams, a casino complex that uses the promotional tagline "Sign Up, Play, Change Your Life." After six years of studies and surveys, Lam views each gambling table as a "microscopic battle," a standoff between science and faith. On one side is the casino, which can reliably calculate its advantage to two decimal points. On the other is a collection of Chinese beliefs about fate and superstition, which, Lam says, "people know are irrational but are part of the culture." He ticked off some received wisdom: To improve the odds, wear red underwear and switch on all the lights before leaving home. To prevent a losing streak, avoid the sight of nuns and monks when traveling to the casino. Never use the main entrance. Always find a side door.

Intrigue, of one kind or another, had clung to Macau since the city's founding myths, which described an act of elegant deception: In 1564, or so the story went, local Chinese fishermen sought the help of a visiting Portuguese fleet for a battle against pirates; the Portuguese disguised their cannon inside Chinese boats and waylaid the bandits at sea. In gratitude, the Chinese granted permission to the Portuguese to stay on the peninsula. Macau became a vital stop between India and Japan, but eventually nearby Hong Kong built a better port, and Macau had to find alternative specialties: opium, prostitution, and gambling. When the Dutch-born writer Hendrik de Leeuw visited in the 1930s for his book *Cities of Sin*, he included Macau as home to "all the riffraff of the world, the drunken shipmasters; the flotsam of the sea, the derelicts, and more shameless, beautiful, savage women than any port in the world. It is a hell."

For most of its history, Macau looked as much Mediterranean as Chinese, with baroque Catholic churches and rows of cafés shaded by drooping palms, where old émigrés sipped *cafe da manhã* over the *Jornal Tribuna*. But by the time I arrived, it had a touch of the Persian Gulf: air-conditioned luxury hotels and high-rises, with sports cars idling in the sunshine. Government tax revenue in Macau was often more than double the budget, and like Kuwait, Macau distributed checks to its residents under a program named the Wealth Partaking Scheme. Un-employment was below 3 percent. "What Las Vegas did in seventy-five years, we are doing in fifteen," Paulo Azevedo, the publisher of *Macau Business* and other local magazines, told me when we met for a drink. That pace had left the city short of many things: taxis, roads, housing, medical services. "For dental, I have to go to Thailand," Azevedo said. One month, Macau came close to running out of coins. The casinos had reordered the rhythms of life and work, in ways that were not universally celebrated. Au Kam San, a member of Macau's Legislative Assembly, who worked as a high school teacher, had students who told him, "I can go get a job in a casino right now and earn more than my teacher."

A short drive from the ferry, the Las Vegas tycoon Steve Wynn had a complex with two hotels, where the Louis Vuitton store was said to gen-erate more sales per square foot than any other Louis Vuitton store worldwide. Walking past a tank of luminescent jellyfish, which required a specially designed curtain to sleep at night, the casino PR person who was showing me around told me that Chinese clientele demanded a heightened level of luxury because "everyone is a president or a chair-man." We stopped into the complex's newest Michelin-starred restau-rant, which had an in-house poet who wrote a personal verse for every VIP. I asked a waitress why there was a tiny white leather stool beside each table, and she said, "That's for your handbag."

A generation ago, families buried their jewels in the backyard to avoid political persecution. By 2012, China had surpassed the United States as the world's largest consumer of luxury goods. Though the Chi-nese had no nostalgia for the days of deprivation, they wondered how single-minded acquisitiveness might be changing them. A joke making the rounds described a man on a Beijing street corner who is sideswiped by a sports car, which tears his arm off. He gazes in horror at the wound and cries, "My watch!"

Macau always reminded me of the American Gilded Age. Matthew Josephson, author of *The Robber Barons*, describes how Americans acclimated to sudden fortune in the 1870s. One man, he writes, "had little holes bored into his teeth, into which a tooth expert inserted twin rows of diamonds; when he walked abroad his smile flashed and sparkled in the sunlight." The American political system at the time was subject to criticisms similar to those facing China's political system today:

corruption, lack of rule of law, weakness in the face of corporate monopolies. When strikes and demonstrations raged across the United States in the 1870s and '80s, they were met with force. Give the strikers "a rifle diet for a few days," suggested Thomas Scott of the Pennsylvania Railroad, "and see how they like that kind of bread." Europeans liked to say that America had gone from barbarism to decadence without the usual interval of civilization.

Macau afforded China's new moneyed class the chance to indulge. In designing his casino, Steve Wynn celebrated Chinese superstitions about the path to fortune: when the hotel designers realized that the number of private rooms in the spa was four—an unfortunate number, because it sounds, in Chinese, like "death"—they installed a line of fake doors across the hall to suggest a total of eight, a word in Chinese that sounds like "get rich." In Las Vegas, Wynn had made his name pushing luxury over camp—Picassos over Wayne Newton—but his hotel in Macau still used what casino designers called the "wow feature." Once an hour, tourists gathered in the lobby to watch a hole open in the floor. A giant animatronic dragon climbed out, coiling into the air, red eyes blazing, smoke pouring from its nostrils.

The City of Dreams smells of perfume, cigarettes, and rug shampoo. Chinese gamblers rarely drink when money is on the line, and the low, festive hum is broken now and then by the sound of someone pounding the table in delight or anguish, or exhorting the cards to obey. One night, I settled into the scrum around a baccarat game in which a slim man with heavy eyebrows and a red face shining with sweat was performing "the squeeze": slowly peeling up the edge of his card, while the man beside him shouted "Blow! Blow!" to wish away the high numbers that would make him lose. When the slim man had peeled enough to see the digit, his face twisted in disgust and he tossed the card across the table.

"Americans tend to see themselves in control of their fate, while Chinese see fate as something external," Lam, the professor, said. "To alter fate, the Chinese feel they need to do things to acquire more luck." In surveys, Chinese casino gamblers tend to view bets as investments and investments as bets. The stock market and real estate, in the Chinese view, are scarcely different from a casino. The behavioral scientists Elke

Weber and Christopher Hsee have compared Chinese and American approaches to financial risk. In a series of experiments, they found that Chinese investors overwhelmingly described themselves as more cautious than Americans. But when they were tested—with a series of hypothetical financial decisions—the stereotype proved wrong, and the Chinese were found to take consistently larger risks than Americans of comparable wealth.

I had come to expect that Chinese friends would make financial decisions that I found uncomfortably risky: launching businesses with their savings, moving across the country without the assurance of a job. One explanation, which Weber and Hsee call "the cushion hypothesis," is that traditionally large Chinese family networks afford people confidence that they can turn to others for help if their risk-taking does not succeed. Another theory is more specific to the boom years. "The economic reforms undertaken by Deng Xiaoping were a gamble in themselves," Ricardo Siu, a business professor at the University of Macau, told me. "So people got the idea that taking a risk is not just okay; it has utility." For those who have come from poverty to the middle class, he added, "the thinking may be, If I lose half my money, well, I've lived through that. I won't be poor again. And in several years I can earn it back. But if I win? I'm a millionaire!"

China's prevailing approach to risk reminded me of Lin Yifu, the defector from Taiwan, who had placed his bet on the new China. Though his journey was more dramatic than most, his decision had something in common with that facing any migrant who sets off in search of better prospects—Gong Haiyan and her online dating business, or the students at Crazy English, or, for that matter, the European immigrants who came to America during the Gilded Age. *What do you want to be, and what will you pay to be it?*

In the case of Inveterate Gambler Ping, success and risk-taking drew attention. Four months into Siu's streak, a gossip column in the *Apple Daily*, a popular Hong Kong paper, took note of a "mysterious" figure making the rounds in Macau, said to be amassing a fortune as large as 150 million dollars. "Is he extremely lucky or does he have the genuine magic touch?" the paper asked in January 2008. The next day, a member of Hong Kong's legislature, Chim Pui-chung, a devoted gambler, told the paper that he had heard people hailing the new high roller as the

"God of Gamblers," borrowed from the title of a Hong Kong movie starring Chow Yun-fat. Professional gamblers had a name for guys like that: "shooting stars," because they came out of nowhere, and usually vanished just as fast.

A hot streak of that scale was guaranteed to attract suspicion. Casinos know that their advantage in baccarat (about 1.15 percent) ordains that the chances of winning all but evaporate for a gambler after thirty thousand hands. A dedicated player might draw a thousand hands in a weekend and come out ahead, but after seven months almost nobody should be going home a winner. Not long after the article appeared dubbing Siu the God of Gamblers, his twenty-year-old son received a series of anonymous threatening phone calls. Then one night someone slipped into Celebrating Fortune village and set part of the family house on fire. Finally, Siu's friend Wong Kam-ming, who had introduced him to the VIP rooms, received an angry call. The man on the other end demanded a meeting to discuss the question of Inveterate Gambler Ping's having cheated.


For years nobody embodied the spirit of Macau more than Stanley Ho, a tall, elegant tycoon who dated starlets and dancers, excelled at the tango into his eighties, and was chauffeured around Hong Kong in a Rolls-Royce with the license plate HK-1. After his father lost the family fortune in the stock market, Ho got his start during the Second World War with a trading company in Macau. "By the end of the war, I'd earned over a million dollars—having started with just ten," he said later. He expanded into airlines, real estate, and shipping, and in 1962 he and his associates took over Macau's casinos, gaining a monopoly that lasted forty years and made him one of Asia's richest men. Foreign governments suspected Ho of being too cozy with Chinese organized crime. He denied it, but regulators thwarted his family's efforts to run casinos in the United States and Australia. In keeping with the spirit of his city, he was nonjudgmental in his choice of business partners; he ran horse racing under the Shah of Iran, a gambling boat under Ferdinand Marcos of the Philippines, and an island casino under Kim Jong-il. Intelligence agents were desperate to cultivate Ho for his connections, but the late Dan Grove, a retired FBI agent who served in Hong Kong, told me, "Nobody ever got past first base."

Stanley Ho's Macau monopoly expired in 2002, and foreign competitors surged in to obtain licenses. The first new casino to open was the Sands Macao, backed by Sheldon Adelson, of Las Vegas, whom *Forbes* ranked as the ninth-richest person in the United States. Adelson was Stanley Ho's physical opposite—small and heavy, with electric red hair. The son of a cabdriver from Lithuania, Adelson grew up in Boston's Dorchester neighborhood and ran a spate of businesses—packaging toiletries for hotels, selling a chemical spray to clear ice from windshields—before his big break, in 1979, when he launched COMDEX, a computer trade show. He later bought the old Sands hotel in Las Vegas, created America's largest privately owned convention center, and enriched himself by pairing casinos with exhibition centers. Adelson had coveted Macau as a gateway to 1.3 billion Chinese nationals, and he successfully courted Chinese leaders in Beijing by emphasizing his influence in Republican politics. (He was the single largest individual donor in the 2012 presidential campaign.) In May 2004, he opened his first casino and then embarked on an idea that he described as coming to him in a dream: to replicate the Las Vegas Strip on a stretch of open sea between two islands in Macau. His company constructed a landfill out of three million cubic meters of sand and opened the $2.4 billion Venetian Macao, a supersize replica of the Las Vegas Venetian, with the largest casino floor in the world. He told people that he hoped Macau would someday allow him to overtake Bill Gates and Warren Buffett in wealth.

Unlike Las Vegas, where most of the profits came from coins fed into slot machines, three-quarters of the revenue in Macau was derived from enormous bets made in VIP rooms, where high rollers played around the clock. Casinos relied on Chinese companies known as "junkets," which existed to solve some of the practical problems of running a casino in Macau—namely, that Chinese law barred them from trying to collect gambling debts in the People's Republic. Working through junket operators was a legal bypass around this problem, because the operators could recruit rich customers from across China, issue them credit, and then handle the complicated business of collection. The system was especially attractive to customers who needed to get large quantities of cash out of China. If a corrupt official or executive wanted to hide the proceeds, a junket was a way to hand over cash on one side of the border and recover it on the other, in chips that could then be played and cashed out in clean foreign currency. (Another option was to smuggle it by hand across Macau's relaxed borders, a practice known in laundering circles as "smurfing," named for the fictional blue characters, a reference to the army of small-time couriers involved.)

While the junket industry had many law-abiding members, it had been, for decades, susceptible to the involvement of organized crime. In China, organized crime groups known as "triads" grew out of nineteenth-century political societies; the term *triad* is believed to have originated when three groups merged into a powerful organization. They became involved in loan-sharking and prostitution, and made their presence felt at Macau's casinos, but in recent years triads had become more business-oriented. They set aside squabbles over drugs and petty crime in order to pursue new criminal opportunities associated with a more prosperous People's Republic, including money laundering, financial fraud, and gambling. Gangsters were becoming "gray entrepreneurs," as criminologists put it, and it was growing more difficult to distinguish between triads that had gone into business and businesses that were acting as triads. Men who were once known in the local papers by their nicknames, as reputed triad bosses, reinvented themselves as executives in the gaming industry.

Macau was proving to be especially attractive to corrupt Chinese officials. It played a recurring role in the downfall of Party cadres, who headed to Macau with public funds and returned empty-handed. There was the pair of Party officials named Zhang and Zhang, from Chongqing, who lost more than $12 million at the casinos in 2004. A former Party chief in Jiangsu lost $18 million. A bureaucrat from Chongqing stood out not for scale but for speed: he managed to lose a quarter of a million dollars in just forty-eight hours. So many officials were arrested for squandering public funds in Macau that, by 2009, scholars calculated how much the average official might lose at the gambling tables before getting caught: $3.3 million.

To find untapped millionaires, the junket agents took to scouring the business press, looking for new faces. A thirty-nine-year-old junket agent told me, "Nowadays, in Macau, if a person doesn't gamble at least a few hundred thousand dollars, then he isn't even a real customer." What happens if a customer doesn't pay up? "We go to the city where he is and call him up. Then, if necessary, we wait there for a couple of days. Just to put some pressure on him."

———

A few weeks after Siu Yun Ping's house was set on fire, a group of young men were summoned to a meeting in a parking lot on the outskirts of Hong Kong. The meeting had been called by See Wah-lun, a midlevel captain in one of China's most famous triads, the Wo Hop To.

The triad captain was a thickset man of thirty. He told his men about a plan to extort Siu. As one of them later described it in court, "A boss wanted a man to return some money." The boss was Cheung Chi-tai, a gang leader who was well known to Hong Kong police and U.S. authorities. In the words of a Hong Kong judge, Verina Bokhary, Cheung could "have a say in things" in a VIP room at the Sands Macao, one of the places where Siu had made his baccarat fortune. Once he was suspected of cheating, Cheung's men tried to claw back his winnings.

See Wah-lun unveiled a straightforward plot: they would send Siu a message by ambushing his friend Wong, pinning his car between two others, and then hustling him over to a nearby village, where they had supplied a secluded, run-down building with gloves, hoods, knives, and extendable police batons. The plan was to break Wong's legs and hands. But then See called his guys back: the plan was being upgraded to murder, to guarantee that Siu would know they were serious and would hand over his winnings.

But when See Wah-lun gave his gang the assignment, his men balked. One of the recruits asked, "Do we have to be that serious?"

See was taken aback. "The boss tells you to do it, are you not going to do it?" he said.

Another of the chosen assassins complained that he was supposed to be a guest at a wedding that evening. A third, Lau Ming-yee, didn't like being asked to do the job gratis. "If you are not going to pay someone, then how would that someone help you?" he said later.

Lau was especially uncomfortable because he was acquainted with the intended victim; in his mid-twenties and the son of farmers, Lau had worked as a teahouse delivery boy, crisscrossing the neighborhood in his gold-painted Toyota. He occasionally dropped off food at Wong's village. "Everyone was shocked by the idea of killing anybody, never mind somebody some of us knew," Lau said.

When See outlined Lau's role in the murder, Lau hesitated. The boss was incensed. "What the fuck do you have to think about?" he said.

Under pressure, Lau capitulated; he told the boss he would help out with the murder. But his heart wasn't in it. He had joined the Wo Hop To as a teenager, a small-time soldier under See's command, and it wasn't much of a living. Over the years, he'd worked at a newsstand and an Internet café. He had a girlfriend now, she was pregnant, and he had enough trouble trying to find five-hundred-plus dollars to repair a truck he had hit with his Toyota.

For the hitman Lau Ming-yee, everything about this job stank, and in the predawn hours on the day of the planned attack, he phoned a cop he knew and offered a tip. The two met near a local shrine called the Temple Under a Big Tree, and Lau told him everything—about the murder plot, about the God of Gambling, about the safe house and the hoods and knives. Later, in court, Lau explained, "I am the father of a child and I want to be a responsible man." He had gamed out his options. A plea bargain might mean jail time, but he calculated that he would be out before it mattered—"before my child understands everything."

Within hours, the police arrested five men. They went to trial that fall, and Lau testified against them. They maintained their innocence, but all were convicted of conspiracy to commit grievous bodily harm and acting as members of a triad. See, the ringleader, was sentenced on additional charges of conspiring to commit murder and recruiting others to carry it out. The five men were sentenced to jail for up to fourteen years. (Lau received immunity for his cooperation.) During the investigation, police also briefly detained Cheung Chi-tai, the triad leader, but he didn't spend long in custody. According to John Haynes, See's defense attorney, Cheung "called his lawyer and refused to answer any questions, and as a result he escaped being charged with anything." At sentencing, Haynes lamented that the "small potatoes" were going to jail while the "big boss . . . now sits comfortably, free from any charges, in Macau."

Siu and his friend Wong testified at the trial, and they were asked to estimate how much Siu had amassed during his five-month winning streak. It was a complicated question, because high rollers in Macau often make side bets many times larger than the chips on the table. (In a side bet, a player and a junket agent secretly agree that every hundred-dollar chip is worth a thousand or ten thousand, and then they settle

their wins and losses in private.) In total, Siu the barber estimated that he
had won the equivalent of thirteen million U.S. dollars. Wong put the
figure far higher: at seventy-seven million dollars.

The notion that a former barber had won as much as seventy-seven
million dollars, and outlasted the mobsters charged with getting it back,
attracted the attention of members of the Hong Kong press. For a while
they pursued the God of Gamblers as a minor curiosity, though he declined interviews. A year after the trial, the Hong Kong magazine *Next*
published an article alleging that Siu had cheated by finding a way to
manipulate the system. The article claimed that he had paid off an un-
derling who recorded players' ups and downs, in order to boost his wins
and minimize his losses. The casino hadn't detected the fraud, the magazine surmised, because many of Siu's wagers were "side bets" off the
books, and besides, the junkets hadn't dreamt that a no-name gambler
might take the extraordinary risk of trying to buy off a staff member. Siu
never responded to the article. In any case, local reporters discovered, he
had disappeared.


The God of Gamblers vanished from the local crime pages. Then, in the
fall of 2010, a former executive at the Sands Macao, Steve Jacobs, filed a
wrongful-termination lawsuit that made a range of accusations against
Sheldon Adelson. Jacobs said that he and Adelson had discussed the
God of Gamblers case, and the allegation that triads were involved with
Sands casinos; over Jacobs's objections, he said, Adelson still sought to
"aggressively grow the junket business." Jacobs's suit also accused the
Sands of hiring a Macau legislator in a way that could put the casino at
risk of violating the Foreign Corrupt Practices Act, which bars companies from bribing foreign officials. The casino company denied all the
accusations and said that Jacobs was the one who had failed to distance
the company from the triad boss.

But the U.S. government took notice of the suit: the Department of
Justice and the Securities and Exchange Commission launched investigations of the Sands for potential violations of the Foreign Corrupt Practices Act. Adelson vehemently denied any wrongdoing. "When the
smoke clears, I am absolutely—not one hundred percent but one thousand percent—positive that there won't be any fire below it," he said.

"They want to get all my e-mails. I don't have a computer. And I don't use e-mails. I'm not an e-mail type of person."

Adelson and his peers were discovering that doing business on the frontier of China's boom was risky in ways they had not anticipated. They were discovering just how much their fortunes now hinged on the behavior of others—of Communist Party cadres, Chinese triads, and even a barber with a dream of beating the house. The files of the God of Gamblers case could be read as a string of accidents: Siu's run at the baccarat table; Wong's luck to be assigned an assassin with a conscience; Adelson's misfortune that reporters covered an obscure murder plot involving his casino. But viewed another way, the tale depended as little on luck as a casino does. It was, rather, about the fierce collision of self-interests, a fable of China in its own Gilded Age.

In its excesses, its plots, its moral flexibility, Macau opened a window on the anxious new era in the People's Republic. In China, in the days of nearly universal poverty, there had been hardly anything to steal, and little reason to consider the moral pressures exerted by the prospect of sudden fortune. But China's combination of new wealth and opaque government was proving to be almost perfectly engineered for abuse.

By 2007, when Siu Yun-Ping hit his streak in Macau, the China scholar Minxin Pei noted that nearly half of all Chinese provinces had sent their chief of transportation to jail. Pei calculated that corruption of one kind or another was costing China 3 percent of its gross domestic product—more than the national budget for education.

For the Chinese government, Macau's roguish success posed a dilemma: how much should it be allowed to continue? China could have brought Macau's boom to an end by fiat—citizens needed a special permit to go to the city, and China opened and closed the flow of visitors at will—but cracking down on Macau posed political problems. Macau was a place where China's winners—those who built bare-handed fortunes, the members of the new Middle-Income Stratum—could go to indulge in the gains of their prosperity. So long as they didn't concern themselves with the state's inner workings, the state did not overly concern itself with theirs. On a flight between Macau and Beijing, I sat beside a former military officer who now owned real estate and a string of factories. He told me that he visited Macau once a month "to let off steam" and he spent much of that particular flight scrutinizing his latest acquisition: a twelve-thousand-dollar Vertu cell phone, encased in alligator skin and equipped with a button that connected him to a full-time concierge.

For the moment, the leaders of Macau, like their brethren in Beijing, saw no reason to change. When I contacted Manuel Joaquim das Neves, Macau's top casino regulator, he said, "Macau is not Las Vegas," and it took me a moment to realize that he was invoking Vegas as a standard of prim moral constraint. "Macau has attracted more than twenty billion dollars in foreign investment in the casino industry alone," he went on. "In short, the public interest has been well served." It was a point of view consistent with the way the Party talked about its success in China: "Development is the only hard truth," Deng had said, and for many people, that view was correct.

Four years after Siu hit his hot streak, I got word through a friend in Hong Kong that he might be back in his old neighborhood, not far from the dismantled squatters' camps where he grew up. He was said to have worked out a deal for protection from another triad, the Wo Shing Wo. I took the train out to look for him. His neighborhood lay in a lush river delta framed by green hills on the horizon. The summer heat had broken, and construction seemed to be under way everywhere, as old villages were being converted into enclaves of villas and cul-de-sacs with names such as the Prestige, Sky Blue, and Full Silver Garden.

I found Siu at a construction site near a scrap metal yard, surrounded by marshy fields of water chestnuts and lilies, crosshatched by footpaths. He was in the real estate business, as he'd always wanted to be, and was building fourteen houses whose modern design, heavy on stainless steel and black granite, would have looked at home in Sacramento or Atlanta. When it was finished, the complex would be called the Pinnacle. Siu was wearing a droopy yellow golf shirt, jeans, and muddy sneakers. He seemed subdued, and his voice was raspy. He was barely distinguishable from his crew—tanned, bony middle-aged men from across the Chinese countryside. I arrived around quitting time to find one of them naked, giving himself a bird bath from a bucket of soapy water. When I introduced myself, Siu did not look overjoyed. But I explained that I'd been interested in him for a long time, I'd retraced his path, and I was curious, most of all, about why he took the risks he did. He agreed to talk to me. We settled into folding chairs beside a line of drying laundry and gazed out over the unfinished houses.

I asked where he had gone when he was on the run, and he smiled. "All over China," he said. "I drove by myself. Sometimes I stayed in five-star hotels, and sometimes I stayed in tiny places. I liked Inner Mongolia the best. After a while, I went up to the mountains of Jiangxi and stayed there for eight months. When it began to snow, I nearly froze. I went down from the mountains and came home."

I asked if he had cheated at baccarat. "The reporters just listened to rumors from people who wanted their money back," he said. "Everybody says I was playing tricks at the table. It's not true. I wasn't. When I gambled, there must have been ten people with their eyes on me at any time. How am I supposed to play tricks?"

His denial left open a range of possibilities for manipulating the game. A lawyer for one of the defendants suggested to me that Siu might have been recruited as a minor player in a larger con, and then realized he could turn the caper toward his own benefit. It occurred to me that, if this was true, it meant Siu had allowed everyone else to project their ambitions on to him, before his own desire to get rich prevailed. But, the lawyer, added, "There is so much cheating going on. How can you ever know the truth?"

I asked Siu if he thought the triads were still after him, and he said, "I'm in my mid-fifties, and I'll live to be, what, seventy? So I've got only another decade or so. What do I have to lose? I'm not afraid." He fell silent for a moment, then flashed a weird smile and said, "Besides, if they come for me, I can go for them, too."

He'd stopped going to Macau because of his children, he said. "I don't want them to gamble. Two of them have bachelor's degrees, one has a master's. They don't swear. They're good kids." He went on, "You have to be highly sensitive to be a good gambler. I don't recommend it to everybody. Everyone called me Inveterate Gambler Ping. But I never liked that, because I was never addicted. I gambled because I knew I could win."

As night fell, Siu offered me a lift back to the train station in his black Lexus SUV, parked in the dirt beside us. It was buffed to a shine so

bright that it glowed in the streetlights—the only visible sign of his fortune. The sky was purple with twilight. "There used to be a helicopter
taking me to the Venetian anytime I wanted to go," Siu said. "Now I'm
getting my feet dirty. Real estate is even more lucrative. It's better than
gambling or drugs or anything." He nodded toward the new houses in
progress. "It costs a few million to build one of these, and then I can sell
it for ten million."

# SEVEN

# ACQUIRED TASTE

Once the Got Rich First Crowd had the trappings of fortune—a child in the Ivy League, a reading team to stay up on new books—they wanted the habits of mind. The men and women who had struggled to reach the top of China's Industrial Revolution craved the chance to extend their exercise of choice to a wider world, to matters of taste, art, and the good life—to see, at last, what they had been missing.

In May 1942, Chairman Mao, in his talks on the future of art and literature, said, "There is, in fact, no such thing as art for art's sake, art that stands above classes, art that is detached from or independent of politics." For Mao, culture was a "weapon for uniting and educating the people and for crushing and destroying the enemy." The Party would make sure that art, literature, and other expressions of taste adhered to what it later called the *zhuxuanlu*—"the central melody"—of Chinese society, the Party's distilled understanding of values, priorities, and desires.

The People's Republic became known for paintings of apple-cheeked peasants, films of determined soldiers, and poems about soaring heroism. The style was called "revolutionary realism combined with revolutionary romanticism," and it was shaped by the Party's belief, as culture czar Zhou Yang put it, that "today's ideal is tomorrow's reality." In some cases, artists who focused too much on unflattering facts about the present were accused of "writing about reality," and punished for it.

After Mao died in 1976, the first group of avant-garde artists to step forward named themselves the "Stars," as a rebuttal to what the member Ma Desheng called the "drab uniformity" of what had come before, as a way "to emphasize our individuality." When their first exhibition was excluded from the national museum in 1979, they hung their work on the fence outside and staged a march beneath the slogan "We Demand Political Democracy and Artistic Freedom." For much of the nineties, authorities arrested performance artists for appearing in the nude, shut down experimental shows, and bulldozed underground artists' villages.

But the influx of money transformed the relationship between artists and the government. By 2006, Chinese painters such as Zhang Xiaogang were selling pieces for close to a million dollars, and a younger generation of artists, raised in the boom years, let it be known that they were tired of addressing authoritarianism and politics. Like artists elsewhere, they trained their sights on consumerism, culture, and sex, and they encountered a new generation of speculators and collectors.

Li Suqiao, a curator and collector in Beijing, told me, "I say to my friends, 'Instead of gambling four thousand dollars on a round of golf, you can get a work of art.'" We were at a gallery called New Millennium, and Li had a yellow sweater tied around his neck. At forty-four years old, he had been collecting for five years, after making money in the petroleum industry. He estimated that he spent about two hundred thousand dollars a year on work by young artists. "I have friends who live in villas north of Beijing, and when it comes time to decorate, they'll spend one hundred thousand renminbi on a couch, and one hundred renminbi on a print to hang above it. Sometimes they don't care about the price; they just care about the measurements." As far as Li was concerned, the avant-garde "has nothing do with politics." He said, "Chinese collectors are more interested in current things than in memory and tragedy."

The Party discovered that the best way to deprive Chinese art of its rebellious energy was to embrace it: in 2006, after years of threatening to demolish Factory 798, a former military electronics plant in Beijing that had been turned into a cluster of galleries and studios, the municipal government designated it as a "creative industry area," and tour buses filled the streets around it.

The commercial art market ballooned. Hundreds of contemporary art museums were built across the country. Artists who had lived hand to mouth now sold their work around the world and built dachas beside the Great Wall. The artist Ai Weiwei opened his own restaurant, where he could hold court late into the evening with friends and critics and hangers-on. For Ai Weiwei, the national pursuit of fortune became a subject itself. He commissioned a series of colossal crystal chandeliers that mocked China's new aesthetics. He hung one inside a rusty scaffolding, a cartoon of China's new disparities.

In his first two decades as an artist, Ai Weiwei had produced a fitful, if influential, stream of work: while gambling and trading antiques, he created installations, photographs, furniture, paintings, books, and films. He had been a member of the early avant-garde group the Stars, and he helped establish experimental artist communities on the edge of the capital. Though he had no training as an architect, he founded one of China's most sought-after architecture practices, before moving on to other obsessions.

In *The New York Times*, in 2004, Holland Cotter called him an "artist whose role has been the stimulating, mold-breaking one of scholar-clown." Now, in his early fifties, he had found a rich new vein in China's aspirations. For his contribution to Documenta 12, in 2007, he arranged an expedition to send a thousand and one ordinary Chinese citizens to the site of the festival, in Kassel, Germany. He named the project *Fairytale*, a reference both to Kassel, which was the home of the Brothers Grimm, and to the allure that the outside world had always held for generations of Chinese who were never able to see it.

To recruit travelers, Ai Weiwei turned to the Web with more intensity, and it revealed a vast world he had never known. He realized that "the Internet could be a very powerful tool," he told me. He raised money from foundations and others for the air travel, and his office designed every detail of the experience, down to matching suitcases, bracelets, and dormitory-style living spaces outfitted with a thousand and one restored wooden chairs from the Qing dynasty. It was social sculpture on a Chinese scale, and the logistics would have staggered Joseph Beuys, the German conceptualist who declared that "everyone is an artist." Yet, to Chen Danqing, a painter and social critic, the project carried a special resonance in China, where validation from the West, including visas, once carried near-mythic value. "For the past hundred years, we were always the ones waiting for the Americans or the Europeans or whomever to call our names. *You. Come.*"

---

Chinese attitudes toward Western culture were a mix of pity, envy, and resentment: pity for the barbarians outside the Middle Kingdom, envy for their strength, and resentment for their incursions into China. "Chinese have never looked at foreigners as human beings," Lu Xun wrote. "We either look up to them as gods or down on them as wild animals."

In 1877, when the Qing dynasty was decaying and Western powers were rising, Chinese reformers dispatched a young scholar named Yan Fu to England to investigate the source of British naval power. He concluded that Britain's strength lay not in its weapons but in its ideas, and he returned to China with a trunkful of books by Herbert Spencer, Adam Smith, John Stuart Mill, Charles Darwin, and other Western thinkers. His translations were not perfect—*natural selection* took on a harsher edge as *natural elimination*—but their impact was vast. To Yan and others, evolution was not simply biology; it was political science. Liang Qichao, one of China's leading reformers, concluded that China must "make itself one of the fittest." Admiring the West too zealously was a liability; when activists in the early twentieth century embraced European notions of the individual, they were mocked as "fake foreign devils." Until the final years of Mao's reign, when he established ties with the United States, admiring the West was a punishable offense.

But by the eighties, the West was increasingly seen as a place of possibility and self-creation. A popular soap opera on Chinese television called *Into Europe* told the story of a penniless man from Fujian who arrives in Paris wearing a tattered T-shirt and, within months, becomes a real estate developer. In the climactic scene, he faces a French audience and asks, "What will be different on the new map of Paris two years from now?" He tears away a cloth covering an architectural model and declares, "The beautiful banks of the Seine will be full of Oriental splendor: the Chinatown Investment and Trade Center!" In the show, the French crowd bursts into applause.

The ambivalence in the Chinese view of the West did not go away; it deepened. Young Chinese were growing up watching the NBA and Hollywood movies, while bookstore shelves carried titles such as *China Can Say No*, the bestselling polemic during my first visit to China. The combination could be confounding. When three researchers asked

Chinese high school students, in 2007, for the first five words that came to mind when they thought of America, their answers suggested a kaleidoscopic portrait:

> Bill Gates, Microsoft, the N.B.A., Hollywood, George W. Bush, Presidential Elections, Democracy, War in Iraq, War in Afghanistan, 9/11, Bin Laden, Harvard, Yale, McDonald's, Hawaii, Police Officer to the World, Oil, Overbearing-ness, Hegemony, Taiwan

When I arrived in China, the closest that most Chinese people would ever come to setting foot in the West was "World Park," a Disney-style attraction on the edge of the capital, where tourists could climb miniature Egyptian pyramids, behold a scale model of the Eiffel Tower, and stroll through an ersatz Manhattan. But as people had more money to spend, they explored more ways to spend it. When the Chinese travel industry surveyed the public on its dream destinations, no place scored higher than Europe. Asked what they liked about it, the Chinese put "culture" at the top of the list. (On the negative side, respondents complained of "arrogance" and "poor-quality Chinese food.")

Local newspapers grew dense with ads for exotic holiday travel. It began to feel as if everyone were getting away, and I decided to join them. China's travel agents competed by carving out tours that conformed less to Western notions of a grand tour than to the likes and dislikes of their customers. I scanned some deals online: "Big Plazas, Big Windmills, Big Gorges" was a four-day bus tour that emphasized photogenic countryside in the Netherlands and Luxembourg; "Visit the New and Yearn for the Past in Eastern Europe" had a certain Cold War charm, but I wasn't sure I needed that in February.

I chose the "Classic European," a popular bus tour that would traverse five countries in ten days. Payment was due up front. Airfare, hotels, meals, insurance, and assorted charges came to the equivalent in yuan of about $2,200. In addition, every Chinese member of the tour was required to put up a bond amounting to $7,600—more than two years' salary for the average worker—to prevent anyone from disappearing before the flight home. I was the thirty-eighth and final member of the group. We would depart the next morning at dawn.

I was told to proceed to Door No. 25 of Terminal 2 at Shanghai's

Pudong International Airport, where I found a slim forty-three-year-old man with floppy, parted hair. He wore a gray tweed overcoat and rectangular glasses. He introduced himself as Li Xingshun, our guide. To identify us in crowds, each of us received a canary-yellow lapel badge bearing a cartoon dragon with smoke curling from its nostrils, striding in hiking boots above our group's motto: "The Dragon Soars for Ten Thousand Li." (A *li* is about a third of a mile.)

We settled into coach on an Air China nonstop flight to Frankfurt, and I opened a Chinese packet of "Outbound Group Advice," which we'd been urged to read carefully. The specificity of the instructions suggested a history of unpleasant surprises: "Don't travel with knockoffs of European goods, because customs inspectors will seize them and penalize you." There was an intense focus on staying safe in Europe. "You will see Gypsies begging beside the road, but do not give them any money. If they crowd around and ask to see your purse, yell for the guide." Conversing with strangers was discouraged. "If someone asks you to help take a photo of him, watch out: this is a prime opportunity for thieves."

I had been in and out of Europe over the years, but the instructions put it in a new light, and I was oddly reassured to be traveling with three dozen others and a guide. The notes concluded with a piece of Confucius-style advice that framed our trip as a test of character: "He who can bear hardship will carry on."

We landed in Frankfurt in heavy fog and gathered in the terminal as a full group. We ranged in age from six-year-old Lu Keyi to his seventy-year-old grandfather, Liu Gongsheng, a retired mining engineer, who was escorting his wife, Huang Xueqing, in her wheelchair. Just about everyone belonged to the New Middle-Income Stratum: a high school science teacher, an interior decorator, a real estate executive, a set designer for a television station, a gaggle of university students. There was nothing of the countryside about my companions—the rare glimpse of a horse grazing in a French pasture the next day sent everyone scrambling for cameras—and yet they had only begun to be at home in the wider world. With few exceptions, this was everybody's first trip out of Asia. Li introduced me, the lone non-Chinese member of the group, and everyone offered a hearty welcome. Ten-year-old Liu Yifeng, who had a bowl cut and wore a black sweatshirt covered in white stars, smiled up at me and asked, "Do all foreigners have noses that big?"

We boarded a gold-colored coach, where I took a window seat and was joined by a tall, rangy eighteen-year-old in a black puffy vest and wire-frame glasses. He had dark bangs that dipped beneath the rim of his spectacles and a suggestion of whiskers on his upper lip. He introduced himself as Xu Nuo; in Chinese, the name means "promise," which he liked to use as an English name. Promise was a freshman at Shanghai Normal University, where he studied economics. His parents were seated across the aisle. I asked him why his family had chosen to travel rather than visit relatives over the holiday. "That's the tradition, but Chinese people are getting wealthier," he said. "Besides, we're too busy to travel the rest of the year." We spoke in Chinese, but when he was surprised, he'd say, "Oh, my Lady Gaga!," an English expression he'd picked up at school.

In the front row of the bus, Li Xingshun stood facing the group with a microphone in hand, a posture he would retain for most of our waking hours in the days ahead. In the life of a Chinese tourist, guides play an especially prominent role: interpreter, raconteur, and field marshal, with a duty to relay more than facts; as a Chinese guidebook put it, the guide should "express approval or disapproval, praise or opposition, pleasure or contempt." Li projected a calm, seasoned air. He often referred to himself in the third person, "Guide Li," and he prided himself on efficiency. "Everyone, our watches should be synchronized. It is now seven-sixteen p.m." He implored us to be five minutes early for every departure. "We flew all the way here," he said. "Let's make the most of it."

Guide Li outlined the plan: we would be spending many hours on the bus, during which he would deliver lectures on history and culture, so as not to waste precious minutes at the sights, when we could be taking photographs. He informed us that French scientists had determined that the optimal length of a tour guide's lecture is seventy-five minutes. "Before Guide Li was aware of that, the longest speech I ever gave on a bus was four hours," he added.

Li urged us to soak our feet in hot water before bed—he said it would help with jet lag—and to eat extra fruit in order to balance the European infusion of bread and cheese into our diets. Since it was the New Year's holiday, there would be many other Chinese visitors, and we must be vigilant not to board the wrong bus at rest stops. He introduced our driver, Petr Pícha, a phlegmatic former trucker and hockey player from the Czech Republic, who waved wearily to us from the well of the driver's seat. ("For six or seven years, I drove Japanese tourists all the time," he told me later. "Now it's all Chinese.") Guide Li had something else to say about the schedule: "In China, we think of bus drivers as super-humans who can work twenty-four hours straight, no matter how late we want them to drive. But in Europe, unless there's weather or traffic, they're only allowed to drive for twelve hours!"

He explained that every driver carries a card that must be inserted into a slot in the dashboard; too many hours, and the driver could be punished. "We might think you could just make a fake card or manipu-late the records—no big deal," Li said. "But, if you get caught, the fine starts at eighty-eight hundred euros, and they take away your license! That's the way Europe is: on the surface, it appears to rely on everyone's self-discipline, but behind it all there are strict laws."

We were approaching the hotel—a Best Western in Luxembourg— but first Li briefed us on breakfast. A typical Chinese breakfast consists of a bowl of congee (a rice porridge), a deep-fried cruller, and perhaps a basket of pork buns. In Europe, he warned, in his most tactful voice, "Throughout our trip, breakfast will rarely be more than bread, cold ham, milk, and coffee." The bus was silent for a moment.


We never saw Luxembourg in the daylight. We were out of the Best Western by dawn and were soon back on the Autobahn. Li asked us to make sure we hadn't left anything behind in the hotel, because some of his older travelers used to have a habit of hiding cash in the toilet tank or the ventilation ducts. "The worst case I've had was a guest who sewed money into the hem of the curtains," he told us.

We headed for our first stop: the modest German city of Trier. Though it was not a household name for most first-time visitors to Europe, Trier has been unusually popular with Chinese tourists ever since Com-munist Party delegations began arriving, decades ago, to see the birth-place of Karl Marx. My Chinese guidebook, written by a retired diplomat, described it as the "Mecca of the Chinese people."

We descended from the bus onto a tidy side street lined with peaked-roofed, pastel-colored buildings. The cobblestones were silvery with rain, and Li donned a forest-green felt outback hat and pointed us ahead as he started walking at a brisk pace. We reached No. 10 Brückenstrasse, a handsome three-story white house with green shutters. "This is where Marx lived. Now it's a museum," Li said. We tried the door, but it was locked. Things were slow in the winter, and the museum wouldn't be open for another hour and a half, so Li said that we'd be experiencing Marx's house only from the outside. "The sooner we finish here, the sooner we get to Paris," he had said. Beside the front door was a brass plaque with Marx's leonine head in profile. The building next door was a fast-food restaurant called Dolce Vita.

Li urged us to stay as long as we wanted, but he also suggested a stop at the supermarket on the corner to buy fruit for the ride ahead. We milled around awkwardly in front of Marx's house, snapping photographs and dodging cars, until one of the kids pleaded, "I want to go to the supermarket," and tugged his mother toward the bright storefront. I stood beside Wang Zhenyu, a tall man in his fifties, and we looked up at Marx's head. "Not many people in America know about him, right?" Wang asked.

"More than you might think," I said. I mentioned that I'd expected to see more Chinese visitors.

Wang laughed. "Young people no longer know anything about all that," he said.

Wang was thin and angular with the bearing of a self-made man. He had grown up in the eastern commercial city of Wuxi and had been assigned the job of carpenter, until economic reforms took hold and he went into business for himself. He now ran a small clothing factory that specialized in the production of wash-and-wear men's trousers. He didn't speak English, but when he was building his business he'd decided he needed a catchy, international name, so he'd called the company Ge-rui-te, a made-up word formed by the Chinese characters that he thought sounded most like the English word *great*.

Wang was an enthusiastic tourist. "I used to be so busy but now I want to travel," he said. "I always had to buy land, build factories, fix up my house. But now my daughter's grown and working. I only need to save up for the dowry, which is manageable." I asked why he and his wife had chosen Europe. "Our thinking is, go to the farthest places first, while we still have the energy," he said. Wang and I were among the last to arrive at the supermarket. Our group had lingered in the Mecca of the Chinese People for eleven minutes.

Until recently, Chinese people had abundant reasons not to see the world as a place for pleasure. Traveling in ancient China was arduous. As a proverb put it, "You can be comfortable at home for a thousand days, or step out the door and run right into trouble." Confucius threw guilt into the mix: "While your parents are alive, it is better not to travel far away." Nevertheless, ancient Buddhist monks visited India, and Zheng He, a fifteenth-century eunuch, famously sailed the emperor's fleet as far as Africa, to "set eyes on barbarian regions."

Over the centuries, Chinese migrants settled around the world, but poverty stood in the way of leisure travel, and Mao considered tourism antisocialist. It wasn't until 1978, after his death, that most Chinese gained approval to go abroad for anything other than work or study. First they were permitted to visit relatives in Hong Kong, and later, to tour Thailand, Singapore, and Malaysia. The government remained acutely wary of the outside world. In 1996, my first year in Beijing, it reformed migration laws to make it easier for Chinese to go abroad, though the rules still required people to be "politically reliable" and explicitly excluded anyone found to be "highly individualistic, corrupt, degenerate, or immoral." The next year, the government cleared the way for travelers to venture to other countries in a "planned, organized, and controlled manner." China doled out approvals with an eye to geopolitics. Vanuatu became an approved destination only after it agreed not to give diplomatic recognition to Taiwan.

When government departments began sending people abroad, they sought to prepare the pioneers for every eventuality. A 2002 guidebook called *The Latest Must-Read for Personnel Going Abroad* warned that, beyond Chinese borders, "foreign intelligence agencies and other enemy forces" wage a "battle for hearts and minds" using "reactionary propaganda to topple the leaders of the Chinese Communist Party." If a traveler on official business encountered a journalist, the authors offered a strategy: "Answer in a simple way; avoid the truth and emphasize the empty."

Eighty percent of first-time Chinese travelers were traveling in groups, and they earned a reputation as passionate, if occasionally overwhelming, guests. At a Malaysian casino hotel in 2005, some three hundred Chinese visitors were issued meal coupons bearing cartoon pig faces. The hotel said that the illustrations were simply to differentiate Chinese guests from Muslims, who don't eat pork, but the Chinese tourists took offense and staged a sit-in, singing the national anthem. In some cases, first-time travelers left mixed impressions on their hosts, and after a few incidents the Beijing government published a handbook, *The Chinese Citizens' Guide to Civilized Behavior Abroad*, which had a list of rules, including:

> 3. Protect the natural environment. Do not trample on green areas; do not pick the flowers and fruit; do not chase, grab, feed or throw things at animals.

> 6. Respect people's rights. Do not force foreigners to take pictures with you; do not sneeze in the direction of others.

Nobody in our group was inclined to throw things at animals. The more I read, the more I wondered if the authors of *The Chinese Citizens' Guide to Civilized Behavior Abroad* hadn't been outclassed by the citizens. Most countries begin to send large numbers of tourists overseas only after the average citizen has a disposable income of five thousand dollars. But when China's urban residents were still at half that level, travel agents made such travel affordable by booking tickets in bulk and bargaining mercilessly for hotels in distant suburbs. "Every route is largely determined by the plane tickets," Li explained to me. Wherever the cheapest flights were on a given day, Chinese tours saw opportunity. That was why our route resembled the Big Dipper: it started in Germany and looped through Luxembourg and into Paris, before a long southerly swoop through France, over the Alps, and down into Italy as far as Rome. It might have ended there, but instead it did an about-face and doubled back to Milan.

Europe, initially, was an afterthought. In 2000, more Chinese tourists visited tiny Macau than visited all the countries of Europe combined. But the opportunities did not go unnoticed. Accor, the French hotel group, began adding Chinese television channels and Mandarin-speaking staff. Other hotels moved beds away from windows, as dictated by feng shui. The more the Chinese went to Europe, the cheaper tours became. By 2009 a British travel industry report had concluded that "Europe" was such a successful "single, unified" brand in China that individual countries would be wise to put aside pride and delay promoting "sub-brands" such as France or Italy. Europe was less a region on the map than a state of mind, and bundling as many countries as possible into a single week appealed to workers with precious few opportunities to travel. "In China, if you can get ten things for a hundred dollars, that's still better than getting one thing for a hundred dollars," Guide Li said.

I strolled back to the bus from Marx's house with a young couple from Shanghai: Guo Yanjin, a relaxed twenty-nine-year-old who called herself Karen and worked in the finance department of an auto parts company, and her husband, Gu Xiaojie, an administrative clerk in the department of environmental sanitation, who went by the English name Handy. He had an easy charm and the build of an American football player—six feet tall and barrel-chested. His sweater was maroon and bore an appliqué of a golf bag, but when I asked if he was a golfer, he laughed. "Golf is a rich man's game," he said.

Handy and Karen had saved up for months for this trip and had also received a boost from their parents. Guide Li had urged us not to ruin our vacations by worrying too much about money—he suggested that we pretend the price tags were in yuan instead of euros—but Handy and Karen kept an eye on every cent. Within a few days, they could tell me exactly how much we'd spent on each bottle of water in five countries.

Back on the gold bus, rolling west across the wintry scrub of Champagne-Ardenne, Li wanted to add an important exception to his demands for efficiency. "We have to get used to the fact that Europeans sometimes move slowly," he said. When shopping in China, he went on, "we're accustomed to three of us putting our items on the counter at the same time, and then the old lady gives change to three people without making a mistake. Europeans don't do that." He continued, "I'm not saying that they're stupid. If they were, they wouldn't have developed all this technology, which requires very subtle calculations. They just deal with math in a different way."

He ended with some advice: "Let them do things their way, because if we're rushing, then they'll feel rushed, and that will put them in a bad mood, and then we'll think that they're discriminating against us, which is not necessarily the case."

At times, Guide Li marveled at Europe's high standard of living—bombarding us with statistics on the price of Bordeaux wines or the average height of a Dutchman—but if there was ever a time when Chinese visitors marveled at Europe's economy, this was not that time. Li made a great show of acting out a Mediterranean lifestyle: "Wake up slowly, brush teeth, make a cup of espresso, take in the aroma." The crowd laughed. "With a pace like that, how can their economies keep growing? It's impossible." He added, "In this world, only when you have diligent, hardworking people will the nation's economy grow."

I dozed off, and awoke on the outskirts of Paris. We followed the Seine west and passed the Musée d'Orsay just as the sun bore through the clouds. Li shouted, "Feel the openness of the city!" Cameras whirred, and he pointed out that central Paris had no skyscrapers. At a dock beside the Pont de l'Alma, we boarded a double-decker boat, and as it chugged upriver, I chatted with Zhu Zhongming, a forty-six-year-old accountant who was traveling with his wife and daughter. He had grown up in Shanghai and had ventured into real estate just as the local market was surging. "Whenever you bought something, you could make a ton of money," he said. He was charismatic, with large, dimpled cheeks framing a permanent mischievous smile, and he'd been going abroad since 2004, so others in the group deferred to him. The boat reached Pont de Sully, and turned slowly against the whitecaps on the Seine to head back downriver.

Zhu said that Chinese interest in Europe was motivated in part by a need to understand their own history: "When Europe was ruling the world, China was strong as well. So why did we fall behind? We've been thinking about that ever since," he said. Indeed, the question of why a mighty civilization slumped in the fifteenth century runs like a central nerve through China's analysis of its past and its prospects for the future. Zhu offered an explanation: "Once we were invaded, we didn't respond quickly enough." It was a narrative of victimhood and decline that I'd often heard in China. (Historians also tend to blame the stifling effects of bureaucracy and authoritarianism, among other factors.) But Zhu did not trace all China's troubles to foreign invaders. "We cast aside our three core ideas—Buddhism, Taoism, and Confucianism—and that was a mistake. We were taught Marxist revolutionary ideas from 1949 to 1978." He paused and watched his wife and daughter snapping photographs at the boat's railing, an orange sun sinking behind the buildings. "We spent thirty years on what we now know was a disaster," he said.

The boat docked, and we headed to dinner, walking through the crowds amid the din of the city for the first time. We passed a young couple in a doorway making out. Karen hugged Handy's arm, their heads swiveling. We followed Li into a small Chinese storefront, down a flight of stairs, and into a hot, claustrophobic hallway flanked by windowless rooms jammed with Chinese diners. It was a hive of activity invisible from the street—a parallel Paris. There were no empty seats, so Li motioned for us to continue out the back door, where we turned left and entered a second restaurant, also Chinese. Down another staircase, into another windowless room, where dishes arrived: braised pork, bok choy, egg-drop soup, spicy chicken.

Twenty minutes later, we climbed the stairs out into the night, hustling after Li to the Galeries Lafayette, the ten-story department store on the Boulevard Haussmann. The store appeared happily poised for an onslaught from the East: it was decked in red bunting and cartoon bunnies for the Year of the Rabbit. We received Chinese-language welcome cards promising happiness, longevity, and a 10 percent discount.

The next day, at the Louvre, we picked up another Chinese-speaking guide, a hummingbird of a woman, who shouted, "We have lots to see in ninety minutes, so we need to pick up our feet!" She darted ahead beneath a furled purple umbrella, which she used as a rallying flag, and without breaking stride, she taught us some French using Chinese sounds: *bonjour* could be approximated by pronouncing the Chinese characters *ben* and *zhu*, which mean, fittingly, "to chase someone." We raced after her through the turnstile, and Wang Zhenyu, the pants manufacturer, tried out his new French on the security guard: *"Ben zhu, ben zhu!"*

The guide advised us to focus most on the *san bao* ("the three treasures"): the Winged Victory of Samothrace, the Venus de Milo, and the *Mona Lisa*. We crowded around each in turn, flanked by other Chinese tour groups as identifiable as rival armies: red pins for the U-Tour travel agency, orange windbreakers for the students from Shenzhen. We'd been going nonstop since before dawn, but the air was charged with diligent curiosity. When we discovered that the elevators were a long detour from our route, I wondered how Huang Xueqing, in her wheelchair, would get to see much of the museum. Then I saw that her relatives hoisted her chair while she hobbled up and down each marble stairway, and rolled her in front of the masterpieces.

By nightfall, another day of touring Europe's sights had kindled a sense of appreciation, albeit with a competitive streak. While we waited for tables, at a Chinese restaurant, Zhu brought up the Zhou dynasty (1046–256 B.C.E.), the era that produced Confucius, Lao-tzu, and other pillars of Chinese thought. "Back then, we were damn good!" Zhu told a group of us. His wife, Wang Jianxin, rolled her eyes. "Here we go again," she said. Her husband was wearing a recently purchased Eiffel Tower baseball cap with blinking battery-powered lights. He turned to me in search of a fresh audience. "Really, during the Zhou dynasty we were practically the same as ancient Rome or Egypt!"

In the middle of a seven-hour drive from Paris to the Alps, my seatmate Promise rooted around in his backpack and pulled out a crumpled edition of *The Wall Street Journal* that he'd picked up at the hotel in Luxembourg. He studied each page in silence and elbowed me for help when he came across a headline related to China: EU FINDS HUAWEI GOT STATE SUPPORT. The story said that European trade officials believed that the big Chinese technology company Huawei was receiving unfairly cheap loans from state banks. "Does the American Constitution prevent companies from receiving government support?" Promise asked. I asked Promise if he used Facebook, which was officially blocked in China but reachable with some tinkering. "It's too much of a hassle to get to it," he said. Instead, he used Renren, a Chinese version, which, like other domestic sites, censored any sensitive political discussion. I asked what he knew about Facebook's being blocked. "It has something to do with politics," he said, and paused. "But the truth is I don't really know."

This kind of remove among urbane Chinese students was familiar. They lived with unprecedented access to technology and information, but also with the Great Firewall, the vast infrastructure of digital filters and human censors that blocked politically objectionable content from reaching computers in China. Many young Chinese regarded the notion of the firewall as insulting, but the barriers were just large enough to keep many people from bothering to get around them. The information about the outside world that filtered through was erratic: Promise could talk to me at length about the latest Sophie Marceau film or the merits of various Swiss race car drivers, but the news of Chinese leaders accruing large private fortunes had not reached him. So many foreign ideas were flooding China at once that people made sense of them partly by grouping the world into manageable pieces. In Beijing, a Chinese dining guide called Dianping offered eighteen separate categories of Chinese cuisine, but everything outside of Asia (Italian, Moroccan, Brazilian) was grouped under one heading: "Western Food."

That night, we stayed in the Swiss town of Interlaken, where Guide Li had promised us "truly clean air," a treat for residents of any large Chinese city. I stepped outside to look around town with Zheng Dao and her daughter, Li Cheng, a nineteen-year-old art major. We strolled past luxury watch shops, a casino, and the Höhematte, a vast green where locals put on yodeling and Swiss wrestling events. Midway through the trip, the daughter was politely unmoved. "Other than different buildings, the Seine didn't look all that different from the Huangpu," she said. "Subway? We have a subway. You name it, we've got it." She laughed.

As Li Cheng walked on ahead with friends, her mother told me that she wanted her daughter to see differences between China and the West that ran deeper than "hardware." Our guide had mocked Europe's stately pace, but Zheng said her countrymen had come to believe that "if you don't elbow your way on to everything you'll be last." A car paused for us at a crosswalk, and Zheng drew a contrast: "Drivers at home think, 'I can't pause. Otherwise, I'll never get anywhere,'" she said.


By the final days of the trip, the advice and efficiency that had been so reassuring in the beginning were wearing thin. On the bus, people asked if we could stop at a Western restaurant; we had been in Europe for a week and had yet to sit down to a lunch or a dinner that was not Chinese. (Nearly half of all Chinese tourists in one market survey reported eating no more than one "European-style" meal on a trip to the West.) But Li warned us that Western food can take too long to serve, and if we ate it too fast, it would give us indigestion. "Save it for your next trip," he said, and everyone consented. In Milan, he reminded us again to be on guard against thieves, but Handy the sanitation specialist was dubious. "Italy is not as chaotic as they made it seem," he said. "It sounded really terrifying."

I had begun to wonder how much longer tours like this might endure. Solo tourism was already growing in popularity among young people, and even in the course of our time together my fellow tourists had wearied of hustling so much. In Milan, we had thirty minutes on our own, so Karen and Handy and I stepped into the cool interior of the Duomo. Handy peered up at soaring sheets of brilliant stained glass. "That looks exhausting," he said. "But it's beautiful."

The Italian papers were full of news that Prime Minister Berlusconi was about to be charged with sleeping with a teenager. Guide Li was diplomatic. "What a unique man he is!" he said. The drive across Italy that day had put him in a reflective mood about life at home. "You might wonder now and then whether it would be good to promote democracy," he said. "Of course, there are benefits: people enjoy freedom of speech and the freedom to elect politicians. But doesn't the one-party system have its benefits, too?" He pointed out the window to the highway and said that it had taken decades for Italy to build it, because of local opposition. "If this were China, it would be done in six months! And that's the only way to keep the economy growing." Li was so boosterish that I might have taken him for a government spokesman, except that his comments were familiar from my day-to-day conversations in Beijing. "Analysts overseas can never understand why the Chinese economy has grown so fast," he said. "Yes, it's a one-party state, but the administrators are selected from among the elites, and elites picked from one-point-three billion people might as well be called super-elites."

Li's portrait of the West contained at least one feature of unalloyed admiration. He mentioned a Western friend who had quit his job to go backpacking and find his calling in life. "Would our parents accept that? Of course not! They'd point a finger and say, 'You're a waste!'" he said. But in Europe, "young people are allowed to pursue what they want to pursue."

He went on: "Our Chinese ancestors left us so many things, but why do we find it so difficult to discover new things? It's because our education system has too many constraints." Our group was even more attentive than usual. At the very moment that American parents were wondering if they had something to learn from China's hard-nosed "tiger mothers," Chinese parents were trying to restore creativity to the country's desiccated education system. One mother, Zeng Liping, told me that teachers had frowned upon her bringing her sixth grader to Europe. "Before every school vacation, the teachers tell them, 'Don't go out. Stay at home and study, because very soon you'll be taking the exam to get into middle school.'" But Zeng had made her peace with being out of step. She had quit a stable job as an art teacher and put her savings into starting her own fashion label. "My bosses all said, 'What a shame that you're leaving a good workplace.' But I've proved to myself that I made the right choice."

In Rome the next day, we stopped at the Trevi Fountain and strolled up to the vast splendor of St. Peter's Square. Zhu said the scale reminded him of Beijing. "It's just like the old days, when Chinese people used to go to Beijing just to catch a glimpse of the Communist Party." He laughed.

We wandered down the block and sat down on a windowsill to rest. Zhu lit a cigarette. He'd been thinking about the varying fortunes of great powers. I asked if he believed American politicians who say they have no objections to China's rise. He shook his head. "No way. They'll let us grow, but they'll try to limit it. Everyone I know thinks that." Ultimately, he said, in the politest way he could think of, Americans would need to adjust to a weaker position in the world, just as China once did. "You are so used to being on top, but you will drop to second place. It won't be immediately—it'll take twenty or thirty years—but our GDP will eventually surpass yours." I was struck that, for all his travels, Zhu saw an enduring philosophical divide between China and the West: "two different ways of thinking," as he put it. "We will use their tools and learn their methods. But fundamentally, China will always maintain its own way," he said.

His sentiment didn't inspire much optimism about China's future alongside the West. On some level, it was hard to argue with him; the prospect that a richer China would naturally become a more Western, democratic China was no longer as convincing to me as it had been in my student days, when I was drawn to Beijing by the tragic potential of Tiananmen Square. The China that I inhabited now was, by turns, inspiring and maddening, home to both Bare-Handed Fortunes and black jails, a fierce curiosity about the world and a defensive pride in China's new place in it. My busmates had answered the call to go West, but if they struggled to make sense of what they found, I could sympathize; I was struggling to make sense of a land "unfettered" but subject to the Party in Power.

If it was naïve to imagine that China's opening would simply draw it closer to the West, it was also naïve, perhaps, to dismiss the power of more subtle changes. Modern Chinese travel, like the modern Chinese state, was predicated on the fragile promise that it would impose order on a chaotic world, by shepherding its citizens and keeping them safe from threats that could include Western thieves, Western cuisine, and Western culture. In the flesh, the West that our group encountered was, indeed, more Europe than "Europe"—unkempt and unglamorous in ways they hadn't expected. And yet, behind the prosperity gospel about Chinese one-party efficiency, my busmates caught unredacted flickers of insight, glimpses of humaneness and openness and a world once forbidden. By declaring, in effect, an end to the revolution, the Party in Power had hoped that its people would now step beyond politics and get on with living. But it would never be that easy.

When Promise finally put down his wilted copy of *The Wall Street Journal*, there were no trumpets. He said simply, "When I read a foreign newspaper, I see lots of things I don't know about." On this first trip, there was much they would never see, but mile by mile, they were discovering how to see it at all.

# PART II
# TRUTH

# EIGHT

# DANCING IN SHACKLES

The most intriguing building in Beijing was not celebrated for its architecture. Facing the Avenue of Eternal Peace, next door to China's equivalent of the White House, was a modern, three-story green office block with a pagoda roof that perched on top like a toupee. What impressed me was that the building did not, on paper at least, exist. It had no address, no sign, and it appeared on no public charts of the Party structure. The first time I asked what it was, the guard said, "I can't tell you that. It's a government organ." Over time, I came to think of it as, simply, the Department.

Every capital has its secret departments, but the odd thing about this one and its aversion to publicity was that it was the Central Publicity Department. The "Publicity" in the title was for English purposes; the Chinese name was the Central Propaganda Department, and it was one of the People's Republic's most powerful and secretive organizations—a government agency with the power to fire editors, silence professors, ban books, and recut movies. By the time I settled in China, the Department, and its offices across the country, had control over two thousand newspapers and eight thousand magazines; every film and television program, every textbook, amusement park, video game, bowling club, and beauty pageant was subject to its scrutiny. The propagandists decided what ads could go on every billboard from the Himalayas to the Yellow Sea. They administered the largest fund for the social sciences, which gave them veto power over scholarly research that did not, for instance, heed their ban on the use of certain words to describe China's political system. (One of the banned words was *jiquanzhuyi*—"totalitarianism.") The

Department had a breadth of authority over the realm of ideas in China that Anne-Marie Brady, a scholar who studied it, compared to the "Vatican's influence over the Catholic world."

Orwell wrote that political prose, in any country, is intended to "give an appearance of solidity to pure wind." During the Truman era, Secretary of State Dean Acheson pruned and massaged his facts until they were, in his words, "clearer than truth." But no country has devoted more time and care to the art of propaganda than China, where the emperor Qin Shi Huang governed, in the third century B.C.E., with a policy he called "Keep the Masses Ignorant and They Will Follow." Mao sanctified propaganda and censorship as essential parts of Thought Work, and he relied on them to reframe the Long March as a strategic triumph, not a crushing defeat. Five year after Mao died, his heirs' final act of devotion was to issue an official declaration on Mao's tumultuous reign. They said it was 70 percent correct and 30 percent wrong—an imponderable calculation that would be studied by schoolchildren for decades to come.

The Department almost disappeared. In 1989 the uprising at Tiananmen Square convinced some Party leaders that propaganda was growing impotent in the modern age. But Deng Xiaoping disagreed, and he made a fateful decision—the Party's future survival, he declared, would rest, more than ever before, on two pillars: prosperity and propaganda. Of China's young people who took to the square, he said, "It will take years, not just a couple of months, of education to change their thinking." But the Soviet approach to propaganda had failed them. Deng and his men urgently needed a new approach, and they found it in the holy land of public relations, America, and in a new, if unlikely, role model: Walter Lippmann, a leading American columnist for much of the twentieth century. They overlooked his early anticommunism and hailed his efforts to prevent mass rule and to sway U.S. public opinion to enter World War I. They studied and cited Lippmann's belief in the power of pictures to, in his words, "magnify emotion while undermining critical thought," and they adopted his view that good PR can create a "group mind" and "manufacture consent" for the ruling elite.

To sculpt propaganda for the emerging middle class, they embraced another father of American PR, the late political scientist Harold Lasswell, who wrote, in 1927, "If the mass will be free of chains of iron, it must accept its chains of silver." Party image makers who began their careers denouncing capitalist stooges now studied the success of Coca-Cola, observing, as one Chinese propaganda textbook put it, that Coke proved that "if you have a good image, any problem can be solved." To learn the art of modern spin, the Communist Party studied the masters: a five-day seminar for top propaganda officials made case studies out of Tony Blair's response to mad cow disease and the Bush administration's handling of the U.S. media after 9/11.

In 2004 the Department created a Bureau of Public Opinion, which commissioned surveys and research to measure the pulse of the public without the niceties of voting. Instead of withering away, the world of Thought Work grew in scale and sophistication, until it encompassed, by one estimate, a propaganda officer for every one hundred Chinese citizens. The era of thundering loudspeakers and mimeographed pamphlets was over. Like any competitive enterprise, the Department now measured its effectiveness in page hits and prime-time viewership. It created big-budget advertising campaigns with the help of famous filmmakers such as Zhang Yimou, and it submerged people in a gauzy emotional message that aimed, as one propaganda chief put it, to reach "into their ears, into their heads, and into their hearts." It was more important than ever, Party scholars pointed out, to "make their thinking conform with the dominant ideology, thereby standardizing people's behavior."

Nothing consumed more of the Department's attention than the press. "Never again," President Jiang Zemin vowed after Tiananmen, "would China's newspapers, radio, and television be permitted to become a battlefront for bourgeois liberalism." China, Jiang said, would never succumb to what he called "so-called glasnost." Journalists were still expected to "sing as one voice," and the Department would help them do so by issuing a vast and evolving list of words that must and must not appear in the news. Some rules never changed: Any mention of Taiwan's laws was to refer to them as "so-called laws," while China's political system was so unique that reporters were never to type the phrase "according to international practice" when drawing comparisons to Beijing. When it came to the economy, they were not to dwell on bad news during the holidays, or on issues that the government classified as "unsolvable," such as the fragility of Chinese banks or the political influence of the wealthy. The most ardently forbidden subject was Tiananmen itself; no mention of the 1989 protests or the bloodshed appear in Chinese textbooks; when the government discusses the events of that year, it describes them as "chaos" or "turmoil" organized by a handful of "black hands."

Journalists had little choice but to heed those instructions to such a degree that, even as China became more diverse and clamorous, the world of the news was an oasis of calm—a realm of breathtaking sameness. Newspapers on opposite sides of the country often carried identical headlines, in identical font. In May 2008, when a powerful earthquake struck the province of Sichuan, papers across the country proclaimed in near-perfect unison that the earthquake had "tugged at the heartstrings of the Chinese Communist Party." The next morning, I rounded up the local papers and marveled at their consistency.

One of the few Chinese news sites that had anything different to say was a magazine called *Caijing*. While the state news service, Xinhua, was hailing the People's Liberation Army for its rescue efforts, *Caijing*—the name means "finance and economics"—was ferreting out estimates of the numbers of dead and wounded and reporting that "many disaster victims have yet to receive any relief supplies at all." I wondered why *Caijing*'s writing was different, and I sensed that it might have something to do with the person in charge, a woman named Hu Shuli, who had made her name divining the boundaries of free expression in China. I asked to come see her. I wanted to know how you negotiate with a building that does not exist.

I heard Hu Shuli before I saw her. I was waiting in her office off the newsroom of *Caijing*, a sleek and open gray-brick space on the nineteenth floor of the Prime Tower, in downtown Beijing, when I heard an urgent click-clack of heels down the hallway. She approached the door and then kept on going, sweeping into the newsroom spouting a series of decrees and ideas, before spinning around and heading back in my direction. In advance of my visit, Qian Gang, an editor whom she had known for years, had warned me that Hu moved at a pace "as sudden and rash as a gust of wind."

In her mid-fifties, Hu Shuli was five feet two and slim, with a pixie haircut and a wardrobe of color-coordinated outfits. She was so voluble and pugnacious that she seemed like "a female Godfather," one of her reporters thought upon their first meeting. Another of her colleagues compared the experience of chatting with her to being on the receiving end of machine-gun fire. Wang Lang, an old friend of Hu's and an editor at *Economic Daily*, a state-run newspaper, repeatedly declined her offers to work together, because, he told me, "keeping some distance is better for our friendship." Depending on the point of view, being with her was either thrilling or unnerving. Her boss, Wang Boming, the chairman of *Caijing*'s parent company, SEEC Media Group, told me, half-jokingly, "I'm afraid of her."

In the world of "news workers," as journalists are known in Party-speak, Hu Shuli had a singular profile. She was an incurable muckraker, but had cultivated first-name familiarity with some of China's most powerful Party leaders. Since 1998, when Hu established *Caijing*, with two computers and a borrowed conference room, she had guided the magazine with near-perfect pitch for how much candor and provocation the Department would tolerate. This meant deciding what to cover (rampant corporate fraud, case after case of political corruption), but also what not to cover (Falun Gong, the Tiananmen Square anniversaries, and many other things). Hu had endured as editor long after other tenacious Chinese journalists had been imprisoned or silenced. She was often described in the Chinese and foreign press as "the most dangerous woman in China," though she downplayed it, saying that she was just "a woodpecker," forever hammering at a tree, trying not to knock it down but to make it grow straighter.

*Caijing* had the glossy feel and design of *Fortune*. It was heavy with advertising, for Cartier watches, Chinese credit cards, Mercedes SUVs. The writing could be purposefully dense. But China's propaganda officials were more likely to clamp down on television and mass-market newspapers, which had audiences in the millions, than they were on a magazine that sold only two hundred thousand copies, even if those copies went to many of China's most important offices in government, finance, and academia, giving the magazine extraordinary influence. It had a pair of websites, in Chinese and English, that together attracted about 3.2 million unique visitors every month. Hu wrote a widely quoted column for the print edition and the Web. Every year, she hosted a conference that drew the economic leadership of the Communist Party.

Hu's brio stood out in an industry in which truth often succumbed to political priorities. Not long after the earthquake, Xinhua, the state news service, published a story on its website, detailing how China's Shenzhou VII rocket made its thirtieth orbit of the earth. The story had plenty of gripping detail—"The dispatcher's firm voice broke the silence on the ship." Unfortunately, the rocket had yet to be launched—the news service later apologized for posting a "draft."

But failing to put politics before truth could be hazardous. When Reporters Without Borders ranked countries by press freedom in 2008, the year of the earthquake, China ranked 167th out of 173 countries— behind Iran and ahead of Vietnam. Article 35 of the Chinese constitution guaranteed freedom of speech and the press, but regulations gave the government broad powers to imprison editors and writers for "harming national interests" and other offenses. There were twenty-eight reporters in Chinese jails, more than in any other country. (In 2009, Iran overtook China in this, for the first time in ten years.)

In the face of those risks, I saw in Hu Shuli's magazine the first Chinese publication with the ambition to become a world-class news organization. "It's different from everything you see in China," an economist named Andy Xie told me. "Its existence, in a way, is a miracle."

The first time I visited Hu Shuli at home, I was sure that I was lost. Unlike many of the reporters and editors on her staff, she did not live in one of Beijing's new residential high-rises. She and her husband lived in an old-fashioned concrete housing block, in a three-bedroom apartment with a view of an overgrown garden. The neighborhood was China's old-media stronghold, home to the headquarters of the state radio and to China's film and television censors. In the 1950s, when the building was a privileged residence for Party cadres, the government assigned space in it to Hu's father.

She came from impeccable Communist stock. Her grandfather Hu Zhongchi was a famous translator and editor, and his brother ran a prominent publishing house; Hu's mother, Hu Lingsheng, was a senior editor at *Workers' Daily* in Beijing. Her father, Cao Qifeng, was an underground Communist before taking a post in a trade union. But from a young age, Hu Shuli had instincts that worried her mother. "I always spoke about what I was thinking," she explained.

The Cultural Revolution engulfed China when she was thirteen, and her classes were suspended. Her family suffered: As a prominent editor, Hu's mother was criticized at her newspaper and placed under house arrest. Her father was shunted into a backroom job. Hu became a Red Guard, with others her age, and they traveled the country proclaiming their love for the "reddest of red suns," Mao Zedong. As the movement descended into violence, Hu Shuli sought refuge in books, trying to maintain a semblance of an education. "It was a very confusing time, because we lost all values," she said. A month before her sixteenth birthday, she was sent to the countryside to experience the rural revolution. What she found there astonished her.

"It was ridiculous," she recalled. Farmers had no reason to work. "They just wanted to stay lying in the field, sometimes for two hours. I said, 'Should we start work?' They said, 'How can you think that?'" She went on: "Ten years later, I realized everything was wrong."

For many in her generation, the rustication campaign was a revelation. Another young believer sent to the countryside, Wu Si, recalled to me his first day at an iron foundry. "We'd always been taught to believe that 'the proletariat is a selfless class,' and we believed in it completely," he told me. A few hours after his arrival, a fellow worker approached him and said, "That's enough. You can stop [working] now."

Wu was puzzled. "I don't have anything else to do, so I might as well keep working."

The comrade whispered some advice. "People won't be too happy about that."

If Wu worked a full day, quotas would go up for everyone. He put down his tools. Soon he learned other secrets of survival in the state-owned factories—how to swipe parts from the storeroom, how to build lamps for sale on the black market. For Wu, who would later become a prominent writer and editor, it introduced him to the world of parallel realities. "One narrative was public," he told me, "and one was real."

When colleges resumed classes, in 1978, Hu Shuli secured a seat at People's University in Beijing. The journalism department was hardly her first choice, but it was the best that the school offered. After graduation, she joined *Workers' Daily*, and was assigned, in 1985, to a bureau in the coastal city of Xiamen, which had been designated as a laboratory for the growth of a free market. She was a natural networker—she had a regular bridge game with the mayor—and her interviewees included a promising young cadre in city government whose openness to the free market had earned him the nickname the God of Wealth. His name was Xi Jinping, and years later he would become the president of China.

In 1987, Hu won a fellowship from the World Press Institute to spend five months in America. The experience changed her sense of what was possible. Her paper, *Workers' Daily*, was four pages long, but every town she visited in the United States seemed to have a paper ten or twenty times as long. One evening in Minnesota, she said, "I spent the whole night reading the St. Paul *Pioneer Press*." She returned to China, and in the spring of 1989 the Tiananmen Square movement electrified the Beijing press. Many journalists, including Hu, joined the demonstrations. As soldiers cracked down on the night of June 3, Hu recalls, "I went to the street, then went back to the office and said, 'We should cover this.'" But the decision had already come down: "We weren't going to publish a word about it." Many reporters who had spoken out were fired or banished to the provinces. Her husband, Miao Di, a film professor, thought that Hu might get arrested, but in the end she was suspended for eighteen months.

After her suspension, Hu became the international editor at *China Business Times*, one of the country's first national papers dedicated to covering the new frontiers of the economy. In 1992, she stumbled on a small group of Chinese financiers who had trained overseas and returned home to build the Chinese stock markets. Many of them were the children of powerful Chinese leaders. The group called itself the Stock Exchange Executive Council, and in 1992 it rented a cluster of rooms at Beijing's Chongwenmen Hotel. The members pulled out the beds and set up an office. At one desk was Gao Xiqing, who had earned a law degree at Duke and worked at Richard Nixon's law firm in New York before returning to China. At another was Wang Boming, the son of a former ambassador and vice foreign minister; Wang had studied finance at Columbia and worked as an economist in the research department of the

New York Stock Exchange. They enlisted the support of rising stars in the Party, such as Wang Qishan, who was the son-in-law of a vice-premier, and Zhou Xiaochuan, a reform-minded political scion.

She began hanging around and ended up with a string of scoops and, eventually, an incomparable Rolodex of names destined for China's highest offices. (Wang Qishan reached the Standing Committee of the Politburo; Gao Xiqing became head of China's sovereign wealth fund; Zhou Xiaochuan ran China's central bank.) Later, many people in Beijing whispered that these connections protected Hu, but she insisted that outsiders overestimated her proximity to power. "I don't know their birthdays," she said, of high-ranking officials. "I'm a journalist, and they treat me as a journalist."

In 1998, Hu received a phone call from Wang Boming, one of the hotel room financiers. He was starting a magazine and wanted her to run it. She had two conditions: Wang would not use her pages to promote his other businesses, and he would give her a budget of a quarter of a million dollars (substantial in those days) to pay salaries that were high enough to prevent reporters from taking bribes. Wang agreed. It was no charity: he and his reform-minded allies in the government believed that, as China's economy modernized, it could no longer rely on the tottering state-run press. People could no longer afford to be uninformed.

"You need the media to play its function to disclose the facts to the public and, in a sense, help the government detect evils," Wang told me one morning in his large, cluttered office downstairs from *Caijing*'s headquarters. He was a chain-smoker with a thick brush of gray-flecked black hair, Ferragamo eyeglasses, and a garrulous sense of humor. For all his Party pedigree, his years abroad had altered his understanding of the value of truth. "When I was studying in the States, I needed to make some money to pay my tuition, so I was working for a newspaper in Chinatown—the *China Daily News*," he said. Even as a cub reporter, he relished the chance to follow a trail wherever it led. He laughed. Being a reporter had made him feel like "a king without a crown."

Hu Shuli wasted no time following the trail; her inaugural issue had an explosive cover story revealing that small-time investors had lost millions when a real estate company called Qiong Min Yuan went bust, even though insiders had been tipped off in time to unload their shares. Regulators were incensed; they accused Hu of flouting the restrictions handed down by the Department, and her bosses had to calm the censors by making self-criticisms. But the defining moment in *Caijing*'s rise came when a reporter named Cao Haili, visiting Hong Kong in the spring of 2003, noticed that every person on the train platform seemed to be wearing a surgical mask. What the hell is that about? she thought, and alerted Hu. The Chinese press had been running reports that health officials had contained the spread of a mysterious new virus called SARS. In fact, the epidemic was growing. Newspaper editors in Guangdong Province had been ordered to publish nothing but reassuring stories about the virus.

But Hu Shuli realized those restrictions did not extend to editors outside the province, and she exploited the opening. "I bought a lot of books about breathing diseases, infections, and viruses," she said, and her staff began pointing out errors in government statements. Over the course of a month, *Caijing* produced a series of indispensable reports, and they were planning yet another when the Department put an end to it.

From its headquarters on the Avenue of Eternal Peace, the Department issued a daily stream of directives to editors that outlined the latest dos and don'ts. By definition, these reports were secret—the public was not allowed to learn what it couldn't learn—and when I arrived in 2005, it was less than three months after reporter Shi Tao was sentenced to ten years in prison for describing the contents of a propaganda directive. To prevent further leaks, censors now preferred to deliver instructions orally. Leaders at the headquarters of state television had a special red telephone for this purpose. Other news organizations received instructions at meetings that reporters called "going to class."

For decades the censors had skillfully suppressed unwelcome news (epidemics, natural disasters, civil unrest), but technology and travel were making this increasingly difficult. When the cover-up of the SARS virus became known, Jiao Guobiao, a journalism professor at Peking University, ignored the taboo against acknowledging the Department's invisible authority and wrote, "The Central Propaganda Department is the only dead spot in China that does not operate by rules and regulations; it is a dark empire in which the rays of law do not shine." The university fired him for it.

When I joined Hu Shuli one afternoon, she was running late for an un-usual appointment: she had decided that her top editors needed new clothes, and she had summoned a tailor. As Hu and her reporters grew in prominence, they were spending more and more time in front of crowds or overseas. She was sick of seeing her staff in sack suits and stained short-sleeve button-downs. She offered her editors a deal: buy one new suit and the magazine would pay for another. A pudgy, heavy-lidded tai-lor carried an armful of suits into a conference room, and the staff filed in for a fitting.

"Doesn't it look baggy here?" Hu said, tugging at the underarm of an elegant gray pin-striped jacket being fitted to Wang Shuo, her thirty-seven-year-old managing editor. With his boss prodding at his midsection, he wore an expression of bemused tolerance that I had seen several times on a dog in a bathtub.

"It is rather tight already," Wang protested.

"He feels tight already," the tailor said.

"Hold on!" Hu said. "Think about the James Bond suit in the movies. Make it like that!"

The change implied by Hu's flamboyant internationalism ran deeper than aesthetics. A well-meaning American professor once advised her, "If you stay in China as a journalist, you will never really join the inter-national mainstream." She was determined to prove him wrong, even if it meant working the angles within the Chinese system.

If a magazine like hers broke the rules, the Department gave it a warning known as a yellow card, as in soccer. Three yellow cards in one year, and she could be shut down. The Department wasn't reading sto-ries before publication; on the contrary, it was up to editors themselves to guess how far they could go and compute the risk of wandering past an ill-defined limit. That was a specific kind of pressure, which China scholar Perry Link once compared to living beneath an "anaconda coiled in an overhead chandelier." "Normally, the great snake doesn't move," he wrote. "It doesn't have to. It feels no need to be clear about its prohi-bitions. Its silent constant message is 'You yourself decide,' after which, more often than not, everyone in its shadows makes his or her large and small adjustments—all quite 'naturally.'"

Over the years, Hu learned to live beneath the anaconda by treat-ing China's government as a living, breathing organism; she constantly measured its moods and sensitivities. Wang Feng, one of her deputies, told me, "You can feel her making adjustments. For example, at Monday's editorial conference she might aim at something, and the editors and reporters go ahead and do it. And by Wednesday's editorial conference she will say, 'You know what? I've got more information on this and we should not say that. Maybe we should aim lower.'"

In January 2007, Hu Shuli got her first lesson in going too far. The cover story "Whose Luneng?" described a group of investors who paid a pittance for 92 percent of a ten-billion-dollar conglomerate, with assets ranging from power plants to a sports club. A tangle of overlapping boards and shareholders hid the identity of the new owners, and nearly half of the purchasing capital came from an untraceable source. When *Caijing* attempted to publish a brief follow-up, authorities banned the magazine from newsstands, and Hu's staff was left to tear up printed copies by hand. "Everybody felt humiliated," a former editor said. Hu called it her "largest disaster." (The story had come too close to implicating the children of senior Party leaders—a taboo that trumped even reformists' desire for a more open press.)

In her office one afternoon, I asked Hu why she thought other publications had been punished while *Caijing* had not. "We never say a word in a very emotional or casual way, like 'You lied,'" she said. "We try to analyze the system and say *why* a good idea or a good wish cannot become reality." When I posed the same question to Cheng Yizhong, a former editor in chief of the *Southern Metropolis Daily*, one of China's liveliest papers, who spent five months in jail for angering authorities, he saw it differently. He drew a distinction between his campaign for limiting police powers and Hu's focus on raising government performance. "*Caijing*'s topics haven't affected the fundamental ruling system, so it is relatively safe," he said, adding, "I am not criticizing Hu Shuli, but in some ways *Caijing* is just serving a more powerful or relatively better interest group."

For all her skepticism and intensity, she used the language of loyal opposition. "Some argue that pushing forward with political reform will be destabilizing," she wrote in a 2007 column. "Yet, in fact, maintaining the status quo without any reform creates a hotbed for social turbulence." In other words, political reform was the way to consolidate power, not lose it.

Her approach appealed to reformers in the government who genuinely wanted to solve problems but didn't want to give up power to do so. Some Chinese journalists said that Hu's greatest skill was playing interest groups against one another, whether by amplifying the central government's effort to round up corrupt mayors or by letting one wing of the government thwart a rival wing's agenda. Allow the most powerful group to endure, the theory went, and you could do real, even profitable, journalism. Hu saw censorship as a matter of negotiation; when propaganda officials raged, she tried not to argue. She promised to improve, to pay more attention, to avoid that mistake in the future. "In Chinese, we say that you can bore a hole in a stone by the steady dripping of water," her friend Qian Gang told me. Other journalists preferred a noisier metaphor: they called it "dancing in shackles."

When I asked Hu about the 2008 earthquake, we were in her office, and it was getting late. The afternoon shadows slanted into her windows, and the subject of the disaster, and its epic loss of life, made her pause. She had received the news by text message while hosting a ceremony for scholarship recipients at a hotel in the mountains west of Beijing. She leaned over to her friend Qian Gang, who had covered previous quakes, and asked him for a rough prediction of the damage. He looked at his watch and realized that schools were in session. The casualties among students would be enormous.

Reporting on a disaster of that scale could be politically hazardous. When the country had suffered a previous enormous quake, in 1976, the government silenced news of the death toll for three years. Now, in 2008, Hu Shuli set off for downtown Beijing, working the phone and e-mailing from the car, shouting to her staff to rent a satellite phone and get a crew to Sichuan. Within the hour, the first *Caijing* journalist was on a flight to the quake zone, followed by nine more. They arrived to discover that many government offices had survived, but hundreds of school buildings had collapsed into piles of concrete and rebar. The buildings had gone up during a surge of funding in the nineties, when a demographic bulge in school-age children required new space. But so much money had been siphoned off that designs that called for steel had, in some cases, been built with bamboo instead.

Thousands of children were trapped or dead in the rubble; nobody could even say for sure how many. The Department swiftly banned coverage of the construction problems at the schools. Several Chinese newspapers reported on them anyway, and were punished. But Hu read the mood differently; she calculated that her magazine's status as a business publication could give it the excuse of simply policing the use of public funds. Its success and bravado had also become self-reinforcing: the magazine had gone so far already that conservative branches of the government could no longer be sure which other officials supported it.

Besides, she was a businesswoman and she had to think about competition; the Internet was expanding, and she had to keep up. She thought that a story could be published if it carried the right tone and facts. "If it's not absolutely forbidden," she said, "we do it." On June 9, *Caijing* published a twelve-page investigative report on the earthquake, including the school collapses. It was cool and definitive. According to the report, heedless economic growth, squandered public funds, and rampant neglect of construction standards had led to disaster. In a way that had rarely been articulated before, the report peeled away a layer of mythology that usually clung to China's pursuit of fortune: the boom years were bringing poor stretches of the countryside into a new era, but the costs of that rise were becoming clear. The story detailed how local cadres had cut corners, but it stopped short of assigning responsibility by name. She was called in for criticism but was not punished.

From her perch, straddling the line between the inside and the outside, she had made a judgment call; if she dwelled on the names of specific corrupt officials, it might score a point for accountability, but the scoop would leave her vulnerable to retribution. She told me, "We try not to give any excuses to the cadres who don't want to get criticized." Ultimately, she said, the important question was not "which person didn't use good-quality bricks fifteen years ago" but something deeper. "We need further reform," she said. "We need checks and balances. We need transparency. We say it this way. No simple words. No slogans." It was a game of a certain, subtle kind, and she had won that round. She would not win others yet to come.

# NINE

# LIBERTY LEADING THE PEOPLE

That spring, official China was counting down to the 2008 Summer Olympics in Beijing with the fervor of a state religion. The Party assembled another giant clock beside Tiananmen Square, to tick off the seconds until the games began, and the capital was decked in a slogan that called for unity above all: "One World, One Dream."

I stepped out my front door one morning and found two city workers slathering cement on the redbrick outer wall of my bedroom. Large swaths of the city were being demolished or refurbished to create a clean, modern backdrop for the games. The workers had laid down a smooth bed of cement and were using a ruler and plumb line to carve crisp lines and corners. It took me a moment to realize that they were drawing the suggestion of fake new bricks on top of real old bricks. Facing my front door, on the alley wall, a faded bit of Cultural Revolution–era graffiti declared, in five blocky characters, LONG LIVE CHAIRMAN MAO! With two swipes of the trowel, the Great Helmsman vanished behind the cement.

The urge for perfection extended to the medal race. Sports officials had vowed to pick up more gold than ever before, under a long-term plan they called "The General Outline for Winning Honor at the Olympics, 2001–2010." The plan included the 119 Project, a campaign to win more gold medals in the summer's most competitive events—a list that by China's calculation totaled 119 medals. No variable was left to chance: When organizers searched for a young girl to sing a solo in the opening ceremony, they could not find the optimum combination of voice and aesthetics, so they created a composite, by training one child to lip-sync to the voice of another. A Chinese pork supplier said it was producing specially pampered pigs, to ensure that hormone-fed meat would not cause Chinese athletes to fail their doping tests—but it caused Chinese citizens to begin wondering about their own pork, and the Beijing Olympic Committee had to issue a "Clarification on Olympic Pig-Related Reports," denouncing the pork story as an "exaggerated falsehood."

The more single-minded the Olympic organizers became, the more they encountered things beyond their control. The Olympic torch relay, which China called the Journey of Harmony, would traverse six continents, reach the summit of Mount Everest, and encompass 21,888 runners, more than any previous relay. The Chinese press called the torch the Sacred Flame, and said that once it was lit in Olympia, Greece, it would not be extinguished for five months, until it reached Beijing. At night or on airplanes, when the torch could not be carried, the flame would be kept alight in a set of lanterns.

On March 10, shortly before the Journey of Harmony was to begin, several hundred monks in Lhasa, the capital of Tibet, conducted a march to demand the release of Tibetans detained for celebrating the U.S. government's awarding of the Congressional Gold Medal to the Dalai Lama. Dozens of monks were arrested, and on March 14 a demonstration to protest their detention turned into the worst riots in Tibet since the 1980s; eleven Han civilians and a Tibetan were burned to death after hiding in buildings set on fire by rioters, and a policeman and six civilians died from beatings or other causes, according to the government. The Dalai Lama called for calm, but the Chinese government said the riot had been "premeditated, masterminded and incited by the Dalai clique." Security forces moved in with armored vehicles to control the city, and the authorities began a roundup of suspects, leading to hundreds of arrests. Tibetan exile groups alleged that eighty Tibetans were killed in the crackdown in Lhasa and elsewhere, a claim that China denied.

As the torch passed through London, Paris, and San Francisco, protests against the crackdown in Tibet grew so clamorous that organizers had to extinguish the flame or reroute the path to avoid angry crowds. Chinese citizens, especially students abroad, responded to the criticism with rare fury. When the torch reached South Korea, Chinese and rival protesters fought in the streets. Inside China, thousands demonstrated in front of outlets of Carrefour, a French supermarket chain, in retaliation for what they considered France's sympathy for pro-Tibetan activists. Charles Zhang, who holds a PhD from MIT and is the CEO of Sohu, a leading Chinese Web portal, called for a boycott of French products "to make the thoroughly biased French media and public feel losses and pain."

State-run media revived language from another age. When U.S. Speaker of the House Nancy Pelosi denounced China's management of Tibet, Xinhua called her "disgusting." The magazine *Outlook Weekly* warned that "domestic and foreign hostile forces have made the Beijing Olympics a focus for infiltration and sabotage." The Communist Party secretary in Tibet called the Dalai Lama "a wolf wrapped in a monk's robe; a monster with a human face, but the heart of a beast." In the anonymity of the Web, decorum deteriorated. "People who fart through the mouth will get shit stuffed down their throats by me!" one commentator wrote, in a forum hosted by a state newspaper. "Someone give me a gun! Show no mercy to the enemy!" wrote another. The comments were an embarrassment to many Chinese, but they were difficult to ignore among foreign journalists who had begun receiving threats. An anonymous letter to my fax machine in Beijing warned, "Clarify the facts on China . . . or you and your loved ones will wish you were dead."

As the protests grew, I began trolling the Chinese Web for the most inventive expressions of patriotism. On the morning of April 15, a short video entitled *2008 China Stand Up!* appeared on Sina, the Chinese Web portal. The video's origin was a mystery: it had no host, no narrator, and no signature except the initials CTGZ.

It was a homespun documentary, and it opened with a Technicolor portrait of Chairman Mao, sunbeams radiating from his head. Out of silence came an orchestral piece, thundering with drums, as a black screen flashed, in Chinese and English, one of Mao's mantras: "Imperialism will never abandon its intention to destroy us." Then a cut to present-day photographs and news footage, and a sprint through conspiracies and betrayals—the "farces, schemes, and disasters" confronting China today: the sinking Chinese stock market (the work of foreign speculators who "wildly manipulated" Chinese stock prices and lured rookie investors to lose their fortunes); the dawn of a global "currency war," in which the West intended to "make Chinese people foot the bill" for America's financial woes.

A cut, then, to another front: rioters looting stores and brawling in Lhasa. Words flashed across the scenes: "So-called peaceful protest!" A montage of foreign press clippings critical of China—all of them "ignoring the truth" and "speaking with one distorted voice." The screen filled with the logos of CNN, the BBC, and other news organizations, which gave way to a portrait of Joseph Goebbels. The orchestra and the rhetoric climbed toward a final sequence: "Obviously, there is a scheme behind the scenes to encircle China. A new Cold War!" A cut to pictures of Paris and protesters trying to wrest the Olympic torch from its official carrier, forcing guards to fend them off. The film ended with the image of a Chinese flag, aglow in the sunlight, and a solemn promise: "We will stand up and hold together always as one family in harmony!"

The video by CTGZ, which was just over six minutes long, captured the mood of nationalism in the air, and in its first week and a half online, it drew more than a million hits and tens of thousands of favorable comments. It rose to the site's fourth-most-popular rating. (A television blooper clip of a yawning news anchor was number one.) The film was attracting, on average, two clicks per second, and it became a manifesto for a self-styled vanguard in defense of China's honor, a patriotic swath of society that the Chinese call the *fen qing*, "the angry youth."

I was struck that nineteen years after the demonstrations at Tiananmen Square, China's young elite had risen again, not in pursuit of liberal democracy but in defense of China's name. Nicholas Negroponte, the founder of MIT's Media Laboratory and one of the early ideologists of the Internet, had predicted that the global reach of the Web would transform the way we think about ourselves as countries. The state, he predicted, will evaporate "like a mothball, which goes from solid to gas directly," and "there will be no more room for nationalism than there is for smallpox." In China, things had gone differently. I was curious about CTGZ. The screen name was connected to an e-mail address. It belonged to a twenty-eight-year-old graduate student in Shanghai named Tang Jie, and this was his first video. He invited me down for a visit.

———

The campus of Fudan University, a top Chinese school, radiates from a pair of thirty-story steel-and-glass towers that could pass for a corporate headquarters. I met Tang Jie at the front gate. He wore a powder-blue oxford shirt, khakis, and black dress shoes. He had bright hazel eyes, rounded baby-face features, and a dusting of a goatee and mustache on his chin and upper lip. As I stepped out of a cab, he bounded over to welcome me and tried to pay my taxi fare.

As we walked across campus, Tang admitted he was glad to have a break from his dissertation, which was on Western philosophy. He specialized in phenomenology—specifically, in the concept of "intersubjectivity," as theorized by Edmund Husserl, the German philosopher who influenced Sartre, among others. In addition to Chinese, Tang read English and German easily, but he spoke them infrequently, so at times he swerved, apologetically, among languages. He was working on Latin and ancient Greek. He was so self-effacing and soft-spoken that his voice sometimes dropped to a whisper. There was a seriousness about him; he laughed sparingly, as if he were conserving energy. For fun, he listened to classical Chinese music, though he also enjoyed screwball comedies by the Hong Kong star Stephen Chow. Tang was proudly unhip. Unlike Michael Zhang from Crazy English, Tang had not adopted an English name. The screen name CTGZ was an adaptation of two obscure terms from classical poetry: *changting* and *gongzi*, which together translated as a "noble son in the pavilion." In contrast to other elite Chinese students, Tang had never joined the Communist Party, for fear that it would impugn his objectivity as a scholar.

Tang had invited some friends to join us for lunch, at Fat Brothers Sichuan Restaurant, and afterward we all climbed the stairs to his room. He lived alone in a sixth-floor walk-up, a studio of less than seventy-five square feet that could have been mistaken for a library storage room occupied by a fastidious squatter. Books covered every surface, and great mounds listed from the shelves above his desk. His collections encompassed, more or less, the span of human thought: Plato leaned against Lao-tzu, Wittgenstein, Bacon, Fustel de Coulanges, Heidegger, the Koran. When Tang wanted to widen his bed by a few inches, he laid plywood across the frame and propped up the edges with piles of books. Eventually books overflowed the room, and they stood outside his front door in a wall of cardboard boxes.

Tang slumped into his desk chair. I asked if he had any idea that his video would be so popular. He smiled. "It appears I have expressed a common feeling, a shared view," he said.

Next to him sat Liu Chengguang, a cheerful, broad-faced PhD student in political science who had recently translated into Chinese a lecture on the subject of "Manliness" by the conservative Harvard professor Harvey Mansfield. Sprawled on the bed, wearing a gray sweatshirt, was Xiong Wenchi, who had earned a PhD in political science before taking a teaching job. And to Tang's left sat Zeng Kewei, a lean and stylish banker who had picked up a master's degree in Western philosophy before going into finance. Each of them was in his twenties, the first in his family to go to college, and had been drawn to the study of Western thought. I asked them why.

"China was backward throughout its modern history, so we were always seeking the reasons for why the West grew strong," Liu said. "We learned from the West. All of us who are educated have this dream: grow strong by learning from the West."

Like the Chinese travelers I knew, and the members of Ai Weiwei's *Fairytale*, the young men around me regarded the temptations of the West with a combination of admiration and anxiety. It was a confusing time: they were protesting CNN at the same time that an English study program was running ads in China with the slogan "After a month, you'll be able to understand CNN!"

Tang and his friends were so gracious, so thankful that I'd come to listen to them, that I began to wonder if China's anger that spring should be viewed as an aberration. They implored me not to make that mistake.

"We've been studying Western history for so long, we understand it well," Zeng said. "We think our love for China, our support for the government and the benefits of this country, is not a spontaneous reaction. It has developed after giving the matter much thought."

In fact, their view of China's direction, if not their vitriol, was consistent with the Chinese mainstream. Almost nine out of ten Chinese approved of the way things were going in their country—the highest share of any of the twenty-four countries surveyed that spring by the Pew Research Center. (In the United States, by comparison, just two out of ten voiced such approval.) It was hard to know precisely how common the more assertive strain of patriotism was, but scholars pointed to a Chinese petition against Japan's membership in the UN Security Council. At last count, it had attracted more than forty million signatures, roughly the population of Spain. I asked Tang to show me how he had made his film. He turned to face the screen of his Lenovo desktop PC. "Do you know Movie Maker?" he asked, referring to a video-editing program. I pleaded ignorance and asked if he'd learned from a book. He glanced at me pityingly. He'd learned it on the fly from the Help menu. "We must thank Bill Gates," he said.

One month before Tang Jie made his Internet video debut, China surpassed the United States to become the world's largest user of the Internet. It had 238 million people online; it was still only 16 percent of the population, but each day, nearly a quarter of a million Chinese citizens were going online for the first time, and it was transforming the way ideas whipped around the country. The most vibrant online communities grew to millions of registered members, putting them among China's largest organizations outside the Communist Party.

In a nation divided by dialect, geography, and class, the Web allowed people to find each other in unprecedented ways. A group of Chinese volunteers came together and began translating every word of *The Economist* magazine each week and offering it free to readers. Explaining their goal, the translators wrote, "In the Internet age, the greatest force is not avarice or love or violence, but devotion to an interest." They were young and unabashedly utopian in their faith in technology. "The Web will link you with like-minded people, and release unimaginable energy," they wrote. To avoid the censors, the group was overtly self-censoring. "If the article involves any sensitive topics," they told newcomers, "and you're not sure whether it's permitted, please don't risk it." That self-censorship contained a kind of self-governance: Sites recruited volunteers to remove material that would get the site into trouble. They were known as "forum hosts," and if users thought they were too tough or too lax, they could replace them, a process that became known as "impeachment."

Among the most zealous early users of the Web were Chinese nationalists. In the spring of 1999, when a NATO aircraft, using American intelligence, mistakenly dropped three bombs on the Chinese embassy in

Belgrade, the Chinese Web found its voice. Chinese patriotic hackers plastered the home page of the U.S. embassy in Beijing with the slogan "Down with the Barbarians!" and they caused the White House Web site to crash under a deluge of angry e-mail. "The Internet is Western," one commentator wrote, "but . . . we Chinese can use it to tell the people of the world that China cannot be insulted!" For many, nationalism provided what one young patriot called "our first taste of the sacred rights of freedom of speech."

Like others his age, Tang Jie lived largely online. When the riots erupted in Lhasa in March, he followed the news closely on American and European news sites, in addition to China's official media. He had no hesitation about tunneling under the government firewall. He used a proxy server—a digital way station overseas that connected a user with a blocked website. He watched television exclusively online, because it had more variety and he didn't have a TV in his room. He also received foreign news clips from Chinese students abroad, a population that has grown by nearly two-thirds in the previous decade to some sixty-seven thousand people. Tang was baffled that foreigners might imagine that people of his generation were somehow unwise to the distortions of censorship. "Because we are in such a system, we are always asking ourselves whether we are brainwashed," he said. "We are always eager to get other information from different channels." Then he added, "But when you are in a so-called free system you never think about whether you are brainwashed."

All spring, news and opinions about Tibet were swirling on Fudan's electronic bulletin board system, or BBS. In technology terms, the BBS was an antique—a simple forum with multiple threads of conversation— but Twitter and its Chinese counterparts had yet to take root, and for many Chinese, bulletin boards provided the first experience of entering a digital roomful of strangers and speaking up. On the Fudan BBS, Tang read a range of foreign press clippings deemed by Chinese Web users to be misleading or unfair. A photograph on CNN.com, for instance, had been cropped around military trucks bearing down on unarmed protesters. But an uncropped version showed a crowd of demonstrators lurking nearby, including someone with an arm cocked, hurling something at the trucks. To Tang, the cropping looked like a deliberate distortion.

"It was a joke," he said bitterly. That photograph and others criss-crossed China by e-mail, scrawled with criticism, while people added more examples from the *Times* of London, Fox News, German television, and French radio. It was a range of news organizations, and to those inclined to see it as such, it smacked of a conspiracy. It shocked people such as Tang who had put their faith in the Western press, but more important, it offended them: Tang thought that he was living in the moment of greatest prosperity and openness in his country's modern history, and yet the world still seemed to view China with suspicion. As if he needed confirmation, Jack Cafferty, a CNN commentator, called China "the same bunch of goons and thugs they've been for the last fifty years," a quote that rippled across the front pages in China and for which CNN later apologized. Like many of his peers, Tang couldn't figure out why foreigners were so agitated about Tibet—an impoverished backwater, as he saw it, that China had tried for decades to civilize. Boycotting the Beijing Games in the name of Tibet seemed as logical to him as shunning the Salt Lake City Olympics to protest America's treatment of the Cherokee.

He scoured YouTube in search of a rebuttal, a clarification of the Chinese perspective, but found nothing in English except pro-Tibet videos. He was already busy—under contract from a publisher for a Chinese translation of Leibniz's *Discourse on Metaphysics* and other essays—but he couldn't shake the idea of speaking up on China's behalf.

"I thought, okay, I'll make something," he said.

Before Tang could start, however, he was obligated to go home for a few days. His mother had told him to be back for the harvest season. She needed his help in the fields, digging up bamboo shoots.


Tang was the youngest of four siblings from a farming family near the eastern city of Hangzhou. Neither his mother nor his father could read or write. Until the fourth grade, Tang had no name. He went by Little Four, after his place in the family order. When that became impractical, his father began calling him Tang Jie, an abbreviated homage to his favorite comedian, Tang Jiezhong.

Tang was bookish, and in a large, boisterous household he said little. He took to science fiction. "I can tell you everything about all those

movies, like *Star Wars*," he told me. He was a good though not a spectacular student, but he showed a precocious interest in ideas. "He wasn't
like other kids, who spent their pocket money on food—he saved all his
money to buy books," his older sister Tang Xiaoling told me. None of
his siblings had studied past the eighth grade, and they regarded him as
an admirable outlier. "If he had questions that he couldn't figure out,
then he couldn't sleep," his sister said. "For us, if we didn't get it, we just
gave up."

In high school, Tang improved his grades and had some success at
science fairs as an inventor, but he found the sciences too remote from
his daily concerns. He happened upon a Chinese translation of a fanci-
ful Norwegian novel, *Sophie's World*, by the philosophy teacher Jostein
Gaarder, in which a teenage girl encounters the history of great thinkers.
"It was then that I discovered philosophy," Tang said.

Patriotism was not an overt presence in his house, but it was all
around him. To prevent a recurrence of Tiananmen, the Party had re-
doubled its commitment to Thought Work directed at China's young
people. When Tang Jie was in primary school, president Jiang Zemin
sent a letter to the Education Ministry calling for a new approach to explaining China's history "even to the kids in kindergarten," the president
wrote. The new approach emphasized the *bainian guochi*—the "century
of national humiliation"—an arc of events extending from China's defeat
in the Opium Wars of the mid-nineteenth century to the Japanese occupation of Chinese soil during World War II.

By focusing on "patriotic education," the Party explained, it would
"boost the nation's spirit" and "enhance cohesion." Students were taught
to "never forget national humiliation." The National People's Congress
approved a holiday called National Humiliation Day, and textbooks
were rewritten. *The Practical Dictionary of Patriotic Education* included
a 355-page section on the details of China's humiliations. Nationalism
helped the Party smooth over the paradox of being a socialist vanguard
of a free-market economy. The new textbooks transformed the explanation of China's suffering to deemphasize the role of "class enemies" and
to emphasize the role of foreign invaders. In the Mao years, China had
whitewashed its defeats, but now students took field trips to places where
China had suffered atrocities. To appeal to young men, the Communist
Youth League invested in the development of patriotic video games such

as *Resistance War Online*, in which users took on the role of Red Army soldiers machine-gunning Japanese invaders.

Emotion and policy became harder to separate. When Chinese diplomats denounced the actions of another government, they often said it "hurt the feelings of the Chinese people." They invoked this idea with increasing frequency; one journalist, Fang Kecheng, counted up those occasions and found that China's feelings were hurt only three times between 1949 and 1978, but by the eighties and nineties it was happening an average of five times each year.

When Tang reached Fudan, he met Wan Manlu, a reserved PhD student in Chinese literature and linguistics. They sat side by side at a dinner with friends but barely spoke. Later, Tang hunted down her screen name (gracelittle) and sent her a private message on Fudan's bulletin board. They worked up to a first date: an experimental opera based on "Regret for the Past," a Chinese story.

Their relationship developed in part on the basis of a shared frustration with China's unbridled Westernization. When I met Wan, she told me, "Chinese tradition has many good things, but we've ditched them. I feel there have to be people to carry them on." She came from a middle-class home, and Tang's humble roots and old-fashioned values impressed her. "Most of my generation has a smooth, happy life, including me," she said. "I feel like our character lacks something. For example, love for the country or the perseverance you get from overcoming hardship. Those virtues—I don't see them in myself and many people my age." Of Tang Jie, she said, "From that kind of background, with nobody educated in his family, nobody helping him with his schoolwork, with great family pressure, it's not easy for him to get where he is today."

After we met, I started going back and forth to Shanghai to spend time with Tang Jie. He was part of a group of students devoted to a charismatic thirty-nine-year-old Fudan philosophy professor named Ding Yun. Professor Ding was a translator of Leo Strauss, the political philosopher whose admirers include Harvey Mansfield and other neoconservatives. In America at that time, Leo Strauss was receiving renewed attention because his arguments against tyranny had been popular among neoconservative architects of the Iraq War. One of Strauss's former students at the University of Chicago, Abram Shulsky, had run the Pentagon's Office of Special Plans before the Iraq invasion; another former student was Paul Wolfowitz, then deputy secretary of defense.

Professor Ding had close-cropped hair and stylish rectangular glasses and favored the loose-fitting long-sleeve shirt of a Tang dynasty scholar. "During the nineteen-eighties and nineties, most intellectuals had a negative opinion of China's traditional culture," he told me. In the early years of reform, the word *conservative* had still been tantamount to *reactionary*, but times had changed; he was teaching a Straussian appreciation for the universality of the classics and encouraging his students to revive ancient Chinese thought. He and other scholars were thriving amid a new vein of conservatism that ran counter to China's drive for integration with the world. Professor Ding had watched with satisfaction as Tang Jie and other students developed an appetite for the classics and pushed back against the onslaught of Westernization.

Tang told me, "The fact is we are very Westernized. Now we started reading ancient Chinese books and we rediscovered the ancient China." The young neoconservatives in Shanghai invited Harvey Mansfield to dinner when he passed through Shanghai. They "are acutely aware that their country, whose resurgence they feel and admire, has no principle to guide it," Mansfield wrote in an e-mail to me after his visit. "Some of them see . . . that liberalism in the West has lost its belief in itself, and they turn to Leo Strauss for conservatism that is based on principle, on 'natural right.' This conservatism is distinct from a status-quo conservatism, because they are not satisfied with a country that has only a status quo and not a principle."

This renewed pride affected the way Tang and his peers viewed the economy. They believed the world profited from China but blocked its attempts to invest abroad. Tang's friend Zeng ticked off examples of Chinese companies that had tried to invest in America. "Huawei's bid to buy 3Com was rejected," he said. "CNOOC's bid to buy into Unocal and Lenovo's purchase of part of IBM caused political repercussions. If it's not a market argument, it's a political argument. We think the world is a free market—"

Before he could finish, Tang jumped in. "This is what you, America, taught us," he said. "We opened our market, but when we try to buy your companies, we hit political obstacles. It's not fair."

Their view, which was popular in China across ideological lines, had some validity: American politicians invoked national security concerns, with varying degrees of credibility, to oppose Chinese direct investment. But Tang's view, infused with a sense of victimhood, also obscured some evidence to the contrary: China had succeeded in other deals abroad—its sovereign wealth fund had stakes in the Blackstone Group and in Morgan Stanley—and though China had taken steps to open its markets to foreigners, it remained equally inclined to reject an American attempt to buy an asset as sensitive as a Chinese oil company.

Tang's belief that the United States would seek to obstruct China's rise—"a new Cold War"—extended beyond economics to broader American policy. Disparate issues of relatively minor importance to Americans, such as support for Taiwan and Washington's calls to raise the value of the yuan, had metastasized in China into a feeling of strategic containment.

Tang stayed at his family's farm for five days before he could return to Shanghai and finish his movie. He scoured the Web for photographs, choosing some that were evocative—a man raising his arm in a sea of Chinese flags reminded him of Delacroix's *Liberty Leading the People*—and others that embodied the political moment: a wheelchair-bound Chinese amputee carrying the Olympic flame in Paris, for instance, fending off a protester who was trying to snatch it away.

For a sound track, he typed "solemn music" into Baidu, a Chinese search engine, and scanned the results. He landed on a piece by Vangelis, a Yanni-style pop composer from Greece who was best known for his score for the movie *Chariots of Fire*. Tang's favorite Vangelis track was from a Gerard Depardieu film about Christopher Columbus called *1492: Conquest of Paradise*. He watched a few seconds of Depardieu standing manfully on the deck of a tall ship coursing across the Atlantic. Perfect, Tang thought: "It was a time of globalization."

He collected mistakes from the foreign press—policemen in Nepal identified in a caption as Chinese; Tibetans being arrested in India, not Tibet—and he typed a message: "Stand up to give our voice to the world!" Some title screens in English were full of mistakes, because he was hurrying, but he was anxious to release the video. He posted it to

Sina and sent a note to the Fudan bulletin board. The video began to climb in popularity, and its success raised his spirits. He had discovered that he was not alone in his quest to project his notion of the truth. All over China, people were watching the video and forwarding it and cheering him on.

Professor Ding rejoiced at what his student had achieved. "We used to think they were just a postmodern, Occidentalized generation," Ding said. "Of course, I thought the students I knew were very good, but the wider generation? I was not very pleased. To see the content of Tang Jie's video, and the scale of its popularity among the youth, made me very happy. Very happy."

Not everyone was as pleased. Young patriots were so polarizing in China that some people, by changing the intonation in Chinese, pronounced "angry youth" as "shit youth." If the activists thought that they were defending China's image abroad, there was little sign of success. After weeks of patriotic rhetoric emanating from China, a poll sponsored by the *Financial Times* showed that Europeans were ranking China as the greatest threat to global stability, surpassing America. But the eruption of the angry youth had been most disconcerting to those interested in furthering democracy. By age and education, Tang and his peers inherited a long legacy of activism that stretched from 1919, when nationalist demonstrators demanded "Mr. Democracy" and "Mr. Science," to 1989, when students flooded Tiananmen Square and erected a sculpture inspired by the Statue of Liberty. We were one year away from the twentieth anniversary of that movement, but my experiences with Tang Jie and his friends made clear that prosperity, computers, and Westernization had not pushed China's elite toward democracy in the way that outsiders had expected after Tiananmen. Rather, prosperity and the strength of the Party had persuaded more than a few to postpone idealism as long as life for them kept improving.

The students in 1989 were rebelling against corruption and abuses of power. "Nowadays, these issues haven't disappeared but have worsened," Li Datong, a liberal newspaper editor, told me despairingly one afternoon, as the protests expanded. "However, the current young generation turns a blind eye to it. I've never seen them respond to these major domestic issues. Rather, they take a utilitarian, opportunistic approach."

One caricature of young Chinese held that they knew virtually nothing about the crackdown at Tiananmen Square—known in Chinese as "the June Fourth Incident"—because the authorities had purged it from the nation's official history. That wasn't the full story. In fact, anyone who took a few steps to get on a proxy server could discover as much about Tiananmen as he chose to learn. And yet many young Chinese had adopted the Party's message that the 1989 movement was misguided and naïve. "We accept all the values of human rights, of democracy," Tang Jie told me. "We accept that. The issue is how to realize it."

I met dozens of urbane students and young professionals that spring, and we often got to talking about Tiananmen Square. In a typical conversation, one college senior asked me whether she should interpret the killing of protesters at Kent State in 1970 as a fair measure of American freedom. Liu Yang, a graduate student in environmental engineering, said, "June Fourth could not and should not succeed at that time. If June Fourth had succeeded, China would be worse and worse, not better."

Liu, who was twenty-six, had once considered himself a liberal. As a teenager, he and his friends happily criticized the Communist Party. "In the 1990s, I thought that the Chinese government is not good enough. Maybe we need to set up a better government," he told me. "The problem is that we didn't know what a good government would be. So we let the Chinese Communist Party stay in place. The other problem is we didn't have the power to get them out. They have the army!"

When Liu got out of college, he found a good job as an engineer at an oil services company. He was earning more money in a month than his parents, retired laborers living on a pension, had earned in a year. Eventually he saved enough money that, with scholarships, he was able to enroll in a PhD program at Stanford. He had little interest in the patriotic pageantry of the Olympics until he saw the fracas around the torch in Paris. "We were furious," he said, and when the torch came to San Francisco, he and other Chinese students surged toward the relay route to support it.

I was in San Francisco later that spring, and Liu and I arranged to meet at a Starbucks near his dorm, in Palo Alto. He arrived on his mountain bike, wearing a Nautica fleece pullover and jeans. The date, we both knew, happened to be June 4, nineteen years since soldiers put down the Tiananmen uprising. The overseas Chinese students' bulletin board had been alive all afternoon with discussions of the anniversary. Liu mentioned the famous photograph of an unknown man standing in front of a tank—the most provocative image in modern Chinese history.

"We really acknowledge him. We really think he was brave," Liu told me. But of that generation, he said, "They fought for China, to make the country better. And there were some faults of the government. But finally, we must admit that the Chinese government had to use any way it could to put down that event."

Sitting in the cool quiet of a California night, sipping his coffee, Liu said that he was not willing to risk all that his generation enjoyed at home in order to hasten the liberties he had come to know in America. "Do you live on democracy?" he asked me. "You eat bread, you drink coffee. All these are not brought by democracy. Indian guys have democracy, and some African countries have democracy, but they can't feed their own people.

"Chinese people have begun to think, 'One part is the good life, another part is democracy,'" Liu went on. "If democracy can really give you the good life, that's good. But without democracy, if we can still have the good life, why should we choose democracy?"


When the Olympic torch finally returned to China, in May, for the last leg to Beijing, the Chinese seemed determined to make up for its woes abroad. Crowds overflowed along the torch's route. One afternoon, Tang Jie and I set off to watch the torch traverse a suburb of Shanghai.

At the time, the country was still in a state of shock following the earthquake in Sichuan. It was the worst disaster in three decades, but it also produced a rare moment of national unity. Donations poured in, revealing the positive side of the patriotism that had erupted weeks earlier. But the burst of nationalism that spring had contained a spirit of violence that anyone old enough to remember the Red Guards—or the rise of skinheads in Europe—could not casually dismiss. At Duke University, Grace Wang, a Chinese freshman, tried to mediate between pro-Tibet and pro-China protesters on campus. But online she was branded a "traitor to the race." People ferreted out her mother's address, in the seaside city of Qingdao, and vandalized their home. Nothing came of the threats to foreign journalists. No blood was shed. After the chaos around the torch in Paris, the Chinese efforts to boycott the French chain Carrefour fizzled. China's leaders, awakening to their deteriorating image abroad, ultimately reined in the students with a call for only "rational patriotism."

In the cab on the way to see the torch, I sensed that Tang Jie was uneasy about how fierce the conflict had become. "We do not want any violence," he told me. What he wanted was to persuade his peers in China that finding the truth of the world around them was no longer simply a matter of accepting what they were told by the media, foreign or domestic. "We aren't limited to only two choices. We have our own media, too. We now have people with cameras and recordings. They have the truth." He believed his generation had learned something vital that spring. "Now they know: I must use my own brain."

From far away, it was easy to trivialize China's young nationalists as the pawns of the state, but up close, that image was less persuasive. The government treated online patriots warily because it sensed that they placed their pride in the Chinese nation, not necessarily in the Party. Their passion could swerve in unpredictable ways. After a nationalist website was shut down by censors in 2004, one commentator wrote, "Our government is as weak as sheep!" The government permitted nationalism to grow at some moments but strained to control it at others. The following spring, when Japan approved a new textbook that critics claimed glossed over its wartime atrocities, patriots in Beijing drafted protest plans and broadcast them via chat rooms, bulletin boards, and text messages. As many as ten thousand demonstrators took to the streets, hurling paint and bottles at the Japanese embassy. Despite government warnings to stop, thousands more marched in Shanghai the following week—one of China's largest demonstrations in years—and vandalized the Japanese consulate. At one point, Shanghai police cut off cell phone service in downtown Shanghai to prevent the crowd from organizing.

Xu Wu, a professor at Arizona State University, studied the rise of online nationalism. "Up to now, the Chinese government has been able to keep a grip on it," he told me. "But I call it the 'virtual Tiananmen Square.' They don't need to go there. They can do the same thing online and sometimes be even more damaging."

As Tang Jie and I approached the torch-relay route, he gazed across the crowd and said, "Look at the people. Everyone thinks this is their own Olympics." Vendors were selling T-shirts, headbands, and Chinese flags. Tang told me to wait until the torch passed, because hawkers would cut the prices in half. He was carrying a small plastic bag and fished around in it for a bright red scarf of the kind that Chinese children wear to signal membership in the Young Pioneers, a kind of socialist Boy Scouts. He tied it around his neck and grinned. He offered one to a passing teenager, who politely declined.

The air was stagnant and thick beneath a canopy of haze, but the mood was exuberant. Time was ticking down to the torch's arrival, and the town was coming out for a look: a man in a dark suit, sweating and smoothing his hair; a construction worker in an orange helmet and farmers' galoshes; a bellboy in a uniform with so many gold buttons and epaulets that he looked like an admiral. Some of the younger spectators were wearing T-shirts inspired by China's recent troubles: "Anti-Riot & Explore the Truth" read a popular English message. All around us, people strained for a better view. A woman hung off a lamppost. A young man in a red headband climbed a tree.

The crowd's enthusiasm brightened Tang's mood, reminding him that China's future belonged to him and to those around him. "When I stand here, I can feel, deeply, the common emotion of Chinese youth," he said. "We are self-confident."

Police blocked the road. A frisson swept through the crowd. People surged toward the curb, straining to see over one another's heads. But Tang Jie hung back. He was a patient man.

# TEN

# MIRACLES AND MAGIC ENGINES

Lin Yifu, the soldier who defected by swimming from Quemoy, was studying at Peking University in 1980 when the University of Chicago economist Theodore Schultz visited Beijing to deliver a speech. Lin was assigned to translate because he spoke English from his years in Taiwan. Schultz, who had recently won the Nobel, was impressed; he returned to Chicago and helped arrange a scholarship. Lin Yifu would, again, be a first: the first Chinese student since the Cultural Revolution to study for an American PhD in economics. If that wasn't enough to make him stand out, he was choosing to go to Chicago, the crucible of free-market thought. In 1982, Lin arrived in the United States, and it allowed him to reunite with his wife and children, who went there, too. Since his defection, he and his wife, Chen Yunying, had maintained occasional secret contact. She even sent him a poem that included the line "I understand you, I understand what you did." Once in America, Chen studied for a doctorate at George Washington University.

While in Chicago, Lin embarked on the study of China's rebirth that would captivate him for decades, and his conclusions would prove controversial. After receiving their PhDs, Lin and his wife returned to Beijing in 1987, where he confronted a delicate problem. As a returnee from America, how was he supposed to explain Milton Friedman to socialists?

"I went to all the meetings and I didn't say anything," he told me. Eventually, he found his voice. "They were surprised, because I said words in terms similar to theirs, in a language they can understand," he said. For instance, when, in the late nineties, Chinese warehouses filled up with unsold televisions, refrigerators, and other consumer goods, many economists blamed low income for the problem, but Lin disagreed. "People didn't have the infrastructure for consuming those kinds of products," he said. He became one of the most vocal advocates of heavy investment in rural electricity, running water, and roads, a proposal embraced by the Party in a package of reforms that it rolled out under the slogan "The New Socialist Countryside."

The end of the Cold War, and the crackdown at Tiananmen Square, shook the Chinese establishment politically and economically. Zhao Ziyang, the reformist member of Deng Xiaoping's original economic brain trust, was blamed for not suppressing the demonstrations earlier; think tanks that he had created were dissolved, and several economists went to jail for supporting the protests. Zhao was put under house arrest, where he lived for fifteen years, hitting golf balls into a net in his yard and tape-recording a secret memoir, until his death. The Chinese government effaced him from the official history of the nation's success.

In economic terms, it was a reckoning point: in the two years after Tiananmen, economic growth slumped more dramatically than at any time since 1976; Deng saw his successes slipping away, and he put China's economists back to work. Reform resumed, but to prevent a repeat of Tiananmen, the Party offered its people the essential bargain: greater freedom in economic activities in exchange for less freedom in political life. It had the makings of a paradox: the Party was sparking individual ambition and self-creation in one half of life and suppressing those tendencies in the other. As an economic strategy, the approach put China at odds with the dominant economists in the West who recommended that the collapsing Soviet bloc undertake "shock therapy": cut spending, privatize state-owned companies, and open borders to foreign trade and investment, a recipe that became known as the Washington Consensus.

In 1994, in a small office borrowed from the geography department at Peking University, Lin and four other economists founded the China Center for Economic Research, a think tank designed to attract foreign-trained Chinese scholars. He worked like a man possessed, often hunched over his desk until 1:00 or 2:00 a.m., and back the next morning by 8:00. Among colleagues, he was known as furiously driven and, on some level, unreachable. Over the years, he wrote eighteen books and dozens of papers, and he told his students, "My ambition is to die at my desk." His research center expanded, and as it did, Lin acquired an influential voice, becoming an adviser on the government's five-year plans and other projects. He was not a member of the innermost circle of Party decision-making—he could never be—but it was a remarkable trajectory for a migrant once suspected of being a Taiwanese spy.


Year by year, Lin was becoming increasingly critical of the mainstream Western view—which had promoted shock therapy reforms in the former Soviet Union—and he became ever more convinced that the key to China's rise was the fusion of the market and strong government. In the decade after the Soviet collapse, much of Eastern Europe that had raced to the free market encountered unemployment, stagnation, and political instability, which weakened support for the shock-therapy approach. At the same time, in the 1990s, China's economy, a hybrid that fit into neither end of the spectrum, began to surge. It had unchecked capitalism in some areas and heavy government control in others. The focus on growth was relentless. Whenever the Party faced a choice between growth or the environment, growth won; between social security and growth, growth won. The costs of transformation were harsh. Health insurance and retirement funds evaporated; environmental pollution ravaged the landscape; urban real estate developers demolished large sections of cities to put up new housing. Public discontent grew, but the Party used force and the steady march of prosperity to keep discontent at bay.

Yet, the measurements were clear: In 1949 the average life expectancy was thirty-six, and the literacy rate was 20 percent. By 2012, life expectancy was seventy-five, and the literacy rate was above 90 percent. Columbia University economist Jeffrey Sachs wrote, "China is likely to be the first of the great poverty-stricken countries of the twentieth century to end poverty in the twenty-first century." When China formulated a stimulus plan to combat the effects of the global financial crisis in 2008, so many new airports and highways had been built already that the planners could not immediately decide what else to build.

Lin was forming opinions about the role that political reform plays in economic success, and it was not a position that endeared him to Chinese liberals who called for democratization. He published *The China Miracle*, a book coauthored with Fang Cai and Zhou Li that zeroed in on the disarray produced by the collapse of the Soviet Union, and concluded,

"The more radical the reform, the more violent will be the destructive social conflicts, and opposition to reform." Lin promoted China's "tinkering gradualist approach." In a lecture at Cambridge University in the fall of 2007, he pointed to "the failure of the Washington Consensus reforms." He joked that the shock therapy policies ordained by the IMF seemed more like "shock without therapy," and were destined to lead to "economic chaos." He reminded people that the proponents of the Washington Consensus had warned that China's slow-reform approach would be, in his words, "the worst possible transition strategy," doomed to "result in unavoidable economic collapse." He had become China's most prominent evangelist for its own story of prosperity.

In November 2007, Lin received a phone call from the World Bank, which provides loans and expertise to combat poverty. Its president, Robert Zoellick, was coming to Beijing and wanted to hear Lin's take on China's economy. They met in Zoellick's hotel room, and two months later, the Bank called and offered Lin the job of chief economist. It was another first: he would be the first Chinese citizen—the first of any developing country, in fact—to serve in a post previously occupied only by high-profile Westerners, including the Nobel laureate and Columbia professor Joseph Stiglitz and the former treasury secretary and head of President Obama's National Economic Council Lawrence Summers.

Chairman Mao had considered the World Bank a tool of imperialist aggression, but now China was its third-largest shareholder and openly determined to acquire a greater say in international economic institutions. In June 2008, Lin and his wife moved to Washington, D.C. Everything he brought fit in two suitcases. They rented a house on the edge of Georgetown, with a patio where Lin could write in the open air. They put a treadmill in the kitchen. On business trips, when colleagues went out to socialize, he went up to his hotel room and worked late into the night.

When I visited Lin in Washington, on a broiling August afternoon, I found him in a roomy corner office on the fourth floor of the World Bank headquarters, a thirteen-story edifice a few blocks from the White House. He pushed back from his desk. He was at work, as always, on a paper. "How can a developing country catch up to developed countries?"

he asked. It was the polarizing question at the center of his life's work, and he was now in a position to act on his answer. "We see a lot of failures and only a few successes," he said. Lin had a staff of almost three hundred economists and other researchers, whose work helped the Bank and the governments of poor countries decide on strategies for raising income levels, a subject that had been riven for decades by ideological debate.

Within weeks of his arrival, the planet was hit by the most serious financial crisis since the Great Depression. The crisis posed a conundrum for Lin: Officials from the United States, Europe, and the IMF called on China to raise the value of its currency, to boost the buying power of Chinese consumers and make products from other countries relatively cheaper. Sen. Charles Schumer, Democrat from New York, told reporters, "China's currency manipulation is like a boot to the throat of our recovery." But Lin saw the issue very differently. Forcing China to raise its currency "won't help this imbalance and can deter the global recovery," he told an audience in Hong Kong, arguing that such a move would only depress U.S. consumer demand, because raising the value of the currency would make Chinese exports more expensive, and it would not help the U.S. economy, because Americans don't produce many of the things they buy from China.

The financial crisis was fundamentally altering the formula at the heart of China's boom: demand from America and Europe for Chinese exports was slumping, so, to ward off a slowdown, the government in Beijing tilted the balance toward investment. It pumped public money into railways, roads, ports, and property. The government lowered real estate taxes and urged the banks to lend, and the surge in loans in 2009 was larger than India's entire GDP. Among government officials, the construction craze unleashed vast ambitions: the city of Wuhan planned to build 140 miles of new subway lines in the seven years that New York City set aside to build 2 miles of the Second Avenue subway.

The recession also gave Lin an opportunity to implement his vision. Not long before that, Chinese intellectuals and officials were reluctant to hold up the country's experience as an alternative to the Western way of doing things, for fear that it would fuel rivalry or distract from the fact that most Chinese people are still very poor. While Western countries struggled, China suffered far less damage. A Western diplomat in Beijing told me, "One lesson of the crisis is that we economists should all be humbler. I think we have to accept the possibility that China may become something close to a fully developed economic state without substantial political reform." When World Bank officials visited Beijing to celebrate thirty years since China resumed its Bank membership, Zoellick praised China's reductions in poverty and said, "We, and the world, have much to learn from this."

At the Bank, Lin churned out a series of papers intended to "revisit" the understanding of how poor countries get rich, much if it anathema to the Washington Consensus that prevailed in the 1990s. Writing with the Cameroonian economist Célestin Monga, he argued that governments must "regain center stage." Industrial policy, in which governments seek to support certain sectors, known to critics as "picking winners," has a bad name in the West, he said, and for good reason: it has failed far more often than it has succeeded. But he argued that the only thing worse was *not* having an industrial policy. He pointed to a recent study of thirteen fast-growing economies. "In all the successful countries, the governments play a very proactive role," he told me. He argued for a "soft" industrial policy in which a clamorous free market produced new industries and firms, and the government spotted the best prospects and helped them grow by giving them tax breaks and building infrastructure such as the ports and highways going up all over the Chinese mainland. It was the marriage of Chicago and Beijing: to rise out of poverty, he and Monga wrote, markets were "indispensable," but government would be "equally indispensable."

He used his perch at the World Bank to argue that China's approach had fundamental strengths that other countries could emulate. When he visited developing countries, he made a point to say they reminded him of China three decades ago. "Can other developing countries achieve a performance similar to that achieved by China over the past three decades?" he asked in a speech he called "The China Miracle Demystified." "The answer is clearly yes." He advised poor countries that if they want to get richer, they needed to delay political reform or fall victim to the chaos of post–Soviet Russia. He argued for the virtues of being free not from repression but "from the fear of poverty and hunger, of which I hold vivid childhood memories." When he wrote in his own name, not on behalf of the Bank, he was even more strident: he dismissed the "optimistic, and perhaps naïve, argument put forward by some scholars that democracies . . . are more likely to undertake economic reforms." He quoted Deng Xiaoping, who once said, "The United States brags about its political system, but the president says one thing during the election, something else when he takes office, something else at midterm, and something else when he leaves."

On a warm night in Beijing, a couple of months later, Lin was back in the Chinese capital for several days, and he took a chauffeur-driven black Audi sedan across town to a reception in honor of the tenth anniversary of an MBA program that he had cofounded. It was held in a traditional Chinese courtyard, shaded by wisteria and crab apple trees, which had once been home to the Empress Dowager Cixi. For this evening, however, it had been done up with a red carpet and klieg lights worthy of a fashion show. Wine was flowing, and a hundred or so guests—mostly middle-aged couples, former students and colleagues—were in a festive mood by the time Lin walked in with his wife, who was by now a leading expert on special education in China and a member of the National People's Congress. When the couple arrived, the well-heeled crowd cheered, and guests swarmed them, taking turns giddily posing for photographs with Lin. A television crew moved in for an interview. A teenager requested an autograph. Lin reached a quiet table, but then a guest buttonholed him with news of an exciting opportunity in the golf course construction business. Lin's facial expression was polite but desperate, and the hosts hustled him and his wife off to the refuge of a private area, where he prepared to give a speech.

Lin stepped up to the stage and peered out over the guests. He began by noting the "earth-shaking transformations" in China's economy over the past decade, and he declared, "The next ten or fifteen years are going to be even more spectacular." The crowd applauded. He pointed out that when the Beijing International Executive MBA program began, in 2000, China had fewer than a dozen companies in the Fortune Global 500, while America had nearly two hundred. "I believe that by 2025, when the Chinese economy has become the largest in the world, and shares the stage with America, the Chinese economy will make up twenty percent of the global economy," he said. "There will probably be one hundred Chinese companies in the Fortune 500." He ended with an exhortation: "I hope that as you build China's economy you will also help to build a better, more harmonious society in China."

"Harmonious society" was not a phrase that all Chinese intellectuals were quick to use. It was the slogan favored by President Hu Jintao to signify the goal of a fair and stable society, but Hu's critics had come to use it as a byword for repression and the silencing of dissent. (A website that got shut down was said to have been "harmonized.") Lin meant it in positive terms, which was consistent with his enduring faith in the power of government. In 1999, Yang Xiaokai, a prominent liberal economist, gave a lecture arguing that "without political reform there is no fairness, which leads to public dissatisfaction." Yang was asking if China could become a strong country without democracy. But, in a response, Lin pointed to China's economic lead over India, writing, "Whether it's the pace or quality of economic growth, China is doing better than India." In Lin's view, China was already becoming a strong country without democracy, and he saw little evidence for making a change. When I asked Lin about the debate, he said that he and Yang, who died in 2004, were good friends but disagreed. "He thought that if China wants to be successful, China needs to adopt the British- or U.S.-style constitution first," he said. "I take a different view: I think that we do not know what kind of governance structure is the best in the world."

As Lin's prominence grew, his life was clouded by an extraordinary fact: more than three decades after his swim, he still faced an arrest warrant, issued by the Ministry of Defense in Taiwan for "defecting to the enemy." After so many years, much of the Taiwanese public had come to view his success with hometown pride, and prominent Taiwanese politicians had asked the military to drop the case, but the minister of defense reiterated that if Lin stepped back on Taiwanese soil, he would be arrested and would face military charges of treason.

His older brother, Lin Wang-sung, told reporters, "I don't understand why people regard him as a villain. My brother just wanted to pursue his ambitions." When Lin's father died, in 2002, Lin's family asked for permission for him to attend the funeral, but the military rejected the request, saying he "should bear disgrace throughout his life." He had no choice but to watch the funeral from Beijing via videoconference. He built an altar inside his office and knelt before it. In a eulogy read aloud, he wrote, "When mother was dying, I couldn't be there to help. When father was bedridden, there was still no route home. I can't send them off on the road to the afterworld . . . How great the sin of being unfilial! May the heavens punish me!"

Lin had thrived in the People's Republic by becoming its most ardent economic spokesman. For those who departed from that view, China was becoming a more difficult place to be. A few days after watching Lin's speech about the bright economic future, I went to see Wu Jinglian, who had emerged as one of China's leading economic advisers in the decade after reform began. He was now close to eighty years old, a gnomish man with lively eyes peering out from beneath a thatch of white hair. He worked from a tiny office on the fringe of the city. He remained an official adviser to China's cabinet, but he sounded more like a gadfly. "It's entirely obvious that the biggest problem China faces right now is corruption," he told me. "Corruption is the reason for the gap between rich and poor. Where did this corruption come from? From the fact that government continues to control too many resources."

In a furious stream of essays and books, Wu pointed to crony capitalism and the gap between rich and poor as evidence that China's economic model had run up against the limit of what was possible without the government's permitting greater political openness to mediate competing demands. In recent years, he had gone so far as to argue that China needed to adopt a Western-style democracy, and nationalists had blasted him for apostasy. At one point, the debate turned personal: the *People's Daily* published Internet rumors that Wu was being investigated for spying for the United States. The claim was absurd—the cabinet eventually put out a statement supporting Wu and disputing the charge—but the prominence of the attack made it clear that his critique had inflamed powerful people with access to the *People's Daily*.

I asked Wu if things had settled down. He sighed. "A month or so ago there was an item on a website saying that someone had knocked me unconscious with a brick, but I had survived," he said. There was no truth to the item, and I asked him what he made of it. "It was giving people the hint to use violence," he said. The item was signed "The China Association for the Elimination of Traitors." Wu had no idea who was behind the effort to demonize him, but the various suspects were proliferating: The right-wing nationalist fringe? Powerful figures opposed to reform?

In China, the financial stakes had grown so large that even arcane economic debates became laced with a sense of intense opposition. Wu had recently argued for allowing China's currency to rise in value, and then he read the reaction online. "One of the commentators on that article mentioned where I live and the fact that security is lax," he said. He gave a weak laugh. "Writing that would be against the law in America. In China, no one cares."

As the debate widened, words once benign took on a political edge. Lin Yifu liked to describe the economic boom as the "China miracle," but the liberal writer and critic Liu Xiaobo took issue with the phrase; he wrote that all he could see was "the 'miracle' of systemic corruption, the 'miracle' of an unjust society, the 'miracle' of moral decline, and the 'miracle' of a squandered future." The boom was becoming "a robber baron's paradise," he wrote. "Only with money can the Party maintain control of China's major cities, co-opt elites, satisfy the drive of many to get rich overnight and crush the resistance of any nascent rival group. Only with money can the Party wheel and deal with Western powers; only with money can it buy off rogue states and purchase diplomatic support."

At fifty-one, Liu Xiaobo was as lean and bony as a greyhound, with short hair that narrowed to a widow's peak. He was a chain-smoker with a wry, knowing sense of humor. He had grown up in Manchuria. When he was eleven, his school shut down for the Cultural Revolution—a "temporary emancipation," he called it—and the taste of independence launched him on a life of unconventional thinking. He earned a PhD in literature at Beijing Normal University but did not excel at the genuflections required to thrive in Chinese academia. He believes that Chinese writers "can't write creatively because their very lives don't belong to them." He was not much kinder about Western sinologists, observing that "ninety-eight percent are useless." He did not set out to offend, but he did not shy away from it. "Perhaps my personality means I will crash into brick walls wherever I go," he wrote to the scholar Geremie Barmé. "I can accept it all, even if in the end I crack my skull open."

Liu was the author of seventeen books and hundreds of poems, articles, and essays. Much of his work was fiercely political, and that came with a price: by the spring of 2008, he had served three jail terms, beginning with a conviction for "counterrevolutionary propaganda and incitement" for his role in the demonstrations at Tiananmen Square. He rejected the charges but embraced the label of "black hand," saying it was a "medal of honor" and one of the few things he could keep with him behind bars. In a jailhouse poem, he wrote, "Besides a lie / I own nothing."

Over the years, Liu Xiaobo stopped drawing sharp distinctions between prisons, detention centers, and labor camps. "When I was in prison, I was kept in a small pen with a wall," he told me by phone, during a spell under house arrest. "Since leaving prison, I'm simply kept in a bigger pen that has no wall." While he was in a labor camp in 1996, on charges of "disturbing social order," he married his longtime companion, the artist Liu Xia. Camp guards double-checked that the bride knew what she was doing. "Right!" she replied. "That 'enemy of the state'! I want to marry him!"

When he was released in 1999, after three years away, he returned to their apartment and discovered that it now contained a computer. "A friend had given it to my wife," he recalled in an essay, "and she was already using it to learn typing and go online. She showed me how to use it, and practically every friend who came by to see us in the next few days kept urging me to get on the computer. I tried it a few times, but composing sentences in front of a machine just felt wrong. I avoided it, and kept on writing with a fountain pen."

Only after he submitted his first piece of writing by e-mail did he awaken to the possibilities of technology. "Within a few hours, I had a response from the editor—and the marvelous power of the Internet suddenly struck me." His wife never got her computer back. Liu had lived through the old rituals of dissent, the "bicycle-and-telephone era," as he called it, when intellectuals had to wait for a funeral or an anniversary in order to convene without arousing the government's suspicion of large groups. The Web slashed across dialect, class, and geography such that the editors of China's first online magazine, *Tunnel*, wrote in 1997, "The reason why autocrats could seal our ears and eyes and fix our thoughts is that they monopolize the technology of disseminating information. Computer networks have changed this equation."

That idealism was hardly universal. Around the world, critics of "cyber-utopianism" argued that the Web provided only an illusion of openness, and a weak sense of community; that it strengthened authoritarian governments by creating a safety valve and defusing the pressure for deeper change. But for Liu, those factors did not outweigh the practical benefits of activism in the digital age. For years, the post office had intercepted his manuscripts when he tried to send them abroad; if he was preparing an open letter of protest, he would spend a month crisscrossing the city to find enough like-minded people to sign it. "Then it took several days (at the very least) to reach consensus on questions of content and wording and timing," he wrote. "Next, one had to find a place where a handwritten letter could be typeset and printed. Then copies had to be made." Liu Xiaobo had become an unapologetic cyberutopian. "A few clicks of a mouse, the exchange of a few emails, and it's done," he wrote. "The Internet is like a magic engine, and it has helped my writing to erupt like a geyser."

By the fall of 2008, behind the door of his fifth-floor walk-up in Beijing, Liu Xiaobo was writing something that he suspected would have more impact than anything he'd ever done. Exactly what he was writing had to remain a secret for the moment, but, when it was ready, he would let it loose, abetted by the technology he called "God's gift to China."

One afternoon the previous winter, Liu and I were at a teahouse near his apartment. He looked gaunter than usual, his belt wrapped nearly twice around his waist; his winter coat drooped across his shoulders as if it were on a hanger. His stutter, always in the background, was strong. He coughed over his tea. He was, by now, the country's most prominent dissident, which meant that he was a celebrity among Chinese intellectuals, but almost unknown to the broader Chinese population. His writings had been banned in China for years, and online censors struck down his essays. He published abroad, but he didn't speak English, and he had turned down offers to resettle overseas. China was his home whether the government liked that or not.

I was struck that day by an unexpected calmness about him. His years behind bars had mellowed his rancor, and he was technical and unhurried as he walked me through the arguments in a new open letter—a warning to Chinese leaders that they risked "a legitimacy crisis" if they did not heed growing calls for political reform.

"Western countries are asking the Chinese government to fulfill its promises to improve the human rights situation, but if there's no voice from inside the country, then the government will say, 'It's only a request from abroad; the domestic population doesn't demand it,'" he told me. "I want to show that it's not only the hope of the international community, but also the hope of the Chinese people to improve their human rights situation."

Liu startled me with his optimism. As China knitted itself into the world, he suspected the "current regime might become more confident," he said, and leaned back into his seat, enjoying the sound of his prediction. "It might become milder, more flexible, more open." His duty, as he saw it, was to keep writing and arguing. "Regardless of whether it works or not, I will keep on asking the government to fulfill its promises."

And so he did, growing more ambitious as the months passed. As fall gave way to winter, he and a small group of collaborators were nearing the end of their secret project—a detailed declaration calling for human rights and political reform. "The political reality, which is plain for anyone to see, is that China has many laws but no rule of law; it has a constitution but no constitutional government," they wrote. "The ruling elite continues to cling to its authoritarian power and fights off any move toward political change."

Unlike the usual dissident manifestos, theirs did not confine their argument to a single case or an obscure provision; they called for nineteen fundamental political reforms, including regular elections, independent courts, a ban on political control of the military, and an end to the practice of, as they put it, "viewing words as crimes." They were inspired by Charter 77, a manifesto that Václav Havel and fellow Czech activists had issued more than three decades earlier, united, as they wrote at the time, "by the will to strive individually and collectively for respect for human and civil rights in our country and throughout the world." In China's case, Liu and his coauthors ended their introduction with the suggestion of a ticking clock: "The decline of the current system has reached the point where change is no longer optional."

Among themselves, they resolved to release it to the public that winter, on December 10, 2008—the sixtieth anniversary of the UN Universal Declaration of Human Rights. They called it Charter 08. They had 303 initial signers, but someone needed to be the primary sponsor, and Liu agreed to take that role. To most, it would have been an unappealing prospect. "The first bird that lifts its neck" the Chinese liked to say, "is the one that gets shot."

# ELEVEN

# A CHORUS OF SOLOISTS

The real estate boom swept across Beijing from east to west, from new to old—past the Global Trade Mansion and on to the Drum Tower, and in the fall of 2008, I got priced out of my neighborhood. I found a cheaper place a mile farther west, on a street that had yet to be redeveloped, called Cotton Flower Alley. It was lined with poplar trees and run-down courtyards popular with migrant workers from Shandong, Anhui, and elsewhere, who stuck out because they were shorter, darker, and more alert than city people. The migrants shared bunk beds in tiny rented rooms, except on the hottest nights, when they pulled their mattresses into the street and hoped for wind.

You could learn a fair bit about the economy without leaving the *hutong*. I could eyeball unemployment by the number of day laborers huddled at the corner of Cuttlefish Alley looking for work. They were middle-aged men in dusty, patched-up sport coats and pleather loafers, shifting their weight from foot to foot. As the financial crisis deepened, their numbers tripled. Watching them, I could see why Home Depot had struggled to romanticize DIY home improvements in China. The men held signs that advertised their skills, and each listed his offerings in a way that struck me as the flip side of the young daters who itemized their demands, CAN BUILD SMALL HOMES, DRYWALL, TILE FLOORS, BRICK FLOORS, WATERPROOFING, INTERIOR WALLS, PAINTING, UNCLOG DRAINS, MOLDINGS, DECORATIONS, WATER, ELECTRIC.

Life was fluid, and nobody ever seemed too far from success or failure. A few doors down from my house, a tiny stall selling sesame biscuits opened in February. It had a deli counter facing the street; steam poured out of the opening into the cold. A middle-aged woman in a paper hat and blue apron was barking valiantly to passersby about free samples. Her name was Mrs. Guo and she had a strong Henan accent; she worked the counter while her husband, a tall quiet guy, pounded dough behind her in a cloud of flour and steam. It was a twenty-four-hour operation, if you didn't count the seven hours at night that they slung a sheet across the front and bedded down on the tables.

But after a few weeks, I stopped by for breakfast and found that they'd taped a FOR RENT sign in the window. "We aren't making any money," Mrs. Guo said. Rent was $150 a month, and that was too much. "People just cycle by. This location is no good for walking," she added, and I tried not to look at all the people walking by as we talked. I was stumped. The bra vendor across the alley was doing fine, and the convenience store with the one-yuan hot dogs on a rotisserie did okay. "We're moving down to Fuxingmen"—another old Beijing neighborhood a mile or so south—"and we'll see what happens," she said. A couple of days later, I went back, and their place was already empty. Through the window, I could see nothing but final footprints left in flour. They had opened and closed in seven weeks.

Soon, Mr. Ye arrived. He was a nervous twenty-five-year-old from Fujian Province who had learned the basics of making Beijing-style crêpes and was trying to contend in a competitive market. (The street was lousy with crêpes.) He didn't even last the spring. Before long, the stall got an impressive new sign—THE GREAT MYTHICAL BIRD CONSTRUC-TION SUPPLY SHOP—and I prepared to bring them my hardware needs. But when it opened, it turned out to be a brothel. It had only a single employee—she sat warily in the window, where the biscuit vendor once stood—but the brothel lasted only two weeks. By fall, the place was dark, its fancy sign still perched overhead. It was hard to know what to blame: the financial crisis perhaps, or the location, or simply the relentless churn of modern *hutong* life.

At night, the busiest place on Cotton Flower Alley was the Internet café, a vast, low-ceilinged expanse with row after row of rickety PCs, where glassy-eyed young men sat for hours smoking and playing games. I could find a place like that in almost any town I visited, no matter how remote.

The windows were almost always blacked out, like at a casino, and they struck me as the only places in China where people weren't racing the clock.

For all the energy that the Web gave to intellectuals such as Liu Xiaobo, and the nationalist fever it stirred among Tang Jie and his friends, most of China's online life, as in any country, concerned matters less grave. When researchers noticed a spike, in April 2010, in the number of Chinese users taking steps to get around censors, the cause might have been a surge in political awareness; actually it was a Japanese porn star, Sola Aoi, who had opened a Twitter account, and young Chinese men were sparing no effort to reach it. But there were many ways to get attention on the Chinese Web. Bloggers started identifying photos that had been doctored by Party propagandists to make the crowds look larger or the officials more important. Techniques that had served the Department well for decades were now open to ridicule: a blogger noticed that a state news report on China's newest fighter jet included footage from *Top Gun*. Look closely, and there was Tom Cruise destroying a Soviet MiG.

Online, people were shedding the habit that Orwell called "blackwhite"—the "loyal willingness to say that black is white when Party discipline demands this." Time-honored rituals were losing their effectiveness. When state television showed President Hu Jintao visiting a low-income family in subsidized housing on New Year's Day, the mother told him, "I am so grateful that the Party and the government have built such a great country." But people online promptly discovered that the mother was a civil servant in the city's traffic police; her image as a member of a low-income family was undermined when it was discovered that she had posted photos of herself on vacation, with her daughter, in Shanghai and the resort island of Hainan.

The establishment media was being undermined by the Web. The blogger Ran Yunfei called it a "parallel language system," and the tension between the languages was reviving a strain of irreverence that had languished in China for decades. Autocrats rarely do well with irony, and these were especially hostile to humor: shortly after the revolution in 1949, the Party set up a committee to evaluate Chinese comedy; the committee officially concluded that stand-up comedians should replace satire with "praise." Online, people were less inclined to praise. When

the government unveiled the new headquarters of China Central Television—a pair of tall, slanted towers joined at the top—people started calling it the Big Underpants. Flustered, the Party suggested, the "Window
on Knowledge," or *zhichuang*, which people embraced but pronounced
slightly differently, so that it meant "hemorrhoid."

Online, Chinese teenagers were watching free subtitled episodes of
*Friends* at the very moment that a state-television apparatchik named
Qin Mingxin was fuming to reporters that he had considered putting
*Friends* on Chinese TV until he watched it. "I had thought the play focused on friendship. But after a careful preview I found each episode
had something to do with sex," he said. Even when the Party could control what people saw, it was unnerved by how people reacted. It blessed a
big-budget drama about itself called *The Founding of a Party*, and recruited a long list of movie stars to volunteer their participation. But when
people started to rate the film on a pop culture site called Douban, it got
so many bad reviews that the site abruptly shut down the rating system.

Fundamentally, the culture of the Web was an almost perfect opposite of the culture of the Communist Party: Chinese leaders cherished
solemnity, conformity, and secrecy; the Web sanctified informality, new-
ness, and, above all, disclosure. Four years after the journalist Shi Tao
went to prison for revealing a censorship order, those orders were now
leaking onto the Web within hours of being issued by the Department,
the State Council Information Office, and other agencies. Censors
pulled them down as fast as possible, but other people collected and re-
posted them beyond the firewall, where censors couldn't reach them.
China Digital Times, an overseas news site, created an archive it called
"Directives from the Ministry of Truth," in homage to Orwell. The directives were often as brief and punchy as a tweet, as if the state had adopted the cadences of the technology that bedeviled it. Each read like a
reverse mirror image of a headline in the state press:

> All websites are requested to delete without delay the essay enti-
> tled "Many Massively Corrupt High Officials Receive Stays of
> Execution."

I signed up to receive Directives from the Ministry of Truth delivered
by e-mail, and they came through on my phone with the same buzz that
accompanied the text messages.

*Bzzzzz.*

All websites are requested to remove immediately the article entitled, "In China, 94% Unhappy with Wealth Disproportionately
Concentrated at the Top."

*Bzzzzz.*

Announcement: the Sunshine Yu Lin Golf Club is offering an
unprecedented deal: "Buy One Business Membership, Get Two
Free."

*Bzzzzz.*

All media are not to exaggerate the pay raise received by the People's Liberation Army.

*Bzzzzz.*

All kinds of receipts at great prices. Don't get scammed on the
Web. Whatever you need, call 13811902313.


The Web was a clamor of new voices, and one of the first I noticed was
that of Han Han, a twenty-six-year-old living in Shanghai. His blog had
a teenybopper look to it, with a powder-blue background and a photograph of a yellow Lab puppy in the corner. But day after day, he lam-
pooned the self-importance and hypocrisies of officialdom. Where an
older generation had used euphemism and allegory to hint at the truth,
Han asked directly why the government lowered the flags for the deaths
of politicians but not for disasters that claimed large numbers of civilian
lives. ("I have a Chinese-style solution," he wrote. "Flagpoles should be
doubled in height. This will satisfy all sides.") He flicked around the
edges of rumors that senior leaders had high-priced mistresses. ("If you
spend a hundred yuan on a woman's intimate services, it's obscene; if
you spend a million, it's refined.") He mocked the Party strategy of
trying to drum up support by plastering the Web with pro-government
messages. ("Just because you see a crowd of people standing on a street

corner eating shit doesn't make you want to elbow your way in for a bite.")

Han Han was no dissident. On the spectrum of Chinese politics, he held a highly ambiguous position. At times his was one of China's most outspoken voices. "How many evil things has China Central Television done in the past? Replacing truth with lies, manipulating public opinion, desecrating culture, abusing facts, concealing wrongdoing, covering up problems, and creating fake images of harmony." (That post, like many of his, was struck down by censors, though readers reached it first and circulated it broadly.) His criticism placed him in frequent combat with the "angry youth." When Tang Jie and his friends were circulating nationalist videos in the spring of 2008, Han Han wrote, "How can our national self-respect be so fragile and shallow? . . . Somebody says you're a mob, so you curse him, attack him, and then you say, 'We're not a mob.' This is as if someone says you're a fool, so you hold up a big sign in front of his girlfriend's brother's dog saying 'I Am Not a Fool.' The message will get to him, but he'll still think you're a fool." A pro-government website once listed Han Han among the "slaves of the West" and superimposed a noose on his picture. But he could also be calculatingly elliptical: when he needed to mention a sensitive word that was sure to trigger the Web's automatic filters, he wrote, "sensitive word," and let his readers figure it out.

In September 2008, not long after the Olympics ended, he edged past a movie star to become China's most popular personal blogger, based on the total number of readers he had accumulated. He had attracted more than a quarter of a billion visitors since he began; only China's stock tip blogs were drawing more. I was going to be in Shanghai, and I asked Han Han if I could come by. He suggested I join him on the road. Once or twice a week, he left downtown Shanghai to return to the village where he grew up, in a farmhouse now occupied by his grandparents.

He picked me up in a black GMC van with tinted windows, driven by his friend Sun Qiang. Han had the van for long trips because he was afraid of flying. He was five feet eight inches tall and weighed less than a hundred and thirty pounds. He had the high cheekbones of a Korean

soap star and black eyes shaded by sheepdog bangs. He favored a uniform of grays and whites and denim—Chinese pop culture's prevailing
aesthetic. His manicured, swaggering persona was a world apart from
Liu Xiaobo and the rumpled archetype of the Chinese intellectual. Han
Han had a look, and it owed equal debts to Kerouac and Timberlake. In
person, he was warm and laconic, and he spoke through a smile that
tended to camouflage the searing edge of his comments.

The Web had altered the course of Han Han's life. When he was in
tenth grade, in 1998, he failed seven courses and dropped out. The next
year, he sent a handwritten manuscript to a publisher; it was a novel
called *Triple Door*, about a Chinese high school student slogging through
"hours of endless emptiness," copying lessons "from the blackboard to
the notebook to the exam," while his mother fed him pills intended to
boost his IQ. Han compared China's school system to the manufacture
of chopsticks—a system designed to yield products of "exactly the same
length." Another publisher had pronounced the novel gloomy and out of
step with the times; successful books about Chinese youth were more
often akin to *Harvard Girl*, with the ambitious Ivy Leaguer clenching ice
cubes to build fortitude. But an editor was enthusiastic about Han's novel
and printed thirty thousand copies. They sold out in three days. Another
thirty thousand copies were printed, and they sold out, too.

In the global canon of teen-angst literature, the novel was tame, but
in China it was unprecedented: a scathingly realistic satire of education
and authority, written by a nobody. State television moved to tamp down
the frenzy with an hour-long discussion on its national broadcast, but
the strategy backfired. On TV, Han Han projected insolent glamour,
with a boy-band shag haircut that swept down and across his left eye.
When educators in tweeds and ties fulminated against "rebelliousness"
that "might contribute to social instability," Han smiled, cut them off,
and said, "From the sound of it, your life experience has been even shal-
lower than mine." He was instantly famous—a seductive spokesman for
a new brand of youthful defiance. The Chinese press proclaimed "Han
Han fever."

*Triple Door* went on to sell more than two million copies, putting it
among China's bestselling novels of the past two decades. In the next
several years, Han published four more novels and several essay collections faithful to the subjects he knew best: teenagers, girls, and cars.

They sold millions more, though even his publisher, Lu Jinbo, president of Guomai Culture and Media, did not hail them as literature. "His novels usually had a beginning but no end," Lu told me. In 2006, Han Han started blogging, and his focus took an unmistakable turn toward some of China's most sensitive matters: party corruption, censorship, the exploitation of young workers, pollution, the gap between the rich and the poor. It was as if Stephenie Meyer, the teen-vampire author, had abandoned the *Twilight* series and started directing fans' attention to the misuse of public funds. Han Han was the patron saint of young strivers who saw in him a way to reconcile their dawning sense of skepticism with the material gratification they coveted. In his world, being political no longer meant being poor.

"As soon as I started making money from writing, I started buying sports cars" and racing, he told me, as we inched through rush-hour traffic. "Other drivers looked down on me, because they thought, 'You're a writer; you're supposed to be driving into walls,'" he said.

For nearly a decade, Han had maintained a parallel career as a race car driver with a respectable record in circuit competition for Shanghai's Volkswagen team and in off-road rally races for Subaru. It was a world of sponsorships and champagne showers, disorientingly at odds with his writing life. By and large, his readers cared nothing for auto racing, but the overlapping identities yielded a singular celebrity: he was on the covers of style magazines while independent websites—Han Han Digest, Danwei, ChinaGeeks—translated and analyzed his utterances. He once began a television interview by saying, "If you speak Chinese, you know who I am"—a boast not quite as ridiculous as it sounds.

He was the only government critic with corporate sponsorship, and he was an enthusiastic pitchman attuned to Bobo sensibilities. A low-cost clothing chain called Vancl put his face on ads with the slogan "I am Vancl." Johnnie Walker paired his picture with the line "Dreaming is realizing every idea that flashes through one's mind." He had lent his name to a one-of-a-kind luxury Swiss watch by Hublot, which was auctioned for charity and inscribed, in English, "For Freedom."


Approaching his hometown, Tinglin, we branched off onto smaller roads until we confronted a creek spanned by a concrete bridge that was only inches wider than the van. At the wheel, Sun Qiang hesitated. Han peered through the gap between the front seats and adopted a mock-serious tone: "This bridge is the test!" We crossed intact. "I've had mishaps there many times," Han said.

The fringe of Shanghai was a steadily eroding ring of small farms and factories a short drive from staggering wealth. Mist hung over fallow fields crisscrossed by footpaths. We reached a two-story brick farmhouse fronted by a narrow plot. Han's grandparents—small, swaddled in padded cotton clothes—ambled out to greet us. A golden retriever went berserk. We passed through a living room that contained the cold damp of the countryside, and reemerged in a small courtyard, where Han smiled and indicated for me to climb through a window into his wing of the house. "A small design flaw," he said. "We didn't put a door on this side."

Within was a rural Chinese teenager's fantasy lair: a beat-up Yamaha motorcycle leaned against one wall, a mammoth television screen graced another. A second giant screen was accessorized with a steering wheel and pedals set up for driving games. In the center of the room was a pool table, and Han racked up the balls and broke. He was in constant, restless motion. To indicate his rare and full attention, he turned both his phones facedown as they buzzed and bleated in protest. On the pool table, I made a shot, then flubbed the second. He sank the rest.

The transformation of his hometown figured prominently in Han's view of China. He pointed out an industrial compound in the distance, a chemical manufacturer, which he blamed for fouling the stream where he used to hunt for crawfish. On his blog, he wrote:

> My grandfather can identify the day of the week by the color of the water. The stench is everywhere. The Environmental Protection Bureau says the water quality is normal, though the river is full of dead fish . . . At various points, my hometown has planned to build Asia's largest industrial harbor, and Asia's largest outdoor sculpture garden, and Asia's largest electronics shopping center. So far, all it has produced is thousands of acres of rubble, unfinished and wasted.

Han was often described as a symbol of China's youth, which was not meant entirely as a compliment. He hailed from the first generation born after the death of Mao and the start of the one-child policy—the *baling hou,* or "post-eighty generation"—which served as a reference point in Chinese discussions of values and the national character much the way baby boomers did for Americans: a generation that came of age amid radical social transformations that alienated its members from their parents and left them either newly self-aware or self-indulgent, depending on who was talking.

In his writings, Han jabbed at the official truth about China's rise, urging workers not to cheer headlines of new prosperity when their "low-wage labor adds up to nothing but a single screw in the boss's Rolls-Royce." After a forty-seven-year-old woman burned herself to death to stop a crew that was trying to demolish her home, he wrote, "If you have not burned yourself to ashes . . . if all your family members are alive, that's the standard of a happy life."

We wandered outside into the cold, and I mentioned that his criticism seemed to underplay the benefits of the most prosperous period in Chinese history. He gave me a dubious sideways look. He said the scale of China's growth obscured the details of how the spoils were being divided. "For rally races we travel widely, because they're on dirt roads, often in small, poor places. Young people there don't care about literature or art or film or freedom or democracy, but they know they need one thing: justice. What they see around them is unfair."

To illustrate his point, he mentioned a news clip he'd seen recently about a seventeen-year-old migrant worker who stood in the aisle of a train for sixty-two hours to get home. It was the kind of ordeal that Chinese papers had always featured as portraits of fortitude. But Han had a different view of the man's experience of standing on the train for two and a half days. "The guy had to wear adult diapers," Han said, appalled. It became the basis of his next blog post. Young Chinese, he wrote, were increasingly being "used by the process of urbanization." He laid out the deal that the boom was offering his generation: "Work for a whole year, stand in line for a whole day, buy a full-price ticket, wear diapers, and stand the whole way home—how dignified!"

On the days that Han was writing, he slept until midday and usually worked, fast and alone, into the predawn hours. He was married to Lily

Jin, a high school friend who served as his assistant and gatekeeper. "Han Han trusts people very easily, almost credulously," she told me. "In the past, he's been cheated by publishers, and lost money because of it." When they had a daughter, the event was greeted by the Chinese gossip magazines with all the ceremony of a royal siring ("Han Han Becomes a Father, Talks for First Time about Daughter").

He was a proudly self-described "country bumpkin." Unlike other prominent Chinese critics of the government, he had few ties to the West; he had visited Europe but not America, and he cared little for Western literature. He long ago recognized his "rebel" identity as a cliché—"If I were a rebel, I wouldn't drive an Audi or a BMW," he liked to say—and he kept to quiet rhythms: he didn't smoke, barely drank, and had no interest in nightclubs.

Han's parents had worked for the government: his mother, Zhou Qiaorong, dispensed benefits at a local welfare office; his father, Han Renjun, once wanted to write fiction but dead-ended at a local Party newspaper, and he resented the path of advancement. "He didn't like the kind of life in which you have to drink every day and kiss your leaders' asses," his son told me. Before the parents knew if they were having a boy or a girl, they agreed to name the baby Han Han, the father's abandoned pen name. As the son's work became recognized, his heckling of the establishment complicated their government jobs; he offered to support them financially, and they took early retirement.

When Han was young, his father stacked the literature on low shelves, where the boy could reach it, and kept the orthodox political tracts up high. The more he read, the more he found gaps between "the textbooks and the truth," as Han put it. "I don't believe anyone who truly loves literature can also love Mao Zedong," he told me. "These two things are incompatible. Even putting aside his political performance, or how many bad things he did, or how many people starved to death because of him, or how many people he killed, there is one thing for sure: Mao Zedong was the enemy of writers."

As a student at Songjiang No. 2 High School, he wrote occasionally, and when he was sixteen a Shanghai magazine was looking for young writers to enter the New Concept Essay Contest. He'd entered contests before. "You'd be asked to write about something that you'd done that was good—say, helping an old lady across the street or returning a lost wallet. Never mind that the more realistic scenario would be you putting the wallet in your pocket." But New Concept intended to be different, and Han's assignment in the final round was abstract: a judge dropped a plain piece of paper into an empty glass—that was the topic. "I had some random idea about how the paper falling to the bottom of the glass tells you about life," he told me, adding, "All bullshit." He took first place.

Then he failed his courses and was held back. On the verge of failing again, he dropped out, which made him desperate to publish his manuscript—"to prove myself," he said. "I had told my classmates and teacher that I was a good writer and I could make a living from it, but they said I was crazy." Just a couple of decades earlier, Han could easily have been jailed for his criticisms of the state, but when *Triple Door* was finally released, it electrified young people not just because it was an honest critique of China's education system. In the words of the Shanghai writer Chen Cun, Han's very existence gave them "the right to choose their own idol."

The publisher Lu Jinbo believed that Han's fans gravitated to him for a simple reason: They saw in his life and writings a rare kind of truth. "In China, our culture forces us to say things that we don't really think. If I say, 'Please come over to my place for dinner today,' the truth is I don't really want you to come. And you'll say, 'You're too kind, but I have other arrangements.' This is the way people are used to communicating, whether it's leaders in the newspaper or regular people. All Chinese people understand that what you say and what you think often don't match up. But Han Han isn't like this. He doesn't consider other people's feelings and just says what's on his mind, or he'll say nothing." In short, Lu said, "If Han Han says, 'This is true,' then ten million fans will say, 'This is true.' If he says, 'This is fake,' then it's fake."

Authenticity, or the appearance of it, had become the rarest of assets in China. In the five years since Gong Haiyan encountered fake bachelors online, the epidemic of fraudulence had reached into every corner of life, most dramatically in the case of the dairy industry. In 2008 a milk producer, Sanlu, discovered that farmers had been adding melamine to boost the protein levels, but the company did not order a recall; instead, it persuaded the local government to bar the press from reporting it. By the time the Ministry of Health warned the public, three hundred thousand infants had been sickened; six of them died. Chinese parents who could afford to travel started buying so much baby formula in Hong Kong that the city imposed a legal limit of two cans per person.

Among intellectuals, Han Han was a polarizing figure. Leung Man-tou, a Hong Kong writer and television commentator, raved that Han had the makings of "another Lu Xun," China's most celebrated social critic. The artist Ai Weiwei went a step further, telling a reporter that "Han is more influential than Lu Xun, because his writing can reach more people." But others recoiled at the comparison. When I asked Lydia H. Liu, a literature and media scholar at Columbia University, about him, she said, "Han Han is only a mirror image of the people who like him. So in what ways will that reflection transform them? It will not." She added, "The first thing you see on his blog is not his writing but a Subaru advertisement."

But serving as a mirror for his fans was perhaps his greatest strength. He articulated what others thought but didn't say. While China's boldest intellectuals and dissidents stood out for being flamboyantly atypical, Han excelled at being typical, for allowing his fans to relate to him enough that the principles he espoused felt within reach. His biography bore all the minor victories and humiliations, the reasons for aspiration and cynicism, that accompanied being young and restless in China— and that made him powerful. For two decades since Tiananmen, Chinese young people had been apolitical, not simply because the basic conditions of life had improved but also because the alternative was frightening and hopeless. Han's writing did not reorder the political life of Chinese youth, or force the hand of policymakers, but he was a powerful spokesman for the joys of skepticism.

For all his conflicts with the angry youth, Han Han had something in common with Tang Jie: both were looking for outlets to channel their discontent, and to express an idea of China. They saw themselves as occupying opposing sides of an emerging culture war inside China and yet both were indulging in the new habits of self-creation, and the tentative chance to cultivate political taste. And both were doing it online, unlike an earlier generation of activists who had filled Tiananmen Square. Han Han and Tang Jie had grown up in an era of fortune and aspiration, and despite their disagreements, neither one of them could imagine abandoning the determination to be heard.

When Han Han outgrew the confines of a blog, he started a magazine called *Duchangtuan*, which means "A Chorus of Soloists." His publisher, fearing political repercussions, forced him to cut 50 percent of the contents in the first issue, but some interesting bits stayed in. The cleverest feature was called "Everyone Asks Everyone," a farcical meditation on the way information was withheld in China; readers dreamed up questions—for boyfriends, for government agencies—and editors tried to find the answers, no matter how difficult this was. Ten hours after it went on sale, the magazine was number one in the rankings of Amazon China. Bookstores dedicated separate sales counters to handle the crush. The censors were unnerved. A few days later, my phone buzzed. It was a directive to news editors from the Shanghai office of the Propaganda Department:

> All activities and comments related to Han Han, other than car racing, are not to be reported.

Han prepared a second issue, in December 2010, but the publisher was ordered to stop. Mountains of magazines were pulped. "People got worried," Han told me afterward. We were in the office he'd rented, now half empty. "Maybe they thought, 'Well, you started out as a writer published in *our* magazines, which we control. Now are you trying to take control?'" He wondered what the shutdown said about the future of Chinese culture. "We can't always use pandas and tea," he said. "What else do we have? Silk? The Great Wall? That isn't China."

When *Time* magazine collected candidates for its annual list of the world's most influential people in 2010, Han Han made the list. Chinese authorities were not pleased. They blocked the combination of "Han Han" and "*Time*" from Chinese search engines, and *People's Daily* asked in a headline, IS TIME MAGAZINE SEVERELY NEARSIGHTED? Han was not feeling triumphant; he had no illusions about what an individual was facing in China. He wrote:

> Maybe my writings help people vent some anger or resentment. But beyond that what use are they? This "influence" is an illusion. In China, influence belongs only to those with power, those who can make rain from clouds, who can decide if you live or die,

those who can keep you somewhere between life and death. They are the people with real influence . . . The rest of us are just small characters under a spotlight on the stage. They own the theater, and they can always bring down the curtain, turn off the lights, close the door, and turn the dogs loose inside.

When he posted this, he received twenty-five thousand comments, some laced with desperate devotion ("I'm willing to give my life to defend Han Han—a man with courage and integrity"). The *Time* list had hinged on a public vote, and in the final tally, Han had come in number two world-wide, behind the Iranian opposition leader Mir-Hossein Mousavi.

One afternoon, after watching Han compete in a car race, I found a small, exuberant crowd of fans waiting to catch a glimpse of him. Among them was Wei Feiran, a wiry, spiky-haired nineteen-year-old from Anhui Province, who seemed on the verge of levitating with anticipation. He'd read *Triple Door* when he was in tenth grade and was deeply affected by it. He was inspired by Han's attempt to publish a magazine, and now he and some friends were trying to launch one, too, in the city of Changsha. "I really want to do it well. I'm sort of an idealist," Wei said. "We are doing it by ourselves, with no company or anybody behind us." For the inaugural issue, they wanted to interview Han, so Wei had ridden fourteen hours on a train to find him.

Whenever Han's fans talked to me about his work, they described it as a revelation—"a shot of adrenaline that awakens us from our apathy," as a blogger put it. For a while, Wei Feiran had helped run a fan site that collected and commented on Han's blog posts. "We were forced to shut down by the Ningxia Internet Patrol," Wei said. "Our site had every post he'd ever written, and they said that's too sensitive." Overhearing our conversation, a shy girl in an orange sweater interjected, "Han Han represents the person that all of us want to become, and the things that we all want to do but are never brave enough to try."

Spending time around Han's young admirers often made me think of Michael, the student from Li Yang Crazy English. Michael was a fan of Han's, too, and the next time I saw him, he pulled out his phone to show me an app that he had downloaded with all of Han Han's books in one place.

———

Not long after I met Michael, he started teaching classes outside Crazy English. To attract students, he bought a small amplifier and delivered free lessons in a park in Guangzhou beneath a twenty-five-foot banner that he had worded to suggest some kind of official position: WELCOME THE OLYMPICS, CONVENE THE ASIAN GAMES. ENGLISH VOLUNTEER OUTDOOR ACTIVITIES. Michael borrowed fifty thousand yuan from a neighborhood credit union, over the objections of his parents, who worried that it was too risky. "My whole family was opposed to it," he told me. But, after a couple of months, he had attracted paying students. He also finagled a small contract with the local Olympic propaganda campaign, for recording a hundred sample sentences that volunteers could memorize. "I was so proud," he wrote in his journal. "I made enough money to buy new suits and a tie."

In January 2009 he left Crazy English and teamed up with another teacher to form a company they called Beautiful Sound English. Michael was in charge of sales, and his partner was the head teacher. Michael started booking talks in other cities, and his business gained traction.

The quality of Michael's English always startled me. For someone who had never left China, he was clear and articulate, and he made relatively few mistakes in conversation and in writing—largely because there was almost nothing he wouldn't do in the name of improvement. When a music teacher suggested he hone his pronunciation by holding up a mirror and making exaggerated movements of his mouth, Michael did it even while riding the bus. It attracted strange looks. When another teacher told him to shout even louder than Li Yang recommended, Michael tried that, too. "I didn't obtain my goal," he wrote in his journal. "All I obtained was chronic pharyngitis." A doctor had to prescribe inhalation treatments to repair the damage.

Most of all, Michael scoured the Internet to find English recordings that appealed to him, and then he recited them over and over to hone his accent. He read me one of his favorites: "Something amazing is happening at Verizon Wireless that will change the way America talks. Something big. Something bold. Something new." Listening to him, I realized there was a universal quality to the sound of salesmanship, even if you didn't care what you were selling. He continued: "Introducing nationwide unlimited talk from Verizon Wireless. Now thirty dollars less than ever before, on America's largest and most reliable wireless network. Verizon." Michael grinned.

He especially loved the voices from commercials and radio broad-casters; he switched his tone of voice and reeled off a news flash: "Five people suffered minor injuries when an earthquake measuring six-point-two on the Richter scale struck Taiwan this morning . . . James Pomfret reports." He was working on emulating a particular southern accent. "Hello, this is Vic Johnson. The year before I encountered Bob Proctor's teaching, I earned fourteen thousand twenty-seven dollars." Michael couldn't remember where he'd found it, but he loved the speaker's twang. "Within a handful of years I was earning that in a week. And now it's not uncommon for me to earn that—and a lot more—in a matter of minutes. I don't even want to imagine where my life would be if I hadn't met Bob Proctor."

One part of his life where Michael was not making progress was with girls. Since college, he had had two serious relationships, but they had foundered in part because of his infatuation with studying. "They usu-ally decide that a person who wakes up in the middle of the night to lis-ten to English recordings is kind of ridiculous," he wrote. He was, at heart, a romantic—"If your wife really loves you, she won't care about anything but your soul," he told me—and he was out of step with his generation's attention to finances. He showed me a set of scenes he wrote for his students to practice, and his perspective came through in his classroom exercises:

A: You look good today.
B: Thanks.
A: Do you love me?
B: No, I only love money.

Now and then, Michael asked me to take a look at his Chinese writ-ing, or to polish the grammar of the English passages he wrote for his students. I was often struck by how comfortable he was putting himself at the center of the story. Earlier generations in China were less comfort-able doing this. I asked his father to talk about the three decades he spent working in a coal mine. He said, "All mines are dangerous. It was very hard at that time. We earned about sixty yuan per month." And that was all he had to say on the subject. Michael, by contrast, saw his own life as an epic fable of frustration and triumph. He wrote, "I was extremely lonely and confused from 2002 to 2007. I wanted to be someone great. I didn't want a commonplace life . . . Was I really destined to be a failure? What should I do? Maybe I was doomed to be an ordinary person." The prospect of conformity offended him. He wrote, "Why should I be like everyone else, just because I was born to a poor family?"

He framed the study of English as a matter of moral entitlement. He told his students, "You are the master of your destiny. You deserve to be happy. You deserve to be different in this world."

TWELVE

# THE ART OF RESISTANCE

The harder the Party struggled against the unruly culture of the Chinese Internet, the more unruly that culture became. When, in 2009, authorities declared their intention to rid the Web of "online vulgarity," people responded by inventing a smiling cartoon symbol—a mythical creature that resembled an alpaca—named the Grass Mud Horse, which, in Mandarin, was a homonym for "Fuck Your Mother." Overnight, the Grass Mud Horse was galloping and grazing all over the Internet, singing in music videos and appearing in animated shorts—often cavorting with another cartoon creature, the River Crab, a play on the Party's beloved concept of "harmony," which Lin Yifu had touted to his audience. Each new satire and double entendre was, in effect, a middle finger in the face of the state. The censors issued urgent instructions:

> Any content related to the "Grass Mud Horse" must not be promoted or exaggerated (this goes for any mythical creatures or river crabs as well).

It did no good. Soon, the Grass Mud Horse was on T-shirts and in the form of kid-friendly stuffed animals. Nobody embraced the symbolism as rapturously as the artist Ai Weiwei, who posted a photo of himself nude, leaping into the air, clutching a stuffed Grass Mud Horse over his genitals. He titled the photo "Grass Mud Horse Covering the Middle"—a near-perfect homonym for "Fuck Your Mother, Party Central Committee."

In the years since Ai Weiwei created chandeliers to spoof China's new opulence, and explored the relationship with the West by sending people to Germany, he'd attracted growing recognition as an artist and an architect. His work on public projects put him in contact with politics in a way he had rarely experienced, and he began to see "how it functions, how it works," he said at the time, adding, "Then you have a lot of criticism about how it works." As his criticism grew, Ai Weiwei became China's most determined innovator of provocation. By the time he was hired to serve as artistic consultant to Herzog and De Meuron, the Swiss firm that was designing China's National Stadium for the Olympics in Beijing, his views had begun to take a sharp turn. Before the stadium was completed, he disowned the games as a "fake smile" concealing China's problems.

Ai Weiwei was a Falstaffian figure: capacious belly; meaty, expressive face; and a black-and-white beard that stretched to his chest. The full picture was imposing, until he revealed a whimsical view of the world. "His beard is his makeup," his brother, Ai Dan, told me. The artist lived and worked on the northeast edge of Beijing, in a studio complex that he had designed for himself, a hive of eccentric creativity that one friend called "a cross between a monastery and a crime family." Behind a metal gate painted turquoise, a courtyard planted with grass and bamboo was surrounded by airy buildings in brick and concrete. He and his wife, Lu Qing, also an artist, inhabited one side of the yard, and several dozen assistants occupied the other. Visitors roamed unhindered, as did a geriatric cocker spaniel named Danni and a tribe of semiferal cats that occasionally destroyed Ai's architectural models.

He and his wife had no children. He had an infant son from an extramarital relationship with a woman who worked on one of his films. They lived nearby, and he spent part of every day with them. He had never intended to be a father. "She said, 'Yes, I want to have the baby,'" he told me. "I said, 'I don't normally think I should have a baby, but if you insist, of course, it's your right, and I will bear the full responsibility as a father.'" He was enjoying being wrong about fatherhood. "So-called human intelligence—we shouldn't overestimate it," he told me. "When an accident happens, that can be nice."

Ai spent much of his time on the road; he owned an apartment in Manhattan, in Chelsea. But when he was in China his orbit revolved tightly around his studio, which acquired a role in the cultural life of

Beijing akin to that of Andy Warhol's Factory. He wandered among the buildings day and night, which made it difficult to discern when he was working and when he was not, a distinction that had eroded further in recent years as the line between his art and his life became increasingly indistinguishable. Since discovering Twitter, he had become one of China's most active users, often spending eight hours a day on it. I asked him if it was taking away from his art. "I think my stance and my way of life *is* my most important art," he said. "Those other works might be collectible, something you can hang on the wall, but that's just a conventional perspective. We shouldn't do things a certain way just because Rembrandt did it that way. If Shakespeare were alive today, he might be writing on Twitter." He enjoyed the spontaneity, but he also saw a deeper significance in it for Chinese people; it was, he concluded, their "first chance in a thousand years to exercise their personal freedom of expression" without the state standing between their words and the public.

Ten months after the earthquake in Sichuan, and nine months after Hu Shuli's investigation of the collapsing schools, Ai Weiwei found himself fixated on one detail in particular: the government had declined to count or name the students who had died. Despite repeated requests, it had produced no list, no tally of the casualties, no report on what went wrong. When some parents demanded information too insistently, they were detained. This galvanized and infuriated Ai in a way that more abstract political issues rarely had. "We started to ask very simple questions: Who's dead? What are their names?" he told me. In a blog post that was unusually harsh even for him, Ai wrote of the officials in charge of the disaster area, "They hide the facts in the name of maintaining stability. They intimidate, they jail, they persecute parents who demand the truth, and they brazenly stomp on the constitution and the basic rights of man."

That December he launched what he called a citizens' investigation of the quake, an attempt to document how and why so many schools collapsed—and to collect as many names as possible. He signed up volunteers and sent them to Sichuan to investigate. They collected 5,212 names and cross-checked them with parents, insurance companies, and

other sources. The results filled eighty pieces of paper plastered on a wall
of his office—a spreadsheet containing thousands of names and birth
dates. Each day, Ai's office posted to Twitter a list of the students who
were born on that day who had died in the earthquake. "Today, there are
seventeen," Ai told me one winter morning at the studio. "The most of
any day yet."

We were sitting in his office, and he was, as usual, at the keyboard
tweeting. As we talked, he checked the clock and announced that it was
time to go to the courthouse. Over the past year, his office had sent more
than 150 letters to government agencies seeking information about earthquake victims and construction problems, under the Freedom of Government Information Law. He had yet to receive a substantive response.
Today he planned to file suit against the Ministry of Civil Affairs for not
responding to his requests.

He slid into the passenger seat of a small black sedan, with a driver
and a woman named Liu Yanping, who was overseeing the letter-writing
campaign. "According to the policy, they have to respond within fifteen
working days," she said, clutching a sheaf of papers on her lap. I asked
Liu if she was a lawyer, and she laughed. "For a long time, I was at home
raising my child," she said. "On his blog, Ai Weiwei asked for volunteers,
so I wrote him an e-mail. The work looked interesting, and I was curious." It led to a full-time job and other new experiences: not long after
Liu joined Ai's staff, she was arrested in Sichuan, where she was publi-
cizing the trial of an earthquake activist; she spent two days in police
custody for "disturbing the social order."

We reached the Second Intermediate People's Court of Beijing, a tall
modern tower with a grand arched entry and a modest office at the back
for processing new cases. We passed through a metal detector, where
two young men in guards' uniforms were engrossed in a comic book.
There was a line of bank teller–style windows, and at the one closest to
us, a tiny old woman in a pink padded jacket was bellowing into a rectangular opening in the glass. "How could the other side win without any
evidence?" she shouted. "Did they bribe the head of the court?" On the
opposite side of the glass, two women in uniform were listening with
resigned expressions suggesting that the old woman had been at it for a
while.

Ai and Liu lined up in front of window No. 1 and, when it was their turn, slid the papers through the opening to a middle-aged man in a tan blazer. He looked glassy-eyed and exhausted. He read the papers carefully and identified a problem: "You say that you need the Ministry of Civil Affairs to make this information public, but why are you taking an interest in this?"

Ai leaned over to speak into the opening in the window. "Actually, according to the policy," he said, "everyone has a right to ask for this information—not that you have to agree." After some back-and-forth, Ai and Liu consented to write out a description of their goals, and they found seats in a waiting area full of people holding similar sheaves of paper. "They don't want to accept this," Ai said, "because once it is in the legal pipeline, they have to make some kind of judgment." By the time Ai and Liu reached the window again, an hour had passed. Now they learned that they were using the wrong color ink. Written materials had to be in black, and they had used blue. They sat down again to rewrite them. They got in line again.

"Kafka's castle," Ai murmured. Two hours stretched into three, and I asked him why he was bothering with this if he did not expect a response. "I want to prove that the system is not working," he said. "You can't simply say that the system is not working. You have to work through it." Twenty minutes before closing time, the man behind the glass finally accepted the filing, and Ai and Liu, satisfied, turned to leave. The old woman was still yelling.


Ai Weiwei always sensed that he was born into the wrong family—or, at least, an inauspicious one. His father, Ai Qing, was among China's foremost literary figures. He had joined the Communist Party as a young man and earned a reputation for accessible verse imbued with the spirit of the revolution. He was especially impressed with Chairman Mao, for whom he wrote a poem of praise that began, "Wherever Mao Zedong appears / thunderous applause erupts."

In 1957, when Ai Qing was forty-seven, he and his wife, Gao Ying, a young staff member at the writers' association, had a son. At the time, the Anti-Rightist Campaign, one of Mao's purges of intellectuals, was gathering force, and Ai Qing's devotion to the Party was called into question. He had written a fable, "The Gardener's Dream," that highlighted the need to permit a broader range of creative opinions. In it, a gardener who cultivates only Chinese roses realizes that he is "causing discontent among all the other types of flowers." A fellow poet, Feng Zhi, attacked Ai Qing, saying that he had fallen "into the quagmire of reactionary formalism."

Ai Qing was stripped of his titles and ejected from the writers' association. At night he would bang his head against the wall and demand, "Do you think I am against the Party?" In those wretched weeks, the couple had to name their infant son. The father simply opened the dictionary and dropped his finger onto a character: 威, pronounced *wei*, which means "power." The irony was too great, given the circumstances, so he altered the tone slightly to make it into a different *wei*, 未, which means "not yet." Their son thus became "Not yet, not yet."

The family was ordered out to a remote western stretch of Xinjiang, where Ai Qing was assigned the job of cleaning public toilets, thirteen a day. For extra food, the family collected the severed hooves of sheep discarded by butchers, and piglets that had frozen to death. When the Cultural Revolution began, things worsened. Ai Qing's tormentors poured ink on his face, and children threw stones at him. The family was assigned to live in an underground cavern that had been used as a birthing place for farm animals. They were there for five years. Of his father, Ai told me, "That period in his life was the absolute bottom, the most painful. He attempted suicide several times."

As a child, Ai Weiwei distracted himself by working with his hands, making ice skates and gunpowder. Ai's parents could not shield their sons from what Ai Dan called "the pressure and humiliation and hopelessness." Speaking of his brother, Ai Dan said, "He was a sensitive, fragile child, so he saw and heard more than other people." In his teens, Ai Weiwei wrote a letter to his brother that recalled their childhood: "The sound of smashing furniture and people begging for mercy; the cat being hanged until it was dead . . . the bullying and cursing in front of people. We were so young but we had to bear all the crimes." He resolved never to be a prisoner of the fate his nation might ordain. "I want a better life for myself to control my own destiny."

Ai graduated from high school the year the family was allowed to return to Beijing. He had already awakened to art, and a translator friend of the family gave him banned books on Degas and van Gogh, which he circulated like talismans among his friends. (He also received a book about Jasper Johns, but the images of maps and flags baffled him, and it went "straight into the garbage.") He gravitated to the group of avant-garde artists known as the Stars, but their activism was circumscribed. In 1979, Deng Xiaoping put an end to an incipient political movement called Democracy Wall; its central figure, Wei Jingsheng, was sentenced to fifteen years in prison, on charges of leaking state secrets. After that, Ai Weiwei recalled, "I felt I can no longer live in this country." His girlfriend at the time was moving to the United States to go to school, and in February 1981 he joined her.

In New York, Ai studied English and found a cheap basement apartment near East Seventh Street and Second Avenue. He spent his weekends haunting the galleries, roaming the city, as his brother put it, like "a mud-fish burrowing wherever there is muck." He was intoxicated by the raw energy of the East Village, which to him felt "like a volcano with smoke always billowing out of the top." Joan Lebold Cohen, a historian of Chinese art who got to know many Chinese artists in New York at the time, recalls visiting Ai's building. "The whole place reeked of urine," she said. "His apartment was a single room, no furniture, just a bed on the floor, and a television. And he was riveted to the television." She went on, "It was, I think, the Iran-Contra hearings. And he was so excited about the idea that the government would go through this cleansing, this agony, this ripping itself apart. He just couldn't believe that this was all done publicly."

He did odd jobs—housekeeper, gardener, babysitter, construction worker—but mostly he played blackjack in Atlantic City. (He was such a frequent visitor that, years later, the gaming press reported that gamblers who knew him were stunned to discover that he was also into art.) He earned some money as a sidewalk portrait painter, avoiding customers who were immigrants, like him, because they tried to bargain down the price. Soon, Ai abandoned painting and began exploring the possibilities in objects. He took a violin from a friend, pried off the neck and strings, and replaced them with the handle of a shovel. (The friend was not pleased.)

Ai was accumulating influences. At a poetry reading at St. Mark's

Church-in-the-Bowery, he met Allen Ginsberg, and they struck up an unlikely friendship. But nobody affected him as deeply as Duchamp, whose subversion of orthodoxy was thrilling to Chinese artists raised on academic realism. Ai took to photography and sold breaking-news pictures to the *Times*. He documented protests in Tompkins Square Park, and had his first run-ins with the police. "Being threatened is addictive," he later told a Chinese interviewer. "When those in power are infatuated with you, you feel valued."

The market for Chinese contemporary art, however, was dismal. Joan Cohen recalled, "One curator I approached said to me, 'We don't show Third World art.'" When Cohen contacted the Guggenheim, she says, "not only would the curator not see me but his secretary wouldn't see me." When, in April of 1993, Ai got word that his father was ill, he returned to Beijing. Upon arrival, he discovered that, in the years after Tiananmen, many young Chinese intellectuals had disengaged from public life. A popular T-shirt had a picture of three monkeys covering their ears, eyes, and mouths, and the phrase "Keeping Out of Harm's Way."

In 1999, Ai Weiwei leased some vegetable fields in the village of Caochangdi, on the fringe of Beijing, and sketched out a studio complex in an afternoon. He had no training as an architect, but the design was distinctive, and it attracted a flurry of commissions for buildings and public art installations. Before long, he had one of China's most influential architecture practices, which he named FAKE Design—a nod to his accidental success and his fascination with questions of authenticity. ("I know nothing about architecture," he liked to say.)

As years went by, Ai Weiwei spent more and more of his time on the intersection of politics, free expression, and technology. The Chinese website Sina invited him to host a blog, and at first he used it in an odd way—putting his own life under surveillance by posting dozens, sometimes hundreds, of snapshots each day, depicting his visitors, his cats, his wanderings. The blog gave him a far wider audience than he had ever encountered. He took to commenting on subjects ranging far beyond art. He wrote of a country called "C," ruled by "chunky and witless gluttons" who "spend two hundred billion yuan on drinking and dining and an equal amount on the military budget every year." Unlike journalists who had to heed the directives from the Department, Ai Weiwei was something new; he had no job from which to be fired for speaking out.

He became engrossed in one sensitive issue after another. "He'd be reading the news and he'd say, 'How can this be?'" Zhao Zhao, a younger artist who was working as one of Ai's assistants, told me. "And then the next day, and the day after that, he'd still be saying the same thing." By May 2009 he was one of China's most outspoken voices, and police officers visited Ai and his mother to ask him about his activities. He responded with an open letter, posted online: "Tapping my phone I tolerated. Surveillance of my residence I tolerated. But charging into my house and threatening me in front of my seventy-six-year-old mother I cannot tolerate. You don't understand human rights, but do you know anything about the constitution?" The next day, his blog was shut down.

The intersection of wealth and authoritarianism posed a predicament for members of China's new creative class. They were not the first artists forced to reckon with a society that supported the arts but suppressed free expression. Mies van der Rohe worked with the Nazis and was criticized for it. In China during the Cultural Revolution, artists were barred from playing Bach, Beethoven, and other composers, and had to perform only the permissible "revolutionary operas." The current pressures were more subtle: there had never been more money available for the arts in China, but receiving those spoils required tolerating the limits on expression. Writers, painters, and filmmakers had to decide how much of their work was activism and how much of it was to produce a commodity. They had to balance the pressures from an overheated commercial market, foreign expectations of artists toiling in the People's Republic, and of course the Party.

To understand how that felt, I visited Xu Bing, who rose to prominence in the eighties when he produced some highly controversial work, including *A Book from the Sky*, a set of hand-printed books and scrolls composed entirely of fake pictograms—a critique of China's hidebound literary culture. Xu moved to America and thrived, earning a MacArthur "genius grant" and commanding high prices for his art. Then, in 2008, he startled the Chinese art world by shedding his outsider status and returning to Beijing to become the vice president of the Central Academy of Fine Arts, the nation's top official art school. I met up with Xu Bing at a Beijing museum, where he was installing a set of giant steel phoenixes that dangled from construction cranes. We got a drink and I asked him why he had returned to China in the way he had. "This place, in fact, still has a lot of problems, like the disparity between rich and poor, and migrant labor issues, and on and on. But it really has solved many problems. China's economy is developing so quickly. I'm interested in *why* that has happened.

"My school has meetings constantly," he went on. They are a fact of life in a state-run organization. "The meetings, you discover, are really boring and useless. Sometimes, in meetings, I write literary essays, and people think I'm taking notes, that I'm especially dedicated." He laughed, and continued, "But then sometimes I think about the fact that China is holding meetings every day, and even though these meetings are meaningless, China has still developed so fast. How has this happened? There must be some reason. This is what interests me."

Ai Weiwei occupied an especially awkward niche in the world of Chinese contemporary art: overseas, his reputation (and prices) was growing—he received a coveted commission to fill the cathedral-like Turbine Hall, at Britain's Tate Modern—but, in China, he was never invited to hold a major exhibition, and his relations with fellow artists were tepid. Zhao Zhao told me, "Galleries and magazines send him things, and he doesn't even open them."

I asked Feng Boyi, a curator and critic who had worked with Ai over the years, to describe how other intellectuals regarded Ai. "Some really admire him, especially young people outside of art circles," Feng told me. But among some artists another view prevailed. "They attack him," Feng said. "They say he simply wants to make a fuss. They don't acknowledge his approach."

Many Chinese artists, like other elites, have explored Western liberalism or lived abroad, but as with Tang Jie or the Stanford engineer I met in Palo Alto, the exposure heightened their patriotism and made them suspicious of Western critiques of China. To his detractors, Ai Weiwei was too quick to satisfy Western expectations of "the dissident," too willing to reduce the complexity of today's China into black-and-white absolutes that appealed to foreign sympathies. They accused him of hypocrisy—for criticizing others' passivity in the face of injustice, though his own famous family name and his profile in the West seemed to afford him a level of protection that others did not enjoy. The fact that Ai exhibited mostly abroad fueled criticism that he was happier allowing foreigners to project their moral longings onto him than engaging with China's ambiguities. (At one point, so many commentators online were speculating that he had renounced his Chinese citizenship that Ai felt compelled to post images of his Chinese passport.)

At one point, Ai Weiwei was close friends with Xu Bing, the Mac-Arthur fellow who had joined the Central Academy. But they had grown apart, and I asked Xu what he made of Ai's political activities. "He has held on to certain ideals, like democracy and freedom, that made a deep impression on him—things inherited from the Cold War era," Xu said. "These things are not without value—they have value—and in today's China he has his function. It is meaningful and necessary. But when I came back to China I thought that China is very different than it was when he came back to China." He added, "We can't hold on to a Cold War attitude, particularly in today's China, because China today and China during the Cold War are worlds apart."

Xu said, "Not everyone can be like Ai Weiwei, because then China wouldn't be able to develop, right? But if China doesn't permit a man like Ai Weiwei, well, then it has a problem."


A couple of months after his blog was shut down, Ai Weiwei went to Chengdu, the capital of Sichuan, to attend the trial of Tan Zuoren, an earthquake activist who had been accused of inciting subversion of the state. At 3:00 a.m. on August 12, while Ai was asleep in his hotel, police knocked on the door and ordered him to open it. He replied that he had no way to know if they were who they said they were, and he picked up the phone to dial the police. (He also turned on an audio recorder to capture the scene.) Before his call could go through, the police broke down the door. A struggle ensued, and he was punched in the face, above the right cheekbone. "It was three or four people," he told me. "They were just dragging me. They tore my shirt and hit my head."

The police took him and eleven of his volunteers and assistants to another hotel and detained them there until the end of the day, when Tan's trial was over. Four weeks later, Ai, in Munich to install a show, felt a persistent headache and weakness in his left arm. He went to a doctor, who discovered a subdural hematoma—a pool of blood on the right side of his brain—caused by blunt force trauma. The doctor considered it life-threatening and performed surgery that night. From his hospital bed as he recovered, Ai posted to Twitter copies of his brain scans, the doctor's statements, and photographs of himself in the hospital with a drain protruding from his scalp. Then he went ahead with the biggest exhibition of his career: a vast installation that blanketed an exterior wall of the Munich Haus der Kunst with a mosaic of nine thousand bright-colored custom-made children's backpacks. In giant Chinese characters, the bags spelled out a statement from the mother of a child killed in the quake: "She Lived Happily on This Earth for Seven Years."

In the months after the surgery, Ai fully recovered, though he tired easily and had trouble summoning words. At the same time, he began to notice signs that the government was watching him more closely. His Gmail accounts were hacked and the settings altered to forward his messages to an unfamiliar address. His bank received official inquiries to review his finances. A pair of surveillance cameras appeared on utility poles outside his front gate, focused on the traffic going in and out—notwithstanding the redundancy of monitoring someone who already broadcast the minutiae of his life. When he tried to make DVDs of his documentaries, duplicating services worried that they would be punished for associating with him. "Not even the porno producers will do it," Zuoxiao Zuzhou, a rock musician who works on Ai's media productions, told me.

Ai Weiwei had come to abhor the mode of oblique dissent in China. Traditionally, intellectuals were expected to couch their criticisms of the government in a way that preserved the appearance of unity. As one saying had it, they should "point at the mulberry bush to disparage the ash tree." Ai Weiwei had lost patience with this. When a group of lesser-known artists who were protesting plans to demolish their studios in the name of development approached him for advice, he told them, "If you protest and fail to publish anything about it, you might as well have protested inside your own house." Ai and the other artists staged a march down the Avenue of Eternal Peace, in the center of Beijing—an immensely symbolic gesture, because of the street's proximity to Tiananmen Square. Police blocked them peacefully after a few hundred yards, but their bravado drew attention far beyond the art world. Pu Zhiqiang, a prominent legal activist, told me, "For twenty years, I have thought that protesting on Chang'an Avenue was absolutely off-limits. He did it. And what could they do about it?"

In China, the subversive dynamics of the Internet age—the rebirth of irony, the search for community, the courage to complain—had stirred a hunger for a new kind of critical voice. The editor Hu Shuli and her journalists couldn't satisfy it; they had neither the independence nor the desire to channel popular outrage. Classic dissidents such as Liu Xiaobo were too earnest and elitist to speak for the broader public. Tang Jie and the nationalists alienated people with their ferocity, and Han Han was usually too glib to share a stage with his elders. But Ai Weiwei combined ironclad Red credentials with a populist flair; he spoke in a vernacular that mixed irony, imagination, and rage.

"There are people who say that he is doing some kind of performance art," Chen Danqing, a Chinese painter and social critic, told me. "But I think he long ago surpassed that definition. He is doing something more interesting, more ambiguous." Chen added, "He wants to see how far an individual's power can go."

# THIRTEEN

# SEVEN SENTENCES

The technology that Liu Xiaobo called "God's gift to China" eventually led the police to his front door. For months, authorities had been monitoring his e-mail and online chats. By December 2008 he and his coauthors had collected the first three hundred signatures for the declaration they called Charter 08, and they were preparing to release it. Two days before they could, a team of officers assembled on the landing outside Liu's apartment.

When the authorities led him away, Liu did not resist. His wife, Liu Xia, was not told where he was going or why. Days passed. Liu's lawyer, Mo Shaoping, tried to find out who in the government had custody of his client, or where he had been taken, but the local agency that dealt with political dissidents—the General Affairs Office of the Beijing Public Security Bureau—was, like the Central Propaganda Department, a building that did not exist. It had no listed address and no known phone number. When the lawyer resorted to showing up, in person, at the front door, the staff refused to acknowledge that it was the office he was seeking. Mo was at a loss for what else to do, so he reverted to an older technology: he typed out his request for information, addressed it to the secret office, and slid it into the mailbox.

When Charter 08 was finally released, a few days after Liu's arrest, it turned out that the statement called for gradual, not abrupt change; the authors had modulated their message on purpose. They wanted to reach beyond marginal intellectuals in order to appeal to ordinary men and women who would recoil from the prospect of full-scale instability but might see something of their own struggles in a call for reform. "The decline of the current system has reached the point where change is no longer optional," Liu and his coauthors had written, and they proposed nineteen reforms, such as independent courts and elections for higher office. On paper, their calls for human rights, democracy, and the rule of law bore similarities to the government's own language: the national constitution contained assurances such as Article 35, which guaranteed "freedom of speech, of the press, of assembly, of association, of procession and of demonstration." In practice, however, the constitution had no legal authority over the Party, so it was largely meaningless. When the Party praised "democracy," it meant "democratic centralism," the concept of debate within its own ranks, and unquestioning adherence to final decisions.

Four months passed without any word of Liu's whereabouts. Then, on June 23, 2009, authorities informed his wife that her husband would be prosecuted for "incitement to subvert state power." His trial would begin two days before Christmas. "Incitement to subvert state power" was a crime with Chinese characteristics. Other authoritarian governments generally preferred to jail dissidents for more concrete reasons; in the Soviet Union, Natan Sharansky was imprisoned for being a spy. (He was not.) In Myanmar, the former junta kept Aung San Suu Kyi under house arrest for years for, in their words, "her own safety." But the Chinese government saw no need for those contrivances, and it indicted Liu Xiaobo on the basis of precisely seven sentences from his writings— words that, prosecutors charged, contained "rumor and slander" against the "people's democratic dictatorship." In the case of one of his offending articles, the title alone became a count in the indictment: he had titled an essay, "Change a Regime by Changing a Society."

What the Party did not say was that it considered Liu a special kind of threat. His contacts overseas and his embrace of the Internet merged two of the Party's most neuralgic issues: the threat of a foreign-backed "color revolution" and the organizing potential of the Web. The previous year, President Hu Jintao told the Politburo, "Whether we can cope with the Internet" will determine "the stability of the state."

At Liu's trial that December, the prosecution needed just fourteen minutes to present its case. When it was Liu's turn to speak, he denied none of the charges. Instead, he read a statement in which he predicted that the ruling against him would not "pass the test of history":

I look forward to the day when our country will be a land of free expression: a country where the words of each citizen will get equal respect; a country where different values, ideas, beliefs, and political views can compete with one another even as they peacefully coexist; a country where expression of both majority and minority views will be secure, and, in particular, where political views that differ from those of the people in power will be fully respected and protected; a country where all political views will be spread out beneath the sun for citizens to choose among, and every citizen will be able to express views without the slightest of fears; a country where it will be impossible to suffer persecution for expressing a political view. I hope that I will be the last victim in China's long record of treating words as crimes.

Midway through Liu's statement, the judge abruptly cut him off, saying the prosecution used only fourteen minutes and so the defense must do the same. (Chinese lawyers had never encountered this principle before.) Two days later, on Christmas Day 2009, the court sentenced Liu to eleven years in prison. This was lengthy by Chinese standards; local activists interpreted it as a deterrent to others, in the spirit of the old saying "Kill a chicken to scare the monkeys."

The severity of the sentence was surprising in part because the charter had produced very little public response. Censors had struck it down as soon as it appeared, and it had been poorly timed: Chinese people were still enjoying the afterglow of the Olympics; earlier that spring, the video by the philosophy student Tang Jie had tapped into Chinese sensitivity to Western criticism. Moreover, the financial crisis was expanding, and Chinese leaders' performance on the economy looked skillful compared with that of many Western leaders. Roland Soong, an author and translator, wrote, "Charter 08 was dead on arrival on account of George W. Bush." The new members of the middle class, he predicted, "won't bet their apartments, cars, television sets, washing machines and hopes on a prayer."

At first the government seemed to agree; it scarcely bothered to acknowledge Charter 08 in public. But in the months that followed, the charter began to attract signatures from intellectuals, farmers, teenagers, and former officials. Eventually the number reached twelve thousand—an infinitesimal minority in China's population, but symbolically significant: it was the largest coordinated campaign against one-party rule since 1949. It reflected a community of ordinary people unafraid to sign their names, people who had been living until then, as one of the signers wrote, "in a certain kind of separate and solitary state." The Party could not stay silent. In October 2010 the state press denounced the charter as "totally obsolete," written to "confuse people's thoughts" and bring about "violent revolution." It called on people to remember the Century of Humiliation: "Adopting this kind of charter would reduce China to an appendage of the West; it would put an end to the progress of Chinese society and the happiness of the people."

Two months after Liu's conviction, he appealed his sentence. The appeal was denied. When foreign reporters asked the Foreign Ministry spokesman Ma Zhaoxu for information about the ruling, he objected to the question because, he said, "There are no dissidents in China." Then he tried to lighten the mood: Chinese New Year was approaching, and at the end of the press conference he wished everyone a happy Year of the Tiger, and he held up a stuffed toy tiger. He urged the reporters to be "very careful when asking questions" or the "tiger here might not be very happy with you."

Across town, at his studio, Ai Weiwei read that line—"There are no dissidents in China"—and it lingered with him. Ai's visitors were increasingly using it to describe him, but the word *dissident* struck him as too simple to encompass the new range of dissent that was taking root in China. In the West, it had the ring of defiant moral clarity in the face of repressive power, but in China, becoming a "dissident" was complicated in ways that outsiders often underestimated.

For one thing, China's government didn't provide a simple target; it had succeeded in improving the lives of hundreds of millions of people, even as it deprived them of political liberty. When the government encountered a critic, it often tried to make this argument in the most practical terms: Wen Kejian, a human rights activist who had also been a successful businessman, recalled being visited by police who tried to steer him away from politics by saying, "Look at your shabby car, already seven or eight years old. All your friends already have Benzes." Wen heard them out but considered the police officers' argument as laughable as they considered his. Each side was trying to persuade the other, but they spoke different languages. It was the kind of conversation the Chinese call a "chicken talking to a duck." *Cluck, cluck. Quack, quack.* Neither side understood a thing.

Beyond the obvious pressures from the security forces, becoming a dissident could torpedo your relationships with friends and patrons. In China, intellectuals were often suspicious of dissidents among them who had too many foreign admirers or who appeared less interested in achieving practical gains than in fueling the kind of overt political conflict shunned by classical Chinese thought. Ai Weiwei reveled in confrontation. Now that he was being followed by plainclothes state security agents, he started calling the cops on them, setting off a Marx Brothers muddle of overlapping police agencies: "an absurdist novel gone bad," as he put it. He inverted the usual logic of art and politics: instead of enlisting art in the service of his protest, he enlisted the apparatus of authoritarianism into his art.

At times, he seemed congenitally incapable of cooperation. At one point, he was asked to create a piece that could fill a prominent site in Copenhagen usually occupied by Edvard Eriksen's statue of the Little Mermaid, which was being loaned to Shanghai. Instead of replacing it with a statue, Ai decided to install a live closed-circuit video of the mermaid in her temporary home in China. The Danes thought the oversize surveillance camera that he designed was unattractive. "That's our real life," he said. "Everybody is under some kind of surveillance camera. It's not beautiful."

Whenever a Chinese activist weighed the costs and benefits of dissent, there was always, in the background, the knowledge of what could happen if the government ran out of patience. You just had to recall the name Gao Zhisheng. In 2005, Gao was a lawyer and a rising star; he had been ranked as one of the country's ten best attorneys by the Ministry of Justice in 2001. The more he succeeded in court, the more pugnacious he became, and the more willing he was to take on sensitive cases for practitioners of Falun Gong, the banned spiritual movement. He was jailed for criticizing the government's handling of the law, but he refused to stop, and in September 2007 he saw a group of men approaching him on the sidewalk, and he felt a sharp blow to the neck. A hood was pulled over his head.

Gao was driven to an unknown location, and the hood was removed. He was stripped naked. He was beaten and electrocuted with batons. "Then two people stretched out my arms and pinned me to the ground," he wrote in an account smuggled abroad. "They used toothpicks to pierce my genitals." The torture continued for fourteen days. He was kept in detention for another five weeks. Finally, he was released with the warning never to describe how he was treated or next time "it will happen in front of your wife and children." When a reporter visited him a couple of years later, Gao had renounced his life as an activist. He said, simply, "I don't have the capacity to persevere."

Ai Weiwei looked, again, at the phrase, "There are no dissidents in China." He typed out a string of messages, to his tens of thousands of followers, that tried to make sense of what the government meant by that:

1. All dissidents are criminals.
2. Only criminals have dissenting views.
3. The distinction between criminals and non-criminals is whether they dissent.
4. If you think China has dissidents, you are a criminal.
5. The reason China has no dissidents is because they are criminals.
6. Now, anyone want to dissent from this view?

The Party was so experienced in containing dissidents, of the classic kind, that it was easy to overlook just how rapidly its information problems were proliferating. Because the Internet had long ago exceeded what the censors in the Department could handle, the work of policing the Web fell to several agencies, including the Internet Affairs Bureau. The bureau was honest about the scale of the challenge. The deputy director, Liu Zhengrong, conceded dolefully, "Our biggest challenge is that the Internet is still growing."

In the old media system, censors relied on the anaconda in the chandelier—the knowledge that Hu Shuli and fellow editors would censor themselves in order to protect their right to keep printing—but on the Web, you simply didn't know who was going to write something dangerous until it was written. The censors could strike down comments as fast as possible, but that was still too slow to prevent their being forwarded and saved and digested. On a scale unprecedented in Chinese history, words were being expressed first and censored second.

And this created yet another problem: censorship, once an abstract and invisible process confined to secret directives and newsroom discussions, was now plainly visible. Whenever the authorities took down one of Han Han's blog posts, it was not simply the digital equivalent of intercepting one of Liu Xiaobo's manuscripts at the post office. It was an act witnessed by millions of casual Internet users who, otherwise, were happy to live their lives without ever dwelling on the patronizing mechanics of censorship. It was a signal, as Han Han explained to me, that "there is something that you really don't want me to know. So now I *really* want to know it."

A generation of his fans was growing up to believe that "whatever you're trying to cover up becomes the truth," he said. In a speech, he said, "I can't write about the police, I can't write about the leaders, I can't write about policies, I can't write about the system, I can't write about the judiciary, I can't write about many pieces of history, I can't write about Tibet, I can't write about Xinjiang, I can't write about mass assemblies, I can't write about demonstrations, I can't write about pornography, I can't write about censorship, I can't write about art."

The best the Party could hope for was to prevent an Internet conversation before it began—by automatically filtering sensitive words. Because political issues popped up overnight, the censors had to maintain a constantly updated glossary of taboo terms, much like the list of directives to the media I received on my phone. The Internet Affairs Bureau sent out instructions, sometimes several times a day, to websites across the country. A word might be permissible one day and banned the next. Typing it into Baidu, the Chinese version of Google, yielded a message: "Search results are not displayed because they may not suit the corresponding laws, regulations and policies."

But people adapted just as fast. To get around the filters, they substituted Chinese characters that sounded similar, creating a kind of code, a shadow language, such that when censors blocked Charter 08—*ling ba xianzhang*—people called it *"linba xianzhang."* (Nobody cared that this meant "county magistrate lymph nodes.")

The government was in a race against the imagination, and it was forever trying to catch up. There was no more difficult time of year than

June, when the anniversary of the Tiananmen Square crackdown approached, and people dreamt up oblique ways to discuss it. Beyond
the terms always on the blacklist—*democracy protests, 1989, June 4*—the
censors clamored to add code words as fast as people invented them. I
read the latest list of banned words, and it looked like a commemoration
of its own:

*Fire*
*Crush*
*Redress*
*Never forget*

In the event that these censorship efforts failed, the Party was testing a
weapon of last resort: the OFF switch. On July 5, 2009, members of
China's Muslim Uighur minority in the far western city of Urumqi protested police handling of a brawl between Hans and Uighurs. The
protests turned violent, and nearly two hundred people died, most of
them Han, who had been targeted for their ethnicity. Revenge attacks on
Uighur neighborhoods followed, and in an effort to prevent people from
communicating and organizing, the government abruptly disabled text
messages, cut long-distance phone lines, and shut off Internet access almost entirely. The digital blackout lasted ten months, and the economic
effects were dramatic: exports from Xinjiang, the Uighur autonomous
region, plummeted more than 44 percent. But the Party was willing to accept immense economic damage to smother what it considered a political
threat. In the event of a broader crisis someday, China probably has too
many channels in and out to impose so complete a blackout on a national scale, but even a limited version would have a profound effect.

The Xinjiang uprising was a turning point in many other ways as
well. Over the previous year, Hu Shuli and *Caijing* magazine had proved
that investigative success could be popular. The more information Chinese people received, the more they seemed to crave. Hu Shuli tripled
the size of her newsroom staff, to more than two hundred reporters. The
magazine hired a former investment banker, Daphne Wu, to be the business manager, and she tripled ad sales in two years, to 170 million yuan.
She and Hu had plans far beyond a print magazine: they envisioned "a

whole media information and commentary platform," Wu told me in her office overlooking Beijing. She sounded less like a Chinese news worker than a Silicon Valley executive. "No matter what kind of device you're using, we want to deliver quality stuff," she said.

But as the magazine became more profitable, and adventurous, Hu Shuli's relations with her patron Wang Boming were fraying. The more she traveled, and studied publications abroad, the larger her aspirations became. She wanted her own media enterprise, one that could function at international standards. Wang, by contrast, had other priorities; he had gone into publishing to make some money and to enjoy the minor glamour of life as a media mogul—not to become a political martyr. He was uneasy. When I had talked to him about Hu, a weary look crossed his face that suggested he had gotten more than he bargained for. "We didn't know that this level of risk would come along with it," he said.

In the spring of 2009, the government warned *Caijing* not to investigate financial corruption within the state television system, or a list of other acutely sensitive topics. "But they do it anyway!" Wang said. He dragged hard on a cigarette. Muckraking, he added, was popular with readers but not with advertisers. "On one page is their advertisement, and on the next page is an article saying their company is a fake," he said. "You can't imagine the phone calls we get. *Caijing* never does a positive report. All the corporations talk to Shuli hoping it will be a good article, and it's always negative!"

By the summer, the relationship between the editor and publisher was deteriorating sharply. When the riots broke out in Xinjiang, and the Internet was shut down, propaganda officials allowed only officially approved journalists to get online. Hu Shuli had dispatched three reporters to the scene, though authorities had given her permission to send only two. The third reporter borrowed a friend's press pass to sneak into the press center that had Internet access. He was caught, and officials attempted to search his laptop. He resisted, and scuffled with a guard. Authorities put him on a plane back to Beijing.

The news of that run-in reached the highest ranks of the government. Propaganda authorities had already scolded *Caijing* that year, and now Hu Shuli's patrons drew up a list of measures to put her back under control: from now on, the magazine would submit every cover story for approval; it would accept instructions "without question"; and most important, it would abandon coverage of politics and "return to positive reporting on finance and economics."

Hu Shuli was outraged. "What is the definition of 'political news'?" she demanded of Wang Boming. "And 'positive news'? Who would be the judge of that?" For the next few weeks, she tried to accommodate the new rules. But her bosses rejected one cover story after another. After the third rejection, she feared that her best young editors were ready to quit. When the bosses rejected a fourth story, she published it anyway.

As word spread in Beijing that Hu Shuli was clashing with her backers, she glimpsed a way out. Investors approached her, and she realized that their backing might allow her to wrest away greater control of the magazine. Her tensions with Wang Boming were about more than just editorial freedom. Hers was the most profitable magazine he owned, and she wanted more of the profits to go into expanding the operation, or she feared she would be left behind in the new era of the Web.

She approached Wang with an audacious plan for a management buyout that would divvy up control of the company: 40 percent for investors; 30 percent for her and her editors; and 30 percent for Wang's company. Most important, she wanted ultimate control over editorial decisions. If anyone was going to negotiate with the Department, she wanted to be that person. "I think, as a professional editor, I should be the one to make the last decision," she said.

But in Wang Boming's eyes, the proposal was a betrayal. He had helped her carve out more freedom to practice journalism than anyone else in China—and instead of being grateful, she was asking for more, just as Chinese citizens were asking for more from a ruling class that believed it had already delivered enough. She was being naïve, Wang thought. Or, worse, grandstanding—draping herself in the flag of free speech to disguise her desire to gain control of the company. He rejected the deal.

By September the arrangement was falling apart: the business manager, Daphne Wu, and sixty members of her staff resigned, while, in the newsroom, editors announced that they, too, were leaving, and together they would start over. "Come with us," Hu's deputy, Wang Shuo, told a group of young editors and reporters. The truth was that it wasn't clear what or how they would start again, but each of them had a choice to make. The departing editors, in the hope of encouraging a full-scale walkout, gave their colleagues three days to decide whether to join them.

To the reporters facing the decision, it was a dilemma: Who would provide political protection to Hu Shuli now? Would investors ever gamble on her again? Besides, her reporters had a range of complaints about her management: for all her talk of transparency and checks and balances, she had a dictatorial streak; some of her investigative reporters thought she pulled punches for high-powered friends; and the high salaries she provided in the early days of *Caijing* had failed to keep up with China's surging economy. Her reporters could have tripled their salaries by joining the industries they covered.

And yet, for all this uncertainty, Hu's very existence had a powerful effect on the rising younger journalists around her. "We like to say that every hundred years you have a person like Shuli," Cao Haili, the reporter who worked on the SARS virus, told me. "She is really, really unique. In the States you might have tons of people like that, but in China it's really rare."

On November 9, Hu Shuli left the magazine, and 140 members of the newsroom walked out with her. For Hu, leaving was a choice, even if it was not one she had sought. "You can say we were driven out. You can say we left. It's very hard to say," she told me. She strained to put a positive spin on it. "Maybe we can do something bigger and more interesting," she said. But among Chinese intellectuals, few saw reason for optimism. "She's got blood on her sword and gunpowder on her clothes," Hecaitou, a blogger, wrote. "It will be hard to find another Hu Shuli."

On October 8, 2010, ten months after Liu Xiaobo was convicted, the Nobel Committee awarded him the Peace Prize "for his long and nonviolent struggle for fundamental human rights." He was the first Chinese citizen to receive the award, not counting the Dalai Lama, who had lived for decades in exile. The award to Liu Xiaobo drove Chinese leaders into a rage; the government denounced Liu's award as a "desecration" of Alfred Nobel's legacy. For years, China had coveted a Nobel Prize as a validation of the nation's progress and a measure of the world's acceptance. The obsession with the prize was so intense that scholars had named it the "Nobel complex," and each fall they debated China's odds of winning it, like sports fans in a pennant race. There was once a television debate called "How Far Are We from a Nobel Prize?"

When the award was announced, most Chinese people had never heard of Liu, so the state media made the first impression; it splashed an article across the country reporting that he earned his living "bad-mouthing his own country." The profile was a classic of the form: it described him as a collector of fine wines and porcelain, and it portrayed him telling fellow prisoners, "I'm not like you. I don't lack for money. Foreigners pay me every year, even when I'm in prison." Liu "spared no effort in working for Western anti-China forces" and, in doing so, "crossed the line of freedom of speech into crime."

For activists, the news of the award was staggering. "Many broke down in tears, even uncontrollable sobbing," one said later. In Beijing, bloggers, lawyers, and scholars gathered in the back of a restaurant to celebrate, but police arrived and detained twenty of them. When the announcement was made, Han Han, on his blog, toyed with censors and readers; he posted nothing but a pair of quotation marks enclosing an empty space. The post drew one and a half million hits and more than twenty-eight thousand comments.

Two days after Liu won the prize, his wife, Liu Xia, visited him at Jinzhou Prison in the province of Liaoning. "This is for the lost souls of June Fourth," he told her. Returning to Beijing, she was placed under house arrest. The government barred her, and anyone else, from going to Oslo to pick up the award; the only previous time this had happened was in 1935, when Hitler prevented relatives from going on behalf of Carl von Ossietzky, the German writer and pacifist, who was in a guarded hospital bed after having been in a concentration camp. Liu Xia's telephone and Internet connections were severed, and she was barred from contact with anyone but her mother—the beginning of a campaign of isolation that would last for years.

As the ceremony approached in December, China called on other countries to boycott it. The state press called it "a choosing of sides," and Vice Foreign Minister Cui Tiankai, a savvy diplomat with a graduate degree from Johns Hopkins, asked of fellow nations, "Do they want to be part of the political game to challenge China's judicial system, or do they want to develop a true friendly relationship with the Chinese government and people?" In the event, forty-five countries showed up, and nineteen stayed away, including Iraq, Pakistan, Russia, Saudi Arabia, and Vietnam. (The front page of the *China Daily* declared MOST NATIONS OPPOSE PEACE PRIZE TO LIU.) Outside Liu's apartment in Beijing, crews hastily erected a blue metal construction fence to prevent photographers from shooting images of Liu Xia under house arrest. When the BBC broadcast the ceremony, television screens in China went black.

Over the years, I'd seen this tactic many times. Decades ago, the black screen had been a fair reflection of China's blinkered view of the world, its backwardness and seclusion. But now the instinct to shield the public from unflattering facts was absurdly at odds with the openness and sophistication in other parts of Chinese life, and it seemed to cheapen what ordinary Chinese people had worked so hard to achieve. China was not Hitler's Germany, but Chinese leaders were willing to let themselves be lumped beside the Nazis in the history of the Nobel Prize. Either the strongest forces in the Chinese government were not wise enough to realize the cost, or the wisest forces were not strong enough to persuade the others.

Ordinary Chinese people never heard much about the ceremony. They never heard the presenter quote Liu's words that political reform should be "gradual, peaceful, orderly and controlled." They did not see the prize medal and the certificate placed on an empty blue chair onstage. Inside China, the moment was recorded only as a ghost, of sorts. On the Internet blacklist that winter, the censors inscribed a new taboo search: "the empty chair."

# FOURTEEN

# THE GERM IN THE HENHOUSE

The people in sunglasses did not immediately attract attention. When the first portraits appeared on Chinese social media sites in the fall of 2011, they encompassed a few dozen men and women. Soon there were more people in sunglasses, including kids, foreigners, and cartoon avatars. Bloggers noticed, and word spread. By the time the number passed five hundred, the censors were striking them down, but they continued to circulate anyway, and to those who knew what they were seeing, the pictures were a milestone: arguably China's first viral political campaign. It was a tribute to a man whom virtually none of the participants had ever met: the blind peasant lawyer Chen Guangcheng.

Six years after I'd tried to see Chen at his home in Dongshigu village, his local government had not wavered in its determination to contain the spread of his ideas, even if it meant sequestering him like the carrier of a fever. Around the time of my visit, in the fall of 2005, he was summoned to a meeting with Liu Jie, the local deputy mayor. Liu demanded to know why Chen was speaking to foreign reporters about abuses of the one-child system. "Why could you not address the matter through the normal official channels instead of talking to hostile forces in overseas countries?"

By that point, however, it was becoming clear that, in going public, Chen had crossed a line that the state could no longer tolerate. He was not yet charged with a crime, but he was put under house arrest and his phone was cut. After a couple of months, there was a routine power outage—a common problem in parts of the countryside that were growing fast—and to his surprise, the blackout disabled the phone-jamming equipment that was keeping him in isolation. Chen was able to get a call out to his lawyers in Beijing, who called me, and I dialed Chen's phone. He laughed at the strangeness of the circumstances, and then he paused, as if trying to summon a properly momentous tone for the occasion. "I want to tell the whole world," he said grandly, "that this local government doesn't obey their own law." He was mystified that his attempts to alert the government to abuses of the law had landed him in seclusion. I asked him what was the biggest question on his mind. He said, "I am only wondering if the central government doesn't want to stop this, or doesn't have the ability to stop this."

In March, after Chen had been under house arrest for nearly six months, his brother and fellow villagers fought with police over the conditions of Chen's confinement. Chen was charged with "destruction of property" and "assembling a crowd to disrupt traffic," though his supporters found this hard to square with his physical limitations. The night before his trial, his lawyer was detained; Chen was represented by court-appointed attorneys, who called no witnesses. He was found guilty of destroying property and disrupting traffic and was sentenced to four years and three months in prison.


In the days of the emperors, one way to seek the attention of Chinese leaders—to appeal a court ruling or expose an abuse of power—was to bang a drum installed for that purpose at the gate of the local court. If this failed to elicit a response, people threw themselves in front of the sedan chairs of passing Mandarins. People who succeeded in lodging their complaints became known officially as *yuanmin*—"People with Grievances"—and they were entitled to pursue their claims, level by level, all the way up to the capital.

When the Communist Party came to power, it retained some of the old system: it established the Bureau of Letters and Visits, to receive the People with Grievances, and to steer their cases to the correct branches of government. But by the twenty-first century, the Bureau of Letters and Visits was an antique; its caseload was crushing, its operations a mystery. A study found that the bureau solved about two-tenths of 1 percent of the cases it received. The cases were rarely given a full airing in court, so when People with Grievances lost their cases, or received no word of progress, it only drove some of them deeper into crusades for justice that stretched for years.

The modern heirs of People with Grievances were known as "petitioners," and I often received cold calls from them. They tracked me down in the hope that the attentions of a foreign reporter might force the government to resolve their cases. When they reached me, the least I could do was hear them out, but usually there were few ways for me to help. Their cases were intricate and confusing, and the process of petitioning was an odyssey that left thousands of people marooned on the edge of Beijing in shantytowns known as "petitioner villages," where they stewed amid mountains of wrinkled legal documents. Sometimes I couldn't tell if they were lost in the labyrinth of their disputes because they were unwell, or because they had been driven mad by the odyssey itself.

When the Web appeared, the People with Grievances were some of the first to embrace it. In September 2002 an outbreak of food poisoning in the city of Nanjing killed more than forty people, but the national evening news ignored it; instead, the stories that night included a piece about workers "expressing deep thanks for the compassion" of Party leaders and the opening of a local costume festival. People took to the Web to complain. "Ordinary Chinese people are not human beings?" one asked. Another wrote, "It is more difficult to choke the mouth of the people than to block the flow of a river."

Before long, People with Grievances were using the new technology to locate one another. When a twenty-five-year-old man named Zhang Xianzhu found he was barred from the civil service because he had tested positive for hepatitis, he located others online who had had the same experience, and together they forced a policy change to prevent such discrimination. Soon there were similar campaigns for greater rights on behalf of gays and lesbians, religious believers, and sufferers of diabetes. The instinct to organize spread further into the mainstream.

In 2007 a text message swept through the city of Xiamen denouncing a proposed chemical plant. The language of the message was dire: "The production of this highly poisonous chemical will be like dropping an atomic bomb on the city . . . For the sake of our grandchildren, take action! Join a ten-thousand-person march at 8 a.m. on June 1. Send this message to all your friends in Xiamen." But instead of a rowdy demonstration, organizers called for a "strolling protest," a low-key march that would not provoke a police crackdown. Thousands of men and women turned up—urban, well-heeled members of the New Middle-Income Stratum, some with children in their arms—all strolling calmly in the name of protest. The local government was taken aback: it had always calculated, as Mencius had predicted, that "those with a constant livelihood have a constant heart." But Mencius never mentioned a strolling protest. Was this an attempt to preserve stability or to disrupt it? It certainly wasn't a riot, but it wasn't legal, either. After several days, and back-and-forth with the crowd, the local government agreed to postpone the plan for the chemical plant pending "reevaluation."

The new spirit of protest, both coordinated and moderate, posed a delicate new problem for the authorities. As Jerome Cohen, a China specialist at New York University Law School, put it, "Are they going to have a legal system that can really handle these things and reduce tensions and satisfy wants, or is it all just a sham that will lead people into the streets and into all kinds of protests and a lack of stability and harmony?" Cohen saw Chen Guangcheng's struggle as a test of whether the authoritarian system could accommodate the rising tide of ambitions. Chen once asked Cohen, "What do they want me to do? Go into the streets? I want to go into the courts." In that sense, Cohen said, Chen was "not a dissident, although they may be making him one."

Cohen had known Chen since 2003, when the U.S. State Department's International Visitor Leadership Program invited Chen on a tour of the United States. When the State Department asked Cohen if he had time to see a Chinese lawyer, the professor was on a deadline and asked, "Where'd he go to law school?'"

"He didn't go to law school," the caller said.

"Then why are you bothering me?" Cohen asked.

"This fellow's special. I think you're going to want to see him."

They met, and Cohen told me, "After half an hour, it was clear to me that I was dealing with someone unusual." It was the beginning of an unlikely alliance. At seventy-three, Cohen was tall and bald, with a brilliant white mustache and a fondness for bow ties; he'd clerked for two U.S. Supreme Court justices before he became the first Western lawyer to practice in the People's Republic. He was regarded as the dean of foreign experts on Chinese law. When he and Chen met for a second time, in Beijing, Cohen bought him a stack of law books, and Chen told him, "You'll never understand what I'm up against or what I'm trying to do if you don't come down to Dongshigu village."

Cohen and his wife, Joan (the art historian who, incidentally, had befriended Ai Weiwei in New York), made the trip from New York to Dongshigu. Even after decades of work in China, they were taken aback by the depth of poverty. Cohen met Chen's clients. "You never saw a sadder bunch," Cohen said. "The lame, the beaten down, dwarfs—all kinds of people—denied the license to open a shop if they didn't bribe the authorities, or subject to unfair taxation or police abuse." Cohen spotted the books he had brought for Chen: they were dog-eared. "His wife and his oldest brother had been reading them to him."

Before Cohen left, Chen mapped out his plan: he wanted to spread the law by word of mouth, by training two hundred villagers in the basics of the courts, so that they could take on cases as he had. Cohen asked, "Do you really think the local authorities are going to allow us to hire a hall in the county seat to train people who are going to subvert them and make them miserable?"

"Yes," Chen said.


By the time Chen Guangcheng went to prison, the Party had concluded that its approach to controlling the spread of ideas was too weak. In the spring of 2007, President Hu Jintao told his fellow members of the Politburo that digital filters and human censors were no longer enough. The Party needed to "use" the Web, he said. It must "assert supremacy over online public opinion."

To that end, the Party expanded a corps of what it called "ushers of public opinion," who wandered the Web masquerading as ordinary users, seeking to steer debate rather than extinguish it. They were paid half a yuan for every comment they posted, and their critics named them the "fifty-cent Party." Much like the staff of the Department, they were supposed to be ubiquitous but invisible; they were prohibited from acknowledging that they worked for the Party. But Ai Weiwei put out the word that he would give an iPad to any usher of public opinion who was willing to talk about what it was like. A twenty-six-year-old calling himself W. took the offer. He had studied journalism, found occasional employment in television, but made most of his income as a part-time usher of public opinion.

Each assignment, W. explained, began with an order to "influence public understanding" or "stabilize netizens' emotions." If he openly praised the government, people ignored him or mocked him as a "fifty-center," so he worked the angles: If there was a gathering crowd, he'd throw in a dumb joke or insert a boring advertisement, to encourage casual readers to wander off. If people were criticizing the Party about, say, rising gas prices, he might lob in a grenade of an idea: "If you're too poor to drive, then it serves you right." "Once people see that, they start to attack me," he said, "and gradually the subject moves from gas prices to my comments. Mission accomplished."

W. didn't pretend to be proud of his work. He did it for money, and he didn't tell his family or friends because, he said, it might "harm my reputation." "Everyone has the thirst for exploring the truth, including me . . . We have more freedom of speech than we did. But at the same time, as soon as you get that freedom, you begin to see that certain people have even more freedom. So then we feel unfree again. It's the comparison that's depressing." Ai Weiwei posted the interview with the usher, and within minutes the censors struck it down. It didn't matter; it was already circulating widely.

Skepticism and criticism were like muscles, and they grew with exercise. One by one, tempests of public criticism, known as "Internet incidents," swept across the country. At one point, grassroots labor organizers used online forums and cell phones to mobilize a cascade of strikes at more than forty factories in two months—a surge of unrest that was especially unnerving to the Party, because, of anyone, it knew the potential strength of mobilized workers. Every institution, no matter how obscure, was now being evaluated in public. I once visited a tiny vocational college in rural Sichuan, and, a few years later, when I searched for news about the school, the first thing to come up was a student appeal to the local mayor saying the school had "cheated" students by classifying them on their diplomas as "part-time." "We paid tuition for a full-time degree," the student wrote. "We don't even have the tears to cry." When the graduates complained, they were summoned by local authorities and warned not to make a fuss. "We didn't create any trouble or riot or anything. We didn't violate the law or harm social morals," he wrote. "All we wanted was an explanation."

In Shanghai, a set of parents discovered that, because they were registered in the countryside, the school would not provide health insurance for their child. So they posted a complaint entitled "We Live in a Rigidly Hierarchical Country." "How can this school even try to teach our children to love the Party and love the motherland?" they wrote. In another case, which carried a certain awkward symbolism, a screenwriter on a hit television show called *Striving*, about young men and women making it on their own, took to the Web to complain: "How many viewers do I need to reach in order to make ends meet?"

The Party was in a conundrum of its own making: Over the years, it had squeezed off so many avenues of expression that people had little choice but to engage in the kind of unrest that was the Party's greatest fear. So it responded by clamping down even further, and the cycle continued. When homeowners in the prosperous coastal city of Ningbo held several days of street demonstrations against another proposed chemical complex, the city government eventually agreed to abandon the plant, but for good measure the censors blocked, from the Web, the demonstrators' slogan: "We want to survive, we want to get by."

People even went online to complain when their bribes did not produce the desired effects. A real estate tycoon in Hunan named Huang Yubiao had tried to buy a seat in the provincial legislature, but after handing over fifty thousand dollars, he was told his bribe was too small. (As retribution, he posted a video of the middlemen who had received the money.) Similarly, a young woman named Wang Qian complained that she had offered fifteen thousand dollars to buy a place in the army (a coveted position, because it could open up other patronage options), but her recruiters told her that other cadets had offered more.

Government officials were not the only targets of complaints. Customers complained to the dating entrepreneur Gong Haiyan that they were getting duped by charlatans on her site. People accused her of looking the other way while con men prowled the ranks of the membership. A man was arrested and later sentenced by a Beijing court to two and a half years in jail for swindling a woman he had allegedly met on Jiayuan. The company denied that it bore any responsibility, but its stock nevertheless lost nearly 40 percent of its value. Customers were drifting away. To protect against frauds, the company created a system that let people fortify their profiles by submitting copies of official documents—pay stubs, government IDs, divorce filings—and the more documents you provided, the more stars you earned beside your name. The company hired a team of document experts to hunt for forgeries and ferret out suspicious activity, such as a user who made frequent changes to his name or date of birth.

But more criticism followed. *Jinghua Weekly*, a state-backed newspaper, criticized the company's "V.I.P. High-Level Marriage Hunting Advisers," a team of special matchmakers who dealt only with the richest members, mostly men, lining them up with the most-sought-after female users. The Diamond Bachelors, as these clients were called, spent up to fifty thousand dollars for six matches, which smacked of a high-tech escort service. When I asked Gong about it, she was unapologetic. It was simple supply and demand, she said. "Diamond Bachelors are looking for pretty young women. And some of these pretty women are looking to marry that kind of man," she said. "It's a perfect match."

As a result of all the bad press, Jiayuan's competitors thrived; Internet dating, which hardly existed in China when Gong began, had become an industry worth more than a billion yuan, and the company needed a veteran. In March 2012, with its revenue and its stock price slumping, Jiayuan hired a seasoned tech executive, Linguang Wu, to be co-CEO. The love industry was getting cutthroat. Before Wu joined it, he was running an online shooter game called World of Tanks.

Where people were once dazzled to be online, now their expectations had soared, and they did not bother to hide their contempt for those who sought to curtail their freedom on the Web. Nobody was more despised than a computer science professor in his fifties named Fang Binxing. Fang had played a central role in designing the architecture of censorship, and the state media wrote admiringly of him as the "father of the Great Firewall." But when Fang opened his own social media account, a user exhorted others, "Quick, throw bricks at Fang Binxing!" Another chimed in, "Enemies of the people will eventually face trial." Censors removed the insults as fast as possible, but they couldn't keep up, and the lacerating comments poured in. People called Fang a "eunuch" and a "running dog." Someone Photoshopped his head onto a voodoo doll with a pin in its forehead. In digital terms, Fang had stepped into the hands of a frenzied mob.

Less than three hours after Web users spotted him, the Father of the Great Firewall shut down his account and recoiled from the digital world that he had helped create. A few months later, in May 2011, Fang was lecturing at Wuhan University when a student threw an egg at him, followed by a shoe, hitting the professor in the chest. Teachers tried to detain the shoe thrower, a science student from a nearby college, but other students shielded him and led him to safety. He was instantly famous online. People offered him cash and vacations in Hong Kong and Singapore. A female blogger offered to sleep with him.

Asked why he'd done it, the student described it as an act of desperation: "I do not have a platform where we can equally debate with Fang Binxing," he told a Chinese reporter. "Therefore, I can only resort to this somehow extreme way to express my discontent."


When Chen Guangcheng was released in September 2009, he had served his full term. There were no more charges against him. And yet he returned to Dongshigu village to find that the local government had prepared for his arrival. They had installed steel shutters on the windows of his house, floodlights around the dirt yard, and cameras to keep an eye on the place twenty-four hours a day. They formed a revolving crew of guards to work in shifts. At one point, Cohen and Chen did their best to estimate the cost of the guards, meals, and other expenses required to keep the blind lawyer isolated from the world around him, and it came to seven million dollars.

But as far as Chen was concerned, most of the punishment was mental: now and then, the guards would carry every object from the house out into the courtyard and leave them there for him and his family to bring back in. The guards confiscated his phone and computer and bent the prongs of the television plug so that it was unusable. At one point, Chen managed to smuggle out a short video describing his conditions, but when that was discovered, the guards punished him by rolling him in a blanket and beating him.

The tactic of isolation that worried Chen the most, however, was not about him; the guards barred his six-year-old daughter from going to school. And it was this, it seemed, that galvanized the tech-savvy citizens of Beijing, Shanghai, and other big cities. On October 23, 2011, thirty of them tried to visit Chen, but guards took their cell phones and cameras, pelted them with stones, and forced them out of town. This drama attracted interest from people such as He Peirong, an English teacher in Nanjing, who had never heard of Chen before a friend mentioned the case that fall. "The first thing I did was check the facts of what Chen Guangcheng was saying," she told me. The more she learned about the conditions of his confinement, the more they offended her. "Even if he once broke the law in the course of his work on human rights, I think he already paid his price. The way he was treated after his release shocked me. I never imagined brutality like that was happening in China now. My friends—even some who were police officers—didn't believe what I described to them."

He Peirong posted a photograph of herself in sunglasses, joining the online campaign. She began to blog about Chen's case, and about her intention to visit him on his birthday, November 5. The police, it seemed, were reading; five days before that date arrived, police started following her, driving her to work and advising her not to try to make the trip to the village. At one point, she said, they offered to pay for her to go on vacation if it would keep her away. When she refused, they put her under house arrest until the birthday passed. She was undeterred; along with other Chen supporters, she distributed four thousand bumper stickers bearing Chen's face in the style and colors of an advertisement for KFC, beneath the words "Free CGC." (If police asked, they said it was an ad for free chicken.) The mode of protest was revealing about those who joined it. "Compared to previous human rights activities in China, it was a different kind of support," He Peirong told me. "I think the Chen Guangcheng bumper sticker movement represented the view of the middle class because the only people who could take part were people with cars."

The campaign made international news, and after two weeks, the local government made a concession; it allowed Chen's daughter to go to school. But Chen was still locked in his house. The case was an embarrassment to the government, but the more that Chen and his supporters complained, the more reluctant the government became to show that it was responding to pressure. When a foreign reporter asked about Chen's conditions, during a press conference at the National People's Congress, the question was stricken from the transcript.

# FIFTEEN

# SANDSTORM

Spring is sandstorm season in Beijing. The wind sweeps down from the Mongol Steppe, drawing up loose grains as it travels. Before a storm hits the capital, you can see it coming: the sky turns a pale, otherworldly yellow, and then sand begins to accumulate at the base of the window-panes, like tiny embankments of snow. By March 2011 the *hutong* house where I lived with Sarabeth Berman (then my fiancée, later my wife) was desiccated after the winter. My neighbors were making their first trips of the season to the flower markets on the edge of the capital, to bring home some color. But recently the flower sellers of Beijing had received an unusual order: do not sell jasmine. It was a Chinese favorite, perfect for tea, with small white petals that classical poets associated with inno-cence. But this year, the police told the vendors, no matter what price you are offered, *no jasmine.* And if anyone comes around asking to buy it, jot down the license plate number and call it in.

In Chinese politics, the flower had acquired the aroma of subversion. A few weeks earlier, on December 17, a twenty-six-year-old unemployed graduate in Tunisia named Mohammed Bouazizi was selling fruit with-out a permit when a police officer confiscated his produce and slapped him for complaining. Bouazizi was the sole earner in an extended family of eleven. He visited the provincial headquarters for help, but nobody would see him. Desperate and humiliated, he doused himself in paint thinner and lit a match.

By the time he died, weeks later, his story had sparked demonstra-tions against the authoritarian rule of President Zine El Abidine Ben Ali. Police moved in, cell phone footage spread on YouTube and Facebook, and the protests grew to encompass complaints about corruption, unemployment, inflation, and limits on political freedom. Within a month, the movement had driven the Tunisian president from office and inspired protests across the Arab world. Abroad, people called it the Jasmine Revolution, after Tunisia's national flower, but inside Tunisia, people called it the Dignity Revolution. By any name, the protest drew immediate attention in China. When president Hosni Mubarak fell in Cairo, Ai Weiwei tweeted, "Today, we are all Egyptians."

Chinese leaders projected nonchalance. Zhao Qizheng, the former head of the government's information office, said, "The idea that a Jasmine revolution could happen in China is extremely preposterous and unrealistic." The *Beijing Daily* declared, "Everyone knows that stability is a blessing and chaos is a calamity." In one story, the *China Daily* mentioned the importance of "stability" seven times. But privately, the Party had a different reaction. My phone buzzed. It was a leak from the Department, a message to editors across the country:

> Draw no comparisons between political systems in the Middle East and the system in our country. When the names of leaders in Egypt, Tunisia, Libya, and elsewhere appear in our media, the names of Chinese leaders must never appear nearby.

The Arab Spring unnerved Chinese leaders more than any event in years. "A single spark," Mao observed, "can start a prairie fire." It was easy to overstate the power of technology, but it had clearly aided the opponents of authoritarianism. The other reason the Party was displeased was philosophical: it often argued that men and women in the developing world were more interested in building wealth and maintaining stability than in pursuing "Western notions" of democracy and human rights. This argument became more difficult to believe now that men and women in the Arab world were marching for democracy and human rights.

Some of the potentates, such as the king of Jordan, responded to the Arab Spring by promising to loosen up, in the hope of averting an explosion. But China's leaders chose the opposite course. The lesson they took from Mubarak's fall was the same they had taken from the collapse of the Soviet Union: protests that go unchecked lead to open revolt. The

Politburo sent out Wu Bangguo, one of its most orthodox conservatives, to dust off his theory of the "Five Nos": China would have no opposition parties, no alternative principles, no separation of powers, no federal system, and no full-scale privatization. "If we waver," he told a meeting of three thousand legislators in Beijing, "the state could sink into the abyss."

On Saturday, February 19, an anonymous notice appeared on an overseas Chinese website calling for people to assemble at 2:00 p.m. the next day, in thirteen Chinese cities, and "stroll silently holding a jasmine flower." The government mobilized tens of thousands of police and state security agents to stand by in case of trouble. The military newspaper, the *People's Liberation Army Daily*, warned of a "smokeless war" intent on "Westernizing and dismembering the country."

At the appointed hour of the protests, authorities in Beijing shut down text messaging across much of the city. Most of the people who showed up were foreign journalists. In front of a McDonald's in the shopping district of Wangfujing, a Chinese crowd of about two hundred formed, but it was impossible to know who was protesting, who were police, and who was gawking. One of the people there, to my surprise, was the young nationalist from Shanghai, Tang Jie. "I just wanted to go have a look, and I thought there might be some drama," he told me. "I didn't think anyone would go except reporters. We took pictures of journalists." He laughed. "There was no revolution," he said.

In the three years that I'd known him, Tang had finished his doctorate in philosophy and turned his patriotism into a profession: when his video became a sensation online, it linked him to others with similar ideas, such as Rao Jin, the creator of Anti-CNN.com, a site that criticized Western reporting of China. Rao Jin was forming a production company, and Tang moved to Beijing to join it. They called the company April Media (m4, for short), after the month in which they had risen up to defend the Olympic torch. They translated articles between Chinese and English, churned out videos and lectures, and hoped, as they put it, to "give a true and more objective picture of the world."

A few hours after the attempted protest, Tang Jie heard from a pair of fellow activists who had returned from McDonald's with video of an unusual scene: the U.S. ambassador to Beijing, Jon Huntsman, Jr., had made a brief appearance among the crowds. The ambassador insisted it was a coincidence—he said he was out for a stroll after lunch—but to Chinese nationalists, it was proof that the United States was seeking to foment a "Chinese Jasmine Revolution." In the video, a man in the crowd asks Huntsman, "You want to see China in chaos, don't you?" The ambassador said no, and made a hasty exit, but Tang Jie saw the makings of a hit. He got to work, adding subtitles and overlaying his argument in exploding red bubbles: "Sure, China has many kinds of problems!" he wrote. "But we don't want to be another Iraq! We don't want to be another Tunisia! We don't want to be another Egypt! If the nation descends into chaos, will America and the so-called 'reformers' feed our 1.3 billion people? Don't fucking mess this up!"

By the time he was done, it was three o'clock in the morning, and before he posted the video to the public, he hesitated; his site had been warned by authorities not to comment on the protests or the unrest in the Middle East. "But then I figured I really have to post it," he told me. "Any media organization that had this kind of material on its hands would know it was news." He hit the button, and by day's end, it was a diplomatic incident. The Ministry of Foreign Affairs complained about Huntsman's visit, and Tang was fielding calls from reporters from as far away as Salt Lake City, Huntsman's hometown.

The following week, I visited Tang Jie at his new office in Beijing, in an office complex not far from the Olympic stadium. He looked energized. He had been sleeping on a broken red sofa in the office while he looked for a place to live in Beijing, but the new venture thrilled him. The office had the Ikea aesthetic that I saw at many Chinese start-ups, and there were posters on the walls with inspirational photos: flags in the wind, wheat in fields. The company slogan was "Our Stage. Our Hope. Our Story. Our Faith."

We went downstairs to a cafeteria. Over lunch, I mentioned that I'd gotten to know Han Han, the writer and entrepreneur who was about the same age as Tang. Tang Jie snorted. "He's too simple, sometimes naïve," he said. "He points out some of China's problems, but they are all very shallow observations. He only says things like 'The government is bad.'" I said that Tang's site talked about many of the same issues—corruption, pollution, the need for political reform—but Tang saw it differently. "The difference between us and Han Han is that we're trying to be constructive.

For example, he talks about corruption and high housing prices, and that gets people all riled up. What we're saying is, let's do things step by step. There has to be a process."


Despite the failure of the jasmine protests, organizers called for another attempt the following weekend. A notice on overseas Chinese sites said, "The rights of the Chinese people are something the Chinese people themselves must fight for." It called on the Party to create an independent judiciary, to fight income inequality and corruption, and if it could not, to "exit the stage of history." In their choice of slogans, the organizers combined the practical ("We want to work, we want housing!") with the abstract ("We want fairness, we want justice!").

Just as Chinese students abroad had played a vital role in the nationalist uprising a few years earlier, now another side of that cohort was speaking up. Students in Seoul, Paris, Boston, and elsewhere, writing in the name of what they called the Jasmine Movement, set up a blog and a Facebook page, Google groups, and a Twitter feed. They appealed to "laid-off workers and victims of forced evictions to participate in demonstrations, shout slogans, and seek freedom, democracy, and political reform, to end 'one-party rule.'"

On the ground, however, there was little sign that the activism went beyond the Web. When it was time for the next scheduled protest, the authorities took no chances. They sent hundreds of police officers in plainclothes and in uniform; a SWAT team in body armor were equipped with automatic rifles and attack dogs. Police phoned foreign journalists in advance, warning them to stay away, but scores showed up anyway, and police forcibly dispersed them. Stephen Engle, a reporter for Bloomberg Television, was pinned to the ground, dragged by a leg, and kicked and beaten. A cameraman was set upon by officers and punched and kicked in the face. Later, when reporters asked the Foreign Ministry to investigate, a spokeswoman dispensed with the usual diplomatic assurances and said, bluntly, if journalists seek "to create trouble for China," then "no law can protect them." The protests were over. In a final effort, organizers called on people to go to McDonald's at a designated hour and simply order Set Meal No. 3.

Before long, the retribution began. People who had spoken up in favor of the protests began to vanish, at least temporarily. Some answered their doorbells and disappeared; others were on the sidewalk when they were swept into waiting cars. On the morning of Sunday, April 3, 2011, the artist Ai Weiwei was at the Beijing Capital International Airport, preparing to board a flight to Hong Kong, when he was ushered out of line and into an office. At his studio across town, an assistant peered out of the turquoise gate and found a crowd of police. Officers had also arrived at the home of Ai's son, who lived with his mother not far from the studio. And elsewhere in Beijing, a reporter named Wen Tao, who often chronicled Ai's activities, was wrestled into a black sedan. Three more of Ai's associates were detained in similar scenes.

At the studio, police carried away dozens of computers and hard drives. They took eight assistants into custody, and kept Ai's wife, Lu Qing, at the studio for questioning. As night fell on Beijing, police released the studio assistants, but there was no word on Ai Weiwei or the others. As the news of their arrests began to spread, Internet censors updated the blacklist to include:

Ai Weiwei
Weiwei
Ai Wei
Ai the Fatty

Some more elliptical references escaped the censors and spread rapidly, including one that reimagined the words of theologian Martin Niemöller:

> When a fat man lost his freedom, you said, "It has nothing to do with me, because I am skinny." When a bearded man lost his freedom, you said, "It has nothing to do with me, because I am not bearded." When a man who sold sunflower seeds lost his freedom, you said, "It has nothing to do with me, because I don't sell sunflower seeds." But when they come for the skinny, beardless ones who never sold sunflower seeds, there will be nobody left to speak up for you.

By the middle of April, human rights groups were calling it the largest crackdown on expression since Tiananmen Square two decades earlier. Two hundred people had been questioned or placed under house arrest; another thirty-five were presumed to be in detention. The list included not only old-line dissidents, but also social media celebrities and journalists. When some were released, they described a range of experiences. A lawyer named Jin Guanghong said he was tied to a bed in a psychiatric facility, beaten, and given injections that he could not identify. Some said police encouraged them to remember the fate of Gao Zhisheng, the lawyer who had written of his torture. In the case of activist Li Tiantian, interrogators required her to narrate the details of her sexual history to a roomful of guards. She was also warned never to say how she had been treated. But she published an account online anyway. "Deep down I was so ashamed," she wrote, "as if I was being beaten but remained smiling, saying that I felt no pain. Deprived of choices. Helpless."

As the crackdown deepened, Secretary of State Hillary Clinton accused Chinese leaders of "trying to stop history, which is a fool's errand." The *People's Daily* replied by citing a Pew Research Center poll of twenty countries in which Chinese people expressed the highest level of satisfaction—87 percent. In the midst of this, it was easy to overlook a routine budget report that revealed a surprising milestone: for the first time in history, the People's Republic was spending more on domestic security than on foreign defense; it was devoting more money to policing and surveilling its own people than it was on defending against threats from abroad. But the *People's Daily* said the protests had failed because a "formerly backward and impoverished nation has been turned into the second biggest economy . . . and the whole world holds it in high esteem."


Days passed with no word on Ai's whereabouts. Eventually his mother and older sister did what occurred to them: they posted a handwritten flyer around the neighborhood, buried amid FOR RENT signs and LOST DOG posters. Across the top, they wrote MISSING PERSON:

AI WEIWEI, MALE, 53 YEARS OLD.
On April 3, 2011 around 8:30 a.m., at Beijing Capital International Airport, before boarding a flight to Hong Kong, he was taken away

by two men. More than fifty hours have passed, and his whereabouts remain unknown.

Later that afternoon, the Foreign Ministry announced that Ai was
under investigation for "economic crimes," which, it added, had "nothing
to do with human rights or freedom of expression." *Global Times*, the
Party tabloid, denounced Ai as "a maverick of Chinese society" who
must "pay a price" for his defiance. "China as a whole is progressing and
no one has power to make a nation try to adapt to his personal likes and
dislikes."

From the airport, the artist had been loaded into the back of a white van,
flanked by officers who held his arms. A black hood had been dropped
over his head. When the van rolled to a stop, Ai was brought indoors and
placed in a chair. The hood was pulled away. A well-muscled man with
short hair was standing over him. Ai braced for a beating. Instead, the
guards emptied his pockets, removed his belt, and handcuffed his right
hand to the arm of the chair. He waited in the chair for eight hours.
Then, two interrogators arrived. One opened a laptop. The other lit a
cigarette. The smoker was a middle-aged man in a pin-striped sport coat
with elbow patches. Ai would come to know him as Mr. Li. Over the
next two hours, Mr. Li asked Ai Weiwei about his contacts overseas, the
sources of his income, and the political messages contained in his artwork. He reviewed years' worth of Ai's blog posts and tweets, line by line.
He asked him if the artist knew who was behind the calls for a Jasmine
Revolution. Ai asked to see a lawyer. "The law is not going to help you,"
he was told. "Just obey the orders, and you can make it easier."

For all his anxiety, Ai was also fascinated. After trying to describe the
Party from so many different angles, he was now face-to-face with it. His
questioners seemed to be struggling to understand the world Ai Weiwei
inhabited: Mr. Li quizzed him about the mechanics of arranging a nude
portrait. When they asked him about his finances, the artist said a single
sculpture could sell for eighty thousand dollars, and the interrogator did
not initially believe him.

Mr. Li told him that this arrest had been a year in the making. "We
had a very difficult decision: whether to arrest you or not. But we decided

we had to." He went on, "You made the Chinese government embarrassed, which is against national interests," he told him, adding, "You
became a part of the foreign strategy of 'peaceful evolution.'" Ultimately,
Li said, the state had to "smash you." Li said the artist would likely be
charged with "incitement to subvert state power," the same charge that
had been brought against the writer Liu Xiaobo.

In the days that followed, Ai was never alone. He was transferred to a
military compound and placed in a narrow windowless room with padded walls, like a mental hospital. Two young guards in olive-green uniforms were never more than three feet from him; at times, they sat four
inches from his face. They accompanied him to the toilet and the
shower. When he paced in his cell, they paced with him. They ordered
him to sleep with his hands in full view and to ask permission to touch
his own face. Ai often wondered about these men around him. Did they
picture themselves as defenders of China's quest for fortune? Did they see
themselves as thwarting the selfish, ruinous acts of individuals like him?
Or did they see themselves in a darker light, as the muscles of a body
racked by fears of mortality?

The interrogation continued, but Ai was never physically abused.
Fear gave away to exhaustion. His weight dropped. He took medicine for
diabetes, high blood pressure, a heart condition, and the head injury. A
doctor checked him constantly—sometimes every three hours. He began to lose track of time. He would forget why he was there. He felt as if
he were stumbling around alone, "in a sandstorm," as he put it.

After six weeks, Ai was abruptly given a clean white shirt and ordered
to take a shower. He was about to see his wife. Rumors were circulating
that Ai was being tortured, and the government was under pressure to
refute them. The stagecraft enraged him. He said, "I don't want to see
her, because you told me I have no chance to see a lawyer, and what can
I tell her about what happened this past month and a half?" The offer
was not negotiable. He was told what he could say: He was being investigated for "economic crimes," and he was in good health. He was to say
nothing more.


Ai Weiwei's arrest attracted a level of international notoriety that his art
never had. Overnight he became one of the world's most famous dissi-

dents. Supporters demonstrated outside Chinese embassies. His portrait—the beard and hooded eyes and ham hock cheeks—was projected onto building facades and silkscreened onto T-shirts for sale in Europe and America. The British sculptor Anish Kapoor called for a worldwide protest and dedicated his latest work to Ai—a colossal purple installation inflated inside the Grand Palais in Paris and named *Leviathan*. In *The New York Times*, Salman Rushdie invoked the great battles between art and tyranny—Augustus and Ovid, Stalin and Mandelstam—and wrote, "Today the government of China has become the world's greatest threat to freedom of speech, and so we need Ai Weiwei."

Inside China, the reactions were more complicated. At dinner a few days after Ai disappeared, an American dealer of Chinese art, who had deep roots in the capital, scolded me for writing about the arrest. "Now is the time to back off," she said. She cited a Chinese legal provision that allowed police to hold a suspect for thirty days without charges, and she predicted that Ai would be released according to the letter of the law. "Stop embarrassing China," she said. "Allow the thirty-day process to run its course." Our hostess, a longtime foreign resident who had less confidence in Chinese courts, told the art dealer, "I've spent twenty years being an apologist for China, but there is no way to defend this. You're just fucking wrong." Dinner did not last long.

The truth was that I struggled with the question of how much to write about Ai Weiwei—or, for that matter, the blind lawyer Chen Guangcheng or the Nobel laureate Liu Xiaobo. How much did their ordeals really tell us about China? If the average news consumer in the West read (or watched or heard) no more than one China story a week, should it be about people with dramatic lives or typical lives? The hardest part about writing from China was not navigating the authoritarian bureaucracy or the occasional stint in a police station. It was the problem of proportions: How much of the drama was light and how much was dark? How much was about opportunity and how much was about repression? From far away it was difficult for outsiders to judge, but I found that up close it wasn't much easier, because it depended on where you were looking.

The stereotype of Western journalists was that we paid too much attention to dissidents. It was, we were told, because we sympathized with their hopes for liberal democracy, because they spoke English and knew how to give a sound-bite. Indeed, the inherent drama of an individual standing up to the state was obviously seductive, and it helped explain why the most famous image from China in the past thirty years was not of its economic rise but of the man standing in front of the tank near Tiananmen Square. Whenever I wrote about human rights abuses, I knew to expect that often the most critical reactions came from other expatriates in China. I understood that: foreigners with no reason to probe could spend years in China without ever interviewing someone who had been tortured or locked up without trial, and to them, my focus was misplaced. Dissidents who were famous in New York or Paris were unknown to ordinary Chinese citizens, which suggested that the discussion of democracy and rights was at odds with the everyday concerns of ordinary people.

But those arguments wore thin with me. Popularity always struck me as an odd way to measure the importance of an idea in a country that censored ideas. (A team of Harvard researchers later discovered that news of Ai's arrest was one of the most heavily censored items of the year, which undermined the notion that people in China paid no attention to his arrest.) *Global Times* argued that Ai's worldview was not the "mainstream perception among Chinese society." And in a sense, the paper was right: Ai Weiwei's lifestyle was emphatically outside the mainstream. But when it came to his ideas, this was less clear than it used to be: the collapse of the schools in the earthquake had captivated the attention of ordinary Chinese, not just the urban elite, and in seeking to dignify the deaths of some of China's most vulnerable people, Ai Weiwei was enacting an idea that many others supported. Even if it was a minority, ignoring the impact of a small group of impassioned people struck me as a misreading of Chinese history, in which small groups had often exerted large forces.

Understanding why Ai Weiwei was arrested—or why Gao Zhisheng was abused, or why Liu Xiaobo was in prison—was vital to understanding China. The degree to which it could accept a figure such as Ai Weiwei was a measure of how far China had or had not moved toward a modern, open society.

As one month of detention stretched into two, the arrest of Ai Weiwei proved divisive in China's creative circles: Many were alarmed by his arrest because it indicated that nobody was too famous or well connected to be insulated. But many others had resented his criticisms of fellow intellectuals, and regarded his approach as vain and confrontational. In Beijing, people rolled their eyes at the international outcry. It became fashionable to whisper that Ai Weiwei and Liu Xiaobo were messianic.

Even among those who were aghast, the arrest was clarifying; it allowed them to stake out the limits of what they imagined they could accomplish. When I saw the writer Han Han, he told me, "For Ai Weiwei's disappearance, we can do nothing." We were in a strange venue for a political conversation: an auto racetrack in the suburbs of Shanghai. Gangly fashion models loped by dressed in fractional vinyl outfits: Volkswagen miniskirts, Kia crop tops. Han Han was wearing a silvery racing suit that advertised Volkswagen across his midsection, Red Bull along his cuffs, and Homark Aluminum Alloy Wheels on his right biceps. We were in the team tent, where the air carried the scent of oil and rubber and the sound of cars buzzing through turns like angry bees. Race car drivers strutted in and out, flicking open the tent flaps like the sultans in old movies.

In recent years, Han and Ai Weiwei had maintained a sympathetic but distant relationship. The artist had praised Han's work, and the writer, in his magazine, had published the radiological scan of Ai Weiwei's skull after his brain injury. But now Han chose his words carefully: "If the government thinks Ai is a big problem, it should say so; they have the power if they want to arrest him. It's okay if everybody knows what's happening. The reason they gave was 'economic crimes.' Ai is an artist and he is famous, so if you want to say he committed 'economic crimes,' you need to show us the evidence." But Han Han would not be blogging about it. That was "useless," he told me. "The system can automatically block the name."

As we spoke, I was reminded how easy it was to overlook the distinctions between Chinese individuals who appeared, at first glance, to share ideas. A few days earlier, the London-based writer Ma Jian had speculated in an op-ed piece printed outside China that, with Ai Weiwei under arrest, the next targets would be Han Han and three other prominent critics. "The regime will not stop the persecution until the only voices to be heard are its own 'official' artists," Ma wrote. But lumping Han Han and Ai Weiwei together as liberals seeking political reform obscured deep differences. Han told me, "Ai's criticism is more direct, and he is more persistent on a single issue. For me, I criticize one thing, make them feel terrible, and if they ask me to stop talking about it, then I'll criticize something else. We have a hundred things to talk about."

Divining how far any individual could go in Chinese creative life was akin to carving a line in the sand at low tide in the dark; the political terrain shifted constantly. Ground that was solid one minute could be swamped the next. Han Han maintained a fitful détente with the government, but he permitted few illusions about his willingness to stay on the safe side of lines he could see. He had never made a move to take his activism from the Web to the street, and he opposed the call for multiparty elections. "The Party will win anyway, because they are rich and they can bribe people," he told me. "Let culture be more vibrant and the media be more open." Outsiders often mistook his demand for openness with the outright demand for democracy, but the difference was essential.


On June 22, his eighty-first day in custody, Ai Weiwei was informed that he was going to prison for ten years—or he could be released that afternoon, if he agreed to accept a charge of "tax evasion." He was given a statement to sign. He asked for a lawyer, but the request was denied. "If you don't sign," one of the interrogators told him, "we can never let you go, because we can't finish our job." That moment was a revelation. "You're not really fighting a system," he realized. "You're really dealing with these two persons, very low-ranking, who don't believe you are a criminal but just can't finish their job. And they are very frustrated, too."

The most important term of his release was that he could not talk to foreigners or write on the Web for a year. He signed the statement. Then he was driven to a police station, where his wife was waiting for him. His case would continue, but for now he was free to go. He was astonished. Why had he been released? He could only guess. Was it diplomatic pressure? Premier Wen Jiabao was preparing to visit Britain and Germany, where people were going to protest Ai's arrest, but the only official explanation came from the state news service, which reported that Ai Weiwei's company had evaded "a huge amount of taxes and intentionally destroyed accounting documents." Ai was released on bond, it said, "because of his good attitude in confessing his crimes as well as a chronic disease."

By the time he reached the studio, a crush of television cameras was waiting in the sweltering summer night. His skinny arms poked out of a worn blue T-shirt, and he clutched the waist of his trousers to hold them up. He had lost twenty-eight pounds, and the police still had his belt. Reporters closed in, and he pleaded for understanding. He was not allowed to talk. The mood in the air was strange; it was not clear if this was a victory or a defeat. Like Hu Shuli's departure from *Caijing*, Ai Weiwei's release thrust him into a costly kind of freedom. In the years since the Party had dedicated itself to a "harmonious society"—the vision of a nation without differences—I had watched as the voices within China grew more demanding, and the Party had risen to meet the challenge. The pursuit of truth, which had begun within the confines of institutions such as Hu Shuli's magazine, had expanded over the years to draw in individuals such as Ai Weiwei and Chen Guangcheng, who represented no institutions and were harder for the government to control. Then the pursuit had expanded further to encompass the opinions on the street, now amplified with the help of technology.

With so many voices clamoring at once, the Party's vision of a "central melody," an ideological consensus, was breaking down. Chinese people were turning to one another not only for information but for trust as well. One year after the arrival of the microblogging site Weibo, a study found that 70 percent of Chinese social media users relied on social media as their main source of news; in America, that number was 9 percent.

The Party's ultimate authority, of course, was physical: the ability to lock up its critics. Watching a humbled Ai Weiwei slip past the turquoise gate and into his house—to await the government's next move—I wondered if the Party had recovered the authority that it was losing over expression in China. Through sheer force, it seemed, the Party was setting the terms of expression again. It would take less than a month for me to realize how wrong I was.

# SIXTEEN

# LIGHTNING STORM

Beijing South Railway Station was shaped like a flying saucer—its silvery vaulted ceiling illuminated by skylights. It contained as much steel as the Empire State Building and could handle 240 million people a year, 30 percent more than New York's Penn Station, the busiest stop in America. When Beijing South opened, in 2008, it was the largest station in Asia; then Shanghai stole the crown. In recent years, some three hundred new stations were built or revitalized by China's Railway Ministry, which had nearly as many employees as the civilian workforce of the U.S. government.

On the morning of July 23, 2011, passengers hurried across the station at the final call to board bullet train D301, heading south on the world's largest, fastest, and newest high-speed railway, the Harmony Express. It was bound for Fuzhou, twelve hundred miles away. When passengers reached the platform, they encountered a vehicle that looked less like a train than a wingless jet: a tube of aluminum alloy a quarter of a mile from end to end, containing sixteen carriages and painted in high-gloss white with blue racing stripes. The guests were ushered aboard by female attendants in Pan Am–style pillbox hats and pencil skirts; each attendant, according to regulations, had to be at least five feet five inches tall, and was trained to smile with exactly eight teeth visible. A twenty-year-old college student named Zhu Ping took her seat, then texted her roommate that she was about to "fly" home on the rails. "Even my laptop is running faster than usual," she wrote.

For the Cao family, in the sleeper section, riding in style was a mark of achievement. The parents had immigrated to Queens, New York, two decades earlier and worked their way up to stable jobs as custodians at LaGuardia Airport. They had put two sons through college, become American citizens, and now found themselves back in China on a tour, posing for pictures in matching hats, standing ramrod straight beneath Mao's portrait at Tiananmen Square. Their next stop would be a reunion with relatives in Fuzhou. This was the first vacation of their lives. Their son Henry, who ran a camera supply business in Colorado, was returning, for the first time, to a country he had been raised to remember as poor.

Until recently, China's trains had always been a symbol of backwardness. More than a century ago, when the Empress Dowager was given a miniature engine to bear her about the Imperial City, she found the "fire cart" so insulting to the natural order that she banished it and insisted that her carriage continue to be dragged by eunuchs. Chairman Mao laid tracks across the country, partly for military use, but travel for ordinary people remained a misery of delayed, overcrowded trains nicknamed for the soot-stained color of the carriages: "green skins" were the slowest, "red skins" scarcely better. Even after Japan pioneered high-speed trains, in the 1950s, and Europe followed suit, China lagged behind with what the state press bemoaned as two inches of track per person—"less than the length of a cigarette."

In 2003, China's minister of railways, Liu Zhijun, took charge of plans to build seventy-five hundred miles of high-speed railway—more than could be found in the rest of the world combined. For anyone with experience on Chinese trains, it was hard to picture. "Back in 1995, if you had told me where China would be today, I would have thought you were stark raving mad," Richard Di Bona, a British transportation consultant in Hong Kong, told me. With a total investment of more than $250 billion, the undertaking was to be the world's most expensive public works project since President Eisenhower's Interstate Highway System in the 1950s.

To complete the first route by 2008, Minister Liu, whose ambition and flamboyance earned him the nickname Great Leap Liu, drove his crews and engineers to work in shifts around the clock, laying track, revising blueprints, and boring tunnels. "To achieve a great leap," he liked to say, "a generation must be sacrificed." (Some colleagues called him Lunatic Liu.) The state news service lionized an engineer named Xin Li because he remained at his computer so long that he went partly blind in his left eye. ("I will keep working even without one eye," he told a reporter.) When the first high-speed line debuted with a test run in June 2008, it was 75 percent over budget and relied heavily on German designs, but nobody dwelled on that during the ceremony. When another line made its maiden run, Liu took a seat beside the conductor and said, "If anyone is going to die, I will be the first."

That autumn, to help ward off the global recession, Chinese leaders more than doubled spending on high-speed rail and upped the target to ten thousand miles of track by 2020, the equivalent of building America's first transcontinental route five times over. China prepared to export its railway technology to Iran, Venezuela, and Turkey. It charted a freight line through the mountains of Colombia that would challenge the Panama Canal, and it signed on to build the "pilgrim express," carrying the faithful between Medina and Mecca. In January 2011, President Obama cited China's railway boom in his State of the Union address as evidence that "our infrastructure used to be the best, but our lead has slipped." The next month, the governor of Florida, Rick Scott, blocked construction of America's first high-speed train by rejecting federal funds. Amtrak had unveiled a plan to reach speeds comparable to China's by 2040.

From Beijing, train D301 sped south and east across emerald-green paddies toward the coast. To Henry Cao, who was seated beside a window in the last compartment of the second car, the train seemed to float, describing long elegant turns and shuddering now and then with the *whump* of a train going in the opposite direction. As the sun set, a summer storm was gathering, and Henry watched lightning flicker across the clouds. He stretched out on the fold-down bed in his carriage. At his feet, his mother sat upright. She had short wavy hair and wore a blue-and-white striped shirt. She'd lived nearly half her life in America, but she retained the habits of a Chinese traveler, and she carried more than ten thousand dollars in cash, as well as gifts of jade jewelry, in a fanny pack. Her husband sat across from her, with his iPhone. He captured a wobbly snapshot of the digital speedometer at the end of the carriage; it showed the kilometer equivalent of 188 miles per hour.

At 7:30 p.m., on the outskirts of the city of Wenzhou, lightning struck a heavy metal box beside the tracks. The box, the size of a washer-dryer, was part of a signal system that lets drivers and dispatchers know where trains are. Because tunnels block a radar signal, trains rely largely on hardwired equipment such as the box beside the track, which helps drivers and dispatchers talk to each other and controls a traffic signal, giving the drivers basic commands to stop and go. When lightning struck the box, it blew a fuse, which caused two catastrophic problems: it cut off communication and froze the signal on the color green.

At a nearby station, a technician picked up garbled signals from the tracks. He ordered the repairmen into the storm to investigate and reported the problem to a dispatcher in Shanghai named Zhang Hua. The train carrying the Cao family was still miles away, but another train, D3115, also bound for Fuzhou, with 1,072 people aboard, was ahead of D301. Zhang called D3115 to warn the driver that, because of the faulty signal, his train might shut down automatically. In that case, he should override and run it at a cautious speed until he reached a normal section again. As predicted, the computer brought the train to a halt, but when the driver tried to get it moving it wouldn't start, despite repeated attempts. He called Shanghai six times in five minutes but couldn't get through. On his train, a passenger uploaded to the Web a picture of the carriage in darkness and asked, "What happened to this train after that crazy storm?? It's running slower than a snail now . . . Hope nothing is going to happen."

Zhang the dispatcher was juggling ten trains by now. Hearing nothing further from D3115, he may have figured that it had restarted and moved on. The train carrying the Cao family was already half an hour late, and at 8:24 p.m., Zhang cleared it to go ahead. Five minutes later, the driver of the first train finally succeeded in restarting his engine and began to inch forward. When his train reached a normal section of track, it suddenly appeared on screens across the system, as if from nowhere, and a dispatcher saw what was about to happen. The train behind it had a green light and was charging down the track. The dispatcher alerted the driver: "D301, be careful! There's a train in your zone. D3115 is ahead of you! Be careful, will you? The equipment—" The line cut off.

The driver of D301, Pan Yiheng, was a thirty-eight-year-old railway man with a broad nose and wide-set eyes. In the final seconds, Pan pulled a hand-operated emergency brake. His train was high atop a slender viaduct across a flat valley, and immediately ahead of him was train D3115, moving so slowly that it might as well have been a wall.

The collision impaled Pan on the brake handle, and it hurled Henry Cao into the air. His body tensed for impact. None came. Instead, he was falling—for how long he couldn't tell. "I heard my mother's voice shouting," he told me later. "And then everything went black." His carriage and two others peeled off the tracks, tumbling sixty-five feet to a field below. A fourth car, filled with passengers and spewing sparks, was left dangling vertically from the edge of the viaduct. Henry awoke in a hospital, where doctors removed his spleen and a kidney. He had shattered an ankle, broken his ribs, and suffered a brain injury. When he was alert enough to understand, he learned that his parents were dead. In the chaos of the rescue and recovery, his mother's ten thousand dollars had disappeared.

The Wenzhou crash killed 40 people and injured 192. For reasons both practical and symbolic, the government was desperate to get trains running again, and within twenty-four hours it declared the line back in business. The Central Propaganda Department ordered editors to give the crash as little attention as possible. "Do not question, do not elaborate," it warned. When newspapers came out the next morning, China's first high-speed train wreck was not on the front page.

But instead of moving on, the public wanted to know what had happened, and why. This was not a bus plunging off a road in a provincial outpost; it was dozens of men and women dying on one of the nation's proudest achievements—in a newly wired age, when passengers had cell phones, and witnesses and critics finally had the tools to humiliate the propagandists. It was only three years since the earthquake in Sichuan, which had had an incomparably larger death toll. Yet the train crash reverberated across China in new ways.

People demanded to know why a two-year-old survivor was found in the wreckage after rescuers had called off the search. A railway spokesman said it was "a miracle." But critics jeered, calling his explanation an "insult to the intelligence of the Chinese people." In the days after the crash, the subject of the collision generated ten million messages on

Weibo, from people across the country, with sentiments such as this: "When a country is so corrupt that one lightning strike can cause a train crash . . . none of us are exempt. China today is a train rushing through a lightning storm . . . We are all passengers."

At one point, the authorities dug a hole and buried part of the ruined train, saying they needed firm ground for recovery efforts. When reporters accused them of trying to thwart an investigation, a hapless spokesman replied, "Whether or not you believe it, I believe it," a phrase that took flight on the Internet as an emblem of the government's vanishing credibility. (The train was exhumed. The spokesman was relieved of his duties and was last seen working in Poland.)

Within days, the state-owned company that produced the signal box apologized for mistakes in its design. But to many in China the focus on a single broken part overlooked the likely role of a deeper problem underlying China's rise: pervasive corruption and a moral disregard that had already led to milk tainted by chemicals reaching the market, shoddy schools in the earthquake zone in Sichuan, and unstable bridges rushed into service to meet political targets. A host on state television, Qiu Qiming, became the unlikely voice of the moment when he broke away from his script to ask, on the air, "Can we drink a glass of milk that is safe? Can we stay in an apartment that will not fall apart? Can we travel roads in our cities that will not collapse?"

Prime Minister Wen Jiabao had no choice but to visit the crash site and vow to investigate. "If corruption was found behind this, we must handle it according to law, and we will not be lenient," he said. "Only in this way can we be fair to those who have died." When people asked why Wen had waited five days to visit the site, he replied that he had been so ill that he had spent the past eleven days in bed. (Online, people dug up headlines and photos from those days showing him greeting dignitaries and presiding at meetings.)

The public didn't forget Wen's pledge as the first deadline for the investigation came and went, and they continued to demand a fuller accounting. At last, in December, authorities released an unprecedented detailed report. It acknowledged "serious design flaws," a "neglect of safety management," and problems in bidding and testing. It also blamed fifty-four people in government and industry, beginning with Great Leap Liu. When I spoke to an engineer who worked on the railway's construction, he told me, "I can't pinpoint which step was neglected or what didn't get enough time, because the whole process was compressed, from beginning to end." He added, "There is an expression in Chinese: when you take too great a leap, you can tear your balls."

The railroad minister, Liu Zhijun, did not initially look like a candidate for a dramatic public disgrace. Liu was a farmer's son, small and thin, with bad eyesight and an overbite. He grew up in a village outside the city of Wuhan and left school as a teenager for a job walking the tracks with a hammer and a gauge. He had an innate sense of the path to power. Good penmanship was a rare skill in the provinces, and Liu perfected his hand, becoming a trusted letter writer for bosses with limited education. He married into a politically connected family and was a Party member by age twenty-one. He was a tireless promoter of the railways and of himself, and he ascended swiftly, heading provincial bureaus on his way to the seat of power in Beijing. By 2003, as railroad minister, he commanded a bureaucratic empire second in scale and independence only to the military, with its own police force, courts, and judges and with billions of dollars at his disposal. His ministry, a state within a state, was known in China as *tie laoda*—"Boss Rail."

Liu kept his hair in an untidy black comb-over and wore a style of square horn-rimmed spectacles so common among senior apparatchiks that they were known as "leader glasses." A colleague of Liu's, a railway staffer who worked closely with him, told me, "Ever since the revolution, most Chinese officials look alike. They have the same face, the same uniform, even the same personality. They work step-by-step, and they are content to sit back and wait for promotions. But Liu Zhijun was different." If it was possible to invest a railway job with glamour, he was determined to do so. He liked to convene meetings after midnight and make ostentatious displays of his work habits. Even as he approached the highest ranks of power, he never stopped flattering his superiors. When President Hu Jintao was returning by train to Beijing one summer, Liu hustled up the platform so frantically to greet him that he nearly ran out of his loafers. "I shouted to him, 'Minister Liu, your shoes! Don't fall!'" the staffer recalled. "But he couldn't be bothered. He just kept grinning and running."

Liu's success benefited his brother, Liu Zhixiang, who joined the ministry and soared up through the ranks. He was wisecracking and volatile. In January 2005 he was detained for questioning about embezzlement, bribe-taking, and intentional harm regarding his role in arranging the killing of a contractor who sought to expose him. By then, he was vice chief of the Wuhan Railway Bureau. (The victim was stabbed to death with a switchblade in front of his wife. According to an official legal journal, he had predicted in his will, "If I am killed, it will have been at the hand of corrupt official Liu Zhixiang.") The minister's brother was embezzling such a large share of the ticket sales that he accumulated the equivalent of fifty million dollars in cash, real estate, jewelry, and art. When investigators caught him, he was living among mountains of money so large and unruly that the bills had begun to molder. (Storing cash is one of the most vexing challenges confronting corrupt Chinese officials, because the largest bill in circulation is a hundred-yuan note, worth about fifteen dollars.) He was convicted and received a death sentence that was suspended and later reduced to sixteen years. But instead of serving his time in a facility for serious offenders, he was transferred to a hospital, where he reportedly continued to conduct railway business by phone.

Back in Beijing, Minister Liu surrounded himself with loyal associates. The *capo di tutti capi* was the chief deputy engineer Zhang Shuguang, who once arrived at a railway conference in a fur coat and a white scarf and liked to describe his approach to negotiations as a "clasped fist." For much of his career, he ran the passenger car division, which gave him control over colossal spending choices. "It was all up to a nod of his head," Zang Qiji, a retired member of the Academy of Railway Sciences, told me. Zhang knew little of science, but he aspired to credibility and attempted to secure membership in an élite academic society by having two professors write a book in his name. (He fell short of membership by a single vote.)

Liu bet everything on high-speed railways. To preempt inflation in the cost of land and labor and materials, he preached haste above all. "We must seize the opportunity, build more railways, and build them fast," he told a conference in 2009. Liu's ambitions and Chinese authoritarianism

were a volatile combination. The ministry was its own regulator, virtually unsupervised, and the minister and his aides had no tolerance for
dissenting voices. When professor Zhao Jian, of Beijing Jiaotong University, publicly objected to the pace of high-speed-rail construction, Liu
summoned him and advised him to keep quiet. Zhao refused to back
down, and the university president called him. "He told me not to continue to voice my opinions," Zhao told me. The professor resisted, but
his concerns were ignored—until the crash. "Then it was too late," he
said.

The obsession with speed was all-encompassing. The system was
growing so fast that almost everything a supplier produced found a
buyer, regardless of quality. According to investigators, the signal that
failed in the Wenzhou crash was developed over six months, beginning
in June 2007, by the state-owned China Railway Signal and Communication Corporation. The company had a staff of some thirteen hundred
engineers, but it was overwhelmed by demands on its time, and crash
investigators discovered that those in charge of the signal had performed
only a "lax" inspection, which "failed to discover grave flaws and major
hidden dangers." The office in charge was "chaotic," a place where "files
went missing." Nevertheless, the signal passed inspection in 2008 and
was installed across the country. When the industry gave out awards for
new technology that year, the signal took first prize. But an engineer inside the company subsequently told me that he was not surprised to discover that the job had been rushed.

There were other suspicious factors. In April 2010 the chairman of
Central Japan Railway, Yoshiyuki Kasai, said that China was building
trains that drew heavily on Japanese designs. When Kawasaki Heavy
Industries threatened to sue the Chinese for passing off its technology as
their own, the Railway Ministry in Beijing dismissed the complaint as
evidence of "a fragile state of mind and a lack of confidence." Kasai also
pointed out that China was operating the trains at speeds 25 percent
faster than those permitted in Japan. "Pushing it that close to the limit is
something we would absolutely never do," he told the London *Financial
Times*.

In the days before the crash, the rush to build the railways added a
final, lethal factor to the mix. In June the government had staged the
debut of the most prominent line yet, Beijing to Shanghai, to coincide

with the ninetieth anniversary of the Chinese Communist Party. A full year had been slashed from the construction schedule, and the first weeks of the run were marred by delays and power failures. According to a manager in the ministry, high-speed-rail staff were warned that further delays would affect the size of their bonuses. On the night of July 23, 2011, when trains began to stack up, dispatchers and maintenance staff raced to repair the faulty signal and ignored the simplest solution: stop the trains and repair the signal. Wang Mengshu, a scholar in the Chinese Academy of Engineering who was deputy chief of the committee investigating the crash, told me, "The maintenance people weren't familiar enough with their jobs, and they didn't want to stop the train. They didn't dare."

When the crash occurred, Great Leap Liu was no longer running the Railway Ministry. In August 2010 the National Audit Office had reviewed the books of a big state-owned company and came upon a sixteen-million-dollar "commission" to an intermediary in return for contracts on the high-speed rail. The intermediary turned out to be a representative of a woman named Ding Shumiao, who perhaps more than anyone embodied the runaway riches created by China's railway boom. Ding was an illiterate egg farmer in rural Shanxi—five feet ten, with broad shoulders and a foghorn of a voice. In the 1980s, after Deng Xiaoping launched the country toward the free market, she collected eggs from neighbors to sell on the sidewalk in the county seat. This was illegal without a permit. Her eggs were confiscated, and years later she still talked of her embarrassment. In time, she came to run a small, thriving restaurant, where she gave away food to powerful customers and exaggerated her own success. "If she has one yuan, she'll say she has ten," one of Ding's longtime colleagues told me. "It makes her look more influential, and bit by bit people began to think that they could benefit from their friendship with her."

Her restaurant became a favorite with coal bosses and officials. Soon she was involved in coal trucking. Then she was "flipping carriages," as it's known in the railway business: working her connections to get cheap access to coveted freight routes and, according to Wang, the investigator, reselling the rights "for ten times what she paid." She became friendly with Great Leap Liu around 2003, and with her ties to the railway business, she prospered. Her company, Broad Union, signed joint ventures and supplied the ministry with train wheels, sound barriers, and more. In two years, Broad Union's assets grew tenfold, to the equivalent of $680 million in 2010, according to the state news service.

Ding's given name, Shumiao, betrayed her rural roots, so she changed it to Yuxin, at the suggestion of her feng shui adviser. She was easy to lampoon—Daft Mrs. Ding, people called her—but she had a genius for cultivating business relationships. A longtime colleague told me, "When I tried to teach her how to analyze the market, how to run the company, she said, 'I don't need to understand this.'" The Chinese press chronicled her audacious social ascent. To gain foreign contacts, she backed a club "for international diplomats," which managed to attract a visit in 2010 by Britain's former prime minister Tony Blair. Her lavish receptions drew members of the Politburo. She joined the lower house of the provincial legislature and made so many charitable gifts that in 2010 she ranked No. 6 on the *Forbes* list of China's philanthropists.

Ding was detained in January 2011, and eventually indicted on charges of bribery and illegal business activities. She was convicted of paying fifteen million dollars in bribes to Liu and others to help twenty-three companies secure railway construction contracts worth thirty billion dollars. For her services, her haul was impressive: she received kickbacks from contractors totaling more than three hundred million dollars. Like many others, Ding had discovered what government auditors found out only later: China's most famous public works project was an ecosystem almost perfectly hospitable to corruption—opaque, unsupervised, and overflowing with cash. In some cases, the bidding on contracts was truncated from five days to thirteen hours. In others, the bids were mere theater, because construction had already begun. Cash was known to vanish: in one instance, seventy-eight million dollars that had been set aside to compensate people whose homes had been demolished to make way for railroad tracks disappeared. Middlemen expected cuts of between 1 and 6 percent. "If a project is four and a half billion, the middleman is taking home two hundred million," Wang said. "And of course nobody says a word."

One of the most common rackets was illegal subcontracting. A single contract could be divvied up and sold for kickbacks, then sold again and again, until it reached the bottom of a food chain of labor, where the workers were cheap and unskilled. Railway ministry jobs were bought and sold: $4,500 to be a train attendant, $15,000 to be a supervisor. In November 2011 a former cook with no engineering experience was found to be building a high-speed railway bridge using a crew of unskilled migrant laborers who substituted crushed stones for cement in the bridge's foundation. In railway circles, the practice of substituting cheap materials for real ones was common enough to rate its own expression: *touliang huanzhu*—"robbing the beams to put in the pillars."

With so many kickbacks changing hands, it wasn't surprising that parts of the railway went wildly over budget. A station in Guangzhou slated to be built for $316 million ended up costing seven times that. The ministry was so large that bureaucrats would create fictional departments and run up expenses for them. A five-minute promotional video that went largely unseen cost nearly $3 million. The video led investigators to the ministry's deputy propaganda chief, a woman whose home contained $1.5 million in cash and the deeds to nine houses.

Reporters who tried to expose the corruption in the railway world ran into dead ends. Two years before the crash, a journalist named Chen Jieren posted an article about problems in the ministry entitled, "Five Reasons That Liu Zhijun Should Take Blame and Resign," but the piece was deleted from every major Web portal. Chen was later told that Liu oversaw a slush fund used for buying the loyalty of editors at major media and websites. Other government agencies also had serious financial problems—out of fifty, auditors found problems with forty-nine—but the scale of cash available in the railway world was in a class by itself. Liao Ran, an Asia specialist at Transparency International, told the *International Herald Tribune* that China's high-speed railway was shaping up to be "the biggest single financial scandal not just in China, but perhaps in the world."


In February 2011, five months before the train crash, the Party finally moved on Liu Zhijun. According to Wang Mengshu, investigators concluded that Liu was preparing to use his illegal gains to bribe his way onto the Party Central Committee and, eventually, the Politburo. "He

told Ding Shumiao, 'Put together four hundred million for me. I'm going to need to spread some money around,'" Wang told me. Four hundred million yuan is about sixty-four million dollars. Liu managed to
assemble nearly thirteen million yuan before he was stopped, Wang said.
"The central government was worried that if he really succeeded in
giving out four hundred million in bribes he would essentially have
bought a government position. That's why he was arrested."

Liu was expelled from the Party the following May, for "severe violations of discipline" and "primary leadership responsibilities for the serious
corruption problem within the railway system." An account in the state
press alleged that Liu took a 4 percent kickback on railway deals; another
said he netted $152 million in bribes. He was the highest-ranking official
to be arrested for corruption in five years. But it was Liu's private life that
caught people by surprise. The ministry accused him of "sexual miscon-
duct," and the Hong Kong newspaper *Ming Pao* reported that he had
eighteen mistresses. His friend Ding was said to have helped him line
up actresses from a television show in which she invested. Chinese officials are routinely discovered indulging in multiple sins of the flesh,
prompting President Hu Jintao to give a speech a few years ago warning
comrades against the "many temptations of power, wealth, and beautiful
women." But the image of a gallivanting Great Leap Liu, and the sheer
logistics of keeping eighteen mistresses, made him into a punch line.
When I asked Liu's colleague if the mistress story was true, he replied,
"What is your definition of a mistress?"

By the time the libidinous Liu was deposed, at least eight other senior
officials had been removed and placed under investigation, including
Zhang, Liu's bombastic aide. Local media reported that Zhang, on an
annual salary of less than five thousand dollars, had acquired a luxury
home near Los Angeles, stirring speculation that he had been preparing
to join the growing exodus of officials who were taking their fortunes
abroad. In recent years, corrupt cadres who sent their families overseas
had become known in Chinese as "naked officials." In 2011 the central
bank posted to the Web an internal report estimating that, since 1990,
eighteen thousand corrupt officials had fled the country, having stolen
$120 billion—a sum large enough to buy Disney or Amazon. (The report
was promptly removed.)

In the months I spent talking to people about the rise and fall of Liu

Zhijun, his story seemed to confound both his enemies and his friends. His rivals acknowledged that, unlike many corrupt officials, Liu had actually achieved something in office: he had produced a railway system that, even with problems, was fundamentally changing the sense of distance and time for ordinary people across the country. On the other side, his defenders found themselves awkwardly saying that he was doing nothing that his peers were not. Liu's colleague, an affable former military man, told me that at a certain point corruption had become difficult for Liu to avoid: "Inside the system today, if you don't take bribes, you have to get out. There's no way you can stay. If three of us are in one department, and you are the only one who doesn't take a bribe, are the two of us ever going to feel safe?"

Not long after the crash, I met a subcontractor for the railway and I asked him if things had been cleaned up since Liu's downfall. He let out a humorless laugh. "They made a show of it, but it's still the same rules," he said. "They caught Ding Shumiao, but she's just one person. There are many, many Ding Shumiaos."


Several weeks after the Wenzhou crash, the Railway Ministry announced a series of steps in the name of safety: it recalled fifty-four bullet trains for tests; it halted construction of new lines; and it ordered trains to slow down from a top speed of 217 miles per hour to 186. But before long the railway boom resumed, and the first anniversary of the Wenzhou crash was tightly managed. The state press was ordered not to visit the scene, and survivors were warned to keep their mouths shut. When one of them, a man in his twenties named Deng Qian, tried to visit the site that day, he was tailed by police, who videotaped his movements. "Their message to me was clear: I am now their enemy, their threat," he told me. "I think they will keep an eye on us forever."

Henry Cao spent five months in a Chinese hospital recovering from broken bones, neurological damage, and the loss of his kidney and spleen. After returning to his family in Colorado, he had to close his camera supply business. He and his brother, Leo, flew to China to retrieve their parents' bodies. They asked to hold a memorial in their ancestral village in Fujian, but the government forbade it; the parents were buried in a cemetery on Long Island.

Liu Zhijun would eventually go on trial. The verdict was no mystery—98 percent of Chinese trials end in conviction—but a reliable predictor of Liu's fate was that the Party had already embarked on one of its most enduring rituals. Just as technicians once airbrushed political casualties out of the archives, censors had already taken to the Web to begin excising years' worth of glowing news reports and documentaries that hailed Liu's accomplishments, leaving behind only squibs about his arrest. Before long, Great Leap Liu had been expunged so thoroughly from the history of China's achievements that you might never have known he existed.

By that point, the Wenzhou collision had already come to symbolize the essential risks facing the Communist Party. The crash struck at the middle-class men and women who had accepted the grand bargain of modern Chinese politics in the era after socialism: allow the Party to reign unchallenged as long as it was reasonably competent. The crash violated the deal, and for many, it became what Hurricane Katrina was to Americans: the iconic failure of government performance. It was a merciless judgment. Gerald Ollivier, a senior infrastructure specialist at the World Bank in Beijing, pointed out that trains in China were still by far one of the safest means of transportation. "If you think about it, the China high-speed railway must be transporting at least four hundred million people per year," he said. "How many people have died on the China high-speed railway in the past four years? Forty people. This is the number of people who die in road accidents in China every five or six hours. So, in terms of safety, this is by far one of the safest ways of transportation. The accident this past year was certainly very tragic and should not have happened. But compared to the alternative of moving people by car, it is safer by a factor of at least a hundred."

And yet, in China, people were more inclined to quote a very different statistic: in forty-seven years of service, high-speed trains in Japan had recorded just one fatality, a passenger caught in a closing door. It was becoming clear that parts of the new China had been built too fast for their own good. Three years had been set aside for construction of one of the longest bridges in North China, but it was finished in eighteen months, and nine months later, in August 2012, it collapsed, killing three people and injuring five. Local officials blamed overloaded trucks, though it was the sixth bridge collapse in a single year.

People were no longer satisfied simply with the fortune delivered by China's rise. The fall of Great Leap Liu had dramatized a culture of entitlement run amok. For years, Liu had dedicated himself to enhancing his own prospects along with those of the nation. He had lost his sense of proportion, and the question was whether the government he served had, too.

# SEVENTEEN

# ALL THAT GLITTERS

The first thing that Hu Gang taught me about bribing a judge was the importance of food. "Everyone says no to the first invitation. After three or four invitations, any man agrees—and once you eat together, you're on the way to becoming family." For all the talk about corruption in China, the details about how it actually worked—the subtle mechanics, the rituals, the taboos—remained mysterious to me. Over the years, I had gathered snippets of understanding, from spending time in Macau or learning the story of Great Leap Liu or reading Hu Shuli's investigations, but those provided only fragments of a picture. When I met Hu Gang, he began to fill in the rest.

At first glance, Hu Gang was not an obvious tutor in the dark arts of success. By the time I met him, he was a novelist—a small, fastidious man of fifty, who fussed with worried pride over his daughter and heeded her reminders not to overdo it at lunch. But like many before him, when opportunity was everywhere, he had found it impossible to resist. In college Hu had studied philosophy, and after graduation he began a quiet career in the university's Human Resources Department. When China's economy took off, he found a job at an auction house, selling classical Chinese paintings and earning a commission on every piece. "I discovered that many of the paintings and scrolls that people sent us were bogus, which fascinated me," he told me one day over lunch. "I thought, well, I can still sell these things at a high price, even though, in my heart, I wasn't comfortable with it."

His discomfort did not last. He was so inundated by fake art that he eventually tried his own hand at it, and discovered, to his surprise, that he had a gift for approximating the vigorous brush strokes of a Qi Baishi and the realism of a Xu Beihong. He also expanded his auction business to handle foreclosures, in which a single signature from a judge bestowed the right to a hefty commission on the sale of buildings, land, and other assets. Everyone seemed to be in on the take, Hu said. "So, I began to think, if they can do it, why can't I?"

But as with so much in China, there was competition; many people were jockeying for the chance to bribe a few people with power, and Hu realized immediately that he had to go beyond gifts. He had to build personal connections, and in that regard, he turned out to be a natural; he bribed judges first with cigarettes, then banquets, then trips to massage parlors. Nobody taught him how to do it, but he was a meticulous man, and he developed certain rules to live by: never offer a bribe to a stranger; schedule cash gifts for the fall, when the tuition bills come around. Before long, he was juggling relationships with so many judges that he had to make three trips to a massage parlor in a single day. "Three times, one day," he said, fixing me with a look of alarm. "That's not pleasant. That's exhausting."

For centuries, every generation of Chinese leaders unveiled its own strategy to root out corruption. The fourteenth-century emperor Zhu Yuanzhang ordered thieving officials to be executed, skinned, and stuffed with straw so that their carcasses might be propped up like mannequins for visitors to behold. The effects did not last. High office remained such a reliable path to riches that when a courtier named Heshen was finally brought low in 1799, he was found to have amassed a fortune worth ten times the entire government's annual budget. In 1935 the author and translator Lin Yutang observed, "In China, though a man may be arrested for stealing a purse, he is not arrested for stealing the national treasury."

In the modern age, corruption and growth have flourished together. In the eighties, a carton of Chinese Double Happiness cigarettes and a couple of bottles of Red Star grain alcohol were enough to secure a job transfer or the ration coupon for a washing machine. But in 1992, when the government began to open up the distribution of land and factories for private ownership, the corruption boom was under way. In the first year, the average sum recovered in corruption cases more than tripled, to six thousand dollars. Double Happiness cigarettes eventually gave way to Hermès bags, sports cars, and tuition for children studying abroad. The larger the deal, the higher the cadre needed to approve it, and the bribes moved straight up the ranks. Officials and businessmen looked out for one another by organizing themselves into "protective umbrellas," a step in what Chinese scholars called the "Mafiazation" of the state.

If the effects were abstract at first, they soon became vivid. In case after case, the disasters that enraged the Chinese public were traced back to graft, fraud, embezzlement, and patronage: The schools that collapsed in the Sichuan earthquake had been compromised by kickbacks; the train that crashed in Wenzhou was managed by one of the country's most corrupt agencies. In the case of the tainted infant formula that killed children in 2008, dairy farmers and dealers first bribed state inspectors to ignore the presence of chemicals. Then, when children fell ill, the dairy company bribed news organizations to suppress the story.

With creativity, anything could become a bribe. Businessmen arranged poker games in which the officials were guaranteed to win. Alcohol was such a reliable choice that the state media conceded that sales of the country's most famous liquor, Kweichow Moutai, was "an index for China's corruption." It was selling so well in 2011 that the company paid the largest dividend in the history of China's stock markets. Demand was heavy enough that the company had to ration it to stores.

I once dropped by the home of Mao Yushi, a liberal economist who happened to live near the headquarters of China's powerful planning agency, the National Development and Reform Commission. He pointed out that the commission was surrounded by gift shops selling alcohol and porcelain. Citizens seeking help knew to stock up before going in for their meetings. "All these people from out of town enter the building carrying big bags and small bags, and they leave empty-handed," the economist observed. "When the cadres get off work, they leave the building carrying all the big bags and small bags, but they can't possibly consume everything, so they sell it back to the gift shops, who in turn sell them to yet more people on a mission to Beijing. That's what our street has become."

Public servants—officially earning twenty or thirty thousand dollars a year—became such frequent shoppers at Gucci and Louis Vuitton that high-end boutiques in Beijing ran out of stock whenever the National People's Congress was in session. (Politicians learned to call ahead to reserve their favorite items.) In some cases, a businessman would accompany an official through the aisles, but if that was too conspicuous, he could leave a credit card on file, to be charged as needed. Most of the time, it was hard to know who was paying whom, but occasionally a court case provided a peek at how the money was changing hands. When police in Macau arrested Ao Man Long, the region's secretary for transport and public works, he had a collection of what he called "friendship notebooks," which documented a hundred million U.S. dollars in kickbacks.

The second thing Hu Gang taught me about bribing a judge was that you'll get nothing in return for at least six months. "Friendship is paramount," he said. "A friendship so close that you have no secrets between you." As we talked, he was building a small mountain of pork in his bowl. "Only after you show loyalty can you show skill—that you are able to do what you say you can do, and that you will make it worth his while every time." He narrowed his eyes and chewed in silence for a moment while he thought it over. "With those steps," he said, "anybody can be pinned down, and the bond is unbreakable."

Hu Gang's strategy did not come cheap. In his first year of bribing judges, he spent a quarter of a million yuan on gifts and girls and meals. But after five years, it was paying off handsomely. He had one of the biggest auction houses in town and a modest nest egg of $1.5 million. He was in a rhythm. "I'd sleep until noon and then begin my rounds, which included taking care of everyone's mistresses," he said.

But even then he found something wanting. "If I made three million or five million one year, all I'm thinking about is how to make more the next year. If I'm number three in town, how do I get to be number one? It's like you're running, and once you're running, there is no stopping. You just run and run and run. You don't think about the philosophical implications. Psychologically, you are in a world of your own."

For outsiders, the scale of political corruption in China was often difficult to comprehend, in part because most were insulated from it. Visitors to China, compared to other developing countries, were not hit up for small bribes by customs officers or street cops; unless foreigners used

Chinese schools or public hospitals, they didn't feel the creep of bribery into virtually every corner of Chinese society. On paper, Chinese public education was free and guaranteed, but parents knew to pay "sponsorship fees" to gain entry to top schools; in Beijing, the fees reached sixteen thousand dollars—more than double the average annual salary. Nationwide, 46 percent of parents said in a survey that strong "social connections" or fees were the only way to get their children a good education. By 2011, according to a report by the Chinese Academy of Social Sciences, authorities were opening corruption cases at the rate of one a day for department-level officials, the equivalent of a city mayor.

Paying for power was so common that in 2012 the *Modern Chinese Dictionary*, the national authority on language, was compelled to add the word *maiguan*—"to buy a government promotion." In some cases, the options read like a restaurant menu. In a small town in Inner Mongolia, the post of chief planner was sold for $103,000. The municipal party secretary was on the block for $101,000. It followed a certain logic: in weak democracies, people paid their way into office by buying votes; in a state where there were no votes to buy, you paid the people who doled out the jobs. Even the military was riddled with patronage; commanders received a string of payments from a pyramid of loyal officers beneath them. A one-star general could reportedly expect to receive ten million dollars in gifts and business deals; a four-star commander stood to earn at least fifty million.

Every country has corruption, but China's was approaching a level of its own. For those at the top, the scale of temptation had reached a level unlike anything ever encountered in the West. It was not always easy to say which Bare-Handed Fortunes were legitimate and which were not, but political office was a reliable pathway to wealth on a scale of its own. By 2012 the richest seventy members of China's national legislature had a net worth of almost ninety billion dollars—more than ten times the combined net worth of the entire U.S. Congress.


The combination of so much money and so little transparency was interfering with the Party's most solemn rituals. The year 2012 was to be set aside for tidy political theater—a handoff of power from one generation of senior apparatchiks to another. The plans were precise: on a single day that autumn, the incoming cast would stride across a stage at the Great Hall of the People, politely clapping for one another, in front of a sixty-foot painting of the Great Wall. But barely one month into the year, the plans began to unravel.

Wang Lijun was a former chief of police in the western city of Chongqing; he had been hailed in the Party press for his toughness and innovation, including perfecting the transplanting of organs from executed prisoners. But on February 6 he fled by car to the U.S. consulate in Chengdu and sought protection from the Americans. He told them he had uncovered a murder, and he put the blame on the family of his boss, Bo Xilai, the Party secretary of Chongqing, who was, until that instant, a leading contender to mount the stage that fall at the Great Hall. The victim was a local British businessman named Neil Heywood, a forty-one-year-old man of pale linen suits and a guarded manner, a "character in a Graham Greene novel—always immaculate, very noble, very erudite," as a friend of Heywood's put it to the British press. Heywood had worked part time for a corporate intelligence firm founded by former MI6 officers, and he drove a Jaguar around Beijing with the license plate number 007. (Friends considered him more Walter Mitty than James Bond.) When his body was discovered that winter, in a shabby room at a mountaintop inn called the Lucky Holiday Hotel, police ascribed the death to alcohol, but the police chief told the Americans that Heywood had been working as a problem-solver for the family of Bo Xilai, and when Bo's wife soured on the Englishman, she had him poisoned to death.

Bo was the most charismatic figure in elite Chinese politics, a populist and a back-slapper. As it happened, I had met him on his way up, when he was running the Ministry of Commerce, waiting his turn for a seat on the Politburo. He was a Beijing Brahmin, the tall, camera-ready son of a Party boss, with the soft palms of a crown prince. His wife, Gu Kailai, was a star lawyer who had published a book about her success in the courtroom—"the Jackie Kennedy of China," as an American colleague later put it. When Bo became Party secretary of Chongqing, he sensed an opportunity to outmaneuver liberal rivals, and he reinvented himself as the closest China had to Huey Long. He draped himself in the flag of Maoism and rallied citizens to sing "Red Songs" such as "Unity Is Power" and "Revolutionaries Are Forever Young." He and his police rounded up thousands of tycoons, political rivals, and alleged criminals in a campaign of arrests and torture that he called "Smash the Black."

When I met him, I was trailing the Chicago mayor Richard M. Daley to see what it was like to be an American pol encountering Chinese politics. We were waiting outside Bo's office when he came bursting through the door, laughing and bidding farewell to his previous appointment: a delegation of tall, thin African men, who looked very pleased to be greeted so warmly. I asked one of the ladies serving tea who these guests were.

"Sudan," she said.

At the front door, Bo waved farewell to the Sudanese, pivoted on his heels, and threw an arm around his next visitor. Before I was ushered out of the room, Bo had peppered his welcome with English, a rare flourish for a Chinese official. Last I saw him, seated beside Daley, a fireplug of a man from the South Side of Chicago, Bo Xilai looked like a movie star.

Had the police chief, Wang Lijun, never tried to flee, the world might never have known anything else about Bo Xilai and the world he made. But Wang's revelations were an astonishment. In the end, he received no asylum from the Americans; he walked glumly out of the consulate and into the hands of Chinese authorities, who tried him as a traitor and a taker of bribes—a clear message to anyone else who might consider defecting. But his tale could not be untold, and as it seeped out into the public, it began to corrode some of the myths at the heart of Chinese power.

The rumors of what Wang had said raced across the Web and through the alleyways. The Party censors tried to strike them down, but the political damage to Bo Xilai was fatal. Within two months, he was removed from office, and the government prepared to put him on trial for taking bribes, abusing his power, and other crimes. The Party was desperate to strike a balance between appearing to pursue justice and not allowing the airing of unseemly details. In a one-day show trial, his wife, Gu Kailai, was convicted of killing the Englishman, though it did little to tamp down public suspicions; when she turned up in court looking far heavier than her photos, Chinese viewers speculated that the defendant was a body double who had been paid to take the fall. (No matter how much the government denied it, the myth lingered; the liberal commentator Zhang Yihe wrote, "It reminds us of the boy who cried wolf, and lied and lied until nobody believed him and then he was eaten.") Bo's downfall had a searing legacy. For one thing, it unraveled the fiction of the humble public servant in China. At a time when his official salary was the equivalent of nineteen thousand dollars a year, his extended family was found to have acquired businesses reportedly worth more than a hundred million dollars.

For foreign businesspeople, the fate of the Englishman was discomfiting. It reminded them that even as China grew and developed, gangland habits lingered beneath the surface of Chinese commerce and politics, and occasionally burst through. A British scrap metal trader named Anil Srivastav told me about a testy negotiation he was having over a load of metals. "These people came in and dragged me out. I shouted 'Help!' but nobody looked," he said. "They put me in this van and drove me off." He was later released, but not before thinking, "I've only seen these things in movies."

For the Chinese public, Bo's downfall contained an even more powerful message about the information now swirling around them: a rumor they had swapped online, denounced and banished by the censors, had been transformed overnight into a fact. On Weibo, a user named Jieyigongjiang wrote, "The attacks spread by 'international reactionary forces' have now become truth. So what other 'truths' exposed by foreign media should we believe?"

Scandal was becoming the backbeat to China's rise. The combination of technology, wealth, and epic indiscretion was pulling aside the curtain that once protected Communist Party leaders from outside scrutiny. Never had the citizens of the People's Republic learned so much about the perks of those who ran it. For two years, an obscure Communist Party official named Han Feng recorded more than five hundred entries in a private diary chronicling his life as chief of the Tobacco Monopoly Bureau in the southern city of Laibin. When Han Feng's journal leaked to the Web—he never discovered how—it chronicled a life replete with banquets, extramarital affairs, and leisurely business trips, interspersed with Communist Party rituals. After one typical workday, he wrote:

November 6th, Tuesday (11–25°C, sunny): I edited a speech about "Civilized Manners." At lunch, Li Dehui and others from Xiamen came over and we drank. Then I rested in the company dorm for the afternoon . . . Went to dinner, drank heavily . . . At 10PM, Ms. Tan Shanfang drove over and dragged me to her house. We made love three times, and again at sunrise.

Once his diary leaked, Han was arrested in March 2010. He was tried and sentenced to thirteen years for accepting over a hundred thousand dollars in bribes and real estate. In the political food chain, he was a minnow, and the Party was happy to chuck him overboard; when I read his chronicle, I was struck by the ordinariness of it all; he stood out as neither a thug nor a statesman, just a man doing what he could to grab hold of the benefits that the system dangled above him. (The three most common abuses of public funds—travel, banquets, and cars—became known as the "three publics," and the Finance Ministry once estimated that they cost the country fourteen billion yuan—more than half the national defense budget.) On the last day of the year, Han the tobacco official took stock of his life:

Work went better this year than any year before . . . My authority has grown among the workers . . . My son is doing well, and he's been recommended for graduate school without even having to take the test. After two years, he'll get a job with no problems. My photography skills have reached a new level, and I will try to keep learning forever. Womanizing is on the right track. Hooked up with Little Ms. Pan. Regularly having a good time with Ms. Tan Shanfang, and I enjoy my time with Ms. Mo Yaodai. It's been a fine year, woman-wise, but with so many partners I need to keep an eye on my health.

Over time, Chinese bloggers learned to zoom in on official photos to find evidence of habits that did not match official salaries. They posted photographs of police departments with Maseratis and Porsches painted blue and white. They pointed out that a local real estate official named Zhou Jiugeng was often photographed smoking cigarettes that cost twenty-four dollars a pack, and after a bribery investigation he was sent to prison for eleven years. Another blogger made a specialty of exposing comrades with suspiciously expensive timepieces, and he became known as the Wristwatch Watchdog.

Censors kept as much off the Web as they could, but each new case tore another hole in the image of a Party that had always pledged to be the "first to eat bitterness, the last to benefit." Each new case sounded less like the exception than the rule, and each new detail accentuated the gap between the Party's solemn presentation and the unadorned reality beneath. A woman went online to describe her affair with her boss, Yi Junqing, the head of the Party's Central Compilation and Translation Bureau—in effect, the chief rabbi of Marxist orthodoxy and values. The mistress described how she had paid him in cash to buy her job, and she posted three years' worth of text messages, and a lengthy narrative of sushi, sake, and lunchtime dalliances.

Another case produced a batch of photos—leaked from a computer under repair—that documented the contortions of five men and women in a hotel room orgy. Viewers quickly identified the faces of several government officials. The problem was not embarrassment; it was hypocrisy: not long before that, the government had prosecuted a computer science professor who lived with his mother and, in his spare time, organized group sex—a community in which he was known by the Internet handle Roaring Virile Fire. He was arrested and sentenced to three and a half years for "crowd licentiousness," a relic of the days when the government charged people with "hooliganism" for sex outside of marriage. The case of Roaring Virile Fire became a rallying cry for advocates of privacy, so the news of the cadres' orgy posed something of a public relations challenge to the Party. One county government decided to declare it a case of mistaken identity, which the *People's Daily* summed up with the headline NAKED GUY IS NOT OUR PARTY CHIEF. (It turned out that he was.)

I had trouble staying up-to-date. There was a local Shanxi official caught with four wives and ten kids in the land of the one-child policy. And there was the memorable footage of a Party secretary named Lei Zhengfu in strenuous exertion with a woman one-third his age who, in an added twist, had been hired by a local real estate developer to seduce Lei for blackmail. (He was a portly, ranine figure, and Chinese Web users paired his photo with that of Jabba the Hutt, the blubbery villain from *Star Wars* films.)

The last case I saw before I gave up bothering to keep track of such reports was about the police chief in the county of Usu. When he was found to be in a pair of simultaneous love affairs with women whom he had promoted through the ranks of the police force—while keeping them in a luxurious apartment funded by taxpayers—his office released a clarification that must have felt like good news under the circumstances: the police chief's two mistresses were not *twin* sisters, they were *just sisters*. When I read this detail, I stopped chewing my lunch and looked up, blinking, while I absorbed the full scale of it; the "just sisters" defense seemed to set a new watermark for the image of Chinese public servants.

The ephemera was so absurd that it was easy to overlook that it undermined one of the pillars of Party rule: for thousands of years, Chinese leaders had relied on the notion of *de zhi*—"rule by virtue." "When a prince's personal conduct is correct," Confucius said, "his government is effective without the issuing of orders. If his personal conduct is not correct, he may issue orders, but they will not be followed." Similarly, the Communist Party's authority rested on the notion that even if local bureaucrats were corrupt, its top leaders so exemplified wisdom, justice, and meritocracy that dissent and direct elections were superfluous and obsolete. President Hu Jintao said that "the cultivation of personal moral integrity is considered the most basic quality for an honest official." When the government was seen to be violating the principle of "rule by virtue," public reaction could be intense: in the eighties, the uprising at Tiananmen Square was fed in large part by an upswell in corruption.

In the more recent upswell, the Party's virtue problem was reflected most acutely, perhaps, in a video that captivated people in China even more than the tawdriest clips: when local reporters asked a group of six-year-olds what they wanted to be when they grew up, the kids ran through the usual list—firefighters, pilots, artists—until one small boy said, "I want to be an official."

"What sort of official?" the reporter asked.

"A corrupt official," the boy said, "because they have lots of things."

The news of extraordinary wealth reached ever higher in the ranks. In June 2012, Bloomberg News used corporate documents and interviews to calculate that the extended family of China's incoming president, Xi

Jinping, had accumulated assets worth hundreds of millions of dollars. That wealth was hard for the Party to explain, so it decided not to try: within twenty-four hours, the government blocked the Bloomberg website—it would stay blocked in China for the foreseeable future—and it barred Chinese banks and companies from signing new contracts for use of Bloomberg terminals. It would cost the company millions in lost sales and advertising.

As pressure built on China's leaders, some of their supporters raged against the revelations—and the rage burst through in strange ways that trickled into our lives. One afternoon my wife, Sarabeth, who worked for a nonprofit education organization, received a call from a woman she knew professionally, the wife of a Chinese professor with close ties to the Party. They were a worldly couple—a child in the Ivy League and deep connections with senior leaders—and she asked Sarabeth for a chat at a nearby mall. At Starbucks, beside the Apple Store, the woman asked about my work as a journalist, and if I was friends with Michael Forsythe, a Bloomberg reporter who had published the details about Xi Jinping's family fortune. She had a warning for Sarabeth to relay to me, and for me to relay to Mike. "He and his family can't stay in China. It's no longer safe," she said. "Something will happen. It will look like an accident. Nobody will know what happened. He'll just be found dead."

Sarabeth, whose experience in such matters was limited, was mystified. Was this for real? Why was this woman talking to her about it? Sarabeth absorbed what she could and asked the woman who was behind the threat. "Not his family directly," the woman said, referring to the president. "It's people around him who want to show their loyalty."

I called Mike and reached him in Europe, where he was on vacation with his wife and sons. He told me that he had received the threat, through another intermediary. He had previously met the professor's wife, because she was working as a public relations consultant for members of the president's family. Now he didn't know what to think. Was she trying to help him? Or was she trying to drive him out of the country? The news of their wealth had been a PR disaster, and forcing him to leave might prevent further disclosures. It was the intersection of modern media and gangland politics.

Security experts working for Bloomberg investigated the threat—conducting interviews, examining connections—and in the end they decided that Mike and his family could safely return to Beijing. But the incident was difficult to forget. Within a year, he and his family left the mainland and moved to Hong Kong. (In 2013, he left Bloomberg.)

If the threats and retaliation were intended to suppress the hunt for unwelcome information, they did not succeed. In October *The New York Times* relied on corporate records to calculate that in the years that Prime Minister Wen Jiabao was in office, his family amassed assets worth $2.7 billion. The family was not previously known for its wealth; the father had been a pig farmer, the mother a teacher. But the family fortune was now large enough to rank it on the *Forbes* list of the world's richest families.

The news made a mockery of one of the Party's mantras: before the Communists arrived, they liked to say, China was run by four dominant families, and the Party had handed those fortunes back to the people. Now it was becoming clear that China, on the one hundredth anniversary of the end of the last dynasty, was returning to a form of aristocracy. The scale of privilege and self-dealing struck an especially awkward blow to Wen Jiabao's reputation, because he had put himself forward as one of the Party's liberal standard-bearers. Nicknamed Grandpa Wen for his attentions to the poor, he had declared, "I often say that we should not only let people have the freedom of speech, we, more importantly, must create conditions to let them criticize the work of the government." And yet, by six o'clock on the morning that his family fortune was revealed, his government had blacked out the *Times*—and it, like Bloomberg, would stay blocked.

As a reflection of decision-making, blocking some of the world's most influential news sources was a vivid measure of how much the Party was willing to isolate its people in order to protect itself: it was now barring them from viewing Facebook, Twitter, *The New York Times*, Bloomberg News, and many other sites. Online, the censors raced to protect the image of Premier Wen by screening out new combinations of words, including *prime minister + family* and *Wen + hundreds of millions.*

There was more than money at stake. People documented ways in which official life was healthier than ordinary life. A manufacturer of air purifiers unwittingly sparked an uproar when it released promotional materials crowing that China's officials breathed with the help of two hundred high-grade purifiers installed inside cloistered offices around the capital. "Creating clean, healthy air for our national leaders is a blessing to the people," the company said. Just as the people were getting their minds around that blessing, they learned of a network of "special farms" dedicated to providing Party leaders with safe ingredients. (An Asian Development Bank report estimated in 2007 that three hundred million people in China suffered from food-borne illnesses every year.) After journalists at *Southern Weekly* wrote about the farms, editors across the country were warned never to let them do so again.

The last thing Hu Gang taught me about bribing a judge was that it was worth it. After five years, he was picked up in a routine crackdown on courtroom corruption. In all, 140 judges were caught, including the head of the provincial supreme court. Hu Gang was convicted and served one year in jail.

When he got out, he published a novel under the name Fu Shi, then another book, and when I met him in 2012, he was working on a television script. He had reached conclusions about his experience. "Even though we have a legal system with all kinds of laws and regulations, enforcement is selective," he told me, settling deep into his chair, glassy-eyed from lunch. "When the rules favor the rule-makers, they are applied; when they do not, they are ignored. The rule-maker says, 'I am the only real rule, and I am the most powerful.' Everyone knows this." He laughed. China, he said, functions by "unwritten rules." He continued: "It has always been this way; the problem has just become more pronounced in recent years."

In most countries, the long-term effects of kleptocracy are easy to predict: economists calculate that for every point that a nation's corruption rises on a scale of one to ten, its economic growth drops by 1 percent. (Think Haiti under François Duvalier or Zaire under Mobutu.) But the exceptions are important. In Japan and Korea, corruption accompanied each nation's rise, not its collapse. There is no more conspicuous case than the United States. When promoters of the first transcontinental railroad were found to have secretly paid themselves to build it—the 1872 scandal known as Crédit Mobilier—the scale of plunder was described by the press as "the most damaging exhibition of official and private villainy and corruption ever laid bare to the gaze of the world." Between

1866 and 1873 the country put down thirty-five thousand miles of track, minting enormous fortunes but also, as Mark Twain put it, displaying "shameful corruption." The excesses of the railroad boom led to the Panic of 1873 and subsequent financial crises, before political pressure to curb abuses gained momentum during the Progressive Era.

There were two basic views of how corruption could affect China's future. The optimistic scenario was that it was part of the transition from socialism to the free market, and it nevertheless produced highways and trains that inspired envy even in the developed world. "The Chinese are more successful," then U.S. transportation secretary Ray LaHood told a reporter, "because in their country only three people make the decision. In our country, three thousand people do." The scholar Minxin Pei was less sanguine. He told me that the Party prosecuted only 3 to 6 percent of its members who were engaged in wrongdoing, and only a third of those convicted ever received jail time. When Andrew Wedeman, a political scientist at Georgia State University who studies China, examined patterns of bribes and prosecutions, he expected to find that the mechanics of Chinese corruption followed the hierarchical patronage system found in Japan and Korea. Instead, Wedeman concluded, "the evidence suggests that corruption in contemporary China is essentially anarchy." He wrote that "corruption in China more closely resembled corruption in Zaire than it did corruption in Japan." But unlike Zaire, China punished many people for it; in a five-year stretch, China punished 668,000 Party members for bribery, graft, and embezzlement; it handed down 350 death sentences for corruption, and Wedeman concluded, "At a very basic level, it appears to have prevented corruption from spiraling out of control."

The darker scenario held that the threat posed by Chinese corruption was not economic; it was political. In this view, the compact between the people and their leaders was fraying, the ruling class was scrambling to get what it could in the final years of frenzied growth, and the Party would be no more capable of reforming itself from within than were the Soviets. After the Bo Xilai scandal, some of the Party rank and file had begun to wonder about the Party's health. Four retired officials signed an open letter that asked, "What kind of shape is the Party in when even its highest echelon is embroiled in a story more sinister than any in *One Thousand and One Nights*?" The new leaders, they wrote,

"must disclose . . . their private and family wealth." Chinese leaders believed political reform would lead to instability, but did they believe that
doing nothing would as well? When an economy thrives, citizens can
tolerate even flagrant corruption. But when it slows, that same level of
corruption can become intolerable.

I asked Hu Gang if he thought China would grow past its corruption
boom, just as America and Korea did. He was quiet for a while, and then
he said, "I see our society as an enormous pond. For years, people have
been using it as a restroom, just because we could. And we enjoyed the
freedom of that, even as the pond got filthier and filthier. Now we need
someone who can stand up and tell everyone that the pond has been
fouled and if you continue to pollute it, nobody will survive."

# EIGHTEEN

# THE HARD TRUTH

The English guru Li Yang was going to pieces. In the years after I met him, I'd watched legions of students devote themselves to Crazy English, and all the while he'd grown more bizarre and belligerent. When a tsunami killed tens of thousands of people in Japan in 2011, he called it "God's little punishment" for Japan's invasion of China during World War II. A blogger in Shanghai pronounced him a "superstar whackjob."

For years, Li Yang's most persuasive evidence of sanity was the continued support of his wife, Kim Lee, but in September 2011 she accused him of domestic violence and filed for divorce. In a country where victims of spousal abuse rarely go to police, the charge made national news. Li Yang told a local reporter, "I hit her sometimes but I never thought she would make it public since it's not Chinese tradition to expose family conflicts to outsiders." In the months that followed, Kim Lee emerged as an improbable icon, "a folk hero for China's battered wives," as the Chinese press put it.

Li Yang's business survived the scandal, but the damage to his reputation was a baffling turn of events for the young men and women who had placed so much faith in him. When the student I'd come to know, Michael Zhang, called me one morning to catch up, he said, "He beat his wife so badly. He's not a good father, he's not a good teacher to follow. I hate—" He stopped himself. "No, I don't have to say that I hate him." A few weeks later, I was in southern China and I rode the bus out to see Michael and his parents. They had left the apartment on Gold Panning Road in Guangzhou and had moved to Qingyuan, a smaller city nearby. It was only an hour away, but Qingyuan felt sootier and closer to the countryside. Qingyuan didn't yet have a high-speed train link directly to the capital. While I waited at the bus station for Michael, I stood beside a man carrying his luggage on a whittled tree branch balanced across his shoulders. When Michael arrived, he looked out of place with earphones slung stylishly around his neck and wearing a fashionable windbreaker. He took in the scene around me and seemed eager to portray his new location in a more modern light. "Three years from now, this will be an international city," he said. "I hate Guangzhou. It's full of thieves. I got robbed three times there."

We took a cab across town. He and his parents lived in what might be called the porcelain district, lined with storefronts selling sinks, toilets, and bathroom tile. The road was littered with tiny broken tiles of every color; they looked like confetti. The apartment was on the eighth floor of a gray cement housing block with no elevator. As we climbed the stairs, I listened to the echoes of construction in the distance. In the apartment, Michael's parents were cooking lunch. It was less polished and cosmopolitan than their place in Guangzhou had been, though this apartment was a bit larger, and Michael had his own room. The motivational sayings on the walls mixed his usual optimism with a tinge of frustration. "I have to mentally change my whole life's destiny!" said one. "I can't stand it anymore!" said another.

On top of his wardrobe was a large cardboard box stenciled with the words "Crazy English." I asked what it was, and Michael sighed. It held dozens of Crazy English books that he'd once hoped to sell. "Li Yang is very persuasive," he said. "He persuaded me to fall in love with Crazy English for nine years. He got deep down into my soul. I became totally weird." He laughed. "The Crazy English method is bad," he went on. "A lot of students come to me and say that I've spent nine thousand yuan but my pronunciation is still so poor."

The language business was difficult. After Michael borrowed money to start Basic English, the company operated for two years, but eventually the partnership soured. Michael had been in charge of sales, and he'd struggled to recruit students. By January 2011 the business had collapsed. Michael was broke, and in debt. He spent two miserable weeks in his parents' apartment pacing back and forth, thinking over all that had happened. He told me that the experience had left him with an unforgiving lesson: rely on nobody but yourself.

His family had left Guangzhou to save more money, and now, in the eighth-floor walk-up in Qingyuan, Michael was at work on a solo project: he was writing an English textbook. "My dream is to change the whole Chinese-English education system," he said. He was convinced he could write a successful book if someone gave him a chance. "I have strengths. I am irreplaceable," he said, and I heard echoes of his self-help readings. "Can you believe it?" he asked.

When lunch was ready, we crowded around a table in the living room, where the walls held portraits of competing icons: outside Michael's door, he still had a poster of Li Yang, and on an adjacent wall his mother, who had converted to Christianity, had put a banner that read, CHRIST IS THE PILLAR HOLDING UP THE FAMILY. (When it came to Christianity, Michael was keeping his options open: "I just take the best parts of every religion," he said.)

Michael was eager to tell me about his book idea: he wanted to address the problem that he described dismissively as "exam English," the kind of stilted language that many Chinese students acquired in order to pass the college entrance test. Instead, he wanted to teach the kind of real-world phrases that tend to confuse foreign speakers. He rattled off examples: "Get it. Get up. Knock up. Cheer up. Gimme a break, man. I don't get it, man. I have no idea, man. Shut your mouth, man." He had also identified eight hundred words for his students to repeat, over and over, to hone their pronunciation. When he demonstrated his technique, it sounded like a one-sentence history of modern China: "I can, I can, I can, I can. Suffered, suffered, suffered, suffered. Have, have, have, have."

I watched his parents watching him, and I got the sense that they were used to this. He had turned their home into an ESL classroom, even though, like most of their generation, they spoke no English. They had little choice but to trust that their son was doing something worthwhile. Later that afternoon, Michael and his parents and I went to see their proudest new possession: an apartment under construction for Michael and the wife he hopes to find someday. We walked across the porcelain district; Michael's father wore camouflage army-surplus shoes that blended in with the broken tiles. We reached a tall and slender modern high-rise, with a modern lobby, sleek and clean, and the camouflage shoes suddenly looked out of place. In the middle of the lobby was a scale model of the complex, with tiny working lights and plastic figurines under palm trees. The lobby doubled as a sales center, but there were no buyers that day; China's economy was slowing, and the real estate market in Qingyuan was not what it once was. We planned to visit their new apartment, but that tower was not yet finished, and the elevator panel dangled from wires in a way that didn't look especially safe. Michael poked at the lifeless buttons for a moment and then suggested we visit a model apartment instead.

The walls of the showroom were bare concrete, suggesting either a promising future or a construction project in trouble. We walked out to the balcony and peered down on a lake. From the eighteenth floor, the people below looked as tiny as the figurines in the lobby. The apartment that Michael and his parents could afford was on the other side of the complex, beside the tile stores, not the lake. We stepped back into the elevator, and Michael seemed uncomfortable. Speaking in English, so his parents couldn't understand, he said, "I won't live here. I will put my parents here. I need to be back in a big city like Shenzhen or Beijing or Shanghai. Qingyuan is countryside. Second tier. They just learn 'exam English.' They don't have big dreams here."

As the years passed, I sensed that other young strivers like Michael were growing frustrated as well. Low-skilled jobs weren't the problem— those wages were climbing—but there weren't enough white-collar jobs to employ each year's crop of more than six million new college graduates. Between 2003 and 2009, the average starting salary for migrant workers had grown by nearly 80 percent, but for college graduates, starting wages were flat. When you considered inflation, their income had declined. The young Chinese strivers desperate to become "car-and-home-equipped"—to find a mate and elbow their way into the New Middle-Income Stratum—now knew the truth: China's new fortunes were wildly out of balance. By 2012 a typical apartment in a Chinese city was selling for eight to ten times the average annual income nationwide. (Even at the heights of the American property bubble, the ratio peaked at five to one.) Young men adopted a self-mocking nickname: a man without the connections to get rich or the cash to get married would call himself a *diaosi*—"a thread penis." These young people had been raised in the era of self-creation, with cell phones marketed as "My Turf, My

Decision," and school chants that told them "I am the biggest miracle of nature!" They had reasons to be disenchanted. When it came time to select a single Chinese character to describe the year 2009, people online chose 被 (pronounced *bei*), a passive preposition, as in "to be fired by" or "to be abused by."

A new mood was setting in: China's boom had made almost everyone better off to some degree—average incomes had more than tripled over the past decade—but the gap between rich and poor had ballooned more than the Party ever intended. In 2001 the blunt-spoken premier Zhu Rongji had been asked if he worried that the growing divide might lead to social unrest. "Not yet," Zhu said. He pointed to the measurement of income equality known as the Gini coefficient, which ranges from 0 to 1, with one being extreme disparity in wealth. Chinese officials predicted that China would be stable as long as its Gini stayed below what he called a "danger line" of 0.4. Eleven years later, the number had grown so large that the government simply stopped publishing it, saying the wealthy hid too much of their income to make the statistic credible.

The income gap was not an abstraction: a child born on the remote Qinghai Plateau was seven times more likely to die before the age of five than a child born in the capital. The government was under pressure to act. It could have reformed the tax system—it still had no capital gains or inheritance taxes—but instead it adopted a more immediate strategy: in April 2011, Beijing banned companies from using the word *luxury* in their names and ads. The "Black Swan Luxury Bakery," which was selling wedding cakes for $314,000, had to call itself the "Black Swan Art Bakery." (The ban did not last.)

After years of not daring to measure the Gini coefficient, in January 2013 the government finally published a figure, 0.47, but many specialists dismissed it; the economist Xu Xiaonian called it "a fairy tale." (An independent calculation put the figure at 0.61, higher than the level in Zimbabwe.) Yet, for all the talk about income, it was becoming clear that people cared most of all about the gap in opportunity. When the Harvard sociologist Martin Whyte polled the Chinese public in 2009, he discovered that people had a surprisingly high tolerance for the rise of the plutocracy. What they resented were the obstacles that prevented them from joining it: weak courts, abuses of power, a lack of recourse.

Two scholars, Yinqiang Zhang and Tor Eriksson, tracked the paths of Chinese families from 1989 to 2006 and found a "high degree of inequality of opportunity." They wrote, "The basic idea behind the market reforms was that by enabling some citizens to become rich this would in turn help the rest to become rich as well. Our analysis shows that at least so far there are few traces of the reforms leveling the playing field." They found that in other developing countries, parents' education was the most decisive factor in determining how much a child would earn someday. But in China, the decisive factor was "parental connections." A separate study of parents and children in Chinese cities found "a strikingly low level of intergenerational mobility." Writing in 2010, the authors ranked "urban China among the least socially mobile places in the world."

Even before they had statistics to prove it, people described new divisions emerging in their society; they no longer simply parsed the distinctions between Bobos and DINKs (double income, no kids) and the New Middle-Income Stratum. There was now a line between the white-collar class and what people called the "black-collar class." An anonymous author circulated an essay that defined it: "Their clothes are black. Their cars are black. Their income is hidden. Their life is hidden. Their work is hidden. Everything about them is hidden—like a man wearing black, standing in the dark."

As the sense of opportunity narrowed, the Bare-Handed Fortunes lost some of their luster. Huang Guangyu, an electronics mogul who had ranked as the richest person in China, was sentenced to fourteen years for insider trading and other offenses. In all, authorities executed at least fourteen yuan billionaires in the span of eight years, on charges ranging from pyramid schemes to murder for hire. (Yuan Baojing, a former stockbroker who made three billion yuan before his fortieth birthday, was convicted of arranging the killing of a man who tried to blackmail him.) The annual rich list was nicknamed the "death list."

The Queen of Trash ran into trouble of a different kind. Less than a year after Cheung Yan was celebrated as the richest self-made woman in the world, her reputation in China began to deteriorate. A labor rights group called Students and Scholars Against Corporate Misbehaviour released "Sweatshop Paper," an investigation that accused her company, Nine Dragons Paper, of labor abuses, including industrial accidents, inadequate safety equipment, and discrimination against carriers of hepatitis B, a common ailment in China. The group published parts of the *Nine Dragons Paper Employee Handbook*, whose dos and don'ts included "Respect the leaders. Stop walking when meeting senior leaders and greet them. Stand behind senior leaders when walking together." Workers were subject to a wide range of fines, such as three hundred yuan for spitting out the window of a company bus or cutting the line in the cafeteria; five hundred yuan for napping, permitting an outsider to view the factory, or playing mah-jongg; a thousand yuan and dismissal for organizing a strike or "spreading rumors which cause harm to the company." The handbook also noted that wages were confidential, and that "revealing one's salary" or "asking others" about theirs was grounds for dismissal.

A Chinese newspaper invoked the exploitation of the American Gilded Age to accuse Cheung of "turning blood into gold." People pointed out that she had once said, "If a country does not have both the rich and the poor, it will not become strong and affluent." *Sanlian Shenghuo*, a prominent magazine, wrote that "if she still has any sense," she will resign from her seat on the government advisory body called the Chinese People's Political Consultative Conference. "Every piece of paper produced by Nine Dragons," it wrote, "is soaked with the blood of labor." Even some of China's most energetic cheerleaders of the free market sensed the passing of an era. In an article about Cheung Yan, the magazine *China Entrepreneur* declared, "In Chinese society five years ago, maybe a company that had achieved success in business, while not being perfect in other respects, would have been tolerated and worshipped. But things have changed."

When the report appeared, Cheung responded angrily, saying, "We became wealthy because we found the right business model to change used paper into treasure—not by treating workers harshly." The company gave out more in bonuses than it withheld in penalties, she said. And she questioned the political motives of the labor rights group, suggesting, darkly, that it "received money from Europe."

When I talked to her about it, Cheung told me that the company had ended the practice of fining workers. A more calculating executive might have stopped there, but Cheung edged forward in her chair to explain that, in fact, she still believed fines were a legitimate tactic under the right conditions. "If you don't impose fines, workers are not careful and they will get injured and come back to ask for more compensation," she said. After an investigation, the provincial trade union criticized the penalty system and other management practices but pronounced Nine Dragons "a relatively good enterprise." It was little help: Cheung's comments and the report completed a transformation of her public image. She had become the antihero of an era of unbridled capitalism.

The longer I lived in China, the more it seemed that people had come to see the economic boom as a train with a limited number of seats. For those who found a seat—because they arrived early, they had the right family, they paid the right bribe—progress was beyond their imagination. Everyone else could run as far and fast as their legs would carry them, but they would only be able to watch the caboose shrink into the distance.

At its extremes, the frustration was explosive. By 2010 the number of strikes, riots, and other "mass incidents" had doubled in five years to 180,000 a year—almost 500 incidents a day, according to the government's statistics. On July 24, 2009, steelworkers in Jilin Province, fearing layoffs, attacked the general manager, a young graduate named Chen Guojun, beating him to death with bricks and clubs, and blocking police and ambulances. When the Party broke up disturbances like this, it often said the problem was members of the "masses who didn't know the truth." But more and more, it seemed that the problem was the truth itself. To some degree, the great national footrace that Deng Xiaoping ordained was rigged. The field was not simply tilted against them. They weren't playing the same game.

In January 2010 a nineteen-year-old named Ma Xiangqian jumped from the roof of his factory dormitory at Foxconn Technology, the maker of iPhones and other electronics. He had worked on the assembly line seven nights a week, eleven hours at a stretch, before being demoted to cleaning toilets. In the months after Ma's death, thirteen other Foxconn workers committed suicide. People wondered if it was spreading like a fever, and they pointed out that the cluster of suicides was still under the rate expected for a factory as large as a city.

Foxconn installed nets around the roofs of its buildings and boosted

wages, and the suicides diminished as abruptly as they had begun. Outsiders were quick to imagine a sweatshop, but this explanation was not
quite right. When therapists were brought in to Foxconn to meet workers, they found what sociologists had begun to detect in surveys of the
new middle class: the first generation of assembly-line workers had been
grateful just to be off the farm, but this generation compared themselves
to wealthier peers. "What is the most common feeling in China today?"
the Tsinghua sociologist Guo Yuhua wrote in 2012. "I think many people would say disappointment. This feeling comes from the insufficient
improvement in lives amid rapid economic growth. It also comes from
the contrast between the degree to which individual social status is rising
and the idea of the 'rise of a great and powerful nation.'"

I noticed that people were still invoking *The Great Gatsby* as an anal-
ogy for their moment in China's rise, but now the reference carried a
sinister new connotation. They pointed to a study known as the Great
Gatsby curve, conducted by labor economist Miles Corak, which produced further evidence that China had one of the world's lowest levels of
social mobility. A Chinese blogger read it and wrote, "The sons of rats
will only dig holes . . . Birth determines class." *The Great Gatsby* no longer read as a tale of a self-made man. A blogger wrote, "Mobsters running wild, farmers leaving their land rushing towards the big cities on
the east coast, farming life declining. Money inscribing itself on morality . . . These are the very things China faces today." The Central Propaganda Department let it be known that reports that suggested a shortage
of happiness were not to receive attention. In April 2012 my phone
buzzed:

> All websites are not to repost the news headlined, "UN Releases
> World Happiness Report, and China Ranks No. 112."

When I returned to Beijing from my time with Michael, it was a brilliant
winter day, and I took my bike out for a long lap around the neighborhood. I pedaled down to the Avenue of Eternal Peace. I turned right to
head north again, and I passed the Central Propaganda Department,
squatting beneath its pagoda roof.

In the years since I'd first noticed it, the quest for truth in China had expanded in ways once unimaginable, and the Department had adapted. The Department had helped the Party weather the financial crisis and silence the admirers of the Arab Spring. The Party had jailed Liu Xiaobo and Ai Weiwei, and blunted the publishing ambitions of Han Han. Even the muckraking editor Hu Shuli—the woodpecker who wanted to make the system grow straighter—had run up against the limits of what it could bear. And those efforts reinforced the Party's determination to contain and control the pursuit of truth. China's highest-ranking censor, Liu Binjie, was asked that spring to evaluate his performance over the previous six years. "Objectively speaking," Liu said of his performance, "it was outstanding."

His confidence struck me as premature. In China the affairs of state had always been kept out of view of the public, and been unveiled only at the end as a fait accompli. But now the uncooked ingredients—the deals, the feuds, the peccadillos, the betrayals—were tumbling into the open air to be judged and evaluated. People were assessing whether the values of the system now on display lived up to their own moral aspirations. By 2012 a Chinese person was going online for the first time every two seconds—still, barely half the population was using the Web. Before he went to prison, Liu Xiaobo pointed out that his inspiration, Havel's Charter 77, had appeared more than two decades before the political system around it evolved in the way its authors envisioned. In Havel's view, the key to life under a Communist Party was the maintenance of a double life—the willingness to say one thing in public and another in private, because of fear or interest or a combination of the two. Eventually that double life became untenable.

In China, the double life was eroding. The reality of extreme inequality was now inescapable: one part of China lived in a different material universe from the rest of the country. This was true in many countries, of course, including my own, but in China it was especially deeply felt; the nation was just one generation removed from bitter sacrifices in the name of egalitarianism. Moreover, the gap between the society's meritocratic myth and its oligarchic reality was becoming clear and measurable. In 2012 a team of political scientists (Victor Shih, Christopher Adolph, and Mingxing Liu) challenged one of the essential shibboleths surrounding China's rise: the Party had always maintained that its ruthless devotion to development—"the hard truth," as Deng put it—ensured meritocracy because it rewarded cadres who made the shrewdest economic decisions. But the researchers found no evidence to support this; on the contrary, Chinese officials with good economic track records were no more likely to be promoted than those who performed poorly. What mattered most was their connections with senior leaders.

As the Party's monopoly on information gave way, so did its moral credibility. For people such as the philosophy student Tang Jie, the pursuit of truth did not satisfy their skepticism; it led them to deeper questions about who they wanted to be and whom they wanted to believe. In the summer of 2012, people noticed that another search word had been blocked. The anniversary of the Tiananmen Square demonstrations had just passed, and people had been discussing it, in code, by calling it "the truth"—*zhenxiang*. The censors picked up on this, and when people searched Weibo for anything further, they began receiving a warning: "In accordance with relevant laws, regulations, and policies, search results for 'the truth' have not been displayed."

# PART III

# FAITH

# NINETEEN

# THE SPIRITUAL VOID

"Mao Badge Fever" struck China in the summer of 1966, when the Shanghai United Badge Factory produced a simple aluminum pin—a half inch in diameter, bearing the face of the Chairman. The Cultural Revolution was gathering, and the badges were a sensation. Within weeks, they were in production nationwide; men, women, and children were pinning them above their hearts as testaments to devotion, the more badges the better, spilling down their chests and across their arms.

The Chairman was pictured facing forward or in profile, but never to the right, which was the counterrevolutionary direction. There were badges that glowed in the dark and badges made from U.S. fighter planes downed in Vietnam. The inscriptions hailed the Chairman as the "Messiah of the Working People" and the "Great Savior" and the "Red Sun in Our Hearts."

The Cultural Revolution was Mao's final play for power. After the catastrophe of the Great Leap Forward, his rivals had pushed him aside, so Mao unleashed China's youth to "bombard the headquarters." It gave him a new aura: "Let Mao Zedong's thought control everything," the media declared, and people confessed their sins at the foot of his statues. His *Little Red Book* of quotations became known for mysterious powers: the state press reported that the book had enabled a team of surgeons to remove a ninety-nine-pound tumor; it had helped workers in Shanghai raise the sinking city by three-quarters of an inch.

Mao's touch acquired otherworldly significance: when a Pakistani delegation gave Mao a basket of mangoes in 1968, he regifted them to workers, who wept and placed them on altars; crowds lined up and bowed before the fruit. A mango was flown to Shanghai on a chartered plane, so that workers such as Wang Xiaoping could see it. "What is a 'mango'? Nobody knew," she recalled in an essay. "Knowledgeable people said it was a fruit of extreme rarity, like Mushrooms of Immortality." When the mangoes spoiled, they were preserved in formaldehyde, and plastic replicas were created. A village dentist who observed that one of the mangoes resembled a sweet potato was tried for malicious slander and executed.

At the very moment that Mao was becoming a god, his believers were dismantling China's ancient infrastructure of faith. Karl Marx had considered religion an "illusory happiness" incompatible with the struggle for socialism, and the *People's Daily* called upon the young to "Smash the Four Olds"—old customs, old culture, old habits, and old ideas. Red Guards demolished temples and smashed sacred objects in a surge of violence that the scholars Vincent Goossaert and David A. Palmer describe as the "most thorough destruction of all forms of religious life in Chinese and, perhaps, human history." In some cases, the deification of Mao and the destruction of his enemies became indistinguishable. *The Little Red Book* was used as a "demon-exposing mirror" that could unmask "class enemies," and in two provinces, the fervor descended into cannibalism: class enemies were disemboweled, and their organs were consumed at communal banquets.

By 1969 the cult of Mao was out of control and threatening China's future. The death toll was rising, temples were in ruins, and even the badges had become a problem: China was manufacturing so many of them (between two and five billion in all) that they were diverting aluminum from industrial production. Mao finally ended the craze by saying the metal had to be used to "make airplanes to protect the nation."

After the Chairman died in 1976, collectors and speculators saw a profit-making opportunity, and they accumulated badges as an investment. But the trade was so lucrative that the badge market was swamped with counterfeits. The talismans became a commodity, and I found them buried in the bric-a-brac at the Beijing flea markets. Online, factories now sold them in bulk for seven cents apiece.

Mao's Cultural Revolution destroyed China's old belief systems, but Deng's economic revolution could not rebuild them. The relentless pursuit of fortune had relieved the deprivation in China's past, but it had failed to define the ultimate purpose of the nation and the individual. The truth now lay in plain view: the Communist Party presided over a land of untamed capitalism, graft, and rampant inequality. In sprinting ahead, China had bounded past whatever barriers once held back the forces of corruption and moral disregard. There was a hole in Chinese life that people named the *jingshen kongxu*—"the spiritual void"—and something was going to fill it.

In the winter of 2010 we moved into a small brick house on Guoxue Hutong—the Alley of National Studies. It was a grand title for a dead-end street so narrow and crooked that two cars couldn't pass at the same time. In the spring, it narrowed further when the neighborhood card game took up residence on the shady side of the street.

The Alley of National Studies—surrounded by noisy boulevards, north of the Forbidden City—was a remnant of old Beijing that had fended off demolition because it was wedged between two treasures: the Lama Temple (Beijing's largest Tibetan monastery) and the Confucius Temple (a seven-hundred-year-old shrine to China's most important philosopher). These were surrounded by the city's largest concentration of fortune-tellers, and together they made the neighborhood the most spiritually alive patch of the capital. It had the feel of a chaotic open-air market stocked with not products but creeds.

The name of the alley came from its location: "National Studies" referred to the mix of philosophy, history, and politics at the core of Chinese culture. Defining exactly what this entailed—which history should be taught, which ideas were valid—was fraught, but generations of Chinese thinkers had dreamed of finding the strongest recipe to insulate China from the pressures of Westernization. Liang Qichao, the foremost intellectual of the early twentieth century, called for promoting the "essence of the country," and in recent years, Chinese leaders had recommitted themselves to this idea, in the hope of fastening the remnants of socialism to deeper roots in Chinese culture. They were unnerved by the spread of Western political values, and like the philosophy student Tang Jie, they reembraced the Chinese classics as a defense. A banner went up declaring our neighborhood THE HOLY LAND OF NATIONAL STUDIES.

Our alley had no stores or bars or restaurants. It was only a hundred yards off the main road, Yonghegong Dajie, but the dead end and the old houses made it feel like a village encircled by a city of nineteen million people. One neighbor kept a rooster to greet the dawn. Another took his exercise by snapping a bullwhip in the morning air. We lived in close proximity to one another; at my desk, I listened for the moment, each night, when my neighbor, a widow named Jin Baozhu, fired up her stove at exactly 6:00 p.m.; at 6:05, the hiss of hot oil; at 6:15, dinner.

In its seclusion, life in the alley had an improvisational quality; at Chinese New Year, a neighbor invited us over for fireworks, which were not, strictly speaking, legal. One year they tipped over and fired a rocket into the crowd. Two months later, Mrs. Jin decided to knock down her house and rebuild it with a few extra feet of space that she absorbed from open land. I didn't mind—she needed it; her place was tiny—but my landlord was incensed. He accused her of "stealing sunlight" and filed a lawsuit. They couldn't agree on who owned what, in part because people had seized so much from each other during the Cultural Revolution.

Not far from our front door, an official bulletin board was set aside for "Anti-Cult Warnings and Education." Large Chinese characters across the top read, BE ON THE LOOKOUT FOR CULTS. BUILD HARMONY. With so much spiritual activity in the neighborhood, the government kept a wary eye on it, because it worried about groups that competed for loyalty and devotion. When the spiritual movement Falun Gong emerged in China in the 1990s, and appealed for greater rights and recognition, the Party declared it a cult and rounded up its members in a crackdown that has continued ever since. One poster was headed COUNTERING FALUN GONG'S DAILY PLOTS TO CAUSE TROUBLE AND DESTRUCTION. It said that cults "use computer networks to create and spread rumors that throw social order into disorder." I never heard anyone in the neighborhood talk about joining a cult, but if I did, there was a poster explaining how to respond: DON'T LISTEN, DON'T READ, DON'T SHARE, AND DON'T JOIN.

Outsiders often saw the Chinese as pragmatists with little time for faith, but for thousands of years the country had been knitted together by beliefs and rituals. At one point, Beijing had more temples than any other city in Asia. Daoism and Buddhism flourished alongside a range of indigenous deities: scholars prayed to the God of Literature, the sick appealed to the God of Rheumatism, and artillerymen worshipped the God of Cannons. Beijing attracted pilgrims from thousands of miles away, some of whom made their way by prostrating flat on the ground with every step, like inchworms.

After the Cultural Revolution subsided, Chinese scholars were gradually permitted to reinterpret Marx's belief that religion was "the opiate of the masses," and they argued that he was referring to religion in the Germany of his day, not religion itself. By then, China was pursuing material satisfaction, and people found that it could satisfy only some of their yearnings; on the existential questions—meaning, self-cultivation, life itself—it was a dead end. Now and then, a surge of patriotism provided a form and direction to people's lives, but it was, as the Japanese author Haruki Murakami wrote of the nationalism in his own country, "like cheap liquor": "It gets you drunk after only a few shots and makes you hysterical," he wrote, "but after your drunken rampage you are left with nothing but an awful headache the next morning."

By the time we settled in the neighborhood, China was in the midst of a full-fledged revival. The "spiritual void" was now being filled, as one study put it, by a "religious universe, exploding centrifugally in all directions." People did not trust the institutions around them: the Party was ravaged by hypocrisy; the press was crippled by bribery and censorship; the big companies were known for patronage and nepotism. People were placing their faith elsewhere. In the poorest reaches of the countryside, temples were reopening and offering a mix of Daoism, Buddhism, and the folk religions. There were now sixty to eighty million Christians, a community as large as the Communist Party. I met Pentecostal judges and Baha'i tycoons.

Faced with so many options, some people hedged with a bit of spiritual promiscuity: before the school exams each spring, I watched Chinese parents stream past the gates of the Lama Temple to pray for good scores. Then they crossed the street to pray at the Confucius Temple, and some finished the afternoon at a Catholic Church, just in case.

Some of the fastest-growing groups blended religion, business, and self-improvement. I attended the meeting of an organization called "Top Human," which recruited ambitious men and women to sell "inspirational marketing" products that help you "see into your psychology." Local papers asked if it was a "spiritual marketing" program or, perhaps,

a "religion." Eventually the government shut it down, and the founders
went to jail, reportedly on charges of tax evasion.

Over the years, I'd followed the stories of those on the hunt for fortune after so many years of poverty. And I'd traveled the country to meet
truth-tellers of one kind or another. But the longer I stayed in China, the
more I sought to understand the changes that were harder to glimpse—
the quests for meaning. Nothing had caused more upheaval in the last
hundred years of Chinese history than the battle over what to believe. I
wanted to know what life was like for men and women trying to decide
what mattered most, and I didn't have to look far. In the bookstores of
my neighborhood, the Chinese titles included *A Guidebook for the Soul*
and *What Do We Live For?* From my front door, I could walk to every
point on the compass and find a different answer.


Due east of the Alley of National Studies was the Lama Temple, a spectacular complex of brightly painted wood-and-stone pavilions wreathed
in the smoke of incense. It was one of the world's most important Tibetan
monasteries and, to the Chinese government, one of the most sensitive
places in the city. Beijing had once been close to Tibetan Buddhism;
emperors had kept thousands of monks in the capital to pray for protection of the empire. But the Dalai Lama, Tibet's spiritual leader, fled
China in 1959 after rejecting the Communist Party's claims to his homeland and trekking over the mountains to India. In exile, he won the Nobel Peace Prize and helped turn Tibetans, in the words of his friend
Robert Thurman, a Columbia University professor and former monk,
into the "the baby seals of the human-rights movement." Just as Pope
John Paul II had been an icon of opposition to the Soviet empire, the
Dalai Lama became the face of resistance to Chinese rule. After the
uprising in Tibet in the spring of 2008, Chinese leaders accused
the Dalai Lama of fomenting unrest. He denied any involvement, but
they considered him a "wolf in monk's clothing" intent on "splitting the
motherland."

There were always police in uniform and plain clothes around the
temple, which was a curious sight because most of the visitors were not
Tibetans; most were prosperous young Chinese couples who came to
burn incense and pray for a healthy baby. For many of them, Tibet was

China's glamorous Wild West, a chic destination associated with spirituality and rugged individualism. "When I'm in Tibet," a young Chinese rock musician told me, "I can be free."

I knew a number of Han Chinese adherents of Tibetan Buddhism, including a private-equity investor named Lin, who wore Buddhist beads on one wrist and a Swiss watch on the other. He struggled to reconcile his faith with the government's warnings about the Dalai Lama. "When I was learning from my Tibetan teachers, I used to ask them, 'Are you Chinese or Tibetan? Are you going to use my money to buy weapons?'" he said. He had dabbled in psychology and spiritualism, and settled on the Tibetan variety of Buddhism because it felt purer than the Chinese variety, which had been merged with elements of Daoism and other traditions. Of the Dalai Lama, he said, "He's written about sixty books, and I've probably read thirty of them."

We were at an outdoor café in Beijing, and another friend at the table—a restaurateur who happened to be a Communist Party member—gave a theatrical gasp and said, "He is brave for saying that." Lin rolled his eyes, and I got the sense that he enjoyed the audacity that accompanied his faith. "I think the Dalai Lama is not actually a Tibetan separatist," Lin said. "If he were, Tibet would have been out of control by now."

Radiating, in all directions, from the Lama Temple were blocks of tiny storefronts occupied by feng shui consultants, blind soothsayers, and "name-givers," who could reveal, for the right price, the most auspicious name for a baby or a new business. After decades underground, the fortune-telling business was out in the open—and booming. So much about success and failure in China hinged on mysterious factors, on hidden relationships and invisible deals, that people were eager to seek a divine advantage.

The soothsayers advertised their services with signs in the windows: PREDICT THE POLITICAL AND FINANCIAL FUTURE; EVALUATE THE PROSPECTS OF MARRIAGE; IMPROVE A SCORE ON THE COLLEGE-ENTRANCE EXAM. More advanced procedures were available upon request, including, as one sign put it, THE RESOLUTION OF SPELLS, ETCETERA. The shop that belonged to Shang Degang always reminded me of an obstetrician's office; it was papered with photos of smiling clients where the snapshots of thriving kids would be. "This young lady, Peng Yuan, was a nobody when she came to Beijing," he told me one afternoon, tapping a finger on the picture of a woman who had a tense smile and red cheeks. "Now she's a cosmetologist, and she's friends with many famous people." In the photo, she was holding something green and flat. "I made that jade plate for her, and it turned her fortune around."

Master Shang's office was cluttered with not-so-ancient books such as *Wall Street Feng Shui*, and his services mixed Buddhism, Daoism, and a smidgen of hocus-pocus. But his sales pitch hinged mostly on a connection to history: he identified himself as a descendent of Shang Kexi, an ancient general, and on his desk, he kept a leather-bound copy of the Shang family tree, which was four inches thick. It impressed his clients because so many of those family trees were destroyed during the Cultural Revolution. Clients who could never know the details of their own history found some comfort in knowing his. His sign promised SUPERNATURAL SERVICES ONCE AVAILABLE ONLY TO THE UPPER CLASS.

For all Mao's efforts, folk religion still thrived in every corner of life. The first autumn after we moved in, I heard the sound of scratching and digging in the ceiling above my desk. I didn't mind, but after a few weeks my office began to smell a bit like a zoo. Through the window one night, I saw a furry blond creature dart up the tree and disappear into a hole in the roof. I mentioned it to my neighbor Huang Wenyi, and he smiled.

"That's a weasel," he said. "You should be happy!" A weasel, he said, was a sign of imminent wealth, as were hedgehogs, snakes, foxes, and rats. Since those species hung around tombs, they were believed to bear the souls of ancestors. "Don't mess with it," Huang said. I mentioned the animal to our housekeeper, Auntie Ma, and she said sternly, "Don't hit it. Never a hit a weasel."

But the smell over my desk was making it difficult to work. Something had to be done. A few days later, I was standing in the courtyard with an exterminator named Han Changdong. I described what I'd seen. He nodded reassuringly. "That's a weasel," he said. "You're a very lucky man."

"But you're in the business of extermination," I said.

Han shrugged and said, "Chinese people would consider it very auspicious to have a weasel move into a house." As more of the city turned to concrete, Han said, the last wild animals were crowding into the alleys in search of wood and straw. He fished around in his bag of tools. "In my hometown, you'd burn an offering of thanks to the God of Wealth. But this situation is different. We'll sort it out." From his bag, he produced a container of rat poison, which didn't make me feel very good.

"Wait," I said. "Is this a bad idea—spiritually speaking?"

Han considered the question, and said, "You should be fine because you're a foreigner and you don't believe in this."

I wasn't sure what I believed anymore. But it was too late anyway; Han was already stuffing handfuls of pink rat poison into the holes in the roof. He said his work was covered by a one-year money-back guarantee. "If the weasel comes back, call me," he said.

The ceiling was silent again. Two weeks later, the scratching returned—stronger this time. The aroma was intense—the smell of revenge, I thought—but I never again called Han the exterminator for his money-back guarantee. Instead I bought an electric fan to air out my office, and I learned to live with the weasel above.

Of all the neighbors, none was closer to us than the Confucius Temple; it shared a wall with our kitchen. The shrine was one of the city's most tranquil places, a secluded compound built in 1302, with ancient trees and a tall wooden pavilion that loomed above our house like a conscience. In the mornings, I brought a cup of coffee outside and listened to the wake-up sounds next door: the brush of a broom across the flagstones, the squeak of a faucet, the hectoring of the magpies overhead.

It was a small miracle that the temple had survived at all. Thousands of shrines across the country once existed to venerate Confucius, the philosopher and politician who was born in the sixth century B.C.E. He acquired a place in Chinese history akin to that of Socrates in the West, in part because his ideology encouraged order and loyalty. "There is government," Confucius said, "when the prince is prince, and the minister is minister; when the father is father, and the son is son." Confucius linked morality to the strength of the state: "He who exercises government by means of virtue may be compared to the North Star, which holds its place while all other stars turn around it." Chairman Mao believed in "permanent revolution," and when the Cultural Revolution began in 1966, he exhorted young Red Guards to "Smash the Four Olds": old customs, old culture, old habits, and old ideas. Zealots denounced Confucius for fostering "bad elements, rightists, monsters, and freaks," and one of Mao's lieutenants gave the approval to dig up his grave. Hundreds of temples were destroyed. By the 1980s, Confucianism was so maligned that the historian Ying-shih Yu called it a "wandering soul."

One morning in September 2010, I heard a loudspeaker crackle to life inside the temple walls. It was followed by the sound of a heavy bell, then drums and a flute, and a narrator reciting passages from the classics. The performance lasted twenty minutes, and then it was repeated an hour later, and an hour after that, and again the next day. The wandering soul, in one form or another, had been stirring. Beginning in the eighties, when it became clear that something would eventually fill the "spiritual void," the Party was determined to have a hand in filling it. The old proletarian virtues (revolution, class consciousness) were obsolete. The leaders needed a new moral vocabulary suited to the Party in Power, a way to link themselves to the glories of their ancient civilization. China needed a morality and a politics for the New Middle-Income Stratum. The Party was intrigued by the renaissance of Confucius among Chinese communities in Singapore and Taiwan. He was, after all, an indigenous moral icon, firmly embedded in China's "national studies." In Beijing, Confucius was rehabilitated.

The government opened more than four hundred "Confucius Institutes" around the world to teach Mandarin language and history. (Abroad, scholars complained that the Confucius Institutes stifled discussion of controversial issues such as Tibet and Taiwan.) Proponents of the Confucian revival argued that it would defend China from Western "egoist philosophy," and they had taken to comparing the city of Qufu, the philosopher's hometown, to Jerusalem. Near the cave where Confucius was said to have been born, a five-hundred-million-dollar museum-and-park complex began construction; plans called for a statue of Confucius that would be nearly as tall as the Statue of Liberty. In its marketing, Qufu called itself "the Holy City of the Orient." In 2012, it received 4.4 million visitors, surpassing the number of people who visited Israel. The Chinese Association for the Study of Confucius unveiled new traditions, including encouraging couples to renew their wedding vows in front of a statue of the sage. To give him a fresher image, historians unveiled what they called a "standardized" portrait: a kindly old man in a Chinese robe, with his hands crossed at his chest.

Universities unveiled high-priced courses for entrepreneurs who sought "commercial wisdom" in the classics. National Studies Web, a site devoted to Confucian thought, went public on the Shenzhen stock exchange, and some enterprising Confucians launched the International Confucius Festival, sponsored by a Confucius-themed wine company, in which thousands of people filled a local stadium in his hometown, giant balloons floated overhead bearing the names of ancient scholars, and a Korean pop star in an abbreviated outfit delivered a rock performance.

Just as America's conservative movement in the 1960s had capitalized on the yearning for a postliberal retreat to morality and nobility, China's classical revival drew on a nostalgic image of what it meant to be Chinese. It conjured images of a simpler past, recorded in the idealized stories of ancient Chinese history, of noble knights and honest rulers who acted with moral clarity and purpose. Young nationalists such as Tang Jie organized events in which they visited the Confucius Temple dressed in classical scholars' robes and reenacted rituals that most people had long forgotten, if they knew them at all.

The Confucian revival found a market. The biggest surprise best seller of recent years was a collection of Confucian lectures delivered by Yu Dan, a telegenic professor of media studies who served as a political adviser to the Party. She wrote, "To assess a country's true strength and prosperity, you can't simply look at GNP growth and not look at the inner experience of each ordinary person: Does he feel safe? Is he happy?" Skeptics mocked it as Chicken Soup for the Confucian Soul, but Yu became the second-highest-paid author in the country.

A few days after I heard the sounds inside the temple, it convened a celebration of Confucius's birthday for the first time since the Communists came to power in 1949. The event featured speeches by government officials and professors, and a group of children recited passages. I figured that this would probably signal the end of the musical performance—but, in fact, the show played on, and it acquired a regular schedule: every hour, ten to six, seven days a week, rain or shine. The sound echoed off the walls of the Alley of National Studies, and what had begun as a novelty gradually wore grooves into the minds of my neighbors. "I hear it in my head at night," Huang told me one afternoon. "It's like I've been on a boat all day and I can still feel the rocking."

His face brightened with an idea. "You should go tell them to turn down the volume."

"Why me?" I asked.

"Because you're a foreigner. They'll pay attention to you."

I wasn't sure I wanted the kind of attention that comes from complaining about China's most famous philosopher. But I was curious about the show, and I arranged to visit the head of the temple, a man named Wu Zhiyou. He was not what I expected; Wu looked less like a theologian than an actor who'd play the kindly father in a Chinese soap opera: in his midfifties, he had a large, handsome face, a perfect pair of dimples in his cheeks, and a resonant voice that sounded somehow familiar. Before being posted to run the temple, Wu had spent most of his career in the research office of the city's Propaganda Department, and he had a mind for marketing. Of the performance, he said, "This show has attracted people from all levels of society—Chinese and foreigners, men and women, well-educated and less-educated, experts and ordinary people."

I asked if he was very involved in the production. "I'm the chief designer!" he said, eyes shining. "I oversaw every detail. Even the narrator's voice is mine."

The show had been conceived under demanding circumstances, he said. Confucius had been gone for more than two thousand years, but Wu had been given only a month to organize the performance. He hired a composer, recruited dancers from a local art school, and selected lines from the classics to give it some shape. "You need ups and downs and a climax," he said, "just like a movie or a play. If it's too bland, it would never work."

I got the sense that Wu was savoring the chance to bring Confucius to the stage. "In junior middle school, I was always the student leader of the propaganda section of the student council. I love reading aloud and music and art." In his spare time he still did cross-talk comedy routines, the Chinese version of stand-up. Wu, it seemed to me, had succeeded in making the Confucius Temple into his own community theater. He had plans for the future. "We're building a new set that will have ceramic statues of the seventy-two disciples. And we need more lighting. Then, maybe, I can say it is complete."

Wu checked his watch. He wanted me to catch the three o'clock show. Before I left, he gave me a book on the history of the temple, and said, "After you read this book, your questions will no longer be questions."

The stage was in front of a pavilion on the north side of the compound. It had been fitted with stage lights. The cast consisted of sixteen young men and women in scholars' robes; each song-and-dance routine was named for a line from the classics, and they took an upbeat interpretation: "Happiness" was based on the line "Good fortune lies within bad; bad fortune lies within good," and the stage version omitted the ominous half. The finale, "Harmony," linked Confucius and the Communist Party. A pamphlet explained that it conveyed the "harmonious ideology and harmonious society of the ancient people, which will have a positive influence on the construction of modern harmonious society."

I read the book that the temple director gave me, and the details about ancient events impressed me: It recorded who planted which trees seven hundred years ago, and it contained lively portraits of people from the temple's history in a section called "Anecdotes of Elites." But the book was conspicuously silent on some matters, including the years between 1905 and 1981. In the official history of the Confucius Temple, most of the twentieth century was blank.

During my time in China, I had learned to expect renderings of history that felt like the drop-outs in an audio recording, when the music goes silent and resumes as if nothing happened. Some of those edits were ordained from above: the Party barred people from discussing the crackdown at Tiananmen or the famine of the Great Leap Forward because it had never repudiated or accepted responsibility for them, nor had it dealt with the question of what changes might prevent their happening again. For a long time, ordinary Chinese were willing to aid in the forgetting, not only because they were poor and determined to get on with their lives, but also because many had been victims at some moments and perpetrators at others.

But there were other books about the Confucius Temple, and these filled in the blanks—especially about the night of August 23, 1966. It was the opening weeks of the Cultural Revolution, and the order to "Smash the Four Olds" had devolved into a violent assault on authority of all kinds.

That night, a group of Red Guards summoned one of China's most famous writers, Lao She, to the front gate of the Confucius Temple.

He was sixty-seven years old and one of China's best hopes for the Nobel Prize in Literature. He had grown up not far from there, in poverty, the son of an imperial guard who died in battle against foreign armies. In 1924 he went to London and stayed for five years, living near Bloomsbury and reading Conrad and Joyce. He wore khakis because he couldn't afford tweeds. In 1939 he published *Rickshaw Boy*, about an honest, independent-minded young rickshaw puller whose encounters with injustice turn him into, in Lao She's words, a "degenerate, selfish, hapless product of a sick society." Lao She became to Beijing what Victor Hugo was to Paris: the city's quintessential writer. The Party named him a "People's Artist." He resented being asked to produce propaganda, but, like many, he was a loyal servant who poured criticism on his fellow writers when they fell out with the Party.

Now he was the target. A group of Red Guards—mostly schoolgirls between thirteen and sixteen years old—pushed him through the gates of the temple and forced him to kneel on the flagstones beside a bonfire, surrounded by other writers and artists under attack. His accusers denounced him for his links to the West. They shouted, "Down with the anti-Party elements!" and used leather belts with heavy brass buckles to whip the old men and women before them. Lao She was bleeding from his head, but he stayed conscious. For three hours this went on, until, at last, he was brought to a police station, where his wife retrieved him.

The next morning, Lao She rose early and walked northwest from his home to a quiet pond called the Lake of Great Peace. He read poetry and wrote until the sun had set. Then he took off his shirt and draped it over a tree branch. He loaded his pockets with stones and walked into the lake.

When his body was discovered the next day, his son, Shu Yi, was summoned to collect it. The police had found his father's clothes, his cane, his glasses, and his pen, as well as a sheaf of papers that he had left behind. The official ruling on his death explained that Lao She had "isolated himself from the people." Since he was a "counterrevolutionary," he was not allowed to be given a proper burial. In the end, his widow and children loaded his spectacles and his pen into a casket and buried it.

I wondered about the son, Shu Yi, who had gone to retrieve his father's body. He would be in his seventies now, older than his father was when he died. I asked around and discovered that he lived only a few minutes' walk from my house. He invited me over. His apartment was cluttered with books and scrolls and paintings in a way that reminded me of the fortune-teller's shop. Shu had white hair and a heavy, kind face. As we talked, a soft breeze blew in the window from a nearby canal. I asked if he had ever learned more about his father's state of mind at the end.

"It's hard to know exactly, but I think his death was his final act of struggle," he said. He went on: "Many years later, I came upon an article called 'Poets,' which he had written in 1941"—a quarter-century before he died. "He wrote, 'Poets are a strange crowd. When everyone else is happy, the poets can say things that are discouraging. When everyone else is sorrowful, the poets can laugh and dance. But when the nation is in danger, they must drown themselves, and let their deaths be a warning in the name of truth.' "

This sacrifice was a tradition in China, dating to the third century B.C.E., when the poet Qu Yuan drowned himself in protest against corruption. Shu Yi told me, "By doing so, they are fighting back, telling others what the truth really is." His father, he said, "would rather break than bend."

After I met Shu Yi, I went back to see Wu Zhiyou, the head of the temple, and I asked him about the story of the writer's final night. He gave a short sigh and said, "It's true. During the Cultural Revolution, there were struggle sessions here. Afterward, Lao She went home and threw himself in the lake. This can be described as a historical fact."

I asked him why the temple's written history made no mention of it. He struggled to find an answer, and I braced for a bit of propaganda. But then Wu said something that surprised me. "It's too sad," he said simply. "It makes people too sad. I think it's best not to include this in books. It's factual, it's history, but it was not because of the temple. It was because of the time. It doesn't belong in the records of the Confucius Temple."

I understood his point, but it felt incomplete. Lao She was beaten in the temple because it was a place of learning, of ideas, of history; the permission to attack one of China's most famous novelists was, like so much of the Cultural Revolution, the permission to attack what it meant to be Chinese, and in the decades since then the Party and the people had never reconciled all that they lost in those moments. Even if someone wanted to mark the site where Beijing's greatest chronicler ended his life, it would be difficult; the Lake of Great Peace was filled in decades ago, during an extension of the subway system. I often marveled at how much people in China had managed to put behind them: revolution, war, poverty, and the upheavals of the present. My neighbor Huang Wenyi lived next door with his mother, who was eighty-eight. When I once asked her if she had old photos of the family, she said, "They were burned during the Cultural Revolution." And then she laughed, the particular hollow Chinese laugh reserved for awful things.

Every day, groups of civil servants from the hinterlands, and students from around the city, were turning up at the Confucius Temple to get a tour and take in the show. I watched a young guide with a ponytail face a group of middle-aged Chinese women. She held her hands out before her. "This is the gesture for paying respects to Confucius," she said. Her visitors did their best to copy her. For many people in China, I realized, the gaps in history had made Confucius a stranger.

In that vacuum, some people were eager to put the philosopher to more useful political purposes. After Liu Xiaobo won the Nobel Peace Prize, a group of Chinese nationalists organized what they called the "Confucius Peace Prize," and awarded it, the next year, to Vladimir Putin for bringing "safety and stability to Russia." A group of Confucian scholars denounced a plan to build a large Christian church in Confucius's hometown, writing, "We beseech you to respect this sacred land of Chinese culture."

Others were growing weary of this version of Confucius. The insistence on harmony seemed to leave little room for a politics of negotiation, for an honest clash of ideas. Li Ling, a Peking University professor, took aim at what he called the "manufactured Confucius," and wrote, "The real Confucius, the one who actually lived, was neither a sage nor a king . . . He had no power or status—only morality and learning—and dared to criticize the power elite of his day. He traveled around lobbying for his policies, racking his brains to help the rulers of his day with their problems, always trying to convince them to give up evil ways and be more righteous . . . He was tormented, obsessed, and driven to roam, pleading for his ideas, more like a homeless dog than a sage. This was the real Confucius."

When the author published this, he was denounced by Confucians as a "prophet of doomsday." One of his defenders was Liu Xiaobo. Before he went to prison, Liu warned of a mood in which "Confucianism was venerated and all other schools of thought were banned." Instead of invoking Confucius, Liu wrote, intellectuals should be venerating "independence of thought and autonomy of person."

Chinese people came to the Holy Land of National Studies on a quest for some kind of moral continuity. But it rarely ended their search. The Party, to maintain its hold over history, offered a caricature of Confucius. Generations of Chinese had grown up being told to condemn China's ethical and philosophical traditions, only to find that the Party was now abruptly resurrecting them, without granting permission to discuss what had happened in the interim. A neighborhood devoted to protecting the "essence of the country" only seemed to reinforce the reality that there was no single "essence" anymore.

There were signs that liberal intellectuals were not the only ones losing patience with such a forceful embrace of Confucius. In January 2011 a giant statue of the wise man appeared beside Tiananmen Square, the first new addition to such a sensitive spot since Mao's mausoleum was erected a generation ago. Philosophers and political scientists wondered if this meant a change in the Party platform. But then, it was gone. In the middle of the night, three months after it arrived, the statue was moved to a low-profile location in the courtyard of a museum. Why? It remained a mystery: the Central Propaganda Department banned any discussion of it. People were left to joke that Confucius, the itinerant teacher from Shandong Province, had been caught trying to live in Beijing without the proper permit.

# TWENTY

# PASSING BY

There are moments in the life of a country when people stop and look at themselves and wonder if they have lost their way. In China's case, one of those moments arrived on the afternoon of October 13, 2011, in the city of Foshan, in the far southern reaches of the country. Foshan is a market town, the home of enormous open-air emporiums, one after another: Iron and Steel World and Flower and Plant World and Children's Clothing Town, which sells enough clothes each year to dress every kid in America, twice.

One of the biggest, Hardware City, has a permanent population of thirty thousand. It specializes in the unforgiving artifacts of construction: steel chains, power tools, drums of chemicals, and spools of electric cable as thick as a man's wrist. It is a labyrinth of storefronts and alleyways, sprawled across a hundred acres, beneath a rambling roof of tin and plastic that shadows the world beneath in a permanent twilight. Hardware City smells of sawdust and diesel. There are two thousand shops, block after block, and the market has grown so fast and erratically, with no street signs or traffic lights, that it's easy to get lost there.

Just after two o'clock that afternoon, a young mother and shopkeeper named Qu Feifei picked up her daughter from nursery school a few blocks away and turned back toward her home in Hardware City. As a mother, Qu was unabashedly doting: she spent four times as much on a dress for her toddler as she did on one for herself. She and her husband had a tiny storefront called Auspicious Prosperity Rolling Mill Ball Bearings. They lived upstairs, with their kids, aged two and seven, in a dimly lit converted storage space where the ceiling was just high enough for an adult to stand upright.

Qu's husband, Wang Chichang, had worked in Hardware City for eight years. At thirty years old, he had large wide-set eyes and overgrown bangs that reached past his brows. He hailed from a county in Shandong Province once famous for its pears and peaches and now devoted to the production of chemicals. He had studied animal husbandry in vocational school, before trying his luck in Beijing, where he had worked construction, and in a pet shop, before finding his way to Hardware City. After the couple married, Qu had a boy they named Wang Shuo. (It means "Wang the Scholar.") When she had a girl, they paid the fines and named her Wang Yue; everyone called her Little Yueyue, which means "Little Joy." By the time she was two, she was precocious, quick to pick up words from the cartoon program *Smart Tiger,* and content to fuss around with her fake cooking while her parents made dinner in the shop. When mother and daughter returned from school that afternoon, Qu went upstairs to bring in the laundry from the line, while Wang Yue played downstairs. When the mother came back, her daughter was gone. It was nothing unusual—she always flitted back and forth among the neighbors—and Qu went out to find her. As dusk approached, the skies opened, and the autumn rain drummed hard on the roof of the market.

A few blocks away, another young vendor, named Hu Jun, was setting off on the final errands of the day. Like the Wang family, Hu Jun and his wife had a young daughter, and a ball-bearing shop, and they, too, hailed from Shandong Province, though the market was so big that the two families didn't know each other. Hu Jun climbed into a small inexpensive van, which the Chinese call a "bread loaf," and snaked through the crowded alleyways. He was picking up a payment in an unfamiliar part of Hardware City, and he scanned the shop signs as he drove.

Little Yueyue had not gone to see the neighbors. She had gone wandering, and soon she was two and a half blocks from home. To attract customers, the shops that lined the alleys liked to keep some of their goods out front, even though it cluttered the roadside with mounds of merchandise. She passed bundles as tall as she was. The little girl, dressed in a dark shirt and pink trousers, passed a shop on the corner, where a banged-up old computer monitor was recording sixteen different angles from the surveillance cameras out front. The cameras chronicled what happened next. At 5:25, Little Yueyue peered over her shoulder but continued walking. When she turned back to face the road ahead, it was just in time to see the van but too late to avoid being hit by it. Hu Jun would later say that he felt only a slight bump against the tire—a hiccup so small that he assumed that it was market detritus in the road: a bundle of rags, a cardboard box. He never stopped to check.

Little Yueyue was struck twice, first by the front wheel, then by the rear, her upper body, then her lower. She came to rest beside a bale of merchandise, and she lay motionless except for the faint movement of her left arm.

Twenty seconds after she was struck, a man on foot, wearing a white shirt and dark trousers, approached. He looked in her direction and slowed. Then he walked on. Five seconds later, a motorbike passed; the driver peered over his shoulder, toward the child, but did not slow down. Ten seconds after that, another man passed, looked in her direction, and kept walking. Nine seconds later, a small truck approached and it, too, hit Little Yueyue, rolling over her legs and continuing on.

More people passed—a figure in a blue raincoat, a rider in a black T-shirt, a worker loading goods at the intersection. A man on a motorbike stared at her and talked to a shop owner, before they hurried away. Four minutes after the initial collision, the eleventh person to approach was a woman holding the hand of a little girl. She ran a store nearby, and she, too, had picked up her daughter from school. She stopped, asked a shopkeeper about the child in the road, and then darted off, hurrying her daughter away from the scene. On they came: a rider on a motorbike, a man on foot, a worker from the shop on the corner.

At 5:31, six minutes after the girl was hit, a small woman carrying bags of salvaged cans and bottles approached. She was the eighteenth passerby. But she did not pass. She dropped her bags and tried to lift Little Yueyue in her arms. She heard the child groan, and her small body crumpled like dead weight. The woman was an illiterate grandmother named Chen Xianmei, who recycled trash and scrap metal for a living. She pulled the child's body closer to the curb, and then she peered around for help. She approached nearby shopkeepers, but one was busy with a customer; another told her, "That child is not mine." Chen tried the next block, shouting for help, and there she encountered the mother, Qu Feifei, who was searching desperately for her daughter.

Chen led her to the roadside. The mother crouched on the asphalt, wrapped Little Yueyue in her arms, and began to run.

Ambulances are rare in China, so mother and father loaded their daughter into the small family Buick. When they reached Huangqi Hospital, fifteen minutes away, nurses in pink uniforms were attending to a stream of arrivals. The waiting room was clean and well built, but the signs on the walls warned people of the perils that cling to China's health care system. One sign advised them against trying to bribe a doctor for better care; another warned against "Appointment Scalpers." It said, IF A STRANGER CLAIMS TO HAVE A CLOSE RELATIONSHIP WITH A SPECIALIST, AND TRIES TO LEAD YOU OUTSIDE THE HOSPITAL, DON'T BE FOOLED.

Doctors discovered that Little Yueyue had a skull fracture and serious damage to the brain. At first, local reporters figured it was a typical hit-and-run. Then they saw the surveillance video. Instantly, the story of the seventeen passersby began to spread across China, and it provoked a surge of self-recrimination. The writer Zhang Lijia asked, "How can we possibly win respect and play the role of a world leader if this is a nation with 1.4 billion cold hearts?" The video played endlessly on television and online, a morality play about big-city apathy and a coarsening of the spirit. For many, the moment crystallized the sense that the great national competition was leaving some of China's most vulnerable people underfoot. It tapped a well of collective guilt—over infants sickened by contaminated formula, over children trapped in collapsing schools, and over a string of cases in which people had neglected strangers in need. Chinese papers had recently reported the death of an eighty-eight-year-old man who fell at a vegetable market and suffocated from a nosebleed because nobody turned him over.

Local reporters rushed to the scene in Hardware City and filled out the portrait: At a shop on the corner called New China Wholesale Safety Gear, the boss said he'd been busy doing the books, and his wife was cooking dinner. "I heard a child's cry," he told them, "but just for a moment or two, and then it was gone. I didn't give it another thought." The local press tracked down the man on the red three-wheeler, but all he would say was, "I did not notice her," a phrase he repeated ten times. Online, people scoured the video and identified the owner of a plumbing supply store on the corner; he had stepped out of his shop, glanced down, and slipped back inside. He insisted he never saw the wounded child in the road, but people called him "unconscionable" and defaced his website. At the same time, they lionized the scavenger who stopped to help. Reporters asked her, over and over, why she had intervened. The question bewildered her. After the reporters moved on, she asked her daughter-in-law, "What did I have to fear about helping a child?"

The Chinese pride themselves on "humaneness," or *ren*, as it was known, and it was an idea as fundamental to conceptions of morality in China as the principle of "do unto others" was in the West. But in recent years, as a practical matter, kids in China were also raised to be mindful of less inspiring concerns, such as *zuo haoshi bei e*—which means "doing something helpful and getting cheated in the process." It was a fear that came with its own categories as specific as a *pengci'r*—a person who "blames you for breaking a piece of porcelain that was already broken."

For many people, living in China in this day and age felt like living on a newly prosperous island that was surrounded by treacherous currents—stay on dry land, and life could be safe and rewarding; lose your footing for a moment, and the world could collapse. They had so little margin to absorb a disaster in their lives that they felt they had no choice but to keep up their defenses. My friend Faye Li, a journalist whose father was a physics teacher, told me about the day her father was on his bicycle and a car knocked him to the ground. "He got up and rode away as fast as possible," she said, only realizing after he was home that *he* was the victim. He was convinced that someone would try to take advantage of him. She said, "I think, in China, it's easy to get into trouble." Over the years, the risk of being blamed for helping someone was a scenario that appeared over and over in the headlines. In November 2006 an elderly woman in Nanjing fell at a bus stop, and a young man named Peng Yu stopped to help her get to the hospital. In recovery, she accused Peng of causing her fall, and a local judge agreed, ordering him to pay more than seven thousand dollars—a judgment based not on evidence, but on what the verdict called "logical thinking": that Peng would never have helped if he hadn't been motivated by guilt.

That verdict became a sensation, and the more interested I became in the case of Little Yueyue, the more I noticed that practically every person I met had heard about the "Peng Yu case." Often people volunteered similar stories: a helpful young member of the urban middle class done in by a gimlet-eyed scam artist. The lesson never changed: what little you have assembled in life can be gone in an instant. After a young man named Chen was falsely accused of injuring a cyclist, he told reporters, "I really don't know if I will help out again if I encounter a similar situation."

Though the chances of ever becoming an extorted Good Samaritan seemed small, they swelled in the public consciousness because they confirmed the anxieties people felt about their moment in time, the sense that the race to get ahead was eroding China's ethics. And the less people thought of their fellow citizens, the less willing they were to help—and the cycle continued. Zhou Runan, an anthropologist who studied Hardware City, told me that nobody was more alert to the risk of being tricked than migrants far from home. "In America, an individual is the basis of civil society, but in China, the collective is breaking down, and there is nothing yet there to replace it . . . When you come to a new place, you take care of yourself; you make a life with your family at its core—your wife, your husband, your child—and everybody else becomes less important," he said. "You divide your mind."

The Chinese press was quick to reinforce the theory that cases like this reflected the alienation of big-city life: HEARTLESS BYSTANDERS NOT SOLELY CHINESE PROBLEM, declared *Global Times*, and the *People's Daily* described the cases as "unavoidable during the country's process of urbanization." Yet, the more I studied the stories of Little Yueyue and others, the more I found these explanations incomplete.


The Chinese were not the first people to suspect that urbanization was damaging their moral health. In 1964, Americans were shocked by the murder of a twenty-eight-year-old woman named Kitty Genovese in New York. As *The New York Times* described it at the time, "For more than half an hour thirty-eight respectable, law-abiding citizens in Queens watched a killer stalk and stab a woman," and none of them called police or came to her aid. Americans embraced the story because it conformed to their fears of becoming an uncaring urban society, and the "Genovese syndrome," as it was known, became a standard explanation in social psychology.

Except that it wasn't quite true. Years later, researchers returned to witnesses and court records and found that only three or four people who heard her cries understood what was happening to her, and at least one witness probably called the police during the attack. Officers, however, arrived too late to save her. (The story of thirty-eight silent bystanders had been mentioned to the newspaper, not incidentally, by the police commissioner.) In the case of Little Yueyue, apathy might not have been the only explanation for why people hesitated. The anthropologist Yan Yunxiang examined twenty-six cases of Good Samaritans who had been the victims of extortion in China, and he found that, in every instance, the local police and the courts treated the helpers as guilty until proven innocent. In none of the twenty-six cases was the extortionist ever required to provide a witness to back up the accusation; nor was the extortionist ever punished, even after the helper was found to be falsely accused.

In the years of the boom, people had picked up more reasons to fear the law than to trust it. Growing up at a time when law enforcement jobs were sometimes sold to the highest bidder, and judges were regularly available to be bribed, people were bound to be wary. When the China scholar Wang Zhengxu surveyed people in 2008, he found "significantly lower trust in the government and the Party among the post-reform citizens." Police were single-minded in achieving convictions, and a series of cases was coming to light that suggested the consequences of haste. A man named She Xianglin served eleven years for the murder of his estranged wife—until she returned one day to visit her family. It turned out that she had moved to another province and remarried; the defendant, who had been tortured for ten days and ten nights into a false confession, was released in 2005. A study of Chinese attitudes published in the journal *Science* in 2013 found that young Chinese men and women were, in the researchers' words, "less trusting, less trustworthy, more risk-averse, less competitive, more pessimistic, and less conscientious individuals."

Virtually everyone who had passed Little Yueyue insisted that they saw nothing, with the exception of one: the mother who had walked by with her daughter. Her name was Lin Qingfei, and when local reporters tracked her down, she did not flinch from the memory of what passed through her mind that day: "She was crying in a very faint voice . . . There was a young man standing in front of the shop. So I asked him whether the child was his. He waved me off and didn't say anything. My daughter said, 'That little girl is covered in blood.' I was so scared, and I dragged my daughter away." Lin reached her own shop, and she told her husband what she had seen, but he was buried in his work. "Nobody else dared to touch her," Lin said, "so how could I?"

At the hospital, Little Yueyue's parents wondered if their daughter might receive better care if they figured out a way to gain access to one of China's elite hospitals that was off-limits to the regular public. They did an inventory of their relationships in the market and approached a fellow Shandong migrant who connected them to another migrant who owned a shop called King Abrasives, which sold the replacement discs for electric sanders. He was an army veteran; he made a phone call and succeeded in getting the child transferred to the ICU at a military hospital in Guangzhou. He had seen the video. "I recognized a lot of the people who walked by and didn't stop," he said later. When he confronted one of them, he was told, "It's not even your own child; why are you getting wrapped up in something that's not your business!"

By October 15, two days after the collision, Little Yueyue was in a large hospital room with pale turquoise walls, surrounded by tubes and racks of machines. She had received an emergency operation to open the back of her skull, but she was still in critical condition. Her parents turned their attention to finding out who was responsible. They went door-to-door, asking, "Do you know the driver of the bread loaf van in this video?" They hung flyers around Hardware City offering fifty thousand yuan—more than eight thousand dollars—for leads on the identity of the driver. Wang posted a notice online, registering under the name Nu'er Hui Haode, which means "My daughter will be okay."

In the home of the driver, Hu Jun, a dark realization was taking hold. His brother-in-law was the first in the family to see the video. "At that moment, Hu Jun thought back and realized, 'I think I hit something two days ago,'" his lawyer, Li Wangdong, told me. Hu Jun watched the tape. "He went numb from head to toe," Li said.

The driver turned himself in to the police. "It was raining, and the pounding of the rain on the roof was so loud that I didn't hear the child cry. I looked in the mirror on the right-hand side and saw nothing, so I drove on," he told police, according to the *Yangcheng Evening News*. "If

I'd known I had hit someone, I definitely would have stopped." In the hours after the collision, he had not acted much like a guilty man, his lawyer told me. "He didn't wash the car or wipe it down with a rag. When he got home, he wasn't nervous or panicked. In conversation with other shopkeepers, he did nothing unusual."

After the arrest, local reporters pressed the girl's father, Wang Chichang, for a reaction. "I really don't know what to express: Hatred? Anger? What's the use in that? Will hatred make my child recover?" Days passed, and Yueyue remained in the ICU, separated from her parents by a pane of glass. She would not recover. Just after midnight on the morning of October 21, she died of multiple organ failure.

Months after the television cameras moved on from Hardware City, I was in Foshan and decided to visit the scene of the accident. It looked the same as it did on TV: big bundles by the roadside, the twilight from above. I wandered into the nearest storefront, which was called Clever Hardware, and found a man behind a cluttered desk. His name was Chen Dongyang. He was his late fifties, with hair brushed back in the style of Chairman Mao and reading glasses on the tip of his nose. He seemed to guess why I was there, and he offered me a seat. Before I could ask a question, he said that his daughter had been working that day and "she didn't hear a thing."

Chen and I talked for a long time. To him, a conversation about Little Yue was a conversation about what you could trust. "In the past, if you saw something, you knew it was true because who had the time or the money to make something fake?" he said, adding, "Now even the fin on a fish can be fake . . . In the past, if you didn't have enough food, I would give you a bite. That's how it was. But after Reform and Opening Up, it's different. If you have one bite of food and I have one bite, I will try to take yours and have two for myself, and leave you with nothing.

"We've learned all these bad habits from countries like yours," he said, smiling, "and we've forgotten our good traditions. Look at me: I didn't even remember to serve you tea!" He bolted up, looked around the shop for tea, and then gave up and sat back down. I asked him if he wasn't overdoing it a bit on the 'good old days' routine.

"Everyone has some cash in his pocket, but the money isn't safe. You need a sense of security to be comfortable," he said. I asked Chen how he would've responded if he had seen the little girl in the road. He said nothing for a moment.

"If it was before Reform and Opening Up, I would have rushed out and risked my life to save her," he said. "But after? I would probably hesitate. I wouldn't be that brave. That's what I'm trying to say: this is the world we're in now." Chen had a granddaughter, and I asked, "When she grows up, what kind of person do you want her to be?"

"That depends on what's going on in society," he said. "If good people run things, she should be a good person. If it's bad people, well, you have no choice but to be bad."

That night, I had dinner with Chen Xianmei, the grandmother who pulled Little Yueyue from the road. She was perhaps the smallest adult I have ever met: four feet seven inches tall, which the family chalked up to her childhood in the mountains of Guangdong, where food was scarce. She spoke only a local dialect that other people struggled to make out. Her son and his wife were her interpreters, her links to the world. In the mornings, she cooked for workers in Hardware City, and in the afternoons, she hunted for loose screws and scraps. "Every little thing can be resold," she said. On the day of the accident, her family had urged her not to go out because it was raining. But a rainy day was a gold mine, she said, because the other scavengers stayed home.

When people discovered her role in helping Little Yueyue, she became a minor celebrity. News photographers came and posed her in a field harvesting crops to dramatize her humble origins—no matter how many times she tried to explain to them that it wasn't the harvest season. She received six invitations to Beijing, for official celebrations of "good deeds," though, in truth, the experiences in Beijing only made her uncomfortable. "I can't understand what people are saying, and they can't understand what I'm saying," she said.

Local officials and private companies were eager to be photographed with her, and she received about thirteen thousand dollars in rewards. But as her name spread, the experience took an unhappy turn. People in her village saw the publicity she was getting and concluded that she had received far more money than she actually had. Neighbors began asking *her* for loans. No matter what she said, they persisted. They even asked her to pave the road into the village.

Chen Xianmei told me she was grateful for the rewards, but she would have preferred that the local government simply allow her grandson to go to public school: he had a rural *hukou*, which made him ineligible for public kindergarten in the city, so his parents were spending seven hundred yuan a month on a private school, and her reward money wouldn't last forever.

The curious consequences of her good deed spilled over into her son's life. No matter how many times he told his coworkers that he wasn't rich, people were convinced that his mother was hiding a fortune. The pressure became so strong that he left his job. The best new work he could find was exhausting; he was driving a bread loaf van thirteen hours a day.

For the parents of Little Yueyue, donations arrived from around the country. A classroom of local kids sent a cookie tin brimming with small bills. A well-meaning newspaper in the father's home province encouraged people to call him, and he was deluged by the response. In a single five-minute stretch, he counted fifty-one missed calls.

At the same time, a crackpot theory took root on the Web: the whole case was a fraud. The video, the girl, the doctors—it was all a scam, people said. Hannah Arendt once identified a "peculiar kind of cynicism" that takes hold in societies prone to the "consistent and total substitution of lies for factual truth." The response, she wrote, was "the absolute refusal to believe the truth of anything." In an effort to put an end to the rumors, the father invited local reporters to watch him count the donations and put them in a bank. The total came to nearly forty-four thousand dollars. But the suggestion of fraud did not go away. By the end of October, Wang was desperate to be rid of the money as fast as he could. He donated it to two patients in need, and then he and his wife receded from view. The father loathed going out. At night, the parents had recurring dreams about their daughter; in his, he was hugging her and hoisting her on his back; in the mother's dream, Little Yueyue was always wearing a yellow dress, and always laughing. Before long, the family left Hardware City.

In the end, prosecutors decided that Hu Jun did not knowingly flee the scene of the accident. Police had staged a re-creation—spraying the roof of Hardware City from a fire engine to simulate rain—and Hu pleaded guilty to involuntary manslaughter. He apologized to the family, and the lawyer asked for leniency; he submitted snapshots of Hu Jun cradling his own ten-month-old daughter. I noticed that instead of traditional split-back pants, his baby girl wore diapers, perhaps the clearest sign in China of a family's first steps into the middle class. When the video played in the courtroom, Hu Jun hung his head. He was sentenced to two years and six months in prison.

Several weeks after Yueyue died, the city of Shenzhen drafted China's first regulation to protect Good Samaritans from legal liability. It shifted the burden of proof to the accusers, and it laid out punishments for false accusations ranging from a public apology to detention. The law stopped short of requiring passersby to get involved—as they are required to do in Japan, France, and elsewhere—but it was nevertheless China's greatest step yet to amend the law. Over time, I came to feel sorry for the men and women of Hardware City—including, I must say, the ones who passed by. They were conscripted into a parable, but the morality play did not do justice to the layers of their lives. The Chinese public had read the death of Little Yueyue much the way sixties-era Americans had accepted the story of Kitty Genovese, even though, up close, there was more to it.

The clearest evidence against the theory that Chinese people no longer cared about one another was that they *did* care: for every video of people ignoring each other, there were examples of people risking themselves to protect others. When a disturbed man with a knife burst into a primary school in Henan in December 2012 and wounded twenty-two children, surveillance footage showed another man dashing after him, armed with nothing but a broom. For all the atomizing effects of the market age, the culture of giving was not shrinking; it was growing. Private philanthropic organizations, which had been shuttered or taken over by the Party, were returning. Blood donations had grown so much that the old blood merchants who used to go door-to-door, standing peasants on their heads, all but disappeared. After the earthquake in Sichuan in 2008, more than a quarter of a million volunteers went to help; most of them were young and most of them paid their own way to get there. Zhou Runan, the anthropologist, told me, "Young people are training to become fully rounded individuals, not selfish isolated people. That's where the hope is: in the young."

The Party's efforts to promote morality rang ever hollower. When I was talking to people about the case of Little Yueyue, state television was reporting on the sixtieth anniversary of Chairman Mao's discovery of the soldier Lei Feng, that icon of socialist dedication. Lei Feng was all over the bus shelters and posters. The Party had blessed three new movies about him, but the propaganda blitz was a disaster. Nobody wanted to see the Lei Feng movies; the *Global Times* reported the story of a theater that was showing a Lei Feng movie to empty seats, "in case anyone showed up." Online, people mocked Lei Feng; they ran the numbers and concluded that, for Lei to have collected as much manure as he proclaimed, he would have had to encounter a piece of dung every eleven steps for nine hours. Another post suggested that Lei might've been corrupt, spending more on his outfit than his salary would have supported. The two men who posted it were detained. A police statement read, "The glorious image of Lei Feng was being questioned by some Web users. Many Web users reported this to the police, demanding a thorough investigation of the creators of the rumors defaming Lei Feng's image."

I sometimes wondered how things might be different in China if its leaders, instead of flying the flags of Lei Feng and a harmonious society, offered credible signs that they were trying to make their institutions more ethical and trustworthy and honest. In its actions, and its inactions, a state enacts a moral view, at least according to Confucius. "The moral character of the ruler is the wind," he said, "the moral character of those beneath him is the grass. When the wind blows, the grass bends." In its abuses and deceptions, the Chinese government was failing to make a persuasive argument for what it meant to be Chinese in the modern world. The Party had rested its legitimacy on prosperity, stability, and a pantheon of hollow heroes. In doing so, it had disarmed itself in the battle for the soul, and it sent Chinese individuals out to wander the market of ideas in search of icons of their own.

# TWENTY-ONE

# SOULCRAFT

At some point along the way, I lost touch with a friend named Lin Gu. He was a well-connected reporter and self-described social butterfly who took pride in never having turned on the stove in his apartment. When I asked around, a friend told me that Lin had moved to the mountains to begin training as a monk. It was not unheard of; China had recently passed a milestone to become the world's largest Buddhist nation. When Lin returned to Beijing on a break, we had dinner. I met him outside the subway. He was dressed in loose brown cotton, and his head was shaved. He was living in a remote community of two dozen people, about two hours from the nearest city. "It's a cliché, right?" he said and laughed. "The middle-class Chinese monk?"

As a journalist in China, Lin had lived by what he called "a golden rule": doubt everything. At thirty-eight, he grew up after the Cultural Revolution, in the time of plenty, when politics was of little interest. His mother had been a devout member of the Party when she was young, but Lin was put off by devotion. He had an unflattering image of Buddhism: "Old grannies and grandpas getting on their knees and burning incense," he said. In the winter of 2009, Lin splurged on a trip to Thailand for himself and his mother. Before he flew, he visited a bookstore in Chengdu and happened on the memoir of a monk. He was not prepared for the effect it had on him. "I found Buddha to be an inspiration. He invited me to think bravely about this world," Lin said. "Buddha could challenge any social norms, such as the caste system of India," he went on. "He rethought the conceptual framework he had from day one."

Lin spent the trip to Thailand in his hotel room, absorbed in the book—"I never even went to the pool"—and when he returned, he began frequenting a Buddhist institute near his apartment in Beijing. His moment of transformation came when he grasped the idea, as he put it, that "this world is a fantasy." He found it impossible to imagine going back to the work he had before. He asked, "Why should we attach ourselves to money and fame and social status?" He went on, "As a journalist in China you have to dance in chains. You have to maneuver in whatever space you get. You have to play the game with the government and the propaganda officials, and the subject of your stories . . . We waste a lot of energy and time trying to bypass all the obstacles of the propaganda machine. By that time, you are exhausted and the deadline is there. So you don't feel satisfied with the professionalism of your stories, and you envy your Western colleagues who can focus on the writing itself." Buddhism gave him answers that journalism never could. "I've been searching for the truth for a long time," he said.

To live in China in the early years of the twenty-first century was to witness a spiritual revival that could be compared to America's Great Awakening in the nineteenth century. The stereotype of the Chinese citizen content to delay moral questions until he was car-and-home-equipped looked increasingly out of date. The more people satisfied their basic needs, the more they uncovered the truth, the more they challenged the old dispensation. For new sources of meaning, they looked not only to religion but also to philosophy, psychology, and literature for new ways of orienting themselves in a world of ideological incoherence and unrelenting ambition. What obligation did an individual have to a stranger in a hypercompetitive, market-driven society? How much responsibility did a citizen have to speak the truth when speaking the truth was dangerous? Was it better to try to change an authoritarian system from within, or to oppose it from outside, at the risk of having no effect at all?

The search for answers awakened and galvanized people in a way that the pursuit of fortune once had. One night in December 2012, I was on the campus of Xiamen University, on China's southeastern coast, when students massed outside the auditorium—far more of them than the building could handle. I stood inside the doors and watched the growing crowd of young, flushed faces on the other side of the glass. Jittery security guards appealed to the crowd to keep calm. The president of the university had phoned the organizers of that evening's event and cautioned them not to lose control. The object of such fervent anticipation—a figure who had acquired a level of popularity in China "usually reserved for Hollywood movie stars and NBA players," as the *China Daily* put it—was an introverted Minnesota native named Michael J. Sandel. At Harvard, where Sandel was a professor of political philosophy, he taught a popular course called Justice, which introduced students to the pillars of Western thought: Aristotle, Kant, Rawls, and others.

He framed their theories of moral decision-making in real-world dilemmas. *Is torture ever justified? Would you steal a drug that your child needs to survive?* The classes had been filmed for an American public television series and put online. As they began to circulate in China, Chinese volunteers came forward to provide subtitles, and after two years, Sandel had acquired an almost preposterous level of celebrity. His Chinese lectures on Western political philosophy had been watched at least twenty million times. *China Newsweek* magazine named him the "most influential foreign figure" of 2010.

Sandel was a cerebral, meticulous man in his late fifties, with vanishing gray hair and pale blue eyes that regarded the world with a vaguely apprehensive expression. He was more accustomed to life in Brookline, Massachusetts, with his wife and two sons, but he was learning to expect extraordinary reactions abroad, especially in East Asia. In Seoul he lectured to fourteen thousand people in an outdoor stadium; in Tokyo the scalpers' price for tickets to his talks was five hundred dollars. But in China, he had inspired near-religious devotion, and his visits plunged him into an alternative dimension of celebrity. Once, at the airport in Shanghai, the passport-control officer stopped him to gush that he was a fan.

Outside the auditorium in Xiamen, the crowd kept growing, until the organizers finally decided that they had a better chance of keeping the peace if they threw open the doors. So, fire codes notwithstanding, they let the crowd pour into the aisles, until young men and women covered every inch of floor space. Sandel climbed the stage. Behind him, an enormous plastic banner carried the Chinese title of his latest book, *What Money Can't Buy*, in which he asked whether too many features of modern life were becoming what he called "instruments of profit." In a nation where everything seemed to have a price tag—a military commission, a marriage, a seat in kindergarten—his audience was rapt. "I am not arguing against markets as such," he told the crowd. "What I am suggesting is that in recent decades we have drifted, almost without realizing it, from having a market economy to becoming a market society."

Sandel mentioned a story from the headlines: Wang Shangkun was a seventeen-year-old high school student from a poor patch of Anhui province who was illegally recruited in a chat room to sell his kidney for $3,500, a transaction his mother discovered when he returned home with an iPad and an iPhone and then went into renal failure. The surgeon and eight others—who had resold the kidney for ten times what they paid—were arrested. "There are one-point-five million people in China who need an organ transplant," Sandel told the crowd, "but there are only ten thousand available organs in any year." How many here, he asked, would support a legal free market in kidneys?

A young Chinese man named Peter, in a white sweatshirt and chunky glasses, raised his hand and made a libertarian argument that legalizing the kidney trade would squeeze out the black market. Others disagreed, and Sandel upped the stakes. Say a Chinese father sold a kidney and then, "a few years later, he needs to send a second child to school, and a person comes and asks if he would sell his other kidney—or his heart, if he is willing to give up his life. Is there anything wrong with that?"

Peter thought it over, and said, "As long as it's free and transparent and open, rich people can buy life, and it's not immoral." A ripple of agitation passed over the crowd; a middle-aged man behind me shouted, "No!" Sandel settled the room. "The question of markets," he said, "is really a question about how we want to live together. Do we want a society where everything is up for sale?"

"Of the various countries I've visited," Sandel told me the next day, "the free-market assumptions and convictions are more present in China among young people than anywhere, with the possible exception of the United States." What interested him most, however, was the countervailing force—the ripple through the crowd at the idea of selling the second kidney. "If you groped and probed, you found one example after another of the limits of extending market logic to everything," he said.

In China, foreign ideas had a history of sparking fevers. After World

War I, John Dewey toured the country and inspired legions of followers. Later, it was Freud and Habermas. When Sandel visited for the
first time, in 2007, the timing was ripe. Introducing him at Tsinghua
University in Beijing, professor Junren Wan said China had a "crying
heart." Sandel had spent much of his career considering what he called
"the moral responsibility we have to one another as fellow citizens."
After growing up in Hopkins, Minnesota, a suburb of Minneapolis, until
he was thirteen, he moved with his family to Los Angeles, where classmates cut school to go surfing. It grated against his midwestern reserve.
"The formative effect of Southern California," he told me, "was seeing
the unencumbered self in practice." He took an early interest in liberal
politics, went to Brandeis, then Oxford on a Rhodes Scholarship, and
over a winter break, he and a classmate planned to collaborate on an
economics paper. "My friend had very strange sleeping habits," Sandel
said. "I would go to bed, maybe around midnight, and he would stay up
until all hours . . . That gave me the mornings to read these philosophy
books." By the time school resumed, he had read Kant, Rawls, Nozick,
and Arendt, and he set aside economics for philosophy.

In the years that followed, he argued for a more direct conversation
about morality in public life. He said, "Martin Luther King drew explicitly on spiritual and religious sources. Robert Kennedy, when he ran for
president in 1968, also articulated a liberalism with moral and spiritual
resonance." But by 1980, American liberals had put aside the language
of morality and virtue because it came to be seen as "what the religious
right does," he said. "I began to feel that something was missing in this
kind of value-neutral politics, and I think it was no accident that there
was a stretch of time from 1968 until 1992 when American liberalism
was more or less moribund, when it had lost its capacity to inspire."

In China in 2010 a group of volunteers calling itself Everyone's Television had come together to subtitle foreign programs. When it ran out
of sitcoms and police procedurals, it turned to American college courses,
which were becoming available online. Sandel had visited China once
before, to speak to small groups of philosophy students, but when he returned, after his course was online, he found that something had happened. "They told me that, for a seven p.m. lecture, kids were starting to
stake out seats at one thirty," he said. "They had overflow rooms, and I
waded into this spirited mass of people." Sandel had seen his work ignite

in other countries, but never as abruptly as it had in China. As we talked, we tried to make sense of this phenomenon. The Harvard brand didn't hurt, and the professional polish of the public television production made it more fun to watch than other courses. But for Chinese students, his style of teaching was also a revelation: he called upon students to make their own individual moral arguments, to engage in vigorous debate in which there was no single right answer, to think creatively and independently about complex, open-ended issues in a way that was largely unheard of in Chinese classrooms.

Beyond style, however, Sandel sensed a deeper explanation for the intense Chinese interest in moral philosophy. "In the societies where it has caught fire, there has not been the occasion—for whatever reason— for serious public discussion of big ethical questions," he said. Young people especially "sense a kind of emptiness in terms of public discourse, and they want something better." China, in the era of Bobos and Bare-Handed Fortunes, was the land of the unencumbered self, a place in which individuals could unfetter themselves from social bonds and history and make their decisions based on self-interest in a way that was previously impossible. It was ruled by technocrats who publicly espoused a discredited ideology while, in practice, they placed their faith in economics and engineering with pitiless efficiency. When Deng identified prosperity as "the only hard truth," he put China on the path toward abundance on a scale it had never known, but also toward counterfeit medicine, piles of moldering cash, and bachelors who stayed alone as long as they were Triple Withouts. Sandel, and the political philosophy he taught, offered Chinese young people a vocabulary that they found useful and challenging but not subversive, a framework in which to talk about inequality, corruption, and fairness without sounding political. It was a way to talk about morality without having to mention the "just sisters" defense or the ambitions on display in Macau.

Sandel never explicitly challenged the taboos of Chinese politics: the separation of powers, the Party's superiority over law. But occasionally the Chinese authorities brushed him back. Once, a salon of Chinese scholars and writers in Shanghai arranged for him to give a public talk to a crowd of eight hundred, but on the eve of the lecture, the local government canceled it. Sandel asked the organizers, "Did they give a reason?"

"No," they said. "They never give a reason."

At times, Sandel encountered skepticism from Chinese critics. For some, his argument against markets was fine in theory, but gauzy notions of equity triggered Chinese flashbacks of ration coupons and empty store shelves. Others argued that, in China, money was the only way to defend yourself against abuses of power, so limiting markets would only fortify the hand of the state. But after the Xiamen lecture, I watched him speak to several more college groups in Beijing, and it was clear that when Sandel described the "skyboxification" of life—the division of America into a world for the affluent and a world for everyone else—Chinese listeners heard much in common. After thirty years of marching toward a future in which everything was for sale, many people in China were reconsidering.

On his last night in Beijing, Sandel gave a lecture at the University of Business and Economics, and then met with a group of student volunteers who were working on perfecting the translations of his "Justice" lectures. One young woman gushed, "Your class saved my soul." Before Sandel could ask her what she meant, the crowd swept him away for photos and autographs. I hung back and introduced myself. Her name was Shi Ye and she was twenty-four years old. She was getting a master's degree in human resources, and when she came upon Sandel's work, it was "a key to open my mind and doubt everything," she told me. "After a month, I began to feel different. That was one year ago. And today, I often ask myself, what is the moral dilemma here?"

Her parents had been farmers, until her father went into the seafood trade. "I accompanied my mom to visit the Buddha to pray and to put some food on the table as an offering. In the past, I didn't think anything was wrong with that. But a year later, when I accompanied my mom, I asked her, 'Why do you do this?'" Her mother was not pleased by all the questions. "She thinks I am posing a very stupid question. I began to question everything. I didn't say it's wrong or right; I'm just questioning."

Shi Ye had stopped buying train tickets from a scalper because, she said, "when he sells them at a price he chooses, it limits my choices. If he wasn't setting the price, I could decide to buy economy or first class, but now he is taking away my choice. It's unfair." She had begun lobbying her friends to do the same. "I'm still young and I don't have much power to change much, but I can influence their thinking," she said.

Shi Ye was getting ready to graduate, but her discovery of political philosophy had made things more complicated. "Before I encountered these lectures, I was sure I was going to be become an HR specialist and an HR manager and serve the employees in a big company. But now I'm confused; I doubt my original dreams. I hope to do something more meaningful." She didn't dare tell her parents, but secretly she was hoping she wouldn't get a job in human resources. "I might take a gap year and go abroad and travel and take a part-time job to see the world. I want to see what I can do to contribute to society. I would like to travel by myself because in China many travel groups are very commercial. And anyway, travel is all about your own experience."

"Where do you want to go?" I asked.

"New Zealand. The air in Beijing is terrible, and I want to escape to a pure and clean place and rest for a while. And then I will think about the next place. Maybe Tibet."

I grew accustomed to meeting people who had drifted into new realms of belief almost by accident. An economist named Zhao Xiao told me, "If eating Chinese cuisine will make me stronger, then I'll eat it, and if Western food makes me stronger, then I'll eat that." Zhao's pragmatism had served him well; by his mid-forties, he had joined the Party, earned a doctorate at Peking University, and was teaching at prominent schools in the capital when he embarked on a study of whether there were policy lessons to draw from predominantly Christian societies. Zhao concluded that Christianity could help China fight corruption, reduce environmental pollution, and stimulate the kind of philanthropy that led early American Christians to found Harvard and Yale Universities. Then he converted. "We see that the Communist Parties of the Soviet Union and all of Eastern Europe have collapsed, and their countries have collapsed with them," Zhao told me. But in China, the Party survived, he said, "precisely because it continues to change."

The Party was under increasing pressure to change the way it regarded the desire for faith. The Chinese constitution guaranteed freedom of religion, but the right was narrowed by regulations against proselytizing and other activities. Officially, China recognized five religions—Taoism, Buddhism, Islam, Catholicism, and Protestantism— and believers could worship in state-controlled settings. More than twenty million Catholics and Protestants attended churches run by the Chinese Catholic Patriotic Association, and its counterpart the Three-Self Patriotic Movement. But more than twice that number worshipped in unregistered "house churches," which ranged in size from small farmhouse study groups to large semipublic congregations in the cities. The house churches were not legally protected, so authorities could tolerate them one day and shut them down the next, if political orders came down to tighten up. In recent years, the Party had taken haltering steps toward tolerance: unofficially, it had allowed the growth of house churches, though it remained uncompromising in its campaign against Falun Gong, and in the ethnic regions of Tibet and Xinjiang, constraints on Buddhism and Islam sparked frequent unrest.

Despite the risks, the ranks of the faithful were soaring, especially among intellectuals. Over lunch, a human rights lawyer named Li Jianqiang ticked off a long list of his colleagues who had converted and were using the courts to try to win greater recognition for their faith. "They don't care who is in power: Caesar, Mao Zedong, the Communist Party," he told me. "Whoever is in power is in power. But don't hinder my belief in Jesus." Li Fan, a secular liberal writer, told me, "Christianity has probably become China's largest nongovernmental organization." House churches that once stayed out of sight were setting themselves up wherever they could find enough space. I attended an especially rousing sermon in the otherwise impious environment of Sauna City, a nightclub-and-massage complex decked in neon. When I asked the pastor, Reverend Jin Mingri, about it, he grinned and said, "The rent was good."

At thirty-nine, Jin had a shock of wavy gray hair and a lively televangelist flair. Not long ago he was destined for the comforts of quiet, suburban Chinese life: raised in a secular family, he joined the Communist Party and studied at Peking University. But in his junior year, the crackdown at Tiananmen shook his faith in the state. "College students in the eighties were groomed by the country; our fees and living expenses were paid for," he said. All of a sudden he felt "an immense sense of hopelessness." The church was a way out; it promised moral clarity and a sense of being part of an enterprise larger than China. He told his parents he was converting. "They thought I'd gone crazy," he said.

For ten years he preached in China's official Protestant Church.

Then he had an idea. Instead of a classic "house church," with believers squeezed into a living room, he wanted to be "open and independent." "We have nothing to hide," he said. Authorities urged him "not to go down the illegal path," as Jin put it, but he reassured them that he had no interest in confrontation. "Originally, we had an enormous government that controlled everything, but the government has been steadily shrinking, and civil society has grown in strength and size," he told me. "I felt that churches should make good use of that opportunity to expand." In 2007 he found a fifth-floor office space in a quiet corner of Sauna City; the space was bland but large enough for 150 people. The old unwritten rules of being an unregistered church in China included staying small and avoiding the authorities. Jin, however, hung a sign outside his door, printed business cards, and welcomed the police to his events. He named it the Zion Church.

When it opened, the church had a parish of 20 people. Within a year, it had 350—almost all of them under forty years old and highly educated. I visited one Sunday, and it was standing room only. I could hear kids squealing in a playroom next door. Jin was a performer: he preached beside a choir dressed in hot-pink robes, accompanied by drums and an electric guitar. He offered a nondenominational, conservative brand of evangelical Christianity, and he peppered his sermons with references to pop culture and the economy. That day he ended his sermon with an appeal I'd never heard in a church: "Please leave," he pleaded, laughing. "We don't have enough seats for the others who want to come, so please stay for only one service a day."

As I traveled around China, I stopped being surprised by my encounters with Christians. On a trip to the city of Wenzhou, a commercial capital on the eastern seaboard, I went to see the head of the chamber of commerce, one of China's richest men, an industrialist named Zheng Shengtao, who was squired around town in a silver Rolls-Royce. He had ridden the wave of prosperity but had come to believe that when Chinese children were being poisoned by milk, something was wrong. Zheng told me that, since becoming a Christian a decade ago, he had dedicated himself to getting other businessmen to sign an ethical pledge. On his fingers, he ticked off the requirements: no tax evasion; no selling substandard products; no "changing contracts and promises." "What happens if I am trustworthy and others are not?" he asked me. "Don't I end up the loser?"

For young men and women who had grown up with control over their economic and personal lives, the limits on what they could believe seemed antique. I met Ma Junyan, a twenty-five-year-old member of a Christian singing troupe that earned its keep playing for churches. It was all off the books, and I asked Ma if the local government had to approve her group's applications to perform. She gave me a funny look. "Jesus tells us to preach to everyone," she told me. "He never said, 'You have to have this certificate in order to preach.'" The reality was more complicated, but I understood her point: she lived in a world so self-contained that she rarely thought twice about the state. Ma and another fifty or so members of her group shared a dormitory on a small, rutted market street lined with dumpling vendors and vegetable stands. Their group was not legal, strictly speaking, but there was nothing especially furtive about their lives. A banner on the wall read, BEIJING BELONGS TO GOD— a slogan that sounded unremarkable until you remembered that Beijing belongs to the Communist Party.

Ma and the others were practicing a dance routine, with a guitar, piano, and drums. The room was humid and filled with bodies, and the boys, in their teens and twenties, bounced up and down shouting, "It's the power of the Holy Spirit! Nothing can stop it!" I had been to settings like this in America—in West Virginia and the South Side of Chicago— but in China it still startled me. Unlike their parents, Ma and her friends were coming of age at a time when Christianity was no longer a dangerous secret. Western religion had a touch of glamour about it because of high-profile converts such as Yao Chen, the television actress who was the most popular person in Chinese social media. When Ma and her friends finished practicing, they lowered their heads and clenched their eyes tight. Tears streamed down their cheeks. In the center of the scrum, a woman tilted her head up and prayed, "China will be a Christian nation."

That vision—that China would make a wholesale turn toward Western religion—never seemed very likely outside the reveries of the true believers. China seemed more inclined to absorb the most useful parts of Western faiths and philosophies and discard the rest, as it had with

Marxism, capitalism, and other imports. But, viewed another way, in the context of its new overlapping identities, China was already a Christian nation—just as it was a lovesick nation, a muckraking nation, and an iconoclastic nation. It was all those things at once, in a way it had never been before. The Party was not allowing the growth of faith as much as it was trying to keep up with it.

# TWENTY-TWO

# CULTURE WARS

When I visited Ai Weiwei at his studio, it felt odd—subdued and claustrophobic. His assistants were working, designs were tacked to the walls, but Ai lived in legal purgatory, free to make art but barred from leaving the capital. Police required him to check in every time he left his house. "I have to pronounce to them where I have to go and whom I have to meet," he told me. "I basically obey their orders because it doesn't mean anything. I also want to tell them I'm not afraid. I'm not secretive. They can follow me." *ArtReview* magazine had recently published its list of the art world's most powerful players and had ranked Ai Weiwei number one. When a reporter called to ask his reaction, he said it was absurd; he did not "feel powerful at all." He felt fragile and, for the first time in a long while, captive to forces beyond his control.

Ai Weiwei had stepped out of detention and into a larger battle for influence in China's cultural life. Not long after the artist was released, President Hu Jintao vowed to shore up what he called China's "cultural security." He warned that "international hostile forces are intensifying the strategic plot of Westernizing and dividing China." The president called on his countrymen to "sound the alarm and remain vigilant." The Party was awakening to urgent questions: Who was going to define the boundaries of Chinese art, ideas, and entertainment? Who was the public going to trust: the government, the dissidents, the tycoons, the muckrakers?

The Party decided to take the recipe that had worked for the economy—planning, investment, and rule-making—and apply it to the world of culture. Some of the first targets were the choice shows that had come to dominate local television. The state ordered stations to remove "repetitive, excessive, and overabundant programs, including those about love, marriage, and friendship; talent shows; emotional stories; game shows; variety shows; talk shows and reality shows." In three months, it cut the number of them by two-thirds and pledged to return television to the work of promoting "socialist core values."

Artists, writers, and filmmakers were running out of patience. China was opening ten new movie screens a day, but its filmmakers were suffocating. The director Jia Zhangke complained that, to get a movie released in China, "I have to portray all the Communists as superheroes." China churned out more television programming than any other country— more than fourteen thousand shows a year—but other countries didn't want them, so China imported fifteen times as much television content as it exported. When the campy Korean music video called "Gangnam Style" became a surprise hit—the most watched clip in the history of the Internet—Chinese artists complained that they could never have created it because the culture officials that preside over their work would never have permitted a silly spoof of Beijing's high-living elite and would, instead, have insisted that a music video for export be grand and impressive. The artists circulated a bitter comic strip called *Shanghai Style*, in which the creator of a Gangnam-style dance move is not showered in fortune but is, instead, incarcerated for "running crazily all over the place."

Cultural figures were increasingly bitter. The film director Lu Chuan once agreed to produce a short film for the Beijing Olympics, but he was inundated with so many official "directions and orders" that he simply abandoned the project and coined a new term: the *Kung Fu Panda* problem. This describes the fact that the most successful film ever made about two of China's national symbols, kung fu and pandas, had to be made by a foreign studio (DreamWorks), because no Chinese filmmaker would ever have been allowed to have fun with such solemn subjects.

The censors at the State Administration of Radio, Film, and Television had always worked in secrecy; they never publicized their orders, but now directors were taking their complaints to the public. In April 2013 the filmmaker Feng Xiaogang was giving a mundane acceptance speech for the Director of the Year award when he seized the chance to make a bold statement; he cut short his list of thank-yous and said, "For the last twenty years, every director in China has faced a kind of tremendous torment, and that torment is censorship." Feng was no dissident; he'd made a bare-handed fortune on romantic comedies and big-budget epics, but the decades of compromises and concessions were rubbing a raw spot on his professional pride. "To get approval, I have to cut my films in ways that actually make them *worse*," he told the audience. If his point wasn't clear enough, the censors unwittingly drove it home to viewers: while he was speaking, someone in the control booth hit a button just in time to censor Feng's reference to censorship; viewers at home heard him say, "that torment is [beep]."

Some of China's most creative people were concluding that the costs of playing by the rules outweigh the benefits. A few weeks after the director's outburst, the novelist and essayist Murong Xuecun reached his limits. When censors deleted his Weibo account, he published an essay called "Open Letter to a Nameless Censor." "I am fully aware that this letter will cause me nothing but grief," he wrote. "I once had fear, but from now on, I am no longer afraid . . . That is the difference between you and me, my dear nameless censor—I believe in the future, while all you have is the present."

The struggle over creativity extended far beyond films and novels. China's economy was at a turning point: the age of cheap labor was ending, and Chinese leaders were desperately trying to foster innovation that could push the country beyond the assembly line. It was investing more in research and development than any country but the United States, and it had surpassed the United States and Japan to become the largest filer of patents. But many of them had little value; they had been filed to meet political targets or attract funding. China was producing more scientific papers than anywhere but the United States, but on measurements of quality (how often the average paper was cited by others), China was not even in the top ten. Academic fraud was rampant; a journal at the University of Zhejiang used CrossCheck software to scan for plagiarism and found that nearly a third of all the papers it received contained plagiarism or sections copied from previous papers. In a government-backed study of six thousand Chinese scientists, one-third admitted that they had fabricated data or plagiarized.

On the lush campus of Tsinghua University in Beijing, Xue Lan, the dean of the school of public policy, lamented that many of China's institutions were standing in the way of some of the country's most talented young people. For example, he said, in the era that cried out for risk-taking, the time of Bare-Handed Fortunes and Peasant da Vincis, the government launched a small-business innovation fund in 1999, but its bureaucratic DNA told it to place only safe bets. "They are concerned that, given that it's a public fund, if their failure rate is very high, the review will not be very good and the public will say, 'Hey, you're wasting money,'" the dean told me. "But a venture capitalist would say, 'It is natural that you'll have a lot of failures.'" Fostering the development of radical new ideas would take more than declaring the ambition to do so; it would require strong courts insulated from political interference and capable of protecting intellectual property, so that entrepreneurs could trust each other enough to put forward innovations and collaborate; it would require university labs where creative thinkers were free to challenge their bosses without fear of retribution or the interference of the Central Propaganda Department. Zhao Jing, a blogger and analyst who wrote under the name Michael Anti, asked, "If you can become a billionaire by blatantly plagiarizing an American website and then putting it on the market, who's going to go out and innovate?"

At times, the institutional reflex to exert control was breathtakingly counterproductive. At one point, Chinese programmers were barred from updating a popular software system called Node.js because the version number, 0.6.4, corresponded with June 4, the date of the Tiananmen Square crackdown. In another case, a digital design project named for the Swedish town of Falun ran aground because the Great Firewall interpreted the name as a reference to Falun Gong. A few days before Facebook went public, an investment banker and Harvard Business School graduate named Wang Ran, the founder of China eCapital, flipped through the company prospectus and saw a sentence reminding investors that Facebook was blocked in four countries: Iran, North Korea, Syria, and China. Seeing China listed among some of the world's most dysfunctional states was startling. "I don't know about you," he wrote to his millions of social media followers, "but I'm beginning to think this state of affairs is insulting." Behind the sting of that embarrassment was a question—a deep question about China's future: How could China ever hope to invent the next big thing, the next Facebook, if it didn't dare to let its people use this one?

Nobody was challenging the restraints on Chinese culture more conspicuously than Ai Weiwei, and the state finally settled on its strategy for silencing him. In November, five months after his release, the government ordered him to pay $2.4 million for "unpaid taxes and fines" related to three architectural projects: a photo gallery he'd designed in Beijing, and a pair of apartments for paying clients in England and Singapore. Ai Weiwei suspected that those projects had drawn the most official attention because they involved offshore clients and accounts. But instead of accepting the bill, Ai Weiwei challenged it; under the law, if he paid a deposit of $800,000 (one-third of his bill), within fifteen days, he could contest it in court. When news of his plan began to circulate, help poured in: people folded hundred-yuan notes into paper planes and lofted them over the wall and into the studio courtyard. They wrapped cash around apples and oranges and delivered them to his doorstep. They wired him money. "Don't hurry to repay it," one donor wrote. "You can return it when there is a new currency"—a bill, someday, with no portrait of Mao on its face.

The artist was awed by the response. "A young girl walked in with a backpack full of money and said, 'Where do you want this?'" he told me. "'It was the savings for a car, and now I can't buy the car. It's yours.'" He added, "That people would raise their voices and act, to give money to a person the state said is a 'criminal'? This is an unthinkable situation." His accountant posted a running tally of donations. The list of givers was eclectic—I recognized the name of a father whose son had fallen ill from drinking tainted milk—and by the end of the first week, supporters had donated even more money than the artist needed for a deposit. After the subject of his donations became the most trending topic on Weibo, his account was shut down. My phone buzzed with a new order for Chinese journalists:

Delete all online references to the case of Ai Weiwei borrowing money to pay his taxes. Interactive pages must promptly remove messages that seize on this occasion to attack the Party, the government, and the legal system.

The Party tabloid, *Global Times*, suggested that paper planes sailing over the studio wall might constitute "illegal fund-raising," and it delivered a warning: "For 30 years Ai Weiweis have emerged and fallen. But China has kept rising despite their pessimistic predictions. The real social trend is that they will be eliminated." While he awaited a day in court, Ai grew antsy. In winter, the trees outside his house were bare, and the police cameras bulged from lampposts. Ai Weiwei threw stones at them, and the police hauled him in for "attacking a security camera," as officers put it. One of his fans circulated an expression of mock concern: "Was the camera badly injured? Did it need a checkup? Perhaps, a CT scan?"

A few days later we were at his dining room table. Winter sun poured in from the south. Danni, the deaf and ancient cocker spaniel, listed around the room like a drunk. Ai's wife, Lu Qing, came down the stairs into the dining room and headed toward the door. She was unaccustomed to the spotlight; the previous year had brought interrogations and the unfamiliar sensation of speaking on behalf of her husband while he was detained. Her name was on the studio's legal papers, so she had been swept up into the tax case. From the table, Ai Weiwei watched his wife wrap a bright red scarf around her shoulders and bundle up against the cold. She was on her way to submit more paperwork to the court. She clutched a manila folder to her chest and opened the front door a crack. She paused. "You okay?" Ai Weiwei asked her. She nodded, gave a tight smile, and slipped out.

I asked him if he had cheated on his taxes. Frankly, it wouldn't have surprised me—in China, people joke that tax evasion is the national sport. Government researchers estimated in 2011 that tax fraud cost the state ¥1 trillion—about $157 billion—and they found that the largest culprits were, in fact, state-owned enterprises. Several times a day I received spam text messages offering to sell me fake invoices for business expenses I could use to evade taxes. In answer to my question, Ai Weiwei said no. Ordinarily, in a situation like this, I would review the files in his case, but the police had confiscated the company's records, sealed the court proceedings to the public and the press, and when I called the court and the prosecutors, nobody would answer any questions. Even Ai's lawyer, Pu Zhiqiang, had never been allowed to review original documents in the case. I asked the artist if he thought he might win. "No," he said. "We're only winning by revealing the truth."

He was right about not winning. In March 2012 the government denied his request for a hearing about his bill, so he tried another tack: he sued the Taxation Bureau, accusing it of mishandling witnesses and evidence. This time, to his astonishment, the court agreed to hear it. But when he tried to visit the court for the hearing, he received a call from the police: "If you try, you can never make it." His wife and lawyer attended, but the courthouse was surrounded by hundreds of police in uniform and plain clothes who barred journalists and diplomats from approaching it. Hu Jia, an activist who tried to attend, was choked and punched by agents outside his home. The city diverted bus routes to bypass the courthouse. On the one-year anniversary of his arrest, with his phones tapped, his e-mail monitored, and his studio surrounded by surveillance cameras, Ai Weiwei decided to out-bug the police: he set up four webcams in his studio, including one on the ceiling of his bedroom, and he began broadcasting his life on the Web. He called it Weiweicam .com. The cops were flummoxed. After a few weeks, they ordered him to pull the plug. He could not conduct surveillance on himself. He joked about writing a book on tax law, probably a first for a contemporary artist. To him, knowledge of any kind was the most powerful art he could produce. "Their power is based on ignorance," he said. *"We're not supposed to know."*

Ai Weiwei thought he would regain his passport one year after his release, but the anniversary, in June 2012, came and went. He was told he couldn't travel because he was suspected of three additional crimes: bigamy, the illegal exchange of foreign currency, and pornography. The pornography investigation, he was told, centered on a single photo: a nude that he had staged in his studio, of himself in a chair flanked by four women standing and staring into the camera. When his fans heard that he might be charged for it, they began posting nude photos of themselves in solidarity.

When I stopped by one morning that fall, he was morose. The court had ruled against his final appeal of the tax case, and he had returned the donations. The government had closed his production company, Fake Cultural Development Ltd., because it failed to update the annual registration. (That would have been difficult, because the police had seized the documents and stamps to do so.) "It's like you're playing chess with a person from outer space," he said. "They play a way you can never imagine, and the game is designed so that they *must* be the winner. I'm forced to play with them, and no matter how smart I move, I will be the loser."

I had never heard him so pessimistic. He had concluded that the system's greatest vulnerability was not that it didn't agree with his ideas, but that it rejected his very right to contest the Party's ideas at all—his bid for the faith of the public. "Every day I'm waiting to see, maybe an official will knock on the door and say, 'Weiwei, let's sit down, let's have a talk. What's your point? Let me see how ridiculous you are.'"

His son was now three and a half, and I asked Ai how he planned to explain the family's situation to him. He was silent for a long time and his eyes reddened. Then he said that he nursed a strange fantasy about that problem: "I want my son to grow slower," he said. "I don't want him to be mature too soon, to understand." It was the first time I'd heard Ai vote for ignorance over knowledge. "The situation is not explainable. It's not rational. It doesn't really make sense to me. I cannot figure out why it has to be this way." His mood seemed to startle him, and he changed the subject. For all his troubles, he sensed a broader change gathering around him. "I think almost every level of the society today realizes China is facing a great crisis in terms of trust, ideology, moral standards, and many, many other ways . . . It's not going to last. Without change in the basic political structure, China has come to the end. This so-called miracle is not going to last." He said, "After ninety years of success, it is still an underground party. They can never really pronounce their ideas and they can never meet anybody who challenges them intellectually."

Over the years that I'd known him, Ai Weiwei had become as much a symbol as a man; he was the most famous dissident China had ever known. There were books and movies and articles about him. But once the artist became a celebrity, the art world lost patience and seemed eager to find the next voice. (*The New Republic* ran a piece subtitled: "Ai Weiwei: Wonderful Dissident, Terrible Artist.") The behavior that disturbed Ai the most was perhaps that of his fellow Chinese artists. "During my disappearance, almost none of them [asked], 'Where is this person? What kind of crime has he committed?'"

I asked why he thought they had stayed silent.

"I think they're afraid," he said flatly. "If I meet them, they always say they completely agree with me, but if you want them to make a public acknowledgment about their position, they will never do it."

To some, Ai Weiwei imposed an unfair standard on others; he argued that, for an artist or writer or thinker to avoid confrontation, to avoid politics, was craven. When a London exhibit of Chinese art received positive reviews, he blasted it for failing to address "the country's most pressing contemporary issues." He compared it to a "restaurant in Chinatown that sells all the standard dishes, such as kung pao chicken and sweet and sour pork."

The pressure on the creative class stirred conflicts far beyond the world of Ai Weiwei, battles over moral authority and trust that gradually turned personal. In January 2012 a blogger named Mai Tian wrote an essay called "Manmade Han Han," in which he compared the dates and times of Han's blog posts with his car races and concluded that he couldn't have written them. The blogger alleged that Han was a fraud—a composite of ghostwriters, perhaps. In response, Han was dismissive; he offered three million dollars to anyone who could prove it. His fans pointed out mistakes in the accuser's time line, and he withdrew it, but all the talk of fraud captured the attention of an unusual figure named Fang Zhouzi.

Fang was a biochemist with a degree from Michigan State who had leaped to prominence by exposing quack science and academic corruption. In China, this was risky work: Fang was attacked by thugs carrying a hammer and pepper spray, and it turned out that they had been hired by a doctor whom he had accused of fabricating data. Fang's accusations were not always right. He had been sued for libel—winning three suits and losing four, by his count—but in the new culture of skepticism, he attracted a large following. When I met Fang, he told me that he was suspicious of believers of many kinds; over the years, he had criticized Evangelical Christianity and Falun Gong, and he saw a similarity in the depth of faith people placed in Han Han. "What I'm criticizing is that they're trying to make a false idol," he told me. In Fang's telling, the very facts that made Han Han a star now sounded suspect: the sudden rise; the habit of writing fast and alone; the insistence that he preferred driving over writing. In an effort to put an end to the issue, Han Han eventually scanned and released roughly a thousand pages of handwritten writings, but Fang argued that they were copies, conspicuously short of "changes in plot and particulars," and he speculated that Han's writing had been produced by his father, the frustrated novelist, or by writers working for the smooth-talking publisher I'd met.

The collision of Han Han and Fang Zhouzi, two of China's most influential commentators, caused a sensation; it generated fifteen million Weibo posts in two weeks. Some of Han Han's critics went so far as to ask the Taxation Bureau to investigate him; they questioned whether his car races had been fixed; they even accused him of overstating his height. The debate over his authenticity and merit divided Chinese intellectuals along such bitter lines that the novelist Murong Xuecun looked at the mud flying back and forth and observed, "Not since the Cultural Revolution have Chinese intellectuals expressed as much hatred toward each other." Why had this issue, of all things, caused a fight so intense? Yevgeny Yevtushenko, the Soviet-era poet, once asked, "Why is it that right-wing bastards always stand shoulder to shoulder in solidarity, while liberals fall out among themselves?" In Murong's view, China's intellectuals were so beaten down that they were brawling on the floor over scraps. With so many thinkers "spending so much energy fighting over words and ink, we have forgotten to criticize government authority; we have forgotten to pay attention to social welfare. That should worry us."

I visited Han Han and asked him about the accusations. "It's hard to disprove something you never did," he said, and he suggested that his accusers were unhinged. "They're like the people who insist Americans never landed on the moon," he said. I asked if his father ever wrote a piece in the son's name, and he said no. "We have two different ways of writing." His father cared about stories; Han Han cared only about moods. "It's not that my writing is so good—it's not perfect—but it is very distinctive," he said, with a bit of race car bluster. Han Han framed the accusations against him in broader terms. "In this society, people don't trust each other, so they exploit this distrust to attack whomever they want." Of Fang's legions of fans online, he said, "They only trust their computers."

The prospect that Han Han was a confection dreamt up by his father and publisher was, in theory, plausible—or, at least, not much odder than Bo Xilai's wife poisoning a British businessman, or a railway boss with so much stolen cash that it was moldering. In all honesty, some part of me wanted the accusations to be true because it would've made one hell of a story. Twice I met Chinese writers who said they knew of one of "Han Han's ghostwriters," but when I followed the trails, they led nowhere. I had interviewed his father and concluded that either he and his son were magnificent actors or the theory was a fantasy. I decided that Han Han was most likely what he appeared to be: a writer who had been sculpted by the attentions of his marketing team, but not a fraud.

It seemed to me that many of Han Han's critics were raging less against him than against the moment he embodied. To the accusers such as the truth-hunter Fang Zhouzi, who called Han a "false idol," Han's success was a taunt to the classical credentials of intellectual life, because he churned out work at a furious pace, feeding the market with writing that was undercooked. To other critics, Han Han was a fair-weather critic who had shown himself to be too willing to back off the call for change when the risks became too great; after Han Han declined to speak up against Ai Weiwei's detention, their relationship soured, and the artist described the writer as "too acquiescent." I saw, in these critiques, a common root: people had projected what they wanted to see onto Han Han, and then he had defied their projections. In that sense, he was the ultimate amateur, an icon of Me Generation individualist politics. The more I saw his face peering out from bus shelters and subway ads, the more I was reminded of the soldier Lei Feng, the old socialist poster boy. Willingly or not, Han Han had become a kind of Lei Feng in denim—a bearer of a faith that no man could fulfill.

When I stopped by to see Han Han for the last time, in the spring of 2013, I sensed that his years of bearing that faith had taken a toll on him. After all the dancing in shackles—the shuttered magazine, the warnings from the Party—he had moved his office to a quiet villa, shared by small technology companies, in a residential complex in Shanghai. He was running a start-up that produced an Android app called One, which sent users one item a day—a story, a poem, a video. It had attracted three million subscribers in its first six months, but it was obscure enough to avoid the attentions of the Central Propaganda Department. "Since I'm not allowed to do a magazine, we turned it into an app," he told me. We were in a small sunlit conference room on the top floor of the house;

below us, roomfuls of young employees were at computers, working amid the stuffed animals, Ping-Pong tables, and other trappings of start-up life. Han Han said he spent most of his time playing with his daughter and racing his cars. Looking at him in his latest incarnation, the bad-boy author in retirement, I asked him why he had stopped writing about corruption, injustice, and other sensitive subjects. "We have Weibo now. People can find anything they need on there," he said. "I rarely write about politics. For me, it's boring now."

"Boring?" I asked.

"Because the same bad things happen again, again, and again. As a writer, you don't want to repeat yourself. I have other ways to express my anger. Or I can choose not to express it at all."

Depending on the point of view, the arc of Han Han's writing life was either encouraging or dispiriting. When I met him he had been edging toward a collision with the Party, but over the years he and the system had found a way to accommodate each other. His work had far less impact in China than it once did, but it was hard to criticize him for choosing a quieter path; the Party had left little mystery about the perils of uncompromising aspiration—which made it only more striking to me when people who had failed in a bid for greater autonomy chose to go once more into the fray. At one point, in March 2010, I received an invitation to a ceremony in downtown Beijing: the editor Hu Shuli was heading back into the business of muckraking. Less than four months after she had broken with her publisher, she rented a hotel ballroom and packed it with reporters and officials and scholars. She was launching a media group, accompanied by many of the editors and reporters who had followed her out the door from *Caijing*. In a feisty gesture, she named her new venture *Caixin*, which sounded, in Chinese, like "the new *Caijing*."

I took a seat in the crowd and watched Hu step to the podium. She wore a red sequined jacket. She was barely tall enough to be seen over the flower arrangement around the microphone. In a high-pitched voice, she said, "Our editorial policy of objectively covering major economic and social developments in China will not change." Her new venture gave her the share of equity she had always wanted; she and her editors held 30 percent ownership; a group of investors and a relatively progressive Chinese newspaper called *Zhejiang Daily* owned the rest. Being in business with a state-run newspaper carried its own risks, but as the months passed, she gained confidence that *Zhejiang Daily* would live up to its pledge to give her latitude to run her newsroom.

I watched, over the next couple of years, as Hu and her staff strained to reestablish themselves. After the initial excitement over the founding, many reporters left for better salaries or more established news organizations. She made risky bets. At one point, she expanded into a broadcast arm that was too costly and complex, and she abandoned it; people in the newsroom took to calling it Hu's "Great Leap Forward." Still, she continued. The staff broke influential stories about financial fraud and official abuses; in one case, officials in charge of the one-child policy were found to be profiting by confiscating babies and selling them to orphanages for foreign adoptions. Hu wrote blistering editorials that challenged the Party's fundamental argument that democracy is prone to instability. "It is autocracy that creates chaos," she wrote during the Middle East uprising, "while democracy breeds peace. Supporting an autocracy is in reality trading short-term interests for long-term costs."

But as bold as it was, Hu Shuli's voice no longer stood out as distinctively as it had when she launched her first magazine twelve years earlier, simply because so many other voices now contended alongside hers. The corporate misdeeds and corruption that had been the main targets of her work were now revealed, day by day, by ordinary people who had no tools but an Internet connection. Tycoons who once gave exclusive interviews to Hu Shuli were now taking to the Web to express themselves. Even Hu's old magazine, *Caijing*, had rebuilt itself. The publisher Wang Boming—sensing, perhaps, that his glory as a press baron was imperiled— promised readers that he would resist "inappropriate controls from above," and the magazine kept up its focus on investigations. In that sense, Hu Shuli's departure had not stymied investigative reporting; it had doubled the volume of it.


In the spring of 2013, Sarabeth and I began preparing to leave Beijing. After eight years, we wanted the chance to think about China with the help of some distance. We would miss it immensely, and we would be back, but it was time. We started saying goodbye to friends, and I made my last visit to the office of Hu Shuli. Over the years, I had come to see her as a kind of heart monitor for the intellectual life of Beijing; her pulse quickened or slowed to a crawl depending on the pressures and opportunities surrounding independent thought.

When I arrived, the newsroom at Caixin was emptier than the last time I had seen it. I knew that young reporters were slipping away for more glamorous or rewarding jobs. Her office was functional, and sparsely furnished. I asked her if it was getting easier or harder to be a muckraker in China, and she acknowledged the proliferation of competition. "When I started *Caijing*, the problem was that there was nothing to quote! There was only *Caijing!*" she said. Now there are too many things to quote, and you have to decide which is true. So we want to be influential and comprehensive—a trusted source." That was a niche in a society short on trust.

Can you survive on that? I asked.

"It depends on the overall situation in China. If China can change, and the future is bright, we can survive, and grow fast." She left the alternative unsaid, and thought for a moment. Then she continued: "I think it's difficult for China to turn back, so I'm still hopeful." She was now teaching classes part time at Sun Yat-sen University in Guangzhou, and the contact with young people had energized her. "In the university, students ask me, 'We know being a journalist is difficult, so why do you encourage us to be journalists?' I say that if everyone knows it's hard and you insist on doing it anyway, you will get success. Everybody is afraid of it, so they don't compete."

For her, the decision to start over had been about more than the business of publishing. She was faithful to the ideas that had animated her from the beginning. "We didn't want death; we wanted life again," she said. "These young people are very confident and optimistic, and they are leading me. They are all between the ages of about thirty and forty. They are all start-up oriented. They are confident, and they believe in the future. They don't just trust me; they trust in the future. That is not only pressure for me, but also encouragement. They said, 'Why don't we start it ourselves? We can start it again.'" She grinned and said, "Of course, for me it's a lot of pressure. But you need to choose sometimes."

# TWENTY-THREE

# TRUE BELIEVERS

Tang Jie, the patriot, was restless again. In the years since his nationalist video lifted him out of anonymity, he'd lived in Shanghai, Berlin, and Beijing—and barely six months after joining m4, the production company in the capital, he was planning something larger. He wanted to broaden his work from criticizing Western media to criticizing Chinese media as well, and to commenting on politics. He wanted to elevate his punditry beyond the ordinary online scrum to a level that he called "independent media." His cofounders disagreed; they worried that moving beyond a narrow focus would get them shut down. "But for me and the others, we pay close attention to this country and its problems—and that means politics," Tang told me. "*Politics* shares a root with *policy* and *police*, and if you're talking about the rise of a country, it's impossible to avoid the subject. For young people like us, if we don't talk about politics, what do we talk about?"

In August 2011 he walked out with ten members of the staff and launched a new site, named Dujiawang—"Unique Web"—with an ambitious new slogan: "Rise Together with China." In the four years I'd known him, China's online population had doubled—it was now half a billion people—and he wanted to be the Chinese nationalist YouTube. "We want to be more than just an attitude," he said. Tang Jie found an angel investor and raised three million yuan (about half a million dollars) to finance the operation, and he rented a suite of offices in the technology corridor of the capital, next door to the headquarters of the search engine Baidu. He and his colleagues converted a room into a studio for broadcasting interviews and lectures over the Web. To give it a studious look, they found a photograph of a library in Dublin and blew it up to cover the wall as a backdrop.

Their videos examined the Chinese space program and the European debt crisis; Goldman Sachs, Greece, and gun control. They were as suspicious of the West as ever; they criticized the editor Hu Shuli for her calls for political reform and said that bringing liberal democracy to China would be like pasting "a fake Western painting" on top of "an authentic work of calligraphy." Even by China's standards, Tang Jie's nationalism was extreme. At one point, he criticized the state news service for being too soft, and one of its reporters called him a "fifty-center," a reference to the loyal "ushers of public opinion." The state news service called you a shill for the government? I asked. "Correct," he said, grinning. "We thought that was a bit ridiculous."

I'd met wealthy Chinese businessmen who invested in sites like his; in his case, his investor wanted to remain anonymous. "Three million yuan isn't much to him. You couldn't even get an apartment in Beijing with that," Tang said, adding, "We wanted to make a profit, and initially our investor thought we could." But that had proved difficult: in April 2012 the news of the Bo Xilai murder scandal alarmed Party censors, and they unleashed such a broad campaign against online political discussion that it extended to Tang's patriotic website. He received a notice from the Internet Affairs Bureau to shut down for a month for "reorganization." When we talked, he put the best face on it that he could. "'Reorganization' means you have to tell them about yourselves, about who is in management, and they make records of it all, and then you can get back to work," he said. "We understood that they had to do this, or the political commentary would rush in like a flood." He went on: "It was frustrating, but we never stopped working. Even though our own site was shut down, we could send our videos all over the place to other sites."

"Did you think the shutdown was justified?" I asked, and he considered the question.

"I thought they were going too far. There were too many websites shut down," he said, adding, "Of course we hope the atmosphere can be freer. But 'freer' is a very abstract concept . . . We have to stay constructive."

Tang Jie kept the faith. One month of "reorganization" became two, and two became three. His investor lost heart and shut down his funding. Tang Jie began to worry about paying rent and salaries. Finally, in

September, five months after it was blocked, his site was allowed back online—just in time for him to help defend what the government called "sacred territory" in the East China Sea—five small islands and three rocks known, in Chinese, as the Diaoyu Islands. Home to moles and albatrosses, but no human inhabitants, they lay far out to sea. Japan controlled them, but China maintained that it was their rightful owner. For decades the dispute had lain dormant, but the islands were suspected to sit atop valuable oil and gas deposits, and bit by bit, the conflict was turning physical.

In September the Japanese family that owned the islands sold them to their government, and the move triggered protests in Chinese cities; in some places, they grew out of control. In Xian, riot police pushed back a crowd that surrounded a hotel where Japanese tourists were believed to be staying. Elsewhere in town, a Chinese man named Li Jianli was attacked for driving a Japanese car; he was pulled from behind the wheel of his Toyota and beaten with a bicycle lock so severely that he was left partly paralyzed. In Beijing, some shopkeepers hung signs in their windows like this one, in English, at a restaurant: THIS SHOP DOES NOT RECEIVE THE JAPANESE, THE PHILIPPINES, THE VIETNAMESE AND DOG.

In this climate, expressing doubts about the nationalist cause was dangerous. When the economist Mao Yushi, who was eighty-four years old, questioned why the government was spending taxpayer dollars to defend specks of land that produce "no GDP, no tax revenues," he was barraged with late-night phone calls and hecklers who called him a "traitor." A leftist website made a gallery of "Slaves to the West"—a lineup of scholars and journalists, including the editor Hu Shuli and the Nobel laureate Liu Xiaobo, each depicted with a noose around the neck, above the caption AS LONG AS CHINA IS SAFE, THE SLAVES TO THE WEST WILL BE SAFE; WHEN CHINA IS IN TROUBLE, WE'LL GO STRAIGHT TO THEIR HOMES AND SETTLE THE SCORE.

Another demonstration was scheduled to be held outside the Japanese embassy in Beijing, and I rode my bike across town. This time, Chinese police were ready. Paramilitary troops in camouflage and officers in blue uniforms far outnumbered the protesters. The architecture of the Japanese embassy reflected its grim relationship with the host country. It was an embassy designed to be pelted: a six-story gray fortress set back from the road, with windows shielded by steel grates.

Compared to the riots days earlier, however, this was more like a parade. The police allowed the demonstrators to throw water bottles and trash at the embassy gate before ushering them on. As I moved along the road in the surge of protesters, I was struck by how hard the Chinese government was straining to remind the protesters that they were on the same side. I heard the recorded voice of a woman, and it took me a moment to realize that it wasn't coming from the protesters and it wasn't directed at the Japanese. It was a police megaphone appealing for public support:

*We share your feelings. The government's position is clear: It will not tolerate the violation of our national sovereignty. We should support our government, express our patriotic sentiments in a legal, orderly, and rational fashion. We should obey the laws and regulations, and not adopt extreme behavior, or disturb the social order. Please work with us, and obey the instructions of the police.*

Up close, among the men and women on the street, Chinese nationalism looked less like an ideology than another way to find meaning in the boom years. My friend Lu Han, a writer and translator who had no interest in the anti-Japan demonstrations, sensed why others were attracted. She told me, "Growing up in China, there are very few chances for you to feel like that—to be lifted spiritually, to be working on something bigger than yourself, more important than your immediate, ordinary life circle." Nationalism, in that sense, was a kind of religion, and people placed their faith in it just as they did in Confucianism or Christianity or the moral philosophy of Immanuel Kant. The newspaper editor Li Datong told me he believed that the fury of China's young nationalists arose from their "accumulated desire for expression—like a flood that suddenly races into a breach." Because a flood moves in whatever direction it chooses, the young conservatives were, to China's political leaders, an unnerving new force.

The outburst of popular nationalism left Tang Jie conflicted. He was pleased to see the sentiment out in the open, but he was repulsed by the violence; it was not only morally wrong, he thought, but counterproductive. He was eager to draw a distinction between his beliefs and the populist rage. "The young people here are more intellectual than those who go out into the street carrying banners," he told me when I visited him at his headquarters.

It had a roomful of cubicles and a glass-walled office, where we sank into a pair of dusty couches. For all his travels and all the Party's scandals and all his study of Western thought, his conservatism was undimmed. He was eager to make a case for the Chinese political system that it was struggling to make for itself. "In Beijing there are more than ten million commuters crossing the city every day, along with tens of thousands of trucks bringing in food, and bringing out incredible amounts of garbage. When you put all these problems together, it's impossible to do it without a powerful government," he said, adding, "We must understand ourselves. We mustn't ignore what's special about us. In sixty years we have become the second-largest economy in the world—maybe the first, depending on how you measure it—and in that that time, we never colonized anyone."

As we talked, he said something that startled me: Tang felt that public opinion was turning against him. He considered the nationalist protests to be unfocused and fleeting; he was increasingly convinced that the majority in China did not agree with him. "Everything is headed in one direction: the American direction," he said. "It's the mainstream view, and you're not supposed to question it. People say everything has to be more like the United States in economics, law, journalism. That's the conventional wisdom." To my surprise, Tang had come to believe that most people in the government saw it that way, too, even if they didn't voice it. "Ever since opening up became national policy, most government officials are pro-reform, and it's very difficult for them to accept alternative views."

A younger, serious man came in and joined our conversation. His name was Li Yuqiang; he had started as Tang's assistant and moved up to running the site day to day. He, too, was a graduate of a top school— Peking University, where he had studied psychology and software development—and as we talked, he picked up on Tang Jie's argument about the shift in ideology. "The mainstream of Chinese media is liberal; that is common knowledge," Li said, and he ticked off a list of objectives he didn't agree with: "independent legal system, market economy, small government." The younger man saw things in harsher, more confrontational terms. "These people who control the media say they

are liberal, but they act like authoritarians. Alternative views are blocked."
For a second, I thought he was making a joke, but he wasn't: the rising
generation of Chinese nationalists was earnestly complaining about the
lack of free expression.

In China, one of the most difficult things to do was to gauge public
opinion. Polls provided some insight, but only up to a point, because
anyone who spent much time in China was reminded that asking citizens of an authoritarian country for their views on politics, over the
phone, did not produce candid answers. Viewed from afar, the bursts of
nationalism, the occasional violence, could make it appear as if China
were boiling with patriotic anger. But, up close, it was not, and it was difficult to know how many people really shared that sentiment. The Party
had always prided itself on articulating the "central melody" of Chinese
life, but as the years passed, the Party's rendition of that melody seemed
increasingly out of tune with the cacophony and improvisation striking
up all around it. It was impossible to know what "most Chinese" believed
because the state media and the political system were designed not to
amplify public opinion but to impose a shape upon it. Nationalism, like
any other note in the melody, might surge to the surface at one moment
and fade into the background at another, but was it the mainstream
view? The nationalists didn't think so.

The shutdown of Tang's site for five months had taken a heavy toll.
Tang had failed to find another investor willing to back him. "The
money is almost gone," he said. He was having second thoughts about a
career in nationalism. He'd started talking to people about getting back
into teaching. A university in his wife's hometown, Chongqing, had a
part-time opening in the philosophy department, and he took it, dividing his time between teaching Plato's *Republic* in Chongqing and running a nationalist website in Beijing. "We're worried," he said after a
while. "I'll meet someone next week who might fund us, but I doubt
he'll give money to a project that has no guaranteed return." Tang the
scholar had decided he wasn't very good at the business side of things.
"It's not me," he said.

It was getting late. We went back into the video studio with the library backdrop to take a snapshot together. For all his vitriol, I sometimes sensed that Tang Jie envied certain things about the West. He said
to me, "The first time I met you, I asked you what is the most fundamen-

tal value in America, and you said something like liberty. I thought, wow, this country has a state religion, and it has educated its citizens so well that everyone believes it." It was an idealized image, but I took his point. He went on, "You Americans have this basic belief—a common value—but for China, this is still a problem. There are different beliefs—liberal and traditional, Maoism, all sorts of things." I asked how he would describe his own beliefs, and he answered in geopolitical terms. "For several hundred years we've been a prisoner of this Western-centric view, which divided the world into two camps: West and East, democracy and authoritarianism, light and dark. Everything light belonged to the West, and everything dark belonged to the East. This worldview should be overturned." That was as close as he came to faith. "This is my revolution," he said.

As the protests continued that fall, some people pushed back against nationalism. Li Chengpeng, a liberal writer with tens of millions of social media followers, wrote that he'd been a "typical Chinese patriot" until the earthquake in Sichuan. "Patriotism is not about bullying mothers of children who died in the earthquake, while calling for people to stand up to the foreign bullies of our motherland," Li wrote. "[It] is about speaking more truth about dignity for the Chinese people." A popular essay by a Nanjing author pointed out that China was defending sacred territory in the East China Sea while migrant laborers were unable to send their children to school in Beijing. "If Chinese kids can't even go to school in China, what use is more territory?" it asked. There were jokes going around about the "fifty-centers," who could always find a way to defend the Party. If a fifty-center heard someone say, "This egg tastes terrible," he would answer, "How about you try to lay an egg and see how it tastes?"

It was a surprisingly difficult time to be a true believer. The defector Lin Yifu had wrapped up his term at the World Bank that June and returned to Beijing. He was proud of his tenure; he had nudged the Bank to learn from China's experience, to put more emphasis on infrastructure and industrial policy, and he received a respectful send-off. But, privately, he and the Bank parted ways with mutual mixed feelings. He had arrived as an outsider, and he left as one, still; when he encountered critics inside the Bank who doubted his faith in governments to make the best investment decisions, he avoided debates. He had no chemistry with Robert Zoellick, the president who had recruited him. Lin took to saying that he was not only the first chief economist from a developing country, but also the first "to have a good understanding of developing countries."

During his years away, Lin had grown only more evangelical about China's economic approach, but when he returned to Beijing, that view put him out of step with many of his peers. For all China's achievements, it still had a per capita income somewhere between Turkmenistan's and Namibia's. China had succeeded in industrializing a very poor, rural country, but economists were divided over how long that could continue. James Chanos, a hedge fund manager who had predicted the fall of Enron, argued that the Chinese economy rested on a bubble that was "Dubai times a thousand." By 2011 nearly 70 percent of the nation's gross domestic product was going to infrastructure and real estate, a level that no other big country had ever approximated in modern times. Japan, even at the peak of its boom in the 1980s, reached barely half that level. In the rush to invest, companies controlled by provincial and local authorities took out a disproportionately large share of the new loans. Between 2006 and 2010, local authorities opened up for development more than eight thousand square miles of rural land—an area the size of New Jersey. Urbanization was an important part of China's economic success, but it came with costly side effects, including pollution and growing anger over the seizure of valuable land. Local governments' debts ballooned to over a fifth of China's GDP in 2011. The central government would not allow them to issue their own debt, so they raised cash by selling land they already owned or by offering low prices to farmers (the source of many of China's protests).

In Beijing, one of Lin Yifu's former students, a professor named Yao Yang, published a view of China's political and economic future that was strikingly at odds with his mentor's. Yao pointed to the rise of crony capitalism and the gap between rich and poor as evidence that China's economic model had run up against the limit of what was possible without permitting greater political openness "to balance the demands of different social groups." He cited control of the Internet and labor unions, and unsafe working conditions. "Chinese citizens will not remain silent in the face of these infringements, and their discontent will inevitably lead to periodic resistance," he warned. "Before long, some form of explicit political transition that allows ordinary citizens to take part in the political process will be necessary." The article circulated fast; it seemed to capture a mounting frustration among Chinese intellectuals that the state's reluctance to share power had brought reforms to a standstill.

In the years after the financial crisis, most economists had come to believe that, as China's workforce aged, its growth would slow. How soon and how far would depend on how China's government behaved: whether it could control corruption, maintain public support, curb pollution, narrow the gap between rich and poor, and unleash another surge of its people's potential. By 2012 the signs of a slowdown were clear. Many economists were predicting a hard landing—but Lin never wavered. He insisted that China had the potential to keep growing at 8 percent a year until 2030, a position that endeared him to the Foreign Ministry, which arranged press briefings for him to rebut gloomier predictions. A columnist nicknamed him "Ever Increasing Lin" and accused him of "satellite talk"—an unflattering reference to Mao's loyal aides who compared the bogus harvest reports to the success of *Sputnik*. An economics website set up a page with a question across the top: "Can Lin Yifu 3.0 Come Back to Earth?" The *South China Morning Post* wrote, "You don't need to be an eminent international economist to spot the holes in his argument."

I visited Lin at Peking University. He had a large, handsome office in a restored, tile-roofed building in a traditional courtyard, on a remote corner of campus. Since returning from Washington, he was relishing being back at his desk, where he was happiest. Though, seeing him in his office, I was struck by how isolated he seemed. I mentioned the criticism of his firm belief in the current system. He smiled, and acknowledged that his optimism made him a target. "China did very well, but income distribution became an issue, and also corruption became an issue," he said. "And income distribution related to corruption, in a sense, makes it worse. And so people tend to look at it more negatively because of those kind of experiences. They're frustrated."

More than thirty years after Lin had washed ashore as Captain Lin Zhengyi—the suspected spy, the man with "origins unclear"—he had dedicated himself so completely to his new hosts that nothing would steer him from his certainty. He had always described national success as a matter of determination, not unlike the path of his own life. "Success or failure," he wrote, "need not be a matter of destiny." Among his favorite passages was a line from Arthur Lewis, the economist and Nobel laureate, who held that all "nations have opportunities which they may grasp if only they can summon up the courage and the will." But now his views clashed with the mood around him, the sense of narrowing opportunity—the inequality, the passive 被. Lin's views, wrote Huo Deming, a fellow economist at Peking University, "have no market in China."

After seeing Lin in Washington, and now back in Beijing, I sensed that he might always be an outsider. When he had returned to China from Washington, the government in Beijing formally asked Taiwan if it might finally allow Lin to return home, as a gesture of better relations. But Taiwan said no. If Lin stepped back on its soil, he would face military charges of treason. "I have to console my husband all the time, telling him to wait, wait just a little longer," his wife said at the time. "Maybe we can go home when we are a hundred years old."

Lin's response was to pour himself even more deeply into his work. He published three books in three years, and the last time I saw him he gave me the bound galleys for a fourth. I read them, and I enjoyed our conversations. But part of him would remain unknowable to me. I had been drawn to him years earlier by the audacity of his decision to defect. I had imagined it to be the act of an idealist. But over the years, I had come to see a practical side to his choice as well. He was a man who believed, above all, in his own power to achieve his ambitions, and he would do whatever it took to do so. And that, I realized, was fitting. It was the energy of China's boom distilled to its hardest truth: a solitary man who decided that he could realize his future only by going to the People's Republic. Soon I would meet another who believed he could realize his future only by leaving it.

# TWENTY-FOUR

# BREAKING OUT

When the moment arrived, it was at the hour of his choosing. Fifteen months after the blind, self-taught lawyer Chen Guangcheng was locked in his home, seven years after I first tried to visit him, he made up his mind to go. On the morning of April 20, 2012, he lingered in bed. For weeks he had been lying around like this, in the hope of lulling his guards into the false idea that he had fallen ill or resigned himself to his circumstances. By now, he and his wife, Yuan Weijing, knew the guards' rhythms and the angles of their cameras. As morning drifted into the drowsy hours of early afternoon, Chen began to crawl.

He crawled out of the back of the house and across the yard until he reached the base of a stone wall. He clambered and hoisted himself to the top. It was desperate and messy, and when he spilled over the other side, he broke his right foot. He dragged himself into a neighbor's pigsty and burrowed in deep to wait out the daylight. Once darkness was on his side, he began to move again, groping his way toward the edge of the village marked by the waters of the Meng River. It was a route inscribed in his memory from childhood. He limped and stumbled, and when he heard a sound, he flattened himself to the ground. He knew of a bend in the river where he once swam as a boy with his brothers, a point where the water was shallow. And in the dead of night, he waded in.

By the time he reached the other side, Chen was cold and caked in mud, but he was out of the village of Dongshigu. When dawn broke, a villager spotted him and took him to the home of one of Chen's former clients, a peasant named Liu Yuancheng, who pulled him inside and contacted Chen's brother. Word began to spread among his sympathizers.

He Peirong, the English teacher involved in the sunglasses campaign online, learned of the escape in a coded e-mail that read, "The bird has left the cage." It was only a matter of time before local police realized Chen was missing, so the teacher and others set off in two cars, for Shandong, to pick him up and bring him to Beijing.

The drive took twenty hours, and once he was in the capital, he moved constantly, and secretly, from home to home. This was not a solution. The activists who were sheltering him appealed to the U.S. embassy for help. American diplomats weighed the issue—Was it legal? Was it wise?—and concluded that Chen's broken foot was a justification to shelter him on humanitarian grounds. Getting him into the embassy was another matter. They arranged a rendezvous on the edge of the city, and an embassy car went out to meet the car that was carrying Chen from place to place. They discovered that both cars were being tailed by Chinese security. They scrapped the rendezvous point and turned abruptly into an alleyway. The embassy car drew up alongside and opened its doors. The Americans pulled Chen into their car "by the lapels," as one of them later put it to me, and took off for the embassy.

Once they were back inside, and an embassy doctor began to work on Chen's broken foot, the diplomats confronted what might lie ahead. In 1989 a Chinese dissident named Fang Lizhi had taken refuge in the embassy, with his wife, and they spent thirteen months in a secret, windowless room until negotiators could broker a deal to get them to the United States. (The longest embassy guest in State Department history was the Hungarian cardinal József Mindszenty, an opponent of the Soviet-backed government; he entered the U.S. embassy in Budapest in 1956 and stayed for fifteen years.) To make matters more complicated, U.S. secretary of state Hillary Clinton was scheduled to arrive in Beijing in a few days for strategic and economic talks, and both sides were desperate to prevent her trip from colliding with a diplomatic crisis.

American and Chinese negotiators met at the Ministry of Foreign Affairs to find a solution. They began at positions far apart: The Americans suggested Chen could study in Shanghai, where New York University was preparing to open a law school. The Chinese suggested that he should be charged with treason. After three days of talks, the two sides agreed to offer Chen the option of studying in the city of Tianjin. He agreed, and was driven to Beijing's Chaoyang Hospital to be reunited with his family. But that night, when he and his wife and children found themselves alone in the hospital, with no American protection, Chen regretted leaving the embassy. For help, he called friends in the United States. Over the years, Chen's campaign against forced abortions had attracted the support of religious conservatives, including Bob Fu, a Chinese American who headed a Christian advocacy group called ChinaAid. Fu, who had a keen sense of American politics, sounded the alarm: he told reporters that "the U.S. government has abandoned Chen," and Mitt Romney, who was running for president at the time, pronounced it a "day of shame" for his opponent, President Obama. Then Fu orchestrated a memorable scene: at a hearing on Capitol Hill, he held his iPhone up to the microphone for the world to hear Chen Guangcheng speak from his hospital room in Beijing. "I fear for my family's lives," he said, and pleaded for refuge in America. "I have not had a rest in ten years."

A hurried new deal was struck: Chen would go to New York City as a visiting fellow at New York University. When it was announced, Nicholas Becquelin, a China specialist at Human Rights Watch, couldn't help but marvel. "One man managed to make the entire Chinese government bend," he said. On May 19, still on crutches, Chen boarded a flight bound for Newark, accompanied by his wife and kids, aged six and ten. Upon arrival, they were met by a group that included Chen's old friend Jerome Cohen, who was dressed, as always, in a bow tie and blazer. They rode to NYU, where a crowd was waiting. Chen stepped to the microphone and thanked Chinese officials for "dealing with the situation with restraint and calm." In China, the Central Propaganda Department forbade coverage of his arrival; it expanded the online blacklist to include the new search words people were using to discuss Chen's situation:

*Blind Man*
*Shawshank Redemption*
*Light + Truth*
*Sunglasses Brother*

About six months later, on a mild morning in New York, I crossed Washington Square Park and turned south on MacDougal Street. At the US-Asia Law Institute at NYU Law School, Chen was standing in the door of his office when I arrived. It was odd to meet him for the first time in a place so much closer to my hometown than his. His office was immaculate, in gray and white, the air-conditioning humming faintly in the background. He was wearing a short-sleeved button-down shirt and sunglasses with small, silver oval lenses. The walls of the office were bare, and the shelves were largely empty, except for plants and an "I ♥ NY" coffee mug.

Since arriving, Chen had focused mostly on giving speeches, writing a memoir, and coping with the differences between Dongshigu Village and Greenwich Village. Many of his early impressions were sensory: the nautical aroma off the rivers, the tang of pollution. His favorite place was the Botanic Garden, which was a feast for the nose. He'd had some surprises: Unlike the Beijing metro, New York subway stations had no air-conditioning. He'd gone to Washington and visited House Speaker John Boehner, who didn't say much, though Boehner's office had the most comfortable leather chair that Chen had ever felt.

He told me that his greatest concern, at the moment, was for his relatives in China. When police discovered that Chen was missing, they came for his brother, Chen Guangfu; they beat him and put a hood over his head and took him for interrogation. In the midst of it, the man's son, Chen Kegui, cut a police officer with a kitchen knife; he claimed self-defense, but he was sentenced to more than three years in prison. In his office Chen said, "Anyone will protect his own rights if they are violated, or if he sees injustice. It's impossible for people in that situation to go without a fight."

For years I wondered how Chen's ideas of justice and citizenship had taken root, and I asked him now about the connection between his blindness and his activism. "The more inequality you experience, the more you crave equality, the more you want justice," he said. But I sensed that he was bored by the question, by the suggestion that his body had ordained his beliefs, and I realized my assumption ignored his curiosity. "When I was little, I liked to ask older people the questions I couldn't answer," he said. "If the first person didn't have an answer, I asked another, and another, and I would collect different explanations. And then I would think about which seemed the closest to correct."

He recalled riding a tractor as a child and groping every piece of the machine that he could reach. His curiosity extended beyond the physical. He was once with his mother on a train when the conductor confiscated a container of propane from a passenger on the grounds that it was flammable. "I asked, 'Will they give this guy his money back after they resell it?' But my mom wouldn't answer me; she stayed silent, and after a while she got angry and said, 'How can you honestly think they will give him his money back?' But I thought, how can they take someone's property and resell it, and not give him anything?"

Chen credited his father for seeding a sense of possibility in his mind. "He thought that a person has a basic capacity for kindness and justice, and you have to be brave enough to speak." I asked him if he believed the Party would eventually reform itself from within. "That's hard to imagine," he said. "It still believes in the power of violence, that it can control situations, finally, with force." The Party often described Chen and other dissidents as anomalies, but Chen didn't see himself that way. "Twenty-five hundred years ago, Confucius said people take different routes but they will eventually come to the same conclusion. Look at how different Ai Weiwei's background is from mine; he is from an elite family, and I am from a poor family, but we share the pursuit of justice." He drew a comparison. "It's like the surface of water: When it's untouched, it's very peaceful. But when you throw in a pebble, it sends ripples in all directions, and sometimes they intersect. Awareness of your rights operates like that."

As we talked, Chen went online using a braille module—a black machine about the size of a keyboard that produced a physical read-out beneath his fingertips, instead of a display. But when I asked Chen whether the Internet played an important role in China's changes, he sighed and described technology as beside the point. "It's not like everyone in China is relying on the Internet," he said. "There are many other channels. In Chinese we say, 'Word of mouth is faster than the wind. It passes from one person to ten, and from ten to a hundred.'"

Chen was not an easy person to interview. When he found my questions vague or uninspiring, I sensed his impatience, and I found myself stumbling in Chinese. The more I tried to untangle my syntax, the more he attended to his computer. I asked his assistant to help me express what I was trying to say, but after an hour or so, I sensed that our interview had run its course. I thanked him, and he politely walked me to the door.

Walking back across Washington Square Park, I realized that our encounter was difficult in ways I hadn't anticipated. He was argumentative, and I was frustrated. But what had I expected? The only reason he was in New York was that he was constitutionally unwilling to accept ideas that he found unpersuasive. It occurred to me that Chen had been an exile all his life, even when he was in his village: he was blind in a country that made few allowances for it; he was stubborn in a culture that privileged accommodation. How else had he taught himself the law, scaled the walls of his yard, slipped past his guards, and outmaneuvered the diplomats who brokered a deal on his behalf? I was foolish for having expected much else. On some level, I had been drawn to Chen for the same reason I had been drawn to the defecting soldier Lin Yifu, or many of the others over the years: each of them had considered what destiny ordained—and rejected it. Up close, they looked less like the icons and villains their admirers and foes imagined; they were simply the "unbound feet" of Chinese history.

It was not the last time Chen Guangcheng would defy people's expectations. Four months after I met him, he waded into American partisan politics: he allied himself with opponents of abortion, including Bob Fu of ChinaAid and a PR consultant named Mark Corallo, a former spokesman for Attorney General John Ashcroft, who "had a hand in almost every newsworthy piece of Republican crisis management in Washington over the past decade," according to his website. Christopher Smith, a conservative congressman from New Jersey, accused NYU of trying to prevent Chen from meeting with him, and Chen accused the university of refusing to extend his fellowship because it wanted to please the Chinese government. (The school denied both counts.) Chen released a statement that read, "The work of the Chinese Communists within academic circles in the United States is far greater than what people imagine," though he declined to explain what he meant. Chen's falling-out with NYU dismayed many of his supporters, including Jerome Cohen, who said glumly, "I have failed as a teacher." In the fall of 2013, Chen became a senior fellow at the Witherspoon Institute, a conservative research organization opposed to abortion and same-sex marriage. At the same time, in an effort to avoid being pinned to any one ideology, he became a visiting fellow at Catholic University and an advisor to the Lantos Foundation for Human Rights & Justice, a liberal organization that had awarded Chen a prize earlier in the year.

Watching Chen's life veer in a new direction, I sensed that the instincts he honed in China had led him into a political minefield in

America that would have been difficult for anyone to navigate, but especially him. For years he had survived by distrusting authority of all kinds, and in many ways, he had applied that principle to his new life in New York. It alienated him from people who might have helped him. Chen didn't know how long he would stay in America, but history suggested that life in exile would not get easier. In the Soviet era, Solzhenitsyn had holed up in Vermont and raged against enemies real and imagined. After Milan Kundera fled from Prague to Paris, he worried that his work would become as "meaningless as the twittering of birds." Chinese dissidents in particular had struggled abroad: Wei Jingsheng, who spent eighteen years in Chinese prisons, was China's most prominent exile when he arrived in New York, straight from jail, in 1997; within a few years, he had alienated his patrons and other activists, and their attention moved on. Some people were quick to say that Chen was reenacting the fate of previous Chinese exiles. But if his history was any guide, he had more incarnations ahead of him. It struck me as premature to predict his future based on the fate of the countrymen who came before him. Over the course of his life, he had sought, above all, the right to be treated as his own man.

Chen's odyssey from Dongshigu Village to Beijing and New York and onward was so dramatic and specific that it was easy to dismiss it as an oddity. There had always been dissidents escaping authoritarian countries; what did it have to do with the lives of ordinary people in China? But in his determination to escape his circumstances, Chen was enacting a force far larger than he. I had arrived in a country that was driven by the need to put deprivation behind it, where people had been so hungry so recently that they could not initially conceive their ambitions beyond that most essential imperative. But that moment had passed. Chen was motivated by neither fortune nor power; he was driven by an idea about his own fate, and his own dignity, and in this he shared something fundamental with many others.

In March 2013, I got a call from Michael the English teacher. For years he had talked about coming to Beijing, and finally he was getting his chance. He had received a call from a small publishing house; one of its staff members had heard him teach a class and he invited Michael to Beijing for a job writing textbooks. The last time I'd seen him, a couple of months earlier, he'd been in the doldrums, but this opportunity thrilled him. "They found *me*," he told me over the phone, before setting out on the thirteen-hour train ride to the capital. Even for a young man who had lived in the big city of Guangzhou, Beijing still carried the hint of transformative potential, the "crucible," as Mao had put it, in which one could not but be transformed.

When Michael's train arrived, he asked me to help proofread some of his lessons. I invited him over. We met at the Lama Temple subway stop and walked back to my house, past the fortune-tellers and the name-givers. In the living room, he dropped his backpack and pulled out his laptop. In the months since the disgrace of his former idol Li Yang of Crazy English, Michael had decided that Li Yang's attempt to mass-produce English speakers was a mistake; his method touched the lives of many people, but not deeply. "Li Yang always told me, 'You have to make a lot of money in the future.' But I don't want to do that," Michael said. "Money is not the only way of living. It's just one part of life. You have to *be* somebody. Just like Steve Jobs."

Michael had found his new icon. "Steve Jobs is my hero," he said. "Steve Jobs used the iPod to change the music industry, and he used the iPhone Four to change the world. Can you believe it?" After his death in 2011, Jobs had become an object of fascination in China; to his young Chinese admirers, he was a nonconformist who became a billionaire. I met young men who couldn't afford iPhones but could afford Chinese translations of Walter Isaacson's Jobs biography, and they quoted it like scripture. On his laptop, Michael clicked on a video file. It was an old Apple television ad that he had found online. *"Here's to the crazy ones. The misfits. The troublemakers. The round pegs in the square holes . . ."* It ended with the phrase, "Think Different" and, under his breath, Michael said, "Beautiful."

Michael, as always, had some new ideas to share. Some were practical (he wanted to license the rights to publish a short, simplified-English version of the Steve Jobs biography, with phonetic markings to help students pronounce the words correctly) and some were preposterous: he was trying to popularize a marketing word he had dreamed up, *charmiac*, to describe people like him, who were charmed by something to the point of distraction. When I told him it wasn't the best use of his time, he sounded disappointed and said under his breath, "Bruce Lee got *kung fu* into the dictionary." We ran through some of the new lessons Michael had written. In one, he encouraged students to fill in the blank with a description of what drove them: "Jobs's mission was to change the world by technology. Edison's mission was to bring light to the world. Bruce Lee's mission was to make kung fu well known around the world. And my mission is to _____."

Once we were done, we went out to get some fresh air and we passed a poster celebrating the sixtieth anniversary of Mao's discovery of the selfless soldier Lei Feng. The poster said, INHERIT THE BANNER OF LEI FENG, JOIN VOLUNTEER ACTIVITIES. Michael read it and smiled; before he had come upon Li Yang Crazy English, Michael had considered Lei Feng one of his childhood idols. I asked him if he still thought the fables about Lei Feng darning socks and collecting manure were true. He frowned and said, "At least forty percent true, I think." I realized it was a sensible way to answer the question in the country that considered Mao "seventy percent right and thirty percent wrong." Michael wasn't holding Lei Feng to too high a standard, and I felt silly for having raised the question. "If somebody can really touch my deep heart, I'll believe it," he said. Over the years, I'd noticed that Michael incorporated influences from every corner of his life, from his mother's Christianity to own devotion to Crazy English. In one of his lessons, he lumped them into a single paragraph for his students to recite:

> "We're here to put a dent in the universe." This is a classic saying from the Great Jobs. He let me know that the most powerful and valuable thing in our lives is the soul, and its final resting place is faith. There is truly nothing that can influence us more powerfully than faith! Throughout human history—politics, economics, technology, culture, art, or religion—all of it begins with faith. It's just like Jesus, Confucius, Jobs, Bruce Lee, Mao Zedong, and Lei Feng. To create a more beautiful world, they started by changing themselves.

After he had been in Beijing for a few days, Michael called me and said the publishing experience wasn't going well. "They want to control everything," he said. "They don't care about me; they just care about making money. They're older, and they're putting pressure on me," he said. I took a cab over to see him at the publisher's office. It was up in the technology district, not far from where Tang Jie was running his nationalist website. Michael met me at the subway and led me into a complex marked by a sign that read, OFFICE OF VETERINARY DRUG CONTROL. He had no idea why his textbook publisher was based at the Office of Veterinary Drug Control, but he was accustomed to mysterious business arrangements, and he decided not to ask much about it.

It was a weekend, and the place was half empty. Michael was working out of a borrowed office nicely decorated with traditional Chinese furniture and calligraphy. His electronics and notebooks were scattered around. For days, he had been writing English lessons and handing them up to editors to polish, but he was frustrated by their demands. As we talked, someone knocked quickly at the door and peered in. It was the boss—a stumpy man with a puckered face—and Michael made polite gestures of introduction. After he left, Michael made a face and said, "He's always making me crazy. 'What did you write today? Show me what you have.'"

We decided to leave before the boss came back and checked on him again. I asked Michael where he was living, and he led me back out to the street, past a string of food stalls, and into the parking lot behind a supermarket. On one side was a two-story boardinghouse where Michael rented a bed in a room he shared with nine other men. His bunk cost him ¥280 a month—about $1.50 a day. A list of rules in the hallway said the boardinghouse took responsibility for nothing. "Residents," it said, "must carry their valuables (such as laptops) everywhere they go."

When we reached his room, Michael held his index finger to his lips to remind me to be quiet. It was the middle of the day; some of his roommates worked the night shift, so they were asleep now. Inside, it was airless and dank and cramped. There were five sets of metal bunk beds around a tiny patch of floor filled with luggage; in front of the window, a rod was hung with clothes. In the ceiling was a ragged hole the size of a basketball. These kinds of boardinghouses were proliferating on the edges of Chinese cities, where college graduates and job seekers were stacking up, looking for a break. The clusters became known in Mandarin as "ant tribes."

The term reminded me of the book from the seventies about the "Emperor of the Blue Ants." Back then, the metaphor had been a fair description of China's reality, but a generation later, the young and ambitious called themselves ants out of resentment. If China did not begin to integrate them into the cities, the urban underclass would reach five hundred million people by 2030 (half the entire urban population), but the government found this fact uncomfortable, so in December 2010 the agency responsible for unemployment data put out a set of rosy statistics reporting that more than 90 percent of the previous year's college graduates were now employed. People mocked this claim; the Web was rife with testimonials from students who said their schools forced them to describe themselves as "employed" in order to boost the numbers and protect the schools' reputations.

Michael and I stepped back into the noonday sun. After his claustrophobic room, the outdoors felt cool and wide open. He had wanted me to see his boardinghouse, but now he seemed self-conscious. "I can't stand it there," he said as we walked away. The conditions embarrassed him. "Next door, ten girls live together, and we go to the same restroom, the same toilets. I hate it." The problem was not discomfort. "It's a waste of my life," he said. "I can't stay with this kind of people." Some of his roommates were unemployed, and they hung around the room sleeping, eating, and playing video games. "It ruins my energy," he said. "It kills my passion for everything—my life, career."

As we walked, he seemed suddenly aware of how his life looked to another person, and it stirred a vocabulary question. "What is the English word for someone like this?" he asked.

"Like what?" I asked.

"Like me," he said.

I thought about it for a moment, and before I could answer, he volunteered an idea: "*Low society?*" he asked.

"No," I said. "We don't really have a good word in English."

We walked on. "When I need some help in English, I always search the Internet. If I can't find the answer, I ask you," he said. I felt I owed him an answer to his question about himself. He was far better off than those in the countryside, but he was stuck on the margins of success. "I think we can call you 'aspiring middle class,'" I said finally. Michael asked me to write it on a piece of paper from my notebook, and he put it in his pocket.

We stopped in front of a low-end real estate office that had advertisements in the window. I scanned the offerings to see if there were any rentals that might get him out of the Ant Tribe. But the cheapest place on offer was 120 square feet for three hundred dollars a month. It was more than Michael usually earned in a month.

In the end, Michael's experience in the capital did not fulfill his expectations. He didn't trust the men at the publishing house. "They just want to take my work and put their names on it," he said. He decided to go back down south to keep writing a book of his own. Before he left, I took him to lunch. It was partly to say goodbye—I was moving soon—but I also wanted to encourage him to set his sights on a more concrete goal. Rattling around that apartment with his parents in Qingyuan didn't strike me as a perfect plan, and I hoped that he would consider working with other people again. He was careening from one inspiration to another, and his determination to succeed on his own terms only deepened his isolation.

"You don't need to worry about me," he said. "I'm a tough man." Toughness was not what I worried about. If anything, he reminded me of a turtle that Steinbeck once described—inching across a highway, "turning aside for nothing"; it got clipped by a truck and it lay still, before it righted itself and trudged on, "drawing a wavy shallow trench in the dust." When we talked, Michael often seemed torn between wanting to present himself as a success and wanting to admit how difficult things were along the way. He oscillated between bluster and self-pity. One moment, he said, "I hate the English industry," and cursed the people he thought were trying to take his ideas without giving him credit. The next moment, he said, "I want to teach English as a religion. I have a plan for my career: five years, ten years." After a moment, his confidence wavered. "Chinese people are so dirty," he said. "At least forty percent of them."

The truth was that Michael didn't have much time to ruminate. He felt the ticking of the clock. He was twenty-eight years old. "In China, when you're thirty, you have to be financially independent," he said. That was an imposing deadline. He thought about it for a second, and then he brightened. "Maybe next year you'll go into a bookstore and see my books on the shelf," he said. "Can you believe it?" Yes, I said. Somehow I could.

It was a weekend, and for once we lingered at the lunch table. The crowd thinned out. Michael brought up the subject of his father's experience in the coal mines. It had been a supremely dangerous way of life.

Once, in Mine Number Five, where Michael grew up, a single accident killed forty-nine miners. It wasn't unusual; despite recent improvements, an average of sixty coal miners still died in China every week. Michael said of his father, "He worked at least fourteen hours a day. He was up at five a.m., and he didn't say a word to my mother and me. I didn't understand why." Only later did Michael come to understand some of the pressures his father had faced. "He had to support four children going to school," Michael said. "He never complained."

There was, however, a part of his father's life that Michael would never be able to understand. "Many of his friends died, but you can't even find their names in books." For decades the detailed accounting of those who perished in China's mines and work sites and factories—the casualties of China's rise—was classified. The government issued broad statistics, but the details on who died and how remained state secrets. "They just said Mine Number One or Mine Number Two, and that's all," Michael said. The idea that his father's coworkers had died as invisible individuals was so far outside the realm of Michael's view of himself and the world that he found it impossible to absorb. He spent so much of his time fantasizing about recognition—about publishing his work, about the adoration of a crowd, about becoming known—that the idea of namelessness mystified him. He was repelled by anonymity in a way that reminded me of Ai Weiwei's search for the names of the children killed in the earthquake. Michael wasn't remotely interested in politics, but for him, a name was about dignity, and there was nothing political about that.

The next morning, Michael boarded a homebound train. It would take thirteen hours to reach Qingyuan. He hoped to graduate someday to the high-speed trains running from the flying-saucer-shaped station, but that day hadn't yet arrived. For now, he bore the weight of the past that had defined him and the future he wanted so desperately to create. He was divided between the old-world expectation to accommodate and the modern pressure to stand on his own. As always, he wrote about it in a passage for his students to recite, and it sounded, to my ear, like a mantra, a Hail Mary, an incantation. But it was a prayer only to themselves: "I will completely accept everything I was born with," they said, "and I will do my best to change it."

# EPILOGUE

For a fragile moment, in my final months in Beijing, the Communist Party succeeded in transporting a city of twenty million people back to a simpler time. In November 2012 the Party set about cleaning up the capital for its most hallowed occasion in a decade: the Eighteenth Party Congress, a meeting of more than two thousand delegates that would culminate in the unveiling of a new Politburo charged with leading the People's Republic into the future. In preparation, the Central Propaganda Department called on its offices across the country to create an "atmosphere for expression that will facilitate the victorious convening of the Eighteenth Party Congress, and create a mass upsurge of online propaganda." The censors cut off the latest conversations about corruption and intrigue, they blocked the newest double entendre, and they silenced the sources of intolerable humor: When Zhai Xiaobing, a man who worked at an investment fund in Beijing, tweeted a geeky joke that compared the meeting to a new apocalypse movie, he was arrested and held for three weeks.

The Party was no less vigilant against threats in the physical realm. Taxi companies ordered drivers to remove the hand cranks from the rear windows of their cabs, to prevent passengers from distributing what the orders called "balloons that bear slogans or Ping-Pong balls bearing reactionary messages." The windows of public buses were taped shut. The city banned pleasure boats from the lakes, barred the sale of remote-control children's airplanes, and ordered pet pigeons to be confined to their cages—perhaps, though it was never explained, to prevent them from carrying explosives. In front of the Great Hall of the People, special firefighting crews were posted, because Tibetans had taken to lighting themselves on fire in protest of Beijing's political and religious policies in their homeland. As long as the meeting was in session, the only Tibetans at the Great Hall were members of the official Tibetan delegation, who brought news that Lhasa, their capital, had been voted "the happiest city in China" four times in the last five years.

To welcome the gathering, outgoing president Hu Jintao delivered his final public speech. He titled it, "Firmly March on the Path of Socialism with Chinese Characteristics and Strive to Complete the Building of a Moderately Prosperous Society in all Respects." The most memorable line was pithier: "We will never copy a Western political system," he said. The state news service reported on a delegate who was so moved by the speech that she "wept five times"; another said her hands went numb from thirty-five rounds of applause.

After the congress had been in session for a week, I wedged into a crowd of reporters for the moment that everyone had been waiting for: the unveiling of the new Standing Committee of the Politburo. It consisted of seven men: five who would serve for five years, and the president and premier, who were expected to serve for ten. The occasion was called a "Meet the Press" opportunity, though the press was not permitted to ask questions. First onstage was the man who would become president: general secretary of the Party Xi Jinping. He hailed from a fine revolutionary family—his father had been one of the Party's hallowed elders, known as the "Eight Immortals"—and in person, he was a striking contrast to his predecessor. Xi was a ruddy-cheeked bear of a figure, with a rich radio voice and a penchant for roomy Western suits. The full picture evoked Jackie Gleason more than Zhou Enlai. "Our people love life," he said. "They hope for better education, more stable jobs, more satisfactory incomes, more reliable social guarantees, higher-level medical and health services, more comfortable living conditions, a more beautiful environment, and they hope that their children can grow up better, work better, and live better. The wishes of our people for better lives are the goals of our struggles."

His language was refreshing and largely free of Party hymns. And yet the tableau of Xi and the men by his side testified to the Party's determination to prevent its future from looking very different from its past: four out of the seven men who would now lead the country were members of aristocratic Communist families; the Party had once taken pains to avoid the perception of nepotism, but now it placed political reliability above all, and the incoming generation included a larger share of hereditary rule at the top than any time in the history of the People's Republic. Outwardly, the Party had vowed to select officials in a "democratic, open, competitive and merits-based" way, but political watchers had been able to predict the lineup by tracking the backroom negotiations among families, Party elders, and powerful factions. Reform-minded candidates had not been chosen; the winners were committed conservatives. Liu Yunshan was a seasoned propagandist. Zhang Dejiang had received his economics training in North Korea. Their faith in precedent and conformity extended to their looks: All but one of them took the stage in dark suits and red ties. Without exception, their hair was dyed to the same featureless black sheen.

When the seven men appeared together for the first time outside the Great Hall, two weeks later, they chose as a symbolic backdrop not a picture of the future—a technology company, say, or a university—but rather, an exhibit at the National Museum: "The Road to Rejuvenation," a political showcase that depicted, as the museum put it, China's "downfall into an abyss of semi-imperial and semi-feudal society" and its rescue at the hands of the Party. Standing before the exhibit, Xi said, "Everyone has his own ideals, aspirations and dreams . . . The greatest dream of the Chinese people in recent times has been to realize the great revival of the Chinese nation . . . No one will be well-off unless the state and the nation are well-off."

Soon his reference to the "Chinese Dream" was a slogan on billboards and television. In one week, the Chinese Dream appeared twenty-four times on the front page of the *People's Daily*. There was a new talent show called the *Voice of the Chinese Dream*, and the Party dispatched "Spirit Explanation Teams" to nonsocialist countries to spread the word. Scientists were encouraged to submit Chinese Dream research proposals, and artists were urged to make Chinese Dream "masterworks." Xi encouraged the military to have a "strong-army dream," and the Party's propaganda chief, Liu Yunshan, ordered it written into textbooks to ensure that it "enters students' brains."

The Chinese Dream was partly a statement of fact—China *was* reviving—and partly an acknowledgment of China's ambitions. Some aspirations would be easier to fulfill than others. To remain the Party in Power, the Communist Party knew it must continue to allow people to prosper. It planned to build another hundred thousand miles of highways, another fifty new airports, and more than five thousand additional miles of high-speed rail. But the new administration knew that ordinary people had more immediate concerns, and once it was in office, it vowed to boost the lowest incomes and allow depositors to earn more on their savings.

Satisfying the pursuit of truth looked to be more difficult. In its first six decades in power, the Communist Party maintained stability with the help of censorship, secrecy, and intimidation, but it now faced a culture of skepticism and disclosure, and growing freedom from fear. The Central Propaganda Department, with its modern walls and pagoda roof, still stood on the Avenue of Eternal Peace—a monument to double-think. Riding by for the last time, it occurred to me that I would know that Chinese leaders had absorbed the reality around them if the Department got a sign on its headquarters.

Most difficult, perhaps, will be satisfying the pursuit of faith. China is in an ideological stalemate; no political wing can claim to be in the ascendance. There will be more outbursts of nationalism, and new demagogues to play on the feelings of humiliation, but that sentiment could harm the Party more than it fortifies it. By setting China against "universal values," the Party is ensuring that it will face more snubs, more protests, more reminders of Liu Xiaobo's empty chair. Yet it is raising its people to believe that humiliation, and those responsible for it, must not be tolerated.

Thirty years after China embarked on its fitful embrace of the free market, it has no single unifying doctrine—no "central melody"—and there is nothing predestined about what kind of country it is becoming. When the president unveiled the Chinese Dream, he intended it to be unifying, but instead, his people interpreted it as Chinese "Dreams"— plural. I bumped into my neighbor the widow Jin Baozhu, who'd been sued by my landlord for stealing sunlight. Jin had seen the new slogan on the news, and she told me, "What's my Chinese Dream? To live a few more years in my house."

Soon the censors were racing to strike down photos of people holding

handwritten signs reading, MY CHINESE DREAM IS JUSTICE AND FAIR-
NESS and MY CHINESE DREAM IS THAT XI JINPING PROTECTS MY PER-
SONAL SAFETY AND REPRODUCTIVE RIGHTS. When a website run by the
*People's Daily* conducted a "Chinese Dream" survey, asking whether
people supported one-party rule and believed in socialism, 80 percent of
the three thousand respondents replied "no" to both questions, and the
survey was abruptly withdrawn. People used to say that their censored
work had been "harmonized." Now they said it had been "dreamed
away."

Shortly after Xi took office, he acknowledged what many had come to
believe: unless the Party beat back the tide of corruption, that corruption
would "inevitably lead the Party and the nation to perish." He compared
it to "worms breeding in decaying matter," and he vowed to punish not
only low-ranking "flies" but also powerful "tigers." He called on his
comrades to be "diligent and thrifty," and when Xi took his first official
trip, state television reported that he checked into a "normal suite" and
dined not at a banquet, but at a buffet—a revelation so radical in Chinese political culture that the word *buffet* took on metaphysical significance. The state news service ran a banner headline: XI JINPING VISITS
POOR FAMILIES IN HEBEI: DINNER IS JUST FOUR DISHES AND ONE SOUP,
NO ALCOHOL.

Xi called for officials to forgo their motorcades, fresh-cut flowers, and
long-winded speeches. Local bureaucrats raced to enshrine his orders
into new rules, but this only, unwittingly, illuminated the prior state of
affairs: The city of Yinchuan declared that officials must no longer "accept money in envelopes while celebrating weddings, moving into new
houses, or during their children's enrollment in school." The "Four
Dishes and One Soup" campaign was followed by "Operation Empty
Plate," a campaign to encourage officials to finish what they ordered. It
didn't take long for the abrupt drop-off in gluttony to affect the economy:
sales of shark fin (de rigueur for banquets) sank more than 70 percent;
casinos in Macau recorded a drop in VIPs, and Swiss watch exports
dropped by a quarter from the year before. Luxury goods makers mourned.

Wang Qishan, the Party warhorse who had been named the president's new anticorruption czar, was trained as a historian, and he told

his peers to read Alexis de Tocqueville's *The Ancien Régime and the Revolution*. When word got out, it became a best seller, and Chinese readers saw much that they recognized in the tale of indulgent aristocrats, a frustrated merchant class, and a government led by rulers who assumed the middle class would be its backbone of support right up until the moment it helped deprive the king of his head. Tocqueville wrote, "Though it took the world by surprise, it was the inevitable outcome of a long period of gestation." Wang never specified exactly what message he wanted people to draw from the book, though discussion gravitated to Tocqueville's observation that a nation is not unstable when it's poor but, rather, when "it suddenly finds the government relaxing its pressure."

To show its commitment to fighting corruption, the government put the railway boss Liu Zhijun on trial in June 2013. At first, the stagecraft went smoothly. The trial took less than four hours, and Great Leap Liu played his part: he wept, he confessed, and he even found a way to plug the president's new slogan, saying that temptation had distracted him from advancing the goal of the Chinese Dream. To avoid gratuitous discussion of cronyism and graft, prosecutors charged him modestly: abuse of power and taking only $10.6 million in bribes. But when he was given a "suspended death sentence," which would likely be commuted to a prison term of perhaps thirteen years, people called that a whitewash. The *South China Morning Post* asked, "How was he allowed to climb up and carry on for so long? Who were his protectors in the leadership and how much money did they receive? Those are the interesting questions anti-graft investigators have never bothered to explore." To ensure that nobody investigated on their own, the Central Propaganda Department put an end to the discussion. "The Liu Zhijun case is now closed," it told editors. "Media coverage must use only the Xinhua story. Do not produce detailed reports, do not comment, and do not sensationalize."

Great Leap Liu had parting words of his own; he gave his lawyer a message to convey to his daughter: "No matter what you do—stay out of politics." It was a tough business, and it was about to get tougher. Xi Jinping confronted a political problem that his predecessors had not: in the era of cynicism and information, Xi was not elected, but he had to figure out a way to be liked. Chairman Mao once compared his comrades to the fish and the public to the water: "The fish can't survive without the water," Mao said. But now, without ideology, the legitimacy of the Chinese government rested evermore on its satisfying and pleasing the public.

By some essential measures—eliminating hunger, illiteracy, and medical neglect—the public was more satisfied than in most countries. When sociologist Martin Whyte of Harvard first asked people, in 2004, if they were receiving coverage under public medical insurance plans, only 15 percent of those in the countryside said yes; when he asked again in 2009, that share had grown to 90 percent. People still faced wide gaps in coverage, and their insurance provided only the most basic care, but the progress was clear.

Ranking China's approval ratings alongside those of other governments was always flattering for the Party: in May 2013, the Chinese media reported that the Pew Research Center had found that 88 percent of the Chinese it polled were feeling good about the economy—a higher share than any of the countries it polled. But there was more to that story. When a team led by Richard Easterlin, a professor of economics at the University of Southern California, analyzed five long-term studies conducted in China over two decades, the results showed "no evidence that the Chinese people are, on average, any happier . . . If anything, they are less satisfied than in 1990, and the burden of decreasing satisfaction has fallen hardest on the bottom third of the population in wealth. Satisfaction among Chinese in even the upper third has risen only moderately." Overall, they found, "economic growth is not enough; job security and a social safety net are also critical to people's happiness." When polls reported, as they did in 2013, that 93 percent of the Chinese "believed their country's best days lay ahead of them," the results said less about satisfaction than about expectation. "Hope is like a path in the countryside," Lu Xun had said. "Originally there was no path, but once people begin to pass, a way appears."

By fixating on corruption, the president was gambling that if the Party declared war on its own iniquity, the public would focus more on the war than on the iniquity. It was risky: for decades, Party leaders had said, "Fight corruption too little and you'll destroy the country. Fight it too much and you'll destroy the Party." The anticorruption campaign was immediately popular. New grassroots websites such as I Made a Bribe let people report whoever had asked them for baksheesh. Xu Zhiyong, a lawyer who had previously served in Beijing's city legislature, organized a petition calling for high officials to disclose their wealth, and his work attracted several thousand supporters to what he called a New Citizens' Movement.

Soon, the Party grew uneasy with this enthusiasm. My phone buzzed with a notice from the Department:

> When reporting on officials suspected of graft or bribery, or those who have become degenerate, strictly adhere to information from the authorities. Do not speculate, do not exaggerate, do not investigate, and do not quote from things on the Internet.

By summer, the government had seen enough; it shut down I Made a Bribe and detained nearly a hundred people who had embraced the campaign to clean up. Among them was Xu Zhiyong, who was detained and accused of "gathering people to disrupt social order." When people stood up on Xu's behalf, they, too, were arrested; an investor named Wang Gongquan, who had made billions in venture capital, organized a petition for Xu's release but was arrested on charges of disturbing public order. Wang's bare-handed fortune and outspoken comments had attracted a large following online, but the authorities were especially uneasy when plutocrats linked up with activists or took an interest in politics.

In September the government adopted a novel approach to taming the unruly power of the Web: the Supreme People's Court issued a rule stating that any "false defamatory" comment viewed five thousand times, or forwarded five hundred times, could result in a prison sentence of up to three years. Now that the state was struggling to prevent people from speaking out, it would try to prevent them from repeating what they heard. In a speech, Lu Wei, the director of the State Internet Information Office, declared "freedom without order does not exist." In the months that followed, discussions unfolding on Weibo became less provocative, the number of users declined, and people searched for safer platforms.

The official campaign against corruption had its limits. Instead of splurging in public, some government departments moved their banquets in-house by hiring the cooks from luxury hotels. An unofficial new slogan took root: "Eat Quietly, Take Gently, Play Secretly."

The Party's long-term objective was no mystery: if Xi Jinping fulfilled his duty to lead the Party until 2023, China would surpass the record held by the Soviet Union as history's most durable one-party state. The Soviets had been in power for seventy-four years, and Chinese leaders openly feared the Soviet fate. Shortly after taking office, Xi Jinping gave a speech to Party members and asked, "Why did the Soviet Communist Party collapse? An important reason was that their ideals and convictions wavered. Eventually, all it took was a quiet word from Gorbachev to declare the dissolution of the Soviet Communist Party, and the great party was gone. In the end nobody was man enough to come out and resist."

Xi's "man enough" speech opened a new propaganda push: in case people wondered what would happen in the absence of the Party, the *People's Daily* painted a dire picture. After the fall of the Soviet Union, it said, Russians discovered that their "GDP fell by half . . . their ships aged and rusted and collapsed into heaps of scrap metal; oligarchs emerged to plunder state assets; Russians lined up on the sidewalk to face supply shortages; war veterans had to sell their medals in order to buy bread." The paper asked what posed a similar threat to China today. Its answer: the Internet. "Every day, microbloggers and their mentors spread rumors, fabricate bad news about society, create an apocalyptic vision of China's demise, and denigrate the socialist system—all to promote the Euro-American model of capitalism and constitutionalism."

Under Xi Jinping, the Party showed no sign that it saw a way out of its ideological gymnastics. It continued to carry the banner of socialism and the ideas that came with it (Thought Reform, the primacy of the Party in Power), while, on all sides, the Party was confronting unbridled Wild West capitalism and a clamorous market of ideas. If there was an enlightened view within the Party élite about how to resolve this tension, that view was not getting out. Instead, a Party memo leaked in August suggested that at least part of the leadership was getting paranoid. Document No. 9, as it was known, called for eradicating seven subversive strains of thinking. Beginning with "Western constitutional democracy," the list included press freedom, civic participation, "universal values" of human rights, and what it described as "nihilist" interpretations of the

Party's history. The "seven taboos" were delivered to university professors and social media celebrities, who were warned not to cross the line. The *People's Daily* summoned the language of another era and warned that constitutionalism, the call to put the Party under the rule of law, was "a weapon for information and psychological warfare used by the magnates of American monopoly capitalism and their proxies in China to subvert China's socialist system."

The Party had reasons to be nervous: it was trapped in a predicament of its own creation. It had recommitted itself to the suppression of heretical ideas and the maintenance of stability, but that approach was producing more heresy and instability. The Party was rightly convinced that China's future depended on innovating ideas that would be felt around the globe, and yet it feared the reverse: absorbing "global values" was a threat to its survival.

Chinese leaders were facing a choice: to continue growing, they could adopt a more democratic form of government, as South Korea did in the 1980s, or they could recommit themselves to authoritarianism. Historically, the latter approach was risky. Over the long term, authoritarian states do not grow as reliably as democracies; they are fragile, and they tend to thrive only in the hands of visionary individual leaders. "For every Lee Kuan Yew, of Singapore, there are many like Mobutu Sese Seko, of the Congo," according to the Harvard economist Dani Rodrik. In the short term, the Party could succeed at silencing its critics, but in the long term, that was less clear, especially if segments within the Party recalculated their own risks and rewards for loyalty and decided that they had more to gain by siding with the people.

China, once known for its conformity, was home to fiercely opposing forces: Western-style liberals against nationalist conservatives; incumbent apparatchiks against restless plutocrats; Ant Tribes against Bobos; propagandists against cyber-utopians. The question was whether the tensions would be channeled outward, at the West, or inward, at the state. For the moment, it was difficult to envision a coherent challenge to the Party: though the Chinese middle class was galvanized by many of the issues that had animated its peers at the advent of democracy in Taiwan, the Philippines, and South Korea (consumer rights, the environment, labor rights, housing prices, free speech), in China there were very few formal organizations in which people could assemble and produce a coordinated alternative to Party rule.

So far, China's middle-class activists generally sought to reform the government, not replace it. In many countries, a more educated and entrepreneurial middle class has demanded greater control over its affairs. China had already passed the threshold into what political scientists call the "zone of democratic transition"—when a country's per capita income exceeds four thousand dollars, and the correlation with regime change rises sharply. By 2013, China was at a level of eight thousand five hundred dollars. The China scholar Minxin Pei examined the twenty-five autocracies with higher levels of income and a resistance to democratization. He found that twenty-one of them were oil states. China was not.

When it became clear that Xi Jinping was placing his bet on fortifying the status quo, another Party aristocrat, Hu Dehua, the sixty-three-year-old son of a previous Party chief, Hu Yaobang, used the protection afforded by his family name and pedigree to openly criticize the president. The real reason the Soviets fell, Hu Dehua argued, was that they couldn't stop themselves from "appropriating public property by graft and bribery." The Party, Hu said, was indeed facing a crisis. "There are two options: to suppress the opposition or to reach reconciliation with the people," he said. It had faced this choice once before, in 1989; and in an astonishing acknowledgment of the bloodshed at Tiananmen, he asked, "What does this mean: 'man enough'? Is driving battle tanks against your own people 'man enough'?"

From afar, China was often described as marching inexorably toward better days. But inside the country, people were more circumspect. Everything the Chinese had ever gained was by iron and sweat and fire, and they, better than anyone, knew the impermanence of it all—"the unreality of reality," as F. Scott Fitzgerald put it, "a promise that the rock of the world was founded securely on a fairy's wing." In my final months in Beijing, that feeling of fragility took hold more deeply. In July 2013, Paul Krugman, the Nobel Prize–winning economist, wrote in his column in *The New York Times*, "The country's whole way of doing business, the economic system that has driven three decades of incredible growth, has reached its limits."

The economy had slowed to its worst performance since 1990, and some of the ingredients in the recipe of its success were running low.

The one-child policy had sharply reduced the number of young workers who had once made Chinese factories so inexpensive. Between 2010 and 2030, China's labor force would shrink by sixty-seven million people, the equivalent of the population of France. What's more, China was devoting half its GDP to investment—a higher level than any big country in modern times—but growth was still slowing, which meant that investments in new equipment and other capital weren't yielding as much growth as before. China was probably not at risk of an imminent economic collapse. Beijing had three trillion dollars in foreign exchange reserves, and it restricted the flow of money in and out of the country, so a run on the banks was unlikely. The larger danger was that China's local governments had spent so much on building that their debt had doubled since 2010, to almost 39 percent of the nation's gross domestic product. So, instead of putting money into the hands of consumers, China was spending it on staving off municipal defaults, a scenario that reminded people of Japan-style stagnation.

For those inclined to find reminders of eighties-era Japan—its loose credit and its ice cubes chipped from the Arctic—the moment arrived in July, when developers in the Chinese city of Changsha broke ground for the world's tallest building, Sky City. Economists point to a historic correlation between "world's tallest" debuts and economic slowdowns. There is no cause and effect, but such projects are a sign of easy credit, excessive optimism, and inflated land prices—a pattern that dates to the world's first skyscraper, the Equitable Life Building. Built in New York at the height of the Gilded Age, it was completed in 1873, the start of a five-year slump that became known as the Long Depression, and the pattern repeated in decades to follow. *Skyscraper* magazine, a Shanghai publication that treated tall buildings like celebrities, reported in 2012 that China would finish a new skyscraper every five days for the next three years; China was home to 40 percent of the skyscrapers under construction in the world.

In the summer of 2013, Sarabeth and I packed up our house on the Alley of National Studies. When I told the widow Jin Baozhu that we were moving back to America, she advised caution. Though she had never set foot outside China, she was a close watcher of the news. "America is rich, but it has many guns," she said. I booked a pair of one-way tickets to Washington, D.C. We handed off our air purifier to friends, and I knew I was getting nostalgic when I began to contemplate life without the weasel in the ceiling. That spring it gave birth to four cubs, and the five of them would climb out onto the roof at dusk to tumble around. I mentioned this to my neighbor Huang Wenyi, who said it was a very auspicious sign for our move back to America.

I was outside in the alley chatting with Huang one day when a man in a fluorescent orange jumpsuit approached us. Around the neighborhood, the men and women in the orange jumpsuits worked for the district sanitation department. Many were migrants from the countryside; they swept the alleys, cleaned the public restrooms, and collected the trash. Some wore straw farmers' hats that cast a shadow across their faces, and the matching uniforms made it difficult for me to keep them straight. I didn't know if there were three of them or thirty. The man who approached us had tousled hair, sun wrinkles around his eyes, and a smile of jumbled teeth. He pointed to a gray flagstone at our feet.

"Can you see the emperor on that rock?" the sweeper asked.

I thought I'd misheard.

"I can see an image of the emperor right there on that rock," he said.

Huang and I looked at the rock and back at the sweeper. Huang was not interested. "What are you bullshitting about?" he asked. "You have no idea what you're talking about."

The sweeper smiled. "Are you saying you think I'm not a cultured man?" he asked.

"What I'm saying is that you're not making sense," Huang said.

The sweeper gave him a look and turned, instead, to face me. "I can look at anything and pull the essence from it," he said. "It doesn't matter how ordinary something is; in my eyes, it becomes a treasure. Do you believe me?"

Huang was irritated. "Old man," he said, "I'm trying to have a chat with our foreign friend here. Can you not disturb us and go back to your work?"

The sweeper kept talking—faster now, about ancient Chinese poetry, and the writer Lu Xun—some of it too fast, and the references too obscure, for me to understand. He sounded somewhere between interesting and bonkers. Huang, the proud Beijinger, had had enough, and he poked fun at the man's countryside accent. "Come back after you've learned to speak Beijing dialect," he said.

Under his breath, the sweeper said, "As long as it's a dialect of human beings, it's legitimate." But Huang didn't hear him. He'd waved him away and wandered into his house. I introduced myself. The sweeper's name was Qi Xiangfu. He was from Jiangsu Province, and he said he had come to Beijing three months earlier. Why did you come? I asked.

"To explore the realm of culture," he said grandly.

"What kind of culture?"

"Poetry, mainly. Ancient Chinese poetry. During the Tang dynasty, when poetry was the best, every poet wanted to come to Chang'an," he said, invoking the name of the ancient capital, the predecessor to Beijing. "I wanted a bigger stage," Qi told me. "It doesn't matter whether I succeed or fail. I'm here. That's what matters." His explanation reminded me of "the call." When I had arrived in China, it felt as if most of the men and women who were hearing that call were young and hungry, people such as Gong Haiyan and Tang Jie. But in the years since then, the call had drawn in many others. Much as the writer Lu Xun had written, "Once people begin to pass, a way appears."

Qi told me that he competed in poetry competitions. "I won the title of 'Super King of Chinese Couplets.'" In his spare time, he had taken to hosting an online forum about modern Chinese poetry. "You can go online and read about me," he said.

That night, I typed his name into the Web, and there he was: Qi Xiangfu, the Super King of Chinese Couplets. In the photo, he was handsomely dressed in a bow tie and a jacket; he looked young and confident. Chinese poems were hard for me to understand, and many of his especially were impenetrably weird. But I appreciated some moments of grace: "Earth knows the lightness of our feet," he wrote. "We meet each other there / Between heaven and earth."

To my surprise, the more I searched about Qi Xiangfu, the more I found of a life lived partly online. He once wrote a short memoir, in which he described himself in the third person, with the formality usually reserved for China's most famous writers. He wrote that his father died young, and Qi was raised by his uncle. He wrote, of himself, "The first time Qi read Mao's poem 'The Long March,' he resolved that Mao would be the teacher to show him the way. Later, he studied the poetry of Li Bai, Du Fu, Su Dongpo, Lu You, and others, and he made a promise to himself: Become a master of literature."

He described the first time he ever presented one of his poems to a large group—it was played on a speaker at a construction site—and he described a bus trip in which he met, as he put it, "a girl who sympathized." They married, and it "ended his life of vagrancy." There were hints of trouble in his life—at one point, he wrote a plea for donations, saying, "Alas, Comrade Qi is having a difficult time"—but something in the spirit of his online persona captivated me. So much of it would have been impossible just a few years ago: the journey to the city, the online identity, the interior life so at odds with the image he projected to the world. Anybody who scratched beneath the surface of Chinese life discovered a more complicated conception of the good life that had made room for the pursuit of values and dignity alongside the pursuit of cars and apartments.

After I met the street sweeper Qi Xiangfu, I started bumping into him frequently. We swapped phone numbers, and he would send me a poem, now and then, by text message. He typed out the characters on his phone, with the help of a magnifying glass to aid his vision. Many of his poems were heavy with Communist fervor; others were oracular and strange. But I sympathized with anyone trying to make sense of this place in writing, and I admired his persistence. "I've experienced every kind of coldness and indifference from people," he told me, "but I've also given myself knowledge, all the way up to the university level. I don't have a diploma. People look down on me when they see me."

Two weeks before I left China, I bumped into Qi on the street for the last time. He wasn't wearing his uniform; he was in street clothes—a crisp white shirt and a black jacket—on his way to see his daughter, who worked at a restaurant nearby. He had a book under his arm: *Ten Contemporary Authors of Prose*. For the first time, I saw the two personae, online and real-world, in one. What inspires you? I once asked him. "When I write," he said, "anything becomes material. In life, I must be practical, but when I write, it is up to me."

# NOTES ON SOURCES

This book is the result of eight years of reporting and living in China. I moved to Beijing in June 2005 and stayed until July 2013, when my wife, Sarabeth Berman, and I moved to Washington, D.C. The vast majority of my research relied on personal experience and interviews, but I am indebted to a range of scholars, journalists, artists, and authors for their work. In researching and writing this narrative, I conducted hundreds of interviews, read personal journals from my subjects, and obtained hundreds of pages of court documents that explain some of the legal dramas I describe. For news, I relied on foreign and Chinese publications, especially BBC, Bloomberg, *Caijing, Caixin, The Economic Observer, The Economist, Financial Times, The New York Review of Books, The New York Times, South China Morning Post, The Wall Street Journal*, and *The Washington Post*. It would not have been possible to keep track of the changes in China's Internet culture without several websites that provide translation and analysis of journalism, leaked government documents, and social media commentary: Beijing Cream, China Digital Times, ChinaFile, China Media Project, chinaSMACK, Danwei, GreatFire, Shanghaiist, and Tea Leaf Nation.

## PROLOGUE

I am indebted to Yunxiang Yan for sharing with me his recollections of the village of Xiajia, where he was a farmer during the Cultural Revolution and where he later returned, as an anthropologist, for a series of long-term studies. He has documented changes in Xiajia, which is located in Heilongjiang Province, in several detailed works, including *Private Life Under Socialism: Love, Intimacy, and Family Change in a Chinese Village 1949–1999* (Stanford, CA: Stanford University Press, 2003); and *The Individualization of Chinese Society* (Oxford, UK: Berg, 2009).

Lu Xun wrote of hope in his short story "Gu Xiang" (My Old Home), first published in January 1921.

The comparison to Britain, which appears in "Urban World: Cities and the Rise of the Consuming Class," produced by McKinsey Global Institute in 2012, was based on research by Angus Maddison, University of Groningen.

I am grateful to Arthur Kroeber, managing director of GaveKal-Dragonomics, for his help in refining the comparisons of income before reform and after the advent of reform. The income comparison is from the World Bank data for China's GNI per capita, Atlas method (US$).

For a sample of China impressions in another age, see George Paloczi Horvath, *Mao Tse-tung: Emperor of the Blue Ants* (London: Secker and Warburg, 1962).

For background on the Gilded Age, see Mark Twain and Charles Dudley Warner, *The Gilded Age: A Tale of To-day* (Hartford, CT: American Publishing Company, 1874); Richard White, *Railroaded: The Transcontinentals and the Making of Modern America* (New York: W. W. Norton and Company, 2011); and Bill Bryson. *At Home: A Short History of Private Life* (New York: Random House, 2010).

## 1. UNFETTERED

I am thankful to Lin Yifu (né Lin Zhengyi) for sharing his story and his writings with me over many interviews. In addition I relied on official documents about his defection produced by the Ministry of Defense in Taiwan, including the *Diaochao Baogao* of May 20, 2009, and *Jiuzheng'an Wen* of November 26, 2002. Other useful background and detail were contained in Zheng Dongyang, *Lin Yifu: Diedang Renshenglu* (Zhejiang: Zhejiang Renmin Chubanshe, 2010).

I am indebted to Lin Yi-chung, the author and local historian who offered to show me Quemoy and shared his books and recollections about island life during the Cold War.

For a vivid history of Quemoy's role in the conflict between Taiwan and mainland China, see Michael Szonyi, *Cold War Island: Quemoy on the Front Line* (New York: Cambridge University Press, 2008); Michael Shaplen, "Letter from Taiwan," *The New Yorker*, June 13, 1977, p. 72; and Richard James Aldrich, Gary D. Rawnsley, and Ming-Yeh T. Rawnsley, *The Clandestine Cold War in Asia, 1945–65: Westrern Intelligence, Propaganda and Special Operations* (New York: Routledge, 2000).

For background on the relationship between senior leaders at the advent of reform, see Barry Naughton, "Deng Xiaoping: The Economist," *China Quarterly* 135, *Special Issue: Deng Xiaoping: An Assessment* (Sept. 1993): 491–514; Jonathan Spence, *The Search for Modern China* (New York: W. W. Norton and Company, 1990); Zhao Ziyang, *Prisoner of the State: The Secret Journal of Premier Zhao Ziyang* (New York: Simon & Schuster, 2009); and Kate Xiao Zhou, *How the Farmers Changed China: Power of the People* (Boulder, CO: Westview Press, 1996).

## 2. THE CALL

For a narrative history of the demonstrations at Tiananmen Square, see Orville Schell, *Mandate of Heaven: In China, a New Generation of Entrepreneurs, Dissidents, Bohemians, and Technocrats Grasps for Its Country's Power* (New York: Simon & Schuster, 1994).

The relationship between the rise of the Internet and the growth of nationalism is the subject of Xu Wu, *Chinese Cyber Nationalism: Evolution, Characteristics, and Implications* (Lanham, MD: Lexington Books, 2007); and Peter Hays Gries, *China's New Nationalism: Pride, Politics, and Diplomacy* (Berkeley: University of California Press, 2004).

For background on the rise of consumer culture, leisure, and choice, I relied most on Yan's *The Individualization of Chinese Society*, and on Deborah S. Davis, *The Consumer Revolution in Urban China* (Berkeley: University of California Press, 2000); Pál Nyíri, *Mobility and Cultural Authority in Contemporary China* (Seattle: University of Washington Press, 2010); and Li Zhang, *In Search of Paradise: Middle-Class Living in a Chinese Metropolis* (Ithaca, NY: Cornell University Press, 2012).

For statistics and analysis of the scale and pace of Chinese growth, I relied on *The Economist* and *The New York Times*. For information about the Party's "Educational Campaign," I relied most on Anne-Marie Brady, *China's Thought Management* (New York: Routledge, 2012).

Chen Guangcheng generously agreed to discuss his childhood and the influences on his thinking. Parts of my visit to his village were described in the *Chicago Tribune* in 2005. For background and other details on his life, I relied on several news accounts, including Zhang Yaojie, "Chen Guangcheng and Wen Jiaobo: Power vs. Human Rights," *China Rights Forum* 3 (2006), 35–39.

I gained valuable insights into the origins of Internet control, the Great Firewall, and the case of Shi Tao from Rebecca MacKinnon, *Consent of the Networked: The Worldwide Struggle for Internet Freedom* (New York: Basic Books, 2012); and Yang Guobin, *The Power of the Internet in China: Citizen Activism Online* (New York: Columbia University Press, 2013).

Zha Jianying's impressions of Beijing are in her book *China Pop: How Soap Operas, Tabloids, and Bestsellers Are Transforming a Culture* (New York: New Press, 2011). For the history of the city, I turned most often to Geremie Barmé, *The Forbidden City* (London: Profile Books, 2008); and Jasper Becker, *City of Heavenly Tranquility: Beijing in the History of China* (New York: Oxford University Press, 2008).

For background on the history and perceptions of time in China, I relied on Colin A. Ronan, *The Shorter Science and Civilisation in China: An Abridgement of Joseph Needham's Original Text*, volume 4 (Cambridge, UK: Cambridge University Press, 1994); and Wu Hung "The Hong Kong Clock: Public Time-Telling and Political Time/Space," *Public Culture* 9 (1997): 329–54.

## 3. BAPTIZED IN CIVILIZATION

The experience of Taiwanese defectors, including Huang Zhi-cheng, is described in Linda Jaivin, *The Monkey and the Dragon: A True Story About Friendship, Music, Politics and Life on the Edge* (Melbourne: Text Publishing, 2000).

University reactions to Lin Yifu's applications are described in "Lin Yifu zeng xiang du Zhongguo renmin daxue yin 'lai li bu ming' bei ju," *Huanqiu Renwu Zhoukan*, April 14, 2012.

For discussions of individuality; interdependence in Chinese culture, law, and history; and the origins of "Thought Reform," see Geremie Barmé and Linda Jaivin, *New Ghosts, Old Dreams: Chinese Rebel Voices* (New York: Times Books, 1992); Mette Halskov Hansen and Rune Svarverud, eds., *iChina: The Rise of the Individual in Modern Chinese Society*, book 45 (Copenhagen: Nordic Institute of Asian Studies, 2010); Gish Jen, *Tiger Writing: Art, Culture, and the Interdependent Self* (Cambridge, MA: Harvard University Press, 2013); Richard Nisbett, *The Geography of Thought: How Asians and Westerners Think Differently . . . and Why* (New York: Simon & Schuster, 2010); Pál Nyíri, *Mobility and Cultural Authority in Contemporary China* (Seattle: University of

Washington Press, 2010); and Orville Schell and John Delury, *Wealth and Power: China's Long March to the Twenty-First Century* (New York: Random House, 2013).

I benefitted from the help of the writer and translator Joel Martinsen for sharing his conclusions about the Lei Feng phenomenon. His writings on the subject include "A Lei Feng Two-fer," at www.danwei.org/trends_and_buzz/a_lei_feng_twofer.php.

The interview with the doctor who was exiled to the western desert during the Cultural Revolution was conducted by Arthur Kleinman, psychiatrist, anthropologist, and China scholar for Arthur Kleinman, Yunxiang Yan, Everett Zhang, Jing Jun, and Sing Lee, eds., *Deep China: The Moral Life of the Person* (Berkeley: University of California Press, 2011). I am indebted to Dr. Kleinman for discussing these issues with me and for alerting me to the work of his peers and former students.

For information on the language around the self and the advent of individual autonomy, I relied on *Deep China*, especially the chapter entitled "From Commodity of Death to Gift of Life," by Jing Jun. In addition, I consulted Tamara Jacka, *Rural Women in Urban China: Gender, Migration, and Social Change* (Armonk, NY, and London: M.E. Sharpe, 2006); and Mette Halskov Hansen, "Learning Individualism: Hesse, Confucius, and Pep-Rallies in a Chinese Rural High School," *China Quarterly* 213 (March 2013): 60–77.

For the political history of love in China, I consulted Yan, *Private Life Under Socialism* and *Deep China*; as well as Fred Rothbaum and Bill Yuk-Piu Tsang, "Lovesongs in the United States and China: On the Nature of Romantic Love," *Journal of Cross-Cultural Psychology* 29, no. 2 (March 1998): 306–19; and Haiyan Lee, *Revolution of the Heart: A Genealogy of Love in China, 1900–1950* (Stanford, CA: Stanford University Press, 2010).

I also benefited from Gong Haiyan's book *Ai de Hao, Shang Bu Liao* (Beijing: Beifang Funv Ertong Chubanshe, 2011).

## 4. APPETITES OF THE MIND

I am indebted to Gong Haiyan for sharing her story with me and allowing me to visit her at work over the years.

For background on consumption habits and advertising, see Tom Doctoroff, *What Chinese Want: Culture, Communism, and the Modern Chinese Consumer* (New York: Macmillan, 2012); and Cheng Li, ed., *China's Emerging Middle Class: Beyond Economic Transformation* (Washington, D.C: Brookings Institution Press, 2010).

The history of translating the word *mortgage* and the scale of price increases are relayed in Jamil Anderlini, "Chinese Property: A Lofty Ceiling" *Financial Times*, December 13, 2011.

The effect on housing is analyzed in Shang-Jin Wei and Xiaobo Zhang, "The Competitive Saving Motive: Evidence from Rising Sex Ratios and Savings Rates in China," in NBER Working Paper no. 15093 (June 2009).

## 5. NO LONGER A SLAVE

I am grateful to Michael Zhang for sharing his writings with me.

For discussion of the language surrounding class struggle and the middle class, I relied on Li, *China's Emerging Middle Class*, as well as Xing Lu, "An Ideological/Cultural Analysis of Political Slogans in Communist China," *Discourse Society* 10 (1999): 487;

and Andrew Scobell and Larry Wortzel, *Civil-Military Change in China: Elites, Institutes, and Ideas After the 16th Party Congress* (Carlisle, PA: U.S. Army War College, 2004), pp. 258 and 275n5. Chris Fraser, of the University of Hong Kong, helped me understand Mencius, and Cheng Li helped me understand what today's Party leaders make of Mencius.

For a discussion of equality in China compared to other socialist states, the advent of the New Middle-Income Stratum, the Party in Power, the Museum of Revolutionary History, and the *bubozu*, see David S. G. Goodman, *The New Rich in China: Future Rulers, Present Lives* (New York: Routledge, 2008); Anne-Marie Brady, *Marketing Dictatorship: Propaganda and Thought Work in Contemporary China* (Lanham, MD: Rowman and Littlefield, 2009), p. 57; and Jing Wang, "Bourgeois Bohemians in China? Neo-Tribes and the Urban Imaginary," *China Quarterly* 183 (September 2005): 10–27.

Paul Fussell's *Class* is available in Chinese as *"Shenghuo Pinwei: Shehui Dengji de Zuihou Chulu,"* June 1998.

The anonymous essay on archetypes of the middle class is entitled "Bailing Yunluo, Heiling Shengqi." It is available at http://forum.iask.ca/archive/index.php/t-266552 .html.

He Zhaofa's manifesto is published in "Zhongguo de Xiandaihua Xuyao Shijian Shehuixue—Fang Shehui Xue Jia, Zhongshan Daxue Jiaoshou He Zhaofa," *Shehui Magazine,* no. 6 (1994).

The success of *Harvard Girl* is analyzed in Andrew Kipnis, "Suzhi: A Keyword Approach," *China Quarterly* 186 (June 2006): 295–313.

For the history of English in China, see Bob Adamson, *China's English: A History of English in Chinese Education* (Hong Kong: Hong Kong University Press, 2004).


## 6. CUTTHROAT

The artist Cai Guo-qiang has interviewed a number of Peasant da Vincis, and he showcased a selection of their inventions in a 2010 exhibition at the Rockbund Art Museum, Shanghai. The interviews I've included are drawn from his exhibition catalogue, Cai Guo-Qiang, *Peasant Da Vincis.*

For background on Wang Guiping, the self-taught chemist, and the judgment in his trial, see "Jiangsu Sheng Taizhou Shi Renmin Jianchayuan Su Wang Guiping Yi Weixian Fangfa Weihai Gonggong Anquan, Xiaoshou Weilie Chanpin, Xubao Zhuce Ziben An," February 20, 2010. Among the Chinese press accounts that were valuable is Wang Kai, "Qi Er Zaojia Zhe Wang Guiping: Daizou Jiu Tiao Renming de Xiangcun 'Maoxian Jia,'" *Sanlian Shenghuo Zhoukan,* June 2, 2006.

I am grateful to the Hong Kong High Court Registry for approving my request for a transcript of the trial surrounding the plot to murder Wong Kam-ming and the effort to extort Siu Yun Ping. As I prepared my request, I received assistance from Simon N. M. Young, director of the Centre for Comparative and Public Law at the University of Hong Kong. I interviewed Siu Yun Ping at his construction site in 2011. I first learned of Inveterate Gambler Ping from a Reuters article published in March 2010 in collaboration with Matt Isaacs, of the Investigative Reporting Program at the University of California, Berkeley. Isaacs generously provided further information about the case.

For more on Chinese risk behavior, and money in Macau, see Desmond Lam, *The*

*World of Chinese Gambling* (Adelaide: Peacock Publications, 2009); and Elke U. Weber and Christopher Hsee, "Cross-National Differences in Risk Preference and Lay Predictions," *Journal of Behavioral Decision Making* 12 (1999): 165–79.

For U.S. State Department analysis of corruption and money laundering in Macau, see the 2011 *International Narcotics Control Strategy Report, Volume II: Money Laundering and Financial Crime.* I am grateful to Sam M. Ditzion, CEO of the Tremont Capital Group, for his analysis of ATM usage in the United States. Other information related to the nature of organized crime in Macau is found in Roderic Broadhurst and Lee King Wa, "The Transformation of Triad 'Dark Societies' in Hong Kong: The Impact of Law Enforcement, Socio-Economic and Political Change," in *Security Challenges* (Summer 2009); Angela Veng Mei Leong, "Macau Casinos and Organised Crime," in *Journal of Money Laundering Control* 7, no. 4 (Spring 2004); and Zhonglu Zeng and David Forrest, "High Rollers from Mainland China: A Profile Based on 99 Cases," in *UNLV Gaming Research and Review Journal* 13, no. 1 (2009).

## 7. ACQUIRED TASTE

Mao laid out his vision for art and culture in May 1942 at his "Talks at the Yan'an Forum on Literature and Art." This reference is from section 111. For more on socialist realism and the rise of contemporary art, see Schell and Delury *Wealth and Power;* Walter J. Meserve and Ruth I. Meserve, "Evolutionary Realism: China's Path to the Future," in *Journal of South Asian Literature* 27, no. 2 (Summer/Fall 1992): 29–39; and Barbara Pollack, *The Wild, Wild East: An American Art Critic's Adventures in China* (Beijing: Timezone 8, 2010).

For background on Yan Fu's visit to the United Kingdom, the impact of his translations, and China's conflicted relationship with the West, I relied on Schell and Delury, *Wealth and Power.*

The Chinese soap opera *Into Europe* is described in Pál Nyíri, *Scenic Spots: Chinese Tourism, the State, and Cultural Authority* (Seattle: University of Washington Press, 2011).

The survey of high school students is described in Yali Zhao, Xiaoguang Zhou, and Lihong Huang, "Chinese Students' Knowledge and Thinking about America and China," in *Social Studies* 99, no. 1 (2008): 13–22.

## 8. DANCING IN SHACKLES

For the history, structure, and evolution of the Central Propaganda Department, I depended most heavily on two books by Anne-Marie Brady, *Marketing Dictatorship* and *China's Thought Management.* Orwell's comments on political prose are in his essay "Politics and the English Language," 1946.

Hu Shuli was generous with her time and reflections. To understand her career, I benefited from conversations with dozens of other journalists, but especially with Wang Shuo, Qian Gang, David Bandurski, Wu Si, and Li Datong.

For background on the press and freedom of expression China, I consulted He Qinglian, *The Fog of Censorship: Media Control in China* (New York: Human Rights in China, 2008); and Philip P. Pan, *Out of Mao's Shadow: The Struggle for the Soul of a New China* (New York: Simon & Schuster, 2008).

## 9. LIBERTY LEADING THE PEOPLE

I am indebted to Tang Jie for his willingness to meet repeatedly from 2008 through 2013. His video is available at www.youtube.com/watch?v=MSTYhYkASsA. I was fortunate to interview his wife, Wan Manlu, and friends, including Zeng Kewei and Liu Chengguang, who answered hours of questions. For background on official support of Chinese nationalism and the revision of textbooks, see William A. Callahan, *China: The Pessoptimist Nation* (Oxford: Oxford University Press, 2010); Hongping Annie Nie, "Gaming, Nationalism, and Ideological Work in Contemporary China: Online Games Based on the War of Resistance Against Japan," *Journal of Contemporary China* 22, no. 81 (January 2013): 499–517; and Zheng Wang, *Never Forget National Humiliation: Historical Memory in Chinese Politics and Foreign Relations* (New York: Columbia University Press, 2012).

Fang Kecheng reported his findings on the expression "hurt the feelings of the Chinese people" on his blog, www.fangkc.com.

## 10. MIRACLES AND MAGIC ENGINES

In the narrative, I quote from a range of Lin Yifu's papers and books, including Lin Yifu, Fang Cai, and Zhou Li, *The China Miracle: Development Strategy and Economic Reform* (Hong Kong: Chinese University of Hong Kong Press, 2003); *Economic Development and Transition: Thought, Strategy, and Viability* (Cambridge, UK: Cambridge University Press, 2009); Lin Yifu and Célestin Monga, "Growth Identification and Facilitation: The Role of the State in the Dynamics of Structural Change," Policy Research Working Paper 5313, World Bank, May 2010; *New Structural Economics: A Framework for Rethinking Development and Policy* (Washington, D..C.: World Bank Publications, 2012); and *The Quest for Prosperity: How Developing Economies Can Take Off* (Princeton, NJ: Princeton University Press, 2012).

For details about China's economic think tanks, see Barry Naughton, "China's Economic Think Tanks: Their Changing Role in the 1990s," *China Quarterly* (2002).

My account of Liu Xiaobo's writing, use of the Web, and activism draws on my interactions with him and his work. He writes in Chinese, but parts of his work—books, poems, essays, reviews—have been translated. I relied most on several works by Liu and others, including Geremie Barmé, "Confession, Redemption, and Death: Liu Xiaobo and the Protest Movement of 1989," in *The Broken Mirror: China After Tiananmen*, reprinted in *China Heritage Quarterly*, March 2009; Perry Link, *Liu Xiaobo's Empty Chair: Chronicling the Reform Movement Beijing Fears Most* (New York: New York Review of Books, 2011); Liu Xiaobo, Perry Link, and Tienchi Martin-Liao, *No Enemies, No Hatred* (Cambridge, MA: Harvard University Press, 2012); and Liu Xiaobo, *June Fourth Elegies: Poems*, trans. Jeffrey Yang (Minneapolis, MN: Graywolf Press, 2012).

## 11. A CHORUS OF SOLOISTS

To keep up with developments in China's Internet culture, I relied on a range of sites, none more so than China Digital Times. Han Han wrote his blog and books in Chinese. His first and most successful book was *San Chong Men* (Beijing: Zuojia Chubanshe, 2000). In writing about the different ways Michael and Han Han's generation described themselves compared to the way their parents described themselves I benefited from Gish Jen's book *Tiger Writing*, which explores generational differences in the styles of Chinese memoir. For history of the efforts to reform and regulate humor, I benefited from David Moser, "No Laughing Matter: A Hilarious Investigation into the Destruction of Modern Chinese Humor," posted to Danwei, November 16, 2004, online at www.danwei.org/tv/stifled_laughter_how_the_commu.php.

## 12. THE ART OF RESISTANCE
Ai Weiwei is prolific; in addition to his films, artwork, architecture, and books are collections of analysis and translation that scholars and critics have produced. One that covers the period in question is Lee Ambrozy, ed. and trans., *Ai Weiwei's Blog: Writings, Interviews, and Digital Rants, 2006–2009* (Cambridge, MA: MIT Press, 2011).

For background on Ai and the birth of the Chinese avant-garde, I consulted Karen Smith, *Ai Weiwei* (London: Phaidon Press, 2009); Karen Smith, *Nine Lives* (Beijing: Timezone 8 Limited, 2008); Philip Tinari, "A True Kind of Living," *ArtForum* Summer 2007; and Wu Hung, *Making History* (Beijing: Timezone 8, 2008).

Several works in Chinese are invaluable to understanding Ai's family and background, including a candid memoir by his mother: Gao Ying, *Wo he Ai Qing* (Beijing: Renmin Wenxue Chubanshe, 2012); his brother's semifictional take on the family's time in New York: Ai Dan, *Niuyue Zhaji* (Hebei: Huashan Wenyi Chubanshe, 1999); and a detailed biography of his father, Ai Qing: Luo Hanchao and Luo Man, *Shidai de Chui Hao Zhe—Ai Qing Zhuan* (Zhejiang: Hangzhou Chubanshe, 2005).

## 13. SEVEN SENTENCES
Liu Xiabo's courtroom statement was translated by Perry Link and published in Lu, Link, and Martin-Liao, *No Enemies, No Hatred*. The book also contains the story of Wen Kejian's interactions with police. Gao Zhisheng described the conditions of his detention in "Dark Night, Dark Hood and Kidnapping by Dark Mafia: My Account of More Than 50 days of Torture in 2007." He reported his decision to give up activism in an interview with the Associated Press in April 2010.

For details on the evolution of Internet censorship, I relied on a range of sources, including Yang's *The Power of the Internet in China*, and Gady Epstein, "Special Report: China and the Internet," *The Economist*, April 6, 2013; Gary King, Jennifer Pan, and Margaret E. Roberts, "How Censorship in China Allows Government Criticism but Silences Collective Expression," *American Political Science Review* 107, no. 2 (May 2013): 1–18; Evgeny Morozov, *The Net Delusion: The Dark Side of Internet Freedom* (New York: PublicAffairs, 2012); and David Bandurski, "China's Guerrilla War for the Web," *Far Eastern Economic Review* (July 2008).

For discussion of China's "Nobel complex," I benefited from conversations with Julia Lovell, and from her book on the subject, *The Politics of Cultural Capital: China's Quest for a Nobel Prize in Literature* (Honolulu: University of Hawaii Press, 2006).

## 14. THE GERM IN THE HENHOUSE
Chen's recollections of the meeting with Deputy Mayor Liu Jie are contained in Zhang's article "Chen Guangcheng and Wen Jiaobo: Power vs. Human Rights." The

study of the Bureau of Letters and Visits was described by Professor Yu Jianrong. For background on traditions of protest in China, I am grateful to Professor Qiang Fang of the University of Minnesota. I also relied on Xi Chen, *Social Protest and Contentious Authoritarianism in China* (Cambridge, UK: Cambridge University Press, 2011); Ho-fung Hung, *Protest with Chinese Characteristics: Demonstrations, Riots, and Petitions in the Mid-Qing Dynasty* (New York: Columbia University Press, 2013); and Qiang Fang, *Chinese Complaint Systems: Natural Resistance*, Routledge Studies in the Modern History of Asia, vol. 80 (New York: Routledge, 2013).

## 15. SANDSTORM

In addition to my interviews and experiences, there are many published accounts of the events of the abortive "Jasmine Revolution." Details of physical attacks on reporters are contained in accounts by *The Wall Street Journal*, CNN, and the Foreign Correspondents' Club of China. For analysis and chronology, I benefited especially from Scott J. Henderson, "Wither the Jasmine: China's Two-Phase Operation for Cyber Control-in-Depth," *Air and Space Power Chronicles*, Maxwell Air Force Base, AL (First Quarter 2012): 35–47; Dale Swartz, "Jasmine in the Middle Kingdom: Autopsy of China's (Failed) Revolution," American Enterprise Institute for Public Policy Research, no. 1 (April 2011): 1–5.

In our interviews, Ai Weiwei described the conditions of his arrest. I also benefited from Barnaby Martin, *Hanging Man: The Arrest of Ai Weiwei* (New York: Macmillan, 2013).

## 16. LIGHTNING STORM

To reconstruct the train crash of July 23, 2011, I interviewed scores of people, including railway officials, engineers, passengers, investigators, contractors, and local journalists. Most of them must remain anonymous because of the threat of retribution. Among the documents that were most valuable was the official State Council report on the crash investigation, available online as "723 Yongwen Xian Tebic Zhongda Tielu Jialong Shigu Diaocha Baogao," available at www.chinasafety.gov.cn/newpage/contents/Channel_5498/2011/1228/160577/content_160577.htm.

For background on the growth of the Chinese high-speed rail, see Paul Amos, Dick Bullock, and Jitendra Sondhi, "High-Speed Rail: The Fast Track to Economic Development?" World Bank, July 2010; Richard Bullock, Andrew Salzberg, and Ying Jin, "High-Speed Rail—The First Three Years: Taking the Pulse of China's Emerging Program," *China Transport Topics*, no. 4, World Bank Office, Beijing, February 2012; James McGregor, "China's Drive for 'Indigenous Innovation': A Web of Industrial Policies," report commissioned by the U.S. Chamber of Commerce, July 2010.

Details on the life and crimes of Liu Zhijun and his brother, Liu Zhixiang, were gathered from interviews, their trials, and those of other railway figures. I am also indebted to investigative reports by *Caixin* and other Chinese media. Liu Zhixiang's scheme for generating cash and his involvement in the death of a contractor were reported in an official legal journal by Rui Jiyun, "Wuhan Tielu Liu Zhixiang Fubai Da An Jubao Shimo," *Jiancha Fengyun* 10 (2006), at www.360doc.com/content/06/0612/08/142_133043.shtml.

## 17. ALL THAT GLITTERS

Several of Hu Gang's novels and how-to guides draw upon his expertise in the art of bribery, including Fu Shi, *Qing Ci* (Hunan: Hunan Wenyi Chubanshe, 2006); and Fu Shi, *Zhongguo Shi Guanxi* (Beijing: Jincheng Chubanshe, 2011).

Contemporary cases of corruption, including the downfall of Bo Xilai, are widely covered in Chinese and foreign media. Bloomberg News analyzed and compared the net worth of China's National People's Congress to that of U.S. officials. Details on corruption in the People's Liberation Army were reported by John Garnaut in "Rotting from Within: Investigating the Massive Corruption of the Chinese Military," *Foreign Policy*, April 16, 2012. Mao Yushi described the practice of gift giving at the National Development and Reform Commission on his Weibo account, http://weibo.com /1235457821/yibTdoQsS, and it was first reported by Shanghaiist.

For more on the history and evolution of corruption in China, I relied on Melanie Manion, *Corruption by Design: Building Clean Government in Mainland China and Hong Kong* (Cambridge, MA: Harvard University Press, 2004), pp. 114–15; Paolo Mauro, "Corruption and Growth," *Quarterly Journal of Economics* 111, no. 3 (1995): 681–712; Minxin Pei, *China's Trapped Transition: The Limits of Developmental Autocracy* (Cambridge, MA: Harvard University Press, 2006); Minxin Pei, "Corruption Threatens China's Future," Carnegie Endowment for International Peace, Policy Brief no. 55 (2007); and Andrew Wedeman, *Double Paradox: Rapid Growth and Rising Corruption in China* (Ithaca, NY: Cornell University Press, 2012).

## 18. THE HARD TRUTH

To understand the changes in opportunity and mobility in China, I relied on many studies, including Cathy Honge Gong, Andrew Leigh, and Xin Meng, "Intergenerational Income Mobility in Urban China," Discussion Paper no. 140, National Centre for Social and Economic Modelling, University of Canberra, 2010; James J. Heckman and Junjian Yi, "Human Capital, Economic Growth, and Inequality in China," NBER Working Paper no. 18100, May 2012; John Knight, "Inequality in China: An Overview," World Bank, 2013; Yingqiang Zhang and Tor Eriksson, "Inequality of Opportunity and Income Inequality in Nine Chinese Provinces, 1989–2006," *China Economic Review* 21, no. 4 (2010): 607–16. I am thankful for Martin Whyte's advice and judgment on this subject.

## 19. THE SPIRITUAL VOID

For background on faith in China before and after 1949, including the lost temples of Beijing, Mao's cult of personality, and the violence that stemmed from it, I relied on Geremie Barmé, *Shades of Mao: The Posthumous Cult of the Great Leader* (Armonk, NY, and London: M.E. Sharpe, 1996); Jasper Becker, *City of Heavenly Tranquility: Beijing in the History of China* (New York: Oxford University Press, 2008); Vincent Goossaert and David A. Palmer, *The Religious Question in Modern China* (Chicago: University of Chicago Press, 2011); Melissa Schrift, *Biography of a Chairman Mao Badge: The Creation and Mass Consumption of a Personality Cult* (New Brunswick NJ: Rutgers University Press, 2001); Daniel Leese, *The Mao Cult: Rhetoric and Ritual in China's Cultural Revolution* (Cambridge, UK: Cambridge University Press, 2013); and Alfreda Murck, *Mao's Golden Mangoes and the Cultural Revolution* (Zurich: Verlag Scheidegger and Spiess, 2013).

The translation of Confucius—"when the prince is prince"—is from James Legge. For discussion of "National Studies" and the debates around the Confucian revival, I benefited from several essays in "The National Learning Revival," *China Perspectives* 2011/1, published by the French Center for Research on Contemporary China.

I owe a debt to Lao She's son, Shu Yi, who invited me to his home and discussed his father's death, and to the scholar Fu Guangming, whose oral history of the death of Lao She was invaluable.

## 20. PASSING BY

The story of Little Yueyue was reconstructed through interviews, security camera footage, and accounts in the Chinese press. I am especially grateful to Li Wangdong, the attorney for driver Hu Jun, who shared with me his investigative notes and photographs. The anthropologist Zhou Runan provided his detailed report on the social dynamics and history of Hardware City, and his reflections on the case.

For analysis of Good Samaritanism in China, see Yunxiang Yan, "The Good Samaritan's New Trouble: A Study of the Changing Moral Landscape in Contemporary China," *Social Anthropology/Anthropologie Sociale* 17, no. 1 (February 2009): 19–24.

In revisiting the Kitty Genovese case, I received help from Kevin Cook, the author of *Kitty Genovese: The Murder, the Bystanders, the Crime that Changed America* (New York: W.W. Norton, 2014). I also relied upon Rachel Manning, Mark Levine, and Alan Collins, "The Kitty Genovese Murder and the Social Psychology of Helping: The Parable of the 38 Witnesses," *American Psychologist*, September 2007: 555–62.

## 21. SOULCRAFT

In China, allowing a reporter into communities of faith is not without risk. I was fortunate to have those opportunities during my work for the *Chicago Tribune* and for *The New Yorker*. For background, in addition to Goossaert and Palmer's *The Religious Question in Modern China*, I also relied upon Fenggang Yang, *Religion in China: Survival and Revival Under Communist Rule* (New York: Oxford University Press, 2011).

## 22. CULTURE WARS

Murong Xuecun's "Open Letter to a Nameless Censor" was first posted to the Chinese edition of *The New York Times*; the English version is by an anonymous translator. The conflict between Han Han and Fang Zhouzi was widely covered by Chinese journalists and bloggers. Fang's comments that were not from my interview are mostly available on his site: http://fangzhouzi.blog.hexun.com/. A valuable analysis by Joel Martinsen was published at www.danwei.com/blog-fight-of-the-month-han-han-the-novelist-versus-fang-zhouzi-the-fraud-buster/.

## 23. TRUE BELIEVERS

Tang Jie's site, Dujiawang, hosted most of his commentary and videos. I interviewed several World Bank employees familiar with Lin's tenure at the bank. Yao Yang's article on China's economic future was published in *Foreign Affairs* in February 2010 and was titled "The End of the Beijing Consensus: Can China's Model of Authoritarian Growth

Survive?" Chen Yunying described her hope that her husband could return to Taiwan in answer to questions from the Taiwan press in March 2012.

## 24. BREAKING OUT
I am indebted to He Peirong and several U.S. officials involved in the events who shared their perspectives on Chen's escape from Dongshigu Village. Other details in this account draw on Chen's interviews with Spiegel Online and iSUN AFFAIRS, and reports by Human Rights in China, Global Voices, and China Digital Times.

For background on the secrecy surrounding coal mine deaths, see Tu Jianjun, "Coal Mining Safety: China's Achilles' Heel," *China Security* 3, no. 2 (2007): 36–53.

## EPILOGUE
The detention of Zhai Xiaobing was reported by the Congressional-Executive Commission on China. A copy of the prohibition against Ping-Pong balls and balloons was first posted on Weibo by the user Luhuahua. Liu Zhijun's defense attorney Qian Lieyang agreed to an interview that clarified some of the charges in the case. Many of Qi Xiangfu's poems and his memoir are available at several sites, including http://hi.baidu.com/abc87614332.

For background on poll results and satisfaction levels, see Richard A. Easterlin, Robson Morgan, Malgorzata Switek, and Fei Wang, "China's Life Satisfaction, 1990–2010," *PNAS Early Edition*, April 6, 2012.

# ACKNOWLEDGMENTS

None of my grandparents lived to see this book, but they are responsible for its inception. My father's parents, Joseph and Marta Osnos, fled Warsaw when Hitler invaded in 1939. They traveled through Romania, Turkey, Iraq, and India before landing in New York and starting over. (My father, Peter, was born on the way, in Mumbai.) Joseph Osnos went into the air-conditioning business; Marta was a biochemist. I was given a middle name, Richard, from a cousin I never knew—Jan Ryszard—who died as a navigator in the Polish squadron of Britain's Royal Air Force. On my mother's side, my grandfather, Albert Sherer, was an American diplomat, posted with his wife, Carroll, to the Eastern bloc. In Budapest in 1951, the Soviet-backed government accused Albert of spying and gave the family twenty-four hours to leave the country. *The Chicago Daily News* ran the story under the headline REDS BOOT YANKS. Those experiences lingered in our household memory, and I grew up wondering about the unrecorded experiences of life under authoritarianism.

In China, I am indebted, above all, to the people whose lives I have followed in these pages. Revealing too much of oneself—the vulnerabilities, the passions, the private choices—can be perilous in China. But these men and women welcomed me back, year after year, even when it was difficult for them to imagine that there was more to ask. There were, of course, many others in China, some in government, others in remote villages, who need to remain anonymous, and I thank them for the courage to speak to me.

One of the great pleasures of these years has been the companionship of talented friends who work on China: Andrew Andreasen, Stephen

Angle, Michael Anti, Angie Baecker, Bill Bishop, Tania Branigan, Chris Buckley, Laurie Burkitt, Cao Haili, Leslie Chang, Clifford Coonan, Edith Coron, Max Duncan, Simon Elegant, Leta Hong Fincher, Jaime Florcruz, Peter Ford, Michael Forsythe, Paul French, Alison Friedman, John Garnaut, John Giszczak, Tom Gold, Jeremy Goldkorn, Jonah Greenberg, Elizabeth Haenle, Paul Haenle, Peter Hessler, Isabelle Holden, John Holden, Lucy Hornby, Andrew Jacobs, Ian Johnson, Joseph Kahn, Tom Kellogg, Alison Klayman, Elizabeth Knup, Arthur Kroeber, Kaiser Kuo, Christina Larson, Tom Lasseter, Dan Levin, Louisa Lim, Phil Lisio, Julia Lovell, H.S. Liu, Jo Lusby.

Mary Kay Magistad, Mark MacKinnon, Simon Montlake, Richard McGregor, Andrew Meyer, Paul Mooney, Allison Moore, David Murphy, Jeremy Page, Jane Perlez, Nick Platt, Sheila Platt, John Pomfret, Qin Liwen, Simon Rabinovitch, April Rabkin, Austin Ramzy, Chris Reynolds, Tiff Roberts, Andy Rothman, Gilles Sabrie, Michael Schuman, Clarissa Sebag-Montefiore, Susan Shirk, Karen Smith, Kumi Smith, Megan Stack, Anne Stevenson-Yang, Anya Stiglitz, Joseph Stiglitz, Didi Kirsten Tatlow, Philip Tinari, Wang Wei, Joerg Wuttke, Lambert Yam, Eunice Yoon, Kunkun Yu, Jianying Zha, Zhang Lijia, Mei Zhang, and Yuan Li. The late Richard Baum, of UCLA, founded ChinaPol as a resource for the China community, and made us all smarter.

For counsel and expertise, I am especially grateful to Geremie Barmé, Nicholas Bequelin, Ira Belkin, Annping Chin, Don Clarke, Jerome Cohen, Paul Gewirtz, Huang Yasheng, Bill Kirby, Roderick MacFarquhar, Victor Mair, David Moser, Barry Naughton, Minxin Pei, Victor Shih, Xiaofei Tian, Sophie Volpp, and Jeffrey Wasserstrom.

It is hard to imagine life in Beijing without our dearest: Amy Ansfield, Jonathan Ansfield, Hannah Beech, Fannie Chen, Eleanor Connolly, John Delury, Barbara Demick, Michael Donohue, Gady Epstein, Ed Gargan, Deb Fallows, James Fallows, Michelle Garnaut, Jorge Guajardo, Susan Jakes, Jonathan Landreth, Brook Larmer, Dune Lawrence, Woo Lee, Leo Lewis, Jen Lin-Liu, Melinda Liu, Jane Macartney, James McGregor, Alexa Olesen, Philip Pan, Hervé Pauze, Hyeon-Ju Rho, Lisa Robins, Jeff Prescott, Paola Sada, Sarah Schafer, Baifang Schell, Orville Schell, Carla Snyder, Nick Snyder, Craig Simons, Comino Tamura, Tang Di, Alistair Thornton, Tini Tran, Alex Travelli, Alex Wang, Alan Wheatley, Edward Wong, Zhang Xiaoguang.

I extend thanks to the Overseas Press Club and the Asia Society for their support of the work of foreign correspondents, including mine. I owe a special thanks to Herbert Allen III for his support and curiosity; in the years since he first invited me to discuss China, I have learned more from his community than I have provided.

In the course of this book, I received invaluable help at various times from terrific young journalists and researchers, including Gareth Collins, Devin Corrigan, Jacob Fromer, Gu Yongqiang, Houming Jiang, Jordan Lee, Faye Li, Max Klein, Wendy Qian, Amy Qin, Gary Wang, Debby Wu, Xu Wan, and Yang Xiao. They did research, transcriptions, and translations. But nobody spent more time with these subjects, and with me, than Lu Han, and I am indebted to her for her expertise and cool, fair-minded judgment.

Portions of this book draw on reporting I did at the *Chicago Tribune*, where I arrived as a summer intern and stayed for nine extraordinary years, mostly overseas. For sending me abroad, and for friendship, I am grateful to Lisa Anderson, George de Lama, Ann Marie Lipinski, Kerry Luft, Tim McNulty, Paul Salopek, Jim O'Shea, and Howard Tyner.

At *The New Yorker*, my professional home for the last six years, David Remnick, Dorothy Wickenden, and John Bennet made me a writer; their own extraordinary skills and judgment set the standard. Peter Canby's fact-checkers, especially Jiangyan Fan, improve and protect us. Nick Thompson and Amy Davidson provided a place to write and think even when I was immersed in the book. John is an editor with perfect pitch. David and Dorothy, assisted by Anna Altman, read the manuscript when I most needed their eyes. Other friends who read along the way, including Barbara Demick, Gady Epstein, Ian Johnson, and Jeffrey Wasserstrom will see their smart observations reflected throughout.

Before I went to China, I visited Jonathan Galassi at Farrar, Straus and Giroux, and he offered a piece of advice: to find the right book, be patient. When I found the book, he replied with a gift: the chance to work with the brilliant Eric Chinski, who is everything an author could want: meticulous, analytical, tireless, and funny. At FSG, I am grateful as well for the creativity and care of Nayon Cho, Gabriella Doob, Debra Helfand, Chris Peterson, Jeff Seroy, and Sarita Varma.

When we were barely out of our teens, I met Jennifer Joel; when she became a literary agent, I became her client and, thus, the beneficiary of her immense gifts as a reader and an advocate. At ICM, she has been aided by Clay Ezell and Madeleine Osborn, and I thank them all for their expertise and care.

My family, which is vast and devoted, put up with a decade's worth of missed holidays and birthdays, interspersed with visits fogged by jet lag. My extraordinary mother, Susan, raised us to be at home in the world and to stand up for the values that matter; Peter, a newsman and publisher, is, forever, my mentor, inspiration, and coconspirator. My wise sister, Katherine Sanford, and her husband, Colin, fed me and revived me; their children—Ben, Pete, and Mae—showed us what a family can be.

Sarabeth Berman came to Beijing to stay for a year. Then she met me. Seven years later, we returned to America, married. China gave me Sarabeth, and for that alone I am grateful to it. She has given me a second family: Ruth Nemzoff and Harris Berman, Kim Berman and Farzad Mostashari, Mandy Lee Berman and Seth Berman, Rebecca Berman and Franklin Huang. Sarabeth's love, her wisdom to prefer every word be read aloud, and, most of all, her laughter, sustain me. Her innate good judgment makes every sentence better. Nothing that I write, except for this paragraph, is done until she hears it.

# INDEX

abortion, 47
Accor, 105
Acheson, Dean, 118
Adams, Charles Francis, Jr., 6
Adamson, Bob, 69
Adelson, Sheldon, 86, 90–91
Adolph, Christopher, 273
Ai Dan, 182, 186
Ai Qing, 185–86
airline passengers, 4
airports, 151, 360
air quality, 260–61
Ai Weiwei, 97, 136, 175, 181–89, 190–93,
    197, 198, 199, 211–12, 219, 319, 323–28,
    329, 347, 355; arrest and imprisonment
    of, 223–30, 273; release of, 230–31,
    325; tax liability of, 323–25
Alley of National Studies, 279–80, 282,
    287, 368
Amtrak, 234
Analects (Confucius), 45
Ancien Régime and the Revolution, The,
    (Tocqueville), 362
Anti, Michael, 322
Anti-CNN.com, 220
Anti-Rightist Campaign, 185
Ao Man Long, 251
Apple Daily, 84
April Media, 220
Arab Spring, 5, 218–20, 273, 331
Arendt, Hannah, 304
arranged marriages, 45, 46

art, 186–91, 319–32; avant-garde, 95–96;
    commercial market in, 96–97; fake,
    248–49; revolutionary realism, 95
Article 35, 195
ArtReview, 319
Asher, David, 80
Asian Development Bank, 261
aspiration, 4, 56–58, 64–65, 76, 175,
    359–61; authoritarianism vs., 7
Auden, W. H., 77
Au Kam San, 82
Aung San Suu Kyi, 195
authoritarianism, aspiration vs., 7
Azevedo, Paulo, 82

baby formula, 175, 250
Baidu, 143, 200, 333
Banco Delta Asia, 80
banks, 120
Barbie, 55
Bare-Handed Fortunes, 269, 322
Barmé, Geremie, 38
Basic English, 265
Beautiful Destiny (Jiayuan), 51–54, 57
Becquelin, Nicholas, 345
Beijing: Ai's protest in, 192–93; foreign
    invasion of, 33; house prices in, 56;
    labor migration to, 43; as poor city,
    21–22; sandstorms in, 218; subway
    in, 4
Beijing Daily, 219

Beijing International Executive MBA program, 155
Beijing Normal University, 23
Beijing Public Security Bureau, 194
Beijing South Railway Station, 232
Belgrade, 137–38
Bell Tower, 33
Ben Ali, Zine El Abidine, 218
Bennett, James Gordon, 6
Berlusconi, Silvio, 111
Berman, Sarabeth, 218, 259, 331, 368
Beuys, Joseph, 97
black-collar class, 269
Blackstone Group, 143
Blair, Tony, 119, 242
bloggers, 30, 47, 165, 168, 188–89, 204, 205, 207, 215, 256–57, 272, 322, 327
blood contractors, 40, 305
Bloomberg News, 258–60
Bobos, 63, 170, 269
*Bobos in Paradise: The New Upper Class and How They Got There* (Brooks), 62
Boehner, John, 346
Bokhary, Verina, 88
*Book from the Sky*, A (Xu), 189
Bouazizi, Mohammed, 218
Bo Xilai, 253–55, 262, 329, 334
Brady, Anne-Marie, 118
brainwashing, 38
bribes, 90, 125, 184, 250–52, 255–57, 362; as hidden, 251–52; of judges, 249, 251, 261
bride wealth, 56
bridge collapses, 246
Broad Union, 242
Brooks, David, 63
Buddhism, 104, 107, 280, 281, 283, 284, 307, 314
Bureau of Letters and Visits, 208–209
Bureau of Public Opinion, 119
Bush, George W., 119, 196

Cafferty, Jack, 139
*Caijing*, 120, 121–22, 125–30, 330, 331, 332; government approval required for, 202; growth of, 201–202; investors in,

202, 203; management buyout plan of, 203–204, 231
Cao, Henry, 234, 236, 245
Cao, Leo, 245
Caochangdi, 188
Cao family, 232–33, 235–36
Cao Haili, 126, 204
Cao Qifeng, 122–23
Carrefour, 133, 147
Carter, Jimmy, 17
Catholicism, 314
Célestin Monga, 154
cell phones, 4
censorship, 6, 7, 8, 30, 58, 109, 118, 122, 126, 129, 137, 138, 147, 160, 165–68, 176–77, 199–201, 207, 211–13, 214–15, 228, 254, 257, 260, 273, 274, 323, 360–61
Central Intelligence Agency (CIA), 38
Central Japan Railway, 240
Central Publicity (Propaganda) Department, 117–19, 121, 126, 127, 130, 166, 176, 194, 199, 211, 219, 272–73, 288, 293, 329, 345, 357, 360, 364; *Caijing* and, 203; on train crash, 236
century of national humiliation, 140, 197
Charter 08, 162, 194–95, 196–97, 200
Charter 77, 161–62, 273
Chen, 299, 302–303
Chen Danqing, 97, 193
Chen Guangcheng, 27–30, 207, 227, 231, 343–49; escape of, 343–46, 349; house arrest of, 207–208, 215–17; in prison, 210, 211; release of, 215
Chen Guangfu, 346
Chen Guojun, 271
Cheng Yizhong, 128
Chen Jieren, 243
Chen Kegui, 346
Chen Xianmei, 296, 303–304
Chen Yun, 13, 14
Chen Yunying, 16, 34, 35, 149
Cheung Chi-tai, 88, 89
Cheung Yan, 66–67, 269–71
*Chicago Tribune*, 24, 32
Chim Pui-chung, 84–85

China: alleged currency manipulation of, 153; anti-Japanese protests in, 147; average income in, 4; billionaires in, 4; bloggers in, 30, 47, 165, 168, 188–89, 204, 205, 207, 215, 256–57, 272, 322, 327; capitalist reforms in, 13–14, 35, 38–40, 60–61, 84, 150, 151, 241, 271, 278–79, 312, 360; censorship in, 6, 7, 8, 30, 58, 109, 118, 122, 126, 129, 137, 138, 147, 160, 165–68, 176–77, 199–201, 207, 211–13, 214–15, 228, 254, 257, 260, 273, 274, 323, 360–61; central bank of, 125; civil war in, 14, 21; constitution of, 122; creative class in, 189; economic growth in, 12–13, 39, 44, 112, 155–56, 204, 248, 366–67; food in, 4; happiness in, 272; history studies in, 140; housing prices in, 56, 267; inequality in, 5–6, 44, 60, 222, 268; intergenerational mobility in, 269; Internet use in, 22, 29, 30–31, 134, 137, 138, 159–60, 166–68, 169, 195, 199, 200, 209, 213, 214–15, 273, 340, 347; investment in, 39; Japanese occupation of, 140, 264; Japan's Diaoyu Islands dispute with, 335–36; Jasmine protests in, 220–23, 225; labor migration in, 43; land reform in, 12; life expectancy in, 151; literacy rates in, 151, 363; luxury goods in, 5–6; popular approval of, 136; press in, 63, 90, 119–20, 121, 122, 124, 125, 126, 128, 174, 195, 197, 205, 233, 242, 244, 245, 264, 281, 299, 331, 358, 365; real estate boom in, 163; revolution in, 21; special economic zones in, 39–40; spiritual awakening in, 308; stereotypes of, 5; stimulus plan in, 151; stock markets in, 124, 250; tax system in, 268; Tibet protests in, 132–34, 138; travel from, 100–113; Uighur-Han riot in, 201; urban growth in, 25, 299–300; Western culture as perceived by, 98–113
China, U.S. relationship with, 5; Belgrade embassy bombing and, 137–38; and Chinese crackdown on Internet, 31; Mao's establishment of, 98; U.S. recognition of, 17
ChinaAid, 345, 348
*China Business Times*, 124
*China Can Say No*, 23, 98
China Center for Economic Research, 150–51
China Central Television, 166, 168
*China Daily*, 70, 125, 206, 219, 309
China eCapital, 322
*China Entrepeneur*, 270
ChinaGeeks, 170
*China Miracle, The* (Lin, Cai and Li), 151–52
China Mobile, 41
*China Newsweek*, 309
China Railway Signal and Communication Corporation, 240
*China Stand Up!*, 133
Chinese Academy of Social Sciences, 252
Chinese Association for the Study of Confucius, 286
Chinese Catholic Patriotic Association, 315
*Chinese Citizens' Guide to Civilized Behavior Abroad, The*, 105
Chinese classics, 142
Chinese Dream, 359–61
Chinese People's Political Consultative Conference, 270
Chongqing, China, murder in, 253–55
Chow Yun-fat, 85
Christianity, 281, 314–18; Evangelical, 327
*Cities of Sin* (de Leeuw), 81
Civil Affairs Ministry, Chinese, 184
civil war, Chinese, 14, 21
Civil War, U.S., 6
Cixi, Empress Dowager, 155, 233
class, 60–61, 63–64
*Class: A Guide Through the American Status System* (Fussell), 63
Clinton, Hillary, 224, 344
CNN, 134, 136, 138–39
Coca-Cola, 119
Cohen, Jerome, 210–11, 348
Cohen, Joan Lebold, 187, 188, 211
Cold War, 5, 16, 150
college admissions, 66
Colombia, 234
color revolution, 195

COMDEX, 86

Communist Party, Chinese, 5, 6, 7, 22, 34, 52, 67, 135, 145, 150, 185, 186, 241, 289, 317, 365–66; alleged virtue of, 258; censorship by, 199, 200–201, 211–13, 254, 273, 274; Central Committee of, 243; Charter 08 denounced by, 197; class opposed by, 60–61; corruption in, 252–60; culture planned by, 319–20; dissidents contained by, 199; Eighteenth Party Congress of, 357–59; free market fundamentalism disdained by, 39; land reform of, 12; membership of, 26; as "Party in Power," 61–62; propaganda studied by, 119; Seventeenth National Congress of, 62; on values, 95; and Wenzhou train crash, 246

Communist Youth League, 140–41

concubines, 45

Confucianism, 107, 293

Confucius, vii, 45, 109, 258, 285, 286–89, 292–93

Confucius Institute, 286

Confucius Temple, 279, 281, 285, 287, 288, 289–90, 292

Congress, U.S., 31

Congressional-Executive Commission on China, U.S., 80

Conrad, Joseph, 290

Corak, Miles, 272

Corallo, Mark, 348

corruption, 157, 222, 237, 239, 242–47, 248–63, 269–71, 362–64; as anarchic, 262; in art, 248–49; growth and, 249–50; plans for rooting out, 249; punishment of, 262; *see also* bribes

*Cosmopolitan*, 55

Cotter, Holland, 97

Cotton Flower Alley, 163–64

Crazy English, 68–74, 84, 135, 177, 178–80, 264, 265, 351

Crédit Mobilier, 261–62

CTGZ, 134

Cui Tiankai, 205–206

cults, 280–81

Cultural Revolution, 34, 38, 39, 60, 62, 64, 123, 131, 149, 158, 186, 189, 277, 278, 281, 284–85, 289–90, 291, 307, 328

currency, China's alleged manipulation of, 153

cushion hypothesis, 84


Dalai Lama, 132, 133, 204, 282, 283

Daley, Richard M., 254

Danni, 182

Danwei, 170

Daoism, 107, 280, 281, 283, 284, 314

Darwin, Charles, 98

das Neves, Manuel Joaquim, 92

Defense Ministry, Taiwan, 156

Delacroix, Eugène, 13

de Leeuw, Hendrik, 81

De Meuron, 182

democracy, 195, 219

Democracy Forum, 31

Democracy Wall, 187

democratic centralism, 195

Deng Lijun, 40

Deng Qian, 245

Deng Xiaoping, 21, 92, 187; capitalist reforms of, 13–14, 35, 40, 60–61, 84, 150, 241, 271, 278–79, 312; China opened by, 66; Mao's purging of, 13; public relations of, 118; U.S. political system disdained by, 155

Depardieu, Gerard, 143

Dewey, John, 311

Diamond Bachelors, 214

Dianping, 110

Diaoyu Islands, 335

Di Bona, Richard, 233

DiCaprio, Leonardo, 46

Dignity Revolution, 219

Ding Shumiao, 241–42, 244, 245

Ding Yun, 141–42, 144

DINKs (double income, no kids), 63, 269

"Directives from the Ministry of Truth," 166–67

*Discourse on Metaphysics* (Leibniz), 139

divorce, 45, 46

domestic violence, 264

Dong Wenjun, 36

Douban, 166
DreamWorks, 320
Drum Tower, 33, 64, 163
*Duchangtuan*, 176
Dujiawang, 333–34

Easterlin, Richard, 363
*Economic Daily*, 121
*Economist*, 137
economy, Chinese: capitalist reforms in, 13–14, 35, 40, 60–61, 84, 150, 241, 271, 278–79, 312; growth in, 12–13, 39, 44, 112, 155–56, 204, 248, 366–67; investment in, 39; special zones in, 39–40; stimulus plan in, 151; stock markets in, 124, 250; tax system in, 268
education, 174, 266, 267; bribes needed for, 252
Educational Campaign to Maintain the Advanced Nature of the Chinese Communist Party, 26
Egypt, 219
Eisenhower, Dwight D., 233
Engle, Stephen, 222
English, 67–75, 264–69
*English* (Wang), 67
Enron, 340
environment, 151
Environmental Protection Bureau, 171
Equitable Life Building, 368
Eriksen, Edvard, 198
Eriksson, Tor, 269
"Everyone Asks Everyone," 176
*Expert Detective Heng Te*, 3

Facebook, 109, 260, 322
factories, 39, 43, 44, 123, 355
Factory 798, 96
*Fairytale*, 97, 136
Fake Cultural Development Ltd., 325–26
FAKE Design, 188
Falun Gong, 70, 121, 198, 280, 315, 322, 327
Fang Binxing, 214–15
Fang Cai, 151

Fang Kecheng, 141
Fang Lizhi, 344
Fang Qingyuan, 51
Fang Zhouzi, 327–28
Fan Kuan, 37
Faye Li, 298
Federal Bureau of Investigation (FBI), 80, 85
Feng Boyi, 190
Feng Guifen, 67–68
Feng Xiaogang, 320–21
Feng Zhi, 186
financial crisis, 151, 153–54, 196, 334
financial risk, 83–85
*Financial Times*, 144, 240
First Opium War, 23
Fitzgerald, F. Scott, 6, 367
Five Nos, 220
floods, 15
*Forbes*, 61, 86, 242, 260
Forbidden City, 70
Foreign Affairs Ministry, Chinese, 197, 221, 222, 225, 344
Foreign Corrupt Practices Act, 90
Foreign IPO Fever, 64
Forsythe, Michael, 259–60
Foshan, China, 294
*Founding of a Party, The*, 166
*1492: Conquest of Paradise*, 143
Foxconn Technology, 271–72
Fox News, 139
France, 6
Freedom of Government Information Law, 184
free market, 8, 39, 149, 151
friend-making clubs, 46
*Friends*, 166
Front Page, 48
Fu, Bob, 345, 348
Fudan University, 135, 138, 141, 144
Fuerzas Armadas Revolucionarias de Colombia (FARC), 80
Fussell, Paul, 63

Gaarder, Jostein, 140
gambling, 77–87

"Gangnam Style," 320
Gao Xiqing, 124, 125
Gao Ying, 185
Gao Zhisheng, 198–99, 224, 228
Garcia, Jack, 80
"Gardener's Dream, The," 185–86
Gate of Heavenly Peace, 5, 22
General Affairs Office, 194
Genovese, Kitty, 299–300, 305
Germany, 6, 102–104, 105
Germany, Nazi, 6, 206
Gerui-te, 103
Gilded Age, 6, 82–83, 84, 270
Ginsberg, Allen, 188
*Global Times*, 228, 299, 306, 324
Global Trade Mansion, 26, 32, 163
Goebbels, Joseph, 134
Goldman Sachs, 332
Gong Haibin, 42, 48
Gong Hainan, 41–45, 58, 64–65; dating
    website of, 47–49, 50, 51–54, 57, 84,
    213–14; marriage of, 50–51
Gong Haiyan, 84, 174
Goossaert, Vincent, 278
Gorky, Maxim, 45
Got Rich First Crowd, 61, 66, 76, 95
Grass Mud Horse, 181
Great Britain, 6
Great Firewall, 30, 109–10, 214, 215, 322
*Great Gatsby, The* (Fitzgerald), 6, 272
Great Hall of the People, 22, 62–63, 253,
    357–59
Great Leap Forward, 12–13, 64, 277, 289
Great Wall of China, 70, 97
Greece, 334
Greece, ancient, 36–37
Grove, Dan, 85
Guanghong, Jin, 224
Guggenheim Museum, 188
*Guidebook for the Soul*, A, 282
*Guide to Entering Shanghai: For Brothers
    and Sisters Who Come to Shanghai to
    Work*, 43
*Guide to Purchasing Upscale Goods*,
    23–24
Gu Kailai, 253, 254–55
gun control, 334

Guo, Mrs., 164
Guo Jianzeng, 50
Guomai Culture and Media, 170
Guo Yanjin (Karen), 106, 108, 111
Guo Yuhua, 272
Gu Xiaojie (Handy), 106, 108, 111


Häagen-Dazs, 55
Han Changdong, 284–85
Han Chinese, 201, 283
Han Feng, 255–56
Han Han, 167–77, 205, 221, 229–30,
    327–30; censorship of, 176–77, 200, 273
Han Han Digest, 170
Hansen, Mette Halskov, 41
Hardware City, 294–98, 302, 303, 305
Harmony Express, 232–33
*Harvard Girl*, 65
Havel, Václav, 161, 273
Haynes, John, 89
health insurance, 151, 213
Health Ministry, Chinese, 174
*Hebei Economic Daily*, 40
Hecaitou, 204
Helen Keller glasses, 56
He Peirong, 216
Hersey, John, 21
Herzog, 182
Heshen, 249
Heywood, Neil, 253–55
He Zhaofa, 64
highways, 151, 262, 360
history studies, 140
Hitler, Adolf, 205, 206
HIV, 40
Ho, Stanley, 85–86
Holy Land of National Studies, 293
Home Depot, 55
homosexuality, 46
Hong Kong, 23, 81, 104, 153; SARS in,
    126
Horng, Jyimin, 80
House Foreign Relations Committee, 31
housing prices, 56, 267
Hsee, Christopher, 84
*Huainanzi*, 27

Huang Guangyu, 269
Huang Wenyi, 284, 292, 369–70
Huang Xueqing, 100, 109
Huang Yubiao, 213
Huawei, 142
Hublot, 170
Hu Dehua, 366
Hu Gang, 248–49, 251, 263
Hu Jintao, 62–63, 156, 165, 195, 238, 258,
    358; cultural security protected by, 319
Hu Jun, 295, 301–302, 304–305
Hu Lingsheng, 122
Human Rights Watch, 345
hunger, 363
*Hunter*, 3
Huntsman, Jon, Jr., 220–21
Huo Deming, 342
*Hurun Report*, 66
Hu Shuli, 120–30, 193, 248, 273, 332,
    335; government approval required for,
    202–203; and growth of *Caijing*,
    201–202; management buyout plan of,
    203–204, 231; media group launched
    by, 330–31
Husserl, Edmund, 135
*hutongs*, 32
Hu Zhongchi, 122


IBM, 142
*If You Are the One*, 57–58
illnesses, food-borne, 261
IMF, 152, 153
*Imperialism* (Lenin), 13
India, 104, 156
individualism, 36–41
individuality, 54
Industrial Revolution, 4, 30, 95
inequality, 5–6, 44, 60, 222, 268
infant mortality, 268
infrastructure, 39
innovation, 322
International Confucius Festival, 287
*International Herald Tribune*, 243
Internet, 22, 29, 30–31, 134, 137, 138,
    159–60, 166–68, 169, 195, 199, 200,
    209, 213, 214–15, 273, 340, 347

Internet Affairs Bureau, 199, 200, 334
Interstate Highway System, 233
*Into Europe*, 98
investment, 368
Iran, 122, 234, 322
Iran-Contra hearings, 187
Iraq War, 141–42
irrigation system, 15, 36
Islam, 314
Italy, 110–11


Jacobs, Steve, 90
Jaivin, Linda, 38
Japan, 6, 39, 137, 141, 147, 368; China
    occupied by, 140, 264; China's Diaoyu
    Islands dispute with, 335–36;
    corruption in, 261, 262; trains in, 233;
    tsunami in, 264
Jasmine Movement, 220–23, 225
Jasmine Revolution, Tunisia, 218–19, 221
Jianguo Hotel, 22
Jiang Xiaoyuan, 42
Jiang Zemin, 30, 61; history studies
    changed by, 140; propaganda praised
    by, 119
Jiao Guobiao, 126
Jiayuan (Love21.cn), 48–49, 50, 51–54,
    57, 84, 213–14
Jia Zhangke, 40, 320
Jieyigongjiang, 255
Jin, Lily, 172–73
Jin Baozhu, 280, 360, 368–69
*Jinghua Weekly*, 214
Jing Jun, 40
Jin Guanghong, 224
Jinmen (Quemoy), 11, 16, 17, 36, 40, 149
Jin Mingri, 315
Jobs, Steve, 350, 351
Johnnie Walker, 170
John Paul II, Pope, 282
Johns, Jasper, 187
Jordan, 219
Josephson, Matthew, 82
Journey of Harmony, 132–33
*Journey to the West*, 16
Joyce, James, 290

judges, bribing of, 249, 251, 261
junket industry, 78, 86–87, 89–90
Junren Wan, 311
Justice Department, U.S., 90
Justice Ministry, Chinese, 198

Kapoor, Anish, 227
Kawasaki Heavy Industries, 240
Keller, Helen, 56
Kennedy, Robert, 311
Kent State, 145
Khrushchev, Nikita, 6
kidney sales, 310
Kim Jong-il, 85
King, Martin Luther, Jr., 311
Kraft, 55
Krugman, Paul, 367
Kundera, Milan, 349
*Kung Fu Panda* problem, 320
Kweichow Moutai, 250

labor unions, 340
LaHood, Ray, 262
Lake of Great Peace, 290, 292
Lam, Desmond, 81
Lama Temple, 279, 281, 282, 283, 350
Lantos, Tom, 31
Lantos Foundation for Human Rights & Justice, 348
Lao She, 290–92
Lao-tzu, 109
Lasswell, Harold, 118–19
*Latest Must-Read for Personnel Going Abroad, The*, 104
Lau Ming-yee, 88–89
*Law Protecting the Disabled, The*, 27
Lee, Kim, 71, 264
Lee Kuan Yew, 366
Leibniz, Gottfried, 139
Lei Feng, 38, 306, 351
Lei Zhengfu, 257
Lenin, Vladimir, 13, 61
Leung Man-tou, 175
*Leviathan*, 227
Lewis, Arthur, 342

Lhasa, 132, 134, 138
Li, Mr., 225
Liang Qichao, 37, 98, 279
Liao Ran, 243
Liao Zhenzhu, 18
liberalism, 142
*Liberty Leading the People*, 143
Li Bing, 15, 34
Libya, 219
Li Cheng, 110
Li Chengpeng, 339
Li Datong, 144, 336
Li Dehui, 256
Li Fan, 315
Li Jianli, 335
Li Ling, 292–93
Lin, 283
Lin, Wang-sung, 156
Lin Gu, 307–308
Linguang Wu, 214
Lin Huoshu, 15
Link, Perry, 127
Lin Qingfei, 300–301
Lin Yifu (Lin Zhengyi), 11–20, 40, 44, 84, 149–58, 339–41, 348; China Center for Economic Research founded by, 150–51; defection of, 11–12, 14, 18–19, 24–25, 34–36, 149, 340; made chief economist at World Bank, 152; MBA program cofounded by, 155; official file on, 36; Washington Consensus disdained by, 151–52
Lin Yutang, 249
Lin Zhijun, 362
Lippmann, Walter, 118
Li Suqiao, 96
literacy rates, 151, 363
Li Tiantian, 224
*Little Red Book*, 277, 278
Liu, Lydia H., 175
Liu, Mingxing, 273
Liu Binjie, 273
Liu Chengguang, 136
Liu Gongsheng, 100
Liu Jie, 207
Liu Ming Chung, 66
Liu Xia, 159, 205, 206

Liu Xiaobo, 158, 159–61, 165, 169, 193, 200, 227, 229, 241, 248, 273, 293, 335, 360; arrest and indictment of, 194–95, 226; Charter 08 of, 162, 194–95, 196–97; Nobel Peace Prize awarded to, 204–206, 292; in prison, 196–97, 205, 228, 273; trial of, 195–96
Liu Yang, 145–46
Liu Yanping, 184
Liu Yuancheng, 343
Liu Yunshan, 359
Liu Zhengrong, 199
Liu Zhijun, 233–34, 237, 238–40, 243; arrest and trial of, 243–47
Liu Zhixiang, 239
Li Wangdong, 301
Li Xingshun, 100–13
Li Yang, 68–74, 178, 266, 351; abuse scandal of, 264
Li Yuqiang, 337–38
"Long March, The" (Mao), 370
lotteries, 61
Love21.cn (Jiayuan), 48–49, 50, 51–54, 57, 84, 213–14
Lucky Holiday Hotel, 253
Lu Han, 336
Lu Jinbo, 170, 174
Lu Keyi, 100
Lu Qing, 182, 223, 324
Lu Tao, 52
Lu Wei, 364
Luxembourg, 99, 102, 105
Lu Xun, 4, 98, 363, 369

Macau, 77–94, 105, 248, 251; dilemma of success of, 91–92
*Macau Business*, 82
mad cow disease, 119
Ma Desheng, 95
Mai Tian, 327
Ma Jian, 229
Ma Junyan, 317
Malaysia, 104, 105
mangoes, 277–78
Mansfield, Harvey, 136, 141, 142
Mao Badge Fever, 277, 278

Mao Yushi, 250
Mao Zedong, 4–5, 21, 123, 173, 185, 219, 306, 351, 370; on art, 95; bourgeois indulgences disdained by, 24; Deng purged by, 13; Great Leap Forward of, 12–13, 64; imperialism denounced by, 133; individualism disdained by, 38; legends of powers of, 277–78; mausoleum of, 22; permanent revolution beliefs of, 285; private businesses dismantled by, 60; propaganda sanctified by, 118; religion forbidden by, 284; Russian favored over English by, 68; smashing of Four Olds encouraged by, 285–86, 289–90; ties with U.S. established by, 98; train tracks laid by, 233; World Bank disdained by, 152
Marcos, Ferdinand, 85
marriage, 56–57; arranged, 45, 46
Marx, Karl, 14, 61, 102–103, 278, 281
matchmakers, 214
Mattel, 55
Ma Xiangqian, 271
Ma Zhaoxu, 197
Mencius, 61, 210
Miao Di, 124
middle class, 61, 366–67
Mies van der Rohe, Ludwig, 189
migrant workers, 267
Milan, Italy, 111
military, patronage in, 252
milk, 174–75
Mill, John Stuart, 98
Mindszenty, József, 344
*Ming Pao*, 244
mining accidents, 355
Minxin Pei, 91, 262, 367
Mobutu Sese Seko, 366
*Modern Chinese Dictionary*, 252
*Mona Lisa* (Leonardo), 108
*Mongolian Cow Sour Yogurt Super Girl Contest*, 55
Mongol Steppe, 218
morality, 300, 305–306, 308–13
Morgan Stanley, 143
Mount Ma, 17–18

Mousavi, Mir-Hossein, 177
Mo Yaodai, 256
Mubarak, Hosni, 219
Murakami, Haruki, 281
Murong Xuecun, 321, 328
Museum of Revolutionary History, 62
*Must Never Forget*, 23
Mu Zi Mei, 47
Myanmar, 195

naked weddings, 57
Nanjing, China, food poisoning in, 209
National Audit Office, 241
National Development and Reform
    Commission, 250
National Humiliation Day, 140
nationalism, 137–38, 140–41, 336–38
Nationalist Party, 14–16, 35, 39
National Museum, 62, 359
National People's Congress, 140, 155,
    217, 251
National Stadium, 182
National Studies Web, 287
natural right, 142
Nazis, 189
Negroponte, Nicholas, 134
neoconservatives, 141–42
Nepal, 143
Netherlands, the, 99
New Citizens' Movement, 364
New Concept Essay Contest, 173–74
New Middle-Income Stratum, 61, 91,
    100, 210, 267, 269, 286
New Millenium gallery, 96
New Oriental, 68
*New Republic, The*, 326
*New York Times, The*, 22, 26, 97, 188, 227,
    260, 299–300, 367
*Next*, 90
Nine Dragons Paper, 66, 270–71
Ningxia Internet Patrol, 177
Nisbett, Richard, 36–37
Nixon, Richard, 16
Nobel Peace Prize, 204–206, 282, 292
Node.js, 322
North Korea, 80, 322

Obama, Barack, 234, 345
Office of Veterinary Drug Control, 352
Old Zhang, 32
Ollivier, Gerald, 246
Olympics of 2008, 32, 131–33, 139, 145,
    148, 168, 178, 182, 196, 220
One (app), 329–30
one-child policy, 28, 29, 47, 172, 257, 368
"Open Letter to a Nameless Censor," 321
Opium Wars, 140
Orwell, George, 118, 165, 166
*Outlook Weekly*, 133

Palmer, David A., 278
Panic of 1873, 262
Pan Yiheng, 235–36
Paris, 105, 107
patents, 321
patriotism, 23
Peasant da Vincis, 76, 322
Pelosi, Nancy, 133
Peng Yu, 298–99
Peng Yuan, 283–84
*People's Daily*, 23, 157, 176, 224, 257, 278,
    299, 359, 361, 365–66
People's Liberation Army, 21, 36, 120
*People's Liberation Army Daily*, 220
People's University, 123–24
"People with Grievances," 208–209
personal freedom, 36–41
Peter, 310
Philippines, 366
Pícha, Petr, 102
pilgrim express, 234
poetry, 369–71
Police Academy, 61
Politburo, 21, 195, 220, 242, 243;
    Standing Committee of, 125, 358
*Popular Films*, 46
pork, 132
Portugal, 81
*Practical Dictionary of Patriotic
    Education, The*, 140
press, 63, 90, 119–20, 121, 122, 124, 125,
    126, 128, 174, 195, 197, 205, 233, 242,
    244, 245, 264, 281, 299, 331, 358, 365

privacy, 257
Progressive Era, 262
Protestantism, 314
public relations, 118
Public Security Bureau, 39
public services, 39
Putin, Vladimir, 292
Pu Zhiqiang, 193, 324–25

Qian Gang, 120, 129
Qi Baishi, 249
*qing*, 45
Qingdao, 146–47
Qing dynasty, 97, 98
Qin Mingxin, 166
Qin Shi Huang, 118
Qiong Min Yuan, 125–26
Qiu Qiming, 237
Qi Xiangfu, 369–71
Quemoy (Jinmen), 11, 16, 17, 36, 40, 149
Qu Feifei, 294–97
Qufu, 286

railroad boom, U.S., 262
Railway Ministry, Chinese, 232, 245
Ran Yunfei, 165
Rao Jin, 220
Red Army, 141
Red Guards, 39, 146, 285–86, 290
religion, 314–18
Renren, 109
rent, 163, 164
Reporters Without Borders, 122
*Resistance War Online*, 141
retirement funds, 151
revolutionary operas, 189
revolutionary realism, 95
*Rickshaw Boy* (Lao), 290
risk-taking, 83–85
Ritz, 55
Roaring Virile Fire, 257
*Robber Barons, The* (Josephson), 82
Rodrik, Dani, 366
romance, 45–49
Rome, 105, 112–13

Romney, Mitt, 345
Rothbaum, Fred, 45
Rothman, Hal, 79
rule by virtue, 258
Rushdie, Salman, 227

Sachs, Jeffrey, 151
Sandel, Michael J., 309–12
Sands Macao, 86, 88, 90
San Francisco, Calif., 145–46
*Sanlian Shenghuo*, 270
Sanlu, 174
SARS, 126, 204
Sartre, Jean-Paul, 35
Schultz, Theodore, 149
Schumer, Charles, 153
science, 15
*Science*, 300
Scott, Rick, 234
Scott, Thomas, 83
*Sea of Words, The*, 39
Second Intermediate People's Court of
    Beijing, 184–85
Securities and Exchange Commission,
    90
SEEC Media Group, 121
See Wah-lun, 88–89
September 11, 2001, terrorist attacks of,
    119
Seventeenth National Congress, 62
sex, 45–46
Shah of Iran, 85
Shang Degang, 283–84
Shanghai, China, 277, 278; anti-Japanese
    protests in, 147; house prices in, 56
*Shanghai Style*, 320
Shanghai United Badge Factory, 277
Shang-Jin Wei, 56
Sharansky, Natan, 195
She Xianglin, 300
Shih, Victor, 273
Shi Tao, 31, 126, 166
Shi Ye, 313–14
shock therapy, 150, 151–52
shopping, 55–56
Shulsky, Abram, 142

Shu Yi, 290–91
Sichuan: dam in, 15, 34–35; earthquake in, 120, 122, 129–30, 183–84, 236, 250, 305, 339, 355
Sina, 133, 144, 188–89
Singapore, 104, 286, 366
Siu, Ricardo, 84
Siu Yun Ping, 77–79, 84–85, 88, 91, 92–94; trial testimony of, 89–90
Sky City, 368
*Skyscraper*, 368
"Smash the Black," 254
Smith, Adam, 98
Smith, Chris, 31
Sohu, 47, 133
Sola Aoi, 165
Solzhenitsyn, Aleksandr, 349
"Song of the Storm Petrel, The" (Gorky), 45
Soong, Roland, 196
*Sophie's World* (Gaarder), 140
*South China Morning Post*, 70, 341, 362
*Southern Metropolis Daily*, 128
*Southern Weekly*, 261
South Korea, 39, 132, 366; corruption in, 261, 262, 263
Soviet Union, 6, 195; collapse of, 5, 151, 219, 314, 365; propaganda in, 118
speed, 64
Spencer, Herbert, 98
Spirit Explanation Teams, 359
"spiritual void," 279, 281, 286
Sputnik, 12
Stars, 187
State Administration of Radio, Film, and Television, 320–21
state capitalism, 8
State Council, 43, 56
Statue of Liberty, 144
steelworkers' riot, 271
Stiglitz, Joseph, 152
Stock Exchange Executive Council, 124–26
stock markets, Chinese, 124, 250
Strauss, Leo, 141–42
strikes, 271
*Striving*, 213

Students and Scholars Against Corporate Misbehaviour, 269–70
Summers, Lawrence, 152
Sun Qiang, 168, 171
Sun Yat-sen, 37
Supreme People's Court, 364
"Sweatshop Paper," 270
Syria, 322

Taiwan, 15–17, 143, 156–57, 286, 366; in Chinese press, 119; defectors from, 11–12, 18, 36; Nationalist Party's flight to, 14–15
Tang dynasty, 142, 370
Tang Jie, 134–44, 146–48, 165, 168, 175, 190, 193, 196, 279, 287, 333–35; and attempted protest, 220–22; on outbreak of nationalism, 336–37
Tang Xiaoling, 140
Tan Shanfang, 256
Tan Zuoren, 191
Taoism, 107, 280, 281, 283, 284, 314
tax system, 268
telephones, 22
Temple Under a Big Tree, 89
Teng Biao, 30
Thailand, 104
Thought Reform, 38
Thought Work, 140
3Com, 142
*Three Kingdoms, The*, 15
Thunderbolt Operation, 19
Thurman, Robert, 282
Tiananmen Square, 5, 22–23, 62, 131, 293; demonstrations at, 21, 23, 24, 31, 113, 118, 119, 120, 121, 124, 144, 145, 150, 159, 175, 188, 201, 223–24, 258, 289, 322, 367
Tibet, 132–33, 138, 139, 144–45, 146, 282–83, 286, 315, 358
tiger moms, 65, 112
*Time*, 176
*Times* (London), 19
*Titanic*, 46
Tobacco Monopoly Bureau, 255–56
Tocqueville, Alexis de, 362

Top Human, 281–82
trade unions, 39
trains, 232–47, 262, 360; corruption and, 242–47; crash of, 234–38, 240, 243, 245, 246, 250
*Travelers Among Mountains and Streams*, 37
Treasury Department, U.S., 80
triads, 87, 88–91, 92
Trier, Germany, 102–104
*Triple Door* (Han), 169–70, 174, 177
Triple Withouts, 43, 57–58, 312
Tsang, Billy Yuk-Piu, 45
Tsinghua University, 322
Tung Chin-yao, 18–19
Tunisia, 218–19, 221
Turbine Hall, 190
Turkey, 234
Twain, Mark, 6, 262
Twitter, 165, 260

Uighurs, 22, 201
unemployment, 163, 368
United Nations, 16; Security Council of, 137; World Happiness Report of, 272
United States: Chinese relationship with, *see* China, U.S. relationship with; corruption in, 261–62, 263; Deng's criticism of, 155; propaganda in, 118
Universal Declaration of Human Rights, 162
Unocal, 142
Usu, China, 258

vacations, 24
Vancl, 170
Vangelis, 143
Vanuatu, 104
Venetian Macao, 86
Venezuela, 234
Venus de Milo, 108
Verizon Wireless, 178
Vietnam, 122
Vietnam War, 277

*Voice of the Chinese Dream*, 359
von Ossietzky, Carl, 205

W., 212
*Wall Street Feng Shui*, 284
*Wall Street Journal, The*, 109, 113
Wang, 241
Wang, Grace, 146
Wang Boming, 121, 124–25, 202, 203, 331
Wang Chichang, 295
Wang Feng, 128
Wang Gang, 67
Wang Guiping, 77
Wang Jianxin, 109
Wang Jingbing, 58–59
Wang Lang, 121
Wang Lijun, 253, 254–55
Wang Mengshu, 241, 243–44
Wang Qian, 213
Wang Qishan, 125, 361–62
Wang Ran, 322
Wang Shangkun, 310
Wang Shuo, 70, 127, 203
Wang Xiaoping, 278
Wang Yue, 295–98, 300–305, 306
Wang Zhengxu, 300
Wang Zhenyu, 103–104, 108
Wan Manlu, 141
Wan Zhendong, 29
Warner, Charles, 6
Washington Consensus, 150, 151–52, 154
Wealth Partaking Scheme, 82
Weber, Elke, 83–84
Wedeman, Andrew, 262
Weibo, 231, 255, 274, 321, 328, 331, 339
Wei Feiran, 177
Wei Jingsheng, 187, 349
Weiliang Institute of Interpersonal Relations, 65
Weiweicam.com, 325
Wen Jiabao, 230, 237; net worth of, 260
Wen Kejian, 197
Wen Tao, 223
Wenzhou train crash, 234–38, 240, 243, 245, 246, 250
*What Do We Live For?*, 282

*What Money Can't Buy* (Sandel), 309–10

Whyte, Martin, 268, 363

Winged Victory of Samothrace, 108

Witherspoon Institute, 348

Wo Hop To, 88

Wolfowitz, Paul, 142

Wong Kam-ming, 78, 85, 89–90, 91

*Worker's Daily*, 122, 124

working conditions, 340, 355

World Bank, 152, 154–55, 339–40

World Happiness Report, 272

World War I, 118

World War II, 140, 147, 264

Wo Shing Wo, 92

Wrigley, 55

Wu, Daphne, 201–202, 203

Wu Bangguo, 220

Wuhan, China, 153

Wuhan Railway Bureau, 239

Wu Jinglian, 39, 157–58

Wu Shuzai, 76

Wu Si, 123

Wu Zhiyou, 288–89, 291

Wynn, Steve, 82, 83


Xia dynasty, 80–81

Xiajia, China, 3

Xiamen, China, chemical plant denounced in, 209–10

Xian, China, anti-Japanese incident in, 335

Xiaobo Zhang, 56

Xiao Lin, 35

Xiao Long, 35

Xie, Andy, 122

Xi Jinping, 124, 258–59, 358–59, 361, 367

Xinhua, 120, 133, 362

Xinjiang, 315

Xinjiang uprising, 201

Xin Li, 233–34

Xiong Wenchi, 136

Xu Beihong, 249

Xu Bing, 189–91

Xue Lan, 322

Xu Nuo (Promise), 101, 109–10, 113

Xu Wu, 147

Xu Xiaonian, 268

Xu Zhiyong, 364


Yahoo!, 31

Yan'an, 34

Yan Fu, 98

Yang, Jerry, 31

*Yangcheng Evening News*, 301–302

Yang Xiaokai, 156

Yan Yunxiang, 46, 300

Yao Chen, 37

Yao Yang, 340–45

Ye, Mr., 164

Yevtushenko, Yevgeny, 328

Yi Junqing, 257

Ying-shih Yu, 286

Yinqiang Zhang, 269

Yoshiyuki Kasai, 240

Young Pioneers, 148

Yuan Baojing, 269

Yu Dan, 287

Yugoslavia, 14


Zaire, 262

Zang Qiji, 239

Zeng Kewei, 136

Zeng Liping, 112

Zhai Xiaobing, 357

Zha Jianying, 32

Zhang, Charles, 133

Zhang and Zhang, 87

Zhang Dazhong, 65

Zhang Dejiang, 359

Zhang Hua, 235

Zhang Lijia, 297

Zhang Shuguang, 239

Zhang Xiaogang, 96

Zhang Xinwu, 65

Zhang Yihe, 255

Zhang Yimou, 119

Zhang Zhiming (Michael), vii, 72–75, 76, 135, 177, 178–80, 264–65, 272; Basic English started by, 265; in Beijing, 349–55; new apartment of, 266–67; textbook written by, 266

Zhao Jian, 240
Zhao Jing, 322
Zhao Qizheng, 219
Zhao Xiao, 314
Zhao Zhao, 189
Zhao Ziyang, 13, 39, 150
*Zhejiang Daily*, 331
Zheng Dao, 110
Zheng He, 104
Zheng Shengtao, 316–17
Zhou dynasty, 109
Zhou Jiugeng, 256–57

Zhou Li, 151
Zhou Qiaorong, 173
Zhou Runan, 299, 305
Zhou Xiaochuan, 125
Zhu Ping, 232
Zhu Rongji, 268
Zhu Yuanzhang, 249
Zhu Zhongming, 107–108, 109, 112–13
Zion Church, 316
Zoellick, Robert, 152, 154, 340
Zuoxiao Zuzhou, 192